The Church
of the Holy Spirit

Father Nicholas Afanasiev, Easter liturgy, St. Sergius Institute chapel, Paris, circa 1965. Courtesy of Anatole Afanasiev.

The Church

of the Holy Spirit

Nicholas Afanasiev

Translated by Vitaly Permiakov

Edited with an introduction by Michael Plekon

Foreword by Rowan Williams

University of Notre Dame Press

Notre Dame, Indiana

Manufactured in the United States of America

Designed by Wendy McMillen
Set in 10.1/13.5 Nicholas (Shinn Type Foundry) by BookComp, Inc.
Printed on 60# Joy White, 30% PCR paper in the U.S.A. by Thomson-Shore, Inc.

Library of Congress Cataloging-n-Publication Data
Afanasíev, Nikolai.
   [Tserkov Dukha Sviatogo. English]
   The Church of the Holy Spirit / Nicholas Afanasiev ; translated by Vitaly Permiakov ; edited with an introduction by Michael Plekon ; foreword by Rowan Williams.
     p.   cm.
   Includes bibliographical references (p.) and index.
   ISBN-13: 978-0-268-02030-9 (cloth : alk. paper)
   ISBN-10: 0-268-02030-2 (cloth : alk. paper)
   1. Theology, Doctrinal   I. Plekon, Michael, 1948–   II. Title.
   BT75.3.A3313   2007
   230'.19—dc22

2007033425

Contents

THE CHURCH OF THE HOLY SPIRIT

Foreword

Rowan Williams

What is the Church of God? We can craft any number of ingenious an-swers to this question and all of them will be useless unless we give proper weight to what it means to be the Church of *God* — to be the community assembled by divine initiative and divine love before all else.

This is the heart of Nicholas Afanasiev's vision. And he identifies, with surgical sharpness, the paradox that most often distorts the life and understanding of the Church: the point at which we should most clearly be affirming and enacting our common identity as God's guests has become the point at which some of the most dangerous kinds of indi-vidualism and reliance on human reckoning show themselves — at the Eucharist. So often it has ceased to be the moment when the commu-nity sees itself drawn together by the eternal energy of the prayer of Christ, and has turned into a rite performed by a holy caste, whose focus is the production of holy things which are revered from a distance.

The prayer and energy of Christ is the fundamental fact of the Church; and this means that the Holy Spirit is what grounds and unifies the Church, the Spirit poured out at last upon all flesh. Afanasiev sits astonishingly light to a whole complex of issues around the discipline of the Church, the recognition or validation of ministries and the structures that constitute the church as more than local; or rather, he refuses to ad-dress these issues in the context and idiom most familiar to traditional Catholic and Orthodox theology. Whether he manages to construct an alternative that is comprehensive and coherent is much disputed by scholarly readers. But it is a salutary shock to read him if you are pre-occupied with the conventional ways of seeing these matters: at the very least he insists that you go back to a close reading of both the New Testament and the patristic evidence so as to draw out what is most basic and new in the Christian account of the community that gathers at the Lord's Table.

Directly and indirectly, Afanasiev's work, despite some strong criticism in certain quarters, had great influence on the churches — not only the Orthodox churches — in the last quarter of the twentieth century; but it has never been fully available to English-speaking readers. Now, in this welcome and readable translation, we have one of the hidden classics of modern theology laid open. Its vision is timely and profound, as all the historic churches wrestle with questions about their unity and interdependence, about the local and the universal. All praise to Vitaly Permiakov and Michael Plekon for their labours in preparing this version; may it open many readers to the Holy Spirit's challenges to the churches of our generation.

† Rowan, Archbishop of Canterbury
Lambeth Palace, Holy Week 2007

Introduction

The Church of the Holy Spirit—Nicholas Afanasiev's
Vision of the Eucharist and the Church

Michael Plekon

In some ways Fr. Nicholas was a man of one idea, or, it may be better
to say, *one vision*. It is this vision that he described and communicated
in what appeared sometimes as "dry" and technical discussions. A
careful reader, however, never failed to detect behind this appearance a
hidden fire, a truly consuming love for the Church. For it was the
Church that stood at the center of that vision, and Fr. Afanasiev, when
his message is understood and deciphered, will remain for future gen-
erations a genuine renovator of ecclesiology.[1]

Memories and memoirs can be most revealing as well as obscuring.
The recently published selections from Fr. Alexander Schmemann's journals attest to this.[2] The quotation above, however, comes from one of
the typically succinct obituaries Fr. Schmemann was accustomed to
writing and in many ways summarizes not only who Fr. Nicholas
Nicholaievitch Afanasiev (1893–1966) was, but the larger significance of
his work.[3] It is telling that another vignette of Fr. Afanasiev, in the often
acerbic but usually accurate memoirs of Fr. Basil Zenkovsky, both confirms the Schmemann view while adding something which perhaps ob-
scures or even misunderstands the man. Zenkovsky several times notes
Afanasiev's reticent personality, his characteristic diffidence, while at
the same time observing the force with which Fr. Afanasiev expressed
his convictions. Zenkovsky, as later John Meyendorff, curiously faults

Afanasiev for being an historical relativist. I think the methodological precision and rigor of historiography that Afanasiev explicitly discusses both at the beginning and close of *The Church of the Holy Spirit* witnesses otherwise, and strikingly so.

If there is something of an enigma here it is not so much about Afanasiev as a person but about the history of his work in ecclesiology. Born in Odessa in 1893, his father was an attorney who died when Afanasiev was very young. He was the only remaining male in a household comprised of his mother, grandmother, and younger sister. Fr. Afanasiev's wife observed that his personality was deeply tied to the south of the Ukraine, its sunshine, seashore, and countryside, the almost Mediterranean feel of life there.

A gifted student, Afanasiev early on wanted to be a bishop, so attracted was he by the ornate vestments. (He would later point to these as sad relics of a disappeared Byzantium, preserved for no theological reasons in Orthodox liturgical tradition.) Of other possible vocations—teaching, medicine, the priesthood—the first seemed to fit best with his skills and sensibilities. Mathematics became his specialization and it eventually influenced his inscription in the artillery school and then service in this branch of the military in WWI. Afanasiev, like Paul Evdokimov, saw much suffering, death, and destruction in these war years, first in the internal conflict and then in the civil strife following the Russian revolution. Marianne Afanasiev notes that it was Fr. Nicholas's beloved books—Rozanov, Merezhovsky, Soloviev, and especially Alexander Blok's poetry—which sustained him. With thousands of other immigrants he fled in 1920, arriving finally in Belgrade, where he enrolled at the University's theology faculty, returning to the vocational intentions of years before. But it was a hard life as a political exile: new surroundings, a different language, loneliness, a tiny stipend which meant that he shared the extreme poverty of fellow refugees.

It was through membership and then service as treasurer in a Russian association that Afanasiev was integrated into a circle of friendships in which he would remain the rest of his life. There was Kostia Kern and Sergei Sergeivich Bezobrazoff, later Father Kyprian and Bishop Cassian, who would be fellow students and then faculty colleagues at the Paris St. Sergius Theological Institute. Bishop Benjamin (Fedtchenko) and Father Alexis Nelioubov became spiritual fathers to him. Perhaps the most important figure was his "teacher and friend" Basil Zenkovsky, also later to be his colleague in Paris. Probably no one was more influential than Zenkovsky in eventually bringing Fr. Nicholas to his career as a theologian and faculty member at St. Sergius. In Belgrade Afanasiev also participated in the Fraternity of St. Seraphim and most especially in the Students' Movement, later the Russian Christian Students Movement. Through these he was drawn into the eucharistic revival, the "churching of life" in the Movement, inspired by Fr. Sergius Bulgakov. But for all the warmth and attachments of these circles, Afanasiev also experienced in them the rifts and hostilities that he would continue to encounter in the Russian Orthodox church the rest of his life. Already in the 1920s, young and committed Russian Christians were divided on political issues such as the relationship to the Russian state, to Russian history, culture, and spirituality. The ecclesiastical schism that emerged between the Karlovtsky Synod and the Exarchate of the Russian Church in Western Euope, its primate Metropolitan Evlogy (Georgievsky), came to divide families and friends from each other. Afanasiev nevertheless found his love, was married to Marianne Andrusova, and while completing his degree, took a teaching post in religion at a secondary school in Macedonia. Already part of the movement to raise funds for an Orthodox theological school in the West—this was to be St. Sergius, where he spent his entire academic career—Afanasiev immersed himself, as was his character, both in teaching and graduate work. Finally, after some conflict, he decided to become a student of the distinguished historian A. P. Dobroklonsky, a decision that would shape the rest of Afanasiev's scholarly endeavors and perspective.

His mentor's rigorous historiographic research methods would turn Afanasiev into the church historian who refused to turn away from the empirical realities of, say, the Roman or Byzantine imperial laws and courts and the influence—in the end, the domination—of the Church by these. It was also Dobroklonsky who would compel Afanasiev to look beneath a church canon or council to find the cultural and social factors at work with the spiritual actions of the ecclesial body. His first scholarly publications were "The Power of the State and the Ecumenical Councils," "The Provincial Assemblies of the Roman Empire and the Ecumenical Councils," and "Ibas of Edessa and His Era," studies whose imprint will be found very clearly in the present work, *The Church of the Holy Spirit.*

In 1930 Afanasiev came to teach canon law at St. Sergius at the request of its dean, Fr. Sergius Bulgakov, who would also come to have a strong influence on him. From Bulgakov Afanasiev acquired a sense for the centrality of the Eucharist as well as a thorough return to the sources in understanding the Church and its relationship to the world. These very same influences would later be recognized and appreciated by the great liturgical theologian Fr. Alexander Schmemann, himself also a student of Bulgakov, as well as a colleague and protégé of Afanasiev.

Afanasiev would teach canon law, its sources, its history, and its pastoral implications all the rest of his life at St. Sergius, with the exception of the war years. He became a member both of Fr. Bulgakov's seminar and the Fraternity of the Trinity that Fr. Bulgakov led, which incuded writer and social activist Mother

Maria Skobtsova, Sister Joanna Reitlinger the iconographer, intellectuals and scholars such as Lev Zander and his wife Valentina, Boris Sové, Vladimir Weidlé, George Fedotov, Basil Zenkovsky, and Boris Vycheslavtsev, among others.

In addition to canon law, Afanasiev also taught Greek, and work with the New Testament as text further made him expert as an exegete. He was among the St. Sergius faculty majority who defended Fr. Bulgakov from charges of heresy brought by members of the Karlovtsy Synod (later the Russian Orthodox Church Outside Russia), Patriarch Sergius of Moscow, and the later eminent theologian Vladimir Lossky. In 1936 Fr. Bulgakov dedicated one of the volumes of his great trilogy to Afanasiev as a "souvenir of a year of trials." In 1937 Afanasiev would be among the contributors to *Zhivoe Predanie*—"Living Tradition"—the strong statement of those Orthodox theologians who saw tradition as dynamic, theology as creative, and the task of the Church as engagement with the world and the culture within which it lived. All of those already named in the St. Sergius faculty and Trinity Fraternity also contributed.

It is not so difficult to track, in the 1930s, several engagements which converged and set the direction for Fr. Afanasiev's work from the 1940s till his death in 1966. Already mentioned were the deep and painful experiences of conflict and condemnation, and then division among even close friends who were both Russian and Orthodox Christians. Like other immigrants to the West, however, there was an astonishing discovery of the history and authentic faith of Western Christians, both Catholic and Protestant, and then the frustration of the canonical separation of Eastern and Western Christians as a result of the great schism of 1054. There was also Afanasiev's continuing historical research into the social, political, and cultural sources and factors shaping the great ecumenical councils. Add to this the powerful eucharistic revival urged on by Fr. Bulgakov and his circle and you have many of the elements of *The Church of the Holy Spirit*, also of the companion volume which he did not complete, *The Limits of the Church*, as well as the important essay on liturgical renewal, *The Lord's Supper* (1950).

On January 8, 1940, he was taken around the altar in procession by Frs. Bulgakov and Kern and ordained a priest by Metropolitan Evology. Fleeing the Nazi occupation, he and his family spent some months in the non-occupied south, where the work on the ancient church's eucharistic ecclesiology was done at the kitchen table. From 1941 until 1947, throughout WWII, Fr. Nicholas served as the pastor of the Orthodox parish in Tunisia at the request of archbishop Vladimir of Nice. His wife recalls in her memoir his dedication to his people, his love for the liturgical services and his efforts to continue work on what would become *The*

Church of the Holy Spirit even without reference resources. Once again as in Skople and Saint-Raphaël, the family dinner table became Fr. Nicholas's workplace between meals and the vision of the Church as the eucharistic assembly: *epi to auto*— "always everyone and always together for one and the same things" (Acts 2.44)— was both a consolation in the deprivation and suffering of the war years as well as an encouragement to persist in his recovery of "eucharistic ecclesiology." Fr. Nicolas was the faithful pastor of his flock. He took care of all the people in his community whether they were Orthodox or Catholic, Muslim or nonbelievers. Upon his return to St. Sergius he completed the first version of *The Church of the Holy Spirit* and defended it for the doctorate on July 2, 1950. As Marianne Afanasiev describes it, the last two decades of his life were consumed by a full teaching load, his official positions as treasurer of St. Sergius and canon law advisor to the ruling bishop and diocese, and a prominent position in ecclesiology and ecumenical work. As Aidan Nichols points out, there is a wealth of theological insight waiting to be discovered in Fr. Nicholas's many unpublished lectures and studies.

It is remarkable that throughout these busy years from 1947 on, Afanasiev managed to publish numerous articles, many of which formed the body of *The Church of the Holy Spirit, The Lord's Supper,* and the two-thirds companion volume to the first, *The Limits of the Church.*[4] At the recommendation of Patriarch Athenagoras I, Afanasiev was appointed an official ecumenical observer at Vatican II, where his ecclesiological work left its imprint particularly in *Lumen gentium,* the dogmatic constitution on the Church.[5] Both a strong proponent of ecumenical activity as well as a critic of certain of its outcomes, he witnessed in Rome on December 8, 1965, the formal suspension of the anathemas of the eleventh century by Patriarch Athenagoras I and Pope Paul VI. In these last years he published his most powerful ecumenical articles, some assessing the accomplishments as well as the failures of Vatican II and others directed at reunion of the churches. *Una sancta,* dedicated "to the memory of the pope of Love, John XXIII," is the most challenging of these. Chronic illness and the wear and tear of a hard life of severe poverty took their toll on Fr. Nicholas. After a few weeks' illness, during which he believed he saw a young man, a messenger of God, waiting for him in his hospital bedroom, he died on December 4, 1966.

It is not as if Fr. Afanasiev's work was simply forgotten after his death. *The Church of the Holy Spirit,* which he had been revising, was posthumously published in 1971. Perhaps his legacy lived on and was most dramatically effective in the work of Frs. Alexander Schmemann and John Meyendorff. Schmemann turned minds around to the *prima theologia,* a "liturgical theology" which did not dwell only on the details of liturgical history and the rites but sought to encompass all of ecclesial life, with the liturgy as the source of both faith and practice. Schmemann's effort to restore as well as reform the liturgical life of the Orthodox Church was massive in impact. Not only did the language of the people return, rather than Slavonic or ancient Greek, but the prayers were said aloud, especially the *anaphora*, the eucharistic prayer. This alteration was not just didactic in purpose but was intended so that the entire assembly could pray together, or better, as Afanasiev repeatedly stressed, could concelebrate the liturgy with the presider as the baptized, priestly, prophetic, and royal people of God. Further, Schmemann and Meyendorff fought for the "local church," so crucial for Afanasiev, in their efforts to gain autocephaly for their own church body in America with the ultimate goal a united, truly local church in America. Afanasiev is often criticized for having no place for mission or outreach in his ecclesiological view. Yet this alleged deficiency is best addressed by attention not only to what he actually wrote but also to the engagement with culture and society of Afanasiev's own "local church," the Exarchate of Paris and the Orthodox Church in America, shaped by those he helped to form, Frs. Schmemann and Meyendorff.

If all of Fr. Afanasiev's ecclesiological research and interpretation could be summed up, it would be in the line that has now become familiar: "*The Church makes the Eucharist, the Eucharist makes the Church.*" Now, years after Vatican II's dogmatic constitution on the Church, *Lumen gentium*, in which Afanasiev's vision was expressed (credit to him given in the Conciliar *Acta*), we take for granted the eucharistic nature of the Church and the ecclesial nature of the Eucharist; but previously both the Eastern and Western churches saw things otherwise.[6] More often the Church was the canons, the hierarchical structure, the formal ecclesiastical organization, the historical and social institution. More often it was the question of who was in charge, who could do or not do this action. It was a matter of rules, protocols, rubrics, these in turn dependent upon the status of hierarch, cleric, or layperson in a complex internal social structure. The "return to the sources" on the part of so many scholars who were Afanasiev's contemporaries was to both the "mind" and the practice of the Church of the Fathers. The reform here was both restoration of tradition and since that tradition was living, an authentic renewal as well. The way forward was back—to the scriptures, the liturgy, and its texts, to the lived experience of the Church as a community that prayed and served God and the neighbor.

As both the present *Church of the Holy Spirit* and *The Lord's Supper* make clear, individualism was the dominant strain in eucharistic celebration as well as piety. This piety made reception of holy communion a rare event, preceded by extreme ascetic practices of "preparation," *govenie* in the Russian idiom. If one could freeze-frame the year of, say, 1950 on any given Sunday morning at the principal liturgy there would be few if any communicants in Orthodox and Roman Catholic churches and very likely no eucharistic celebration in other communions such as the Anglican, Lutheran, or reformed. The eucharistic nature of the Church and the churchly nature of the Eucharist were by no means dominant in the ecclesial consciousness, nor had they been for years.

Afanasiev was not alone in his efforts to "return to the sources" of the Church's life. In this he was accompanied by that ecumenical *ressourcement* group of scholars whose work later shaped much of the thinking of Vatican II. These included Jean Daniélou, Yves Congar, Oscar Cullman, Gregory Dix, Bernard Botte, I.-M. Dallmais, M. D. Chenu, and Henri de Lubac, among others. The photographs of participants in the first liturgical weeks at St. Sergius Institute (started by Fr. Afanasiev and Fr. Kern in 1953) testify to the ecumenical character of both the "return to the sources" and the efforts in liturgical renewal. Later there was the citation of his name by these and other such as Frs. Schmemann and John Meyendorff, who were graduates. Theologians such as Aidan Kavanagh, J. M-R. Tillard, Bishop Hilarion Alfeyev, Boris Bobrinskoy recognize the importance of his contributions.[7] Though aimed at different issues, Paul Bradshaw's work also confirms the eucharistic shape of ecclesiology.[8] Even his critics indicate a debt to his pioneer work in returning to the ecclesiology of the ancient Church.[9] Relatively few critics outrightly dismiss Afanasiev's framework.[10]

But criticism as well as limitation there must always be. Fr. Afanasiev's work is now over half a century old. He began it in articles even further back, in the 1930s, but the ecclesiological focus crystallized in the late 1940s. Cut off from research libraries and colleagues by his pastoral care of the Orthodox parish in Tunisia during WWII, Afanasiev only completed a first draft of *The Church of the Holy Spirit* in 1948, defending it for his doctoral degree in 1950. He had published many of the chapters as journal articles and he continued this for the second companion volume, *The Limits of the Church*. But *The Church of the Holy Spirit* was only published posthumously, first in Russian in 1971 and in French translation in 1975.

Thus it is necessary to locate *The Church of the Holy Spirit* within the scholarly context of its time, admitting that research has progressed, that other studies would have to be consulted and perhaps even some perspectives modified. Perhaps his interpretation of Cyprian's "universal ecclesiology" is skewed, taking what Cyprian judged to be a description of the local church in Carthage for the Church worldwide. Possibly criticism stems from uneasiness with many of Afanasiev's conclusions, reading for example, anti-clericalism into his critique of the emergence of a clerical caste. I wonder whether or not the assumptions of some Western, Roman Catholic critics originate in the decentralized, localized ecclesiology Afanasiev sketches, one still evident in the Eastern churches and continually baffling, if not problematic, to some Western observers. I would echo Fr. John Meyendorff's criticism of Afanasiev's position on the important reforming Moscow Council of 1917–18.[11] Afanasiev is critical of the Council's use of the representation of the lower clergy and laity by delegates. He also objected to the deliberative role these delegates took in that council. Here and elsewhere he seems to draw a definitive line around the particular ministries of bishops, clergy, and laity, lines that have been blurred virtually on a regular basis through church history.

Yet despite these and other criticisms, the enduring significance of Afanasiev's ecclesiological study both in the present volume and his other writings is acknowledged even by critics. The appearance of this work, *The Church of the Holy Spirit*, in translation will allow both further analysis and criticism as well as assimilation of its conclusions. There is, for example, at present among the Orthodox (members of the episcopate in particular) significant ecclesiastical opposition to the essential conciliar or sobornal nature of the Church's liturgy and structure. But when faced with the empirical history of the Church, it is hard to imagine scholarly refutation of its conciliar nature, East or West. Thus while the restorations and reforms of the Moscow Council of 1917–18 were implemented in only a few local churches, it is still difficult to dismiss the Council's appeals to the liturgy, the scriptures, patristic writings, and the structure and actions of many earlier general and local councils.

Likewise it is difficult to refute the eucharistic shape of the Church that Afanasiev points to in so many sources: the Pauline letters, the gospels, the writings of Ignatius of Antioch, as well as Cyprian of Carthage, whom he views as a proponent of a "universal ecclesiology." Also there are John Chrysostom, Augustine, the Didache, and Justin Martyr, among others. And then there are both the ancient and present texts of the eucharistic liturgy themselves.

Most often the only work of Fr. Afanasiev's that is referred to is his essay, "The Church That Presides in Love," on the question of the primacy of the see of Peter in the churches.[12] There he briefly develops the work that he unfolds in much greater depth in *The Church of the Holy Spirit*. It is a meticulous examination of the early Church's eucharistic ecclesiology. Though often faulted for focusing solely on the Eucharist, the study begins in fact with what happens in *baptism and chrismation*, namely the consecration of each member of the Church as priest, prophet, and king. Contrary to later theology which would divide the Church into clergy and laity on the basis of consecration for ministry, Afanasiev examines the texts of the baptismal liturgy as well as those of ordination and the Eucharist itself to show that all Christians are consecrated to priestly ministry. All the people of God, not just the bishops, presbyters, and deacons, celebrate the Eucharist. More precisely, the Eucharist is concelebrated by all, as the prayers in the plural indicate. Likewise, the same prayers of ordination as well as the testimonies of such fathers as Ignatius of Antioch and Irenaeus of Lyons are scrutinized in the emergence of the office of bishop from that of first presbyter. If the Eucharist cannot be celebrated unless done so by the presiders and the rest of the assembly, it follows that the calling and setting apart of the presiders must be for service. All were consecrated in baptism and chrismation for service to God in the Eucharist. All are also consecrated thereby to further service in the Church and the world, the service depending on one's place (*topos*) or position in the assembly.

Central to the life of the early Church for Afanasiev was the *constant presence and work of the Holy Spirit:* "Where the Spirit is, there is the Church and all grace." Historian that he was, he consistently faulted theologians for neglecting the divine nature and activity of the Church. Nevertheless he also faulted those who would overspiritualize the Church's structures and activities, seeing such as near-Nestorian tendencies. Afanasiev further stresses the communal nature of the Church. It is not just the sum of its members. Rather, like Durkheim, he recognized that as a collectivity it had a social reality *sui generis.* In the Church, no one ever spoke or acted alone but "always and everywhere together" with the others, the *epi to auto* of Acts that punctuates his writings. Fundamental to his vision is *the royal priesthood of all the baptized.* Fr. Michel Evdokimov personally related many Sunday dinners in which Fr. Afanasiev and Fr. Evdokimov's own father, the lay theologian Paul Evdokimov, both on the St. Sergius faculty, would discuss their work; hence their mutual interest in the priesthood of all the baptized, in the connections between the vocations of marriage and monastic life, seemingly opposed to each other, in the assertion of the Church in its fullness in the eucharistic assembly, with all the rest of Christian work and life flowing from this center.

One could easily characterize Afanasiev's view of ecclesiology as pneumatological, for while seeing the Church's primary expression as the eucharistic assembly, what distinguishes the Church from all other institutions is the presence and the gifts of the Spirit. The paramount gift of the Spirit for Afanasiev, as one can read in the last chapter of *The Church of the Holy Spirit,* was the "authority of love" (*vlast' lyubvi*). The early Church was ruled by the Spirit's love, not by laws, clerical elites, or political figures. However, this graced sense of consecrated membership and eucharistic community did not endure very long on its own. In

the chapters that unfold here Afanasiev carefully tracks the emergence of the domi-
nance of law and of a clerical caste in the church. Here too one might emphasize
that for Afanasiev the elements (*panta*) of the church that were not formed within
the purview of love, even if they endured for centuries, would never be properly
"of" the church nor affect its true life as one connected to the kingdom of love.[13]

The other somewhat controversial emphasis of Afanasiev is his insistence
that the structure of the Church is above all local, the immediate community that
celebrates the Eucharist, and that from here the Church extends itself in ministry
to the world. The "local church" was not some isolated, atomic unit over against
the universal "Church of God in Christ." The only church known in the early centuries was the "local church" of this household or this city. That the "local church"
possessed all the fullness of the Church was without question. However, contrary
to his critics, Afanasiev is almost obsessive in his insistence that the local church is
only the church in communion with, along with all the other churches. In formulaic
terms, $1 + 1 + 1 = 1$. The aggregation of many local churches does not constitute a
Church greater than any one of them. This said, it is impossible to fault Afanasiev
for a reduction of the church to its smallest local expression. The "parish" of our
time may indeed be the "local church" in the sense that the early Christians understood it, yet one cannot simply equate today's parish with the "local church" of
which Afanasiev speaks and pit it against, say, the deanery, diocese, national
church, or the church catholic and ecumenical (*oikumene*).

Afanasiev's examination of the early church in *The Church of the Holy Spirit*
as well as his careful application of this to the church of his time remains relevant
for us today, almost over a half century after he completed the first draft of it. Both
the Eastern and Western churches face the external challenges of indifference as
well as the internal ones of extremism and despair. Fr. Afanasiev's analysis and in
particular his critique of the emergence of legalism and clericalism in the Church is
distinctive, a voice not heard in Protestant, Catholic, or Orthodox theological
scholarship and debate. His vision is rooted in the bread and cup on the holy
table and in the Spirit-driven community gathered round it.[14] He ended the introduction to this work much as his colleague and teacher Fr. Sergius Bulgakov
ended many of his books, with the Church's eschatological cry, the name of the
One who was to come and always is coming: the name of the Lord Jesus Christ.
For this reason, his voice deserves to be heard.

Baruch College of the City University of New York
St. Gregory the Theologian Orthodox Church,
Wappingers Falls, New York

Notes

1. Alexander Schmemann, "Fr. Nicholas Afanasiev—†December 4, 1966, In Memoriam," *St Vladimir's Seminary Quarterly* 10 (1966): 4, 209. The imprint of Fr. Afanasiev's writing and teaching can be found throughout the work of Fr. Schmemann and for that matter, Fr. John Meyendorff. See for example, *The Eucharist: Sacrament of the Kingdom*, trans. Paul Kachur (Crestwood, NY: St. Vladimir's Seminary Press, 1988), one of the rare times that Afanasiev is credited explicitly, on 14, 17, 19. Also see 242–244.

2. *The Journals of Father Alexander Schmemann 1973–1983*, ed. and trans. Juliana Schmemann (Crestwood, NY: St. Vladimir's Seminary Press, 2000).

3. Biographical sketches of Fr. Afanasiev by his wife, Marianne, are the source for what follows: "La genèse de L'Église du Saint-Esprit," in both *Tserkov Dukha Sviatogo* (Paris: YMCA Press, 1971) and *L'Église du Saint-Esprit*, trans. Marianne Drobot (Paris: Cerf, 1975) and "Nicolas Afanasieff-essai de biographie," *Contacts* 66, no. 2 (1969): 99–111. A substantial online collection of materials on Fr. Afanasiev is maintained by Andrei Platonov: http://www.golubinski.ru/academia/afanasieffnew.htm (last accessed November 28, 2006). Also see my *Living Icons: Persons of Faith in the Eastern Church* (Notre Dame, IN: University of Notre Dame Press, 2002), 149–177, as well as Richard Gaillardetz, "The Eucharistic Ecclesiology of Nicholas Afanasiev: Prospects and Challenges for Contemporary Ecumenical Dialogue," *Diakonia* 27 (1994): 18–44.

4. See Marianne Afanasiev's discussion in *L'Église du Saint-Esprit*, 20–21, as well as the notes to Nicholas Afanasieff, "L'Église de Dieu dans le Christ," *La pensée orthodoxe* 13, no. 2 (1968): 1–38.

5. See Aidan Nichols, O.P., *Theology in the Russian Diaspora: Church, Fathers, Eucharist in Nikolai Afanas'ev, 1893–1966* (Cambridge: Cambridge University Press, 1989), 253, 270. The reference is to *Acta Synodalia Sacrosancti Concilii Oecumenici Vaticani Secundi* (Vatican City: 1971), vol. 1, pt. 4, 87, note 2; vol. 2, pt. 1, 251, note 27; vol. 3, pt. 1, 254.

6. See for example *The Catechism of the Catholic Church* (New York: Image/Doubleday, 1995), paras. 1118, 1166–1167, 1343, 1396, 1407, 2177.

7. See Aidan Kavanagh, *On Liturgical Theology* (Collegeville, MN: Pueblo/Liturgical Press, 1984), J. M.-R. Tillard, *Church of Churches: Flesh of the Church, Flesh of Christ* (Collegeville, MN: Michael Glazier/Pueblo/Liturgical Press, 1992); Hilarion Alfayev, "Orthodox Theology on the Threshold of the Twenty-first Century," and Boris Bobrinskoy, "The Holy Spirit in Twentieth Century Russian Theology," *The Ecumenical Review*, 52 (July 2000), 309–325 and 326–340.

8. Paul Bradshaw, *Eucharistic Origins* (New York: Oxford University Press, 2004).

9. Over the years critics have included Metropolitan John (Zizioulas), Bishop Kallistos (Ware), Aidan Nichols, Peter Plank, T. Camelot, Paul McPartlan, and John Erickson. See among these Joseph G. Aryankalayil, *Local Church and Church Universal: Towards a Convergence between East and West: A Study on the Theology of the Local Church according to N. Afanasiev and J. M.-R. Tillard with Special Reference to Some of the Contemporary Catholic and Orthodox Theologians* (Fribourg: Université de Fribourg Suisse / Institut d'études œcuméniques, 2004).

10. An exception appears to be Lucian Turcescu, *Dimitru Staniloe: Tradition and Modernity in Theology* (Iasi/Oxford: Center for Romanian Studies, 2002), especially "Eucharistic Ecclesiology or Open Sobornicity," 83–103.

11. John Meyendorff, "Hierarchy and Laity in the Orthodox Church," *Vestnik RSKhD* [Messenger of the Russian Student Christian Movement] (Paris) 39 (1955): 36–45.

12. *The Primacy of Peter,* ed. John Meyendorff (Crestwood, NY: St. Vladimir's Seminary Press, 1992), 91–143.

13. I am indebted to my colleague Fr. Alexis Vinogradov for this insight.

14. Also see Fr. Afanasiev's very bold application of his ecclesiological perspective to the issues of restoring unity among the churches in his essays "*Una sancta*" and "The Eucharist: The Principal Link between the Catholics and the Orthodox," in *Tradition Alive: On the Church and the Christian Life in Our Time: Readings from the Eastern Church,* ed. Michael Plekon (Lanham, MD: Sheed & Ward / Rowman & Littlefield, 2003), 3–30, 47–49.

The Church
of the Holy Spirit

Author's Foreword

The expression *Ecclesia Spiritus Sancti* is found in Tertullian. Trying to reclaim from bishops, possibly from Callistus of Rome in particular, the power "to bind and to loose," Tertullian argued that this power belonged to the "Church of the Spirit," rather than to the "church of the psychics." It seemed to him that the "Great Church" had forgotten its prophetic inspiration, and with all his passionate nature he embraced Montanism, which put prophecy in the foreground.

The conflict of the catholic church with Montanism is perhaps the strangest conflict ever found in church history. Everyday routine and stagnation are inevitable in the life of the church, but the church of the end of the second and beginning of the third centuries by no means intended to deny the gifts of the Spirit. By fighting against Montanism the Church was not rejecting prophecy—that was something it could not do. Rather it was fighting for its own existence. Seeking inspiration, Tertullian did not see that he had entered the path that would lead him out of the Church, since Montanism was destroying the Church, and by destroying the Church it was denying also the gifts of the Spirit.

Contrary to what Tertullian thought, the Church of the Spirit was not that of the "pneumatics," but the church of those whom he contemptuously called the "psychics." He deceived himself as well as those few who were his followers. But he was correct and still is in saying that the only foundation of the life of the Church is the Spirit. The Church is an organism filled with grace not because long ago it received the gifts of the Spirit which it keeps as if a hidden treasure, not because only some receive a charism within it, but because it lives and acts by the Spirit. The Church is the place of the Spirit's activity. Without the Spirit there is no life in the Church, no activity, no ministry; in short, there is no Church. Founded by Christ at the Last Supper, the Church was actualized at Pentecost when the glorified Lord sent the Spirit to his disciples. Beginning with that day the Spirit lives in the Church and the Church lives by the Spirit. The Church of the Spirit—that is what "the Church of God in Christ" was at the time of Tertullian and what it remains today.

The victory over Montanism raised some suspicions regarding prophecy, and in many cases not without reason. Montanism had discredited prophecy, but the Church could not refuse that which constituted its very being—the gifts of the Spirit, prophecy included. It would be strange to abandon the term "the Church of the Holy Spirit" to Montanism and to hold this term in suspicion. It would be even stranger to see in this term an allusion to Montanism specifically because this term existed before Tertullian and before Montanism. Tertullian himself probably borrowed this term from Irenaeus of Lyons. Irenaeus, whom one could not accuse of Montanism, very forcefully expressed what constitutes the very being of the Church: "Wherever the Church is, there is also the Spirit of God, and wherever the Spirit of God is, there is the Church and the fullness of grace."

To some extent Tertullian had anticipated the future course of the Church's history. Immediately after him ecclesial life began to accommodate to other principles. Roman law would penetrate the Church and create in it a stratum which had nothing in common with grace. Leaving aside the question as to whether this penetration of the law into ecclesial life was legitimate we nevertheless should not forget that the Church in its foundation was and always remains the charismatic organism possessing the fullness of grace—*omnis gratia.*

How was this *omnis gratia* expressed in the primitive Church? Was it expressed in life or was it a purely dogmatic statement with which ecclesial life did not correspond or did not correspond fully? Certainly we are not asking whether the life of primitive Christianity was ideal, devoid of any defects or weaknesses. Nowadays we know more about life during the primitive period and are less inclined to idealize it. However inspired ecclesial life was, there were defects then as well as in all subsequent periods. What we ask is whether the Spirit was indeed the foundation of the Church's entire life.

Modern theology grants primitive Christianity the status of a charismatic time par excellence in the Church's history. What does this mean? Does it have an absolute or relative force? Did charisma really belong to all? It appears that it did not, for according to the affirmations of modern theology not all the ministries were charismatic. If some were established by God—"and God appointed some," as the apostle says—others were established by the local churches which created for themselves the ministries necessary to their existence. Among these were the ministries that became the foundation of the entire ecclesial structure in subsequent history, those of bishops and presbyters. Therefore, when in the history of the Church the charismatic ministries gradually disappeared, all ecclesial ministries passed to non-charismatics. As the charismatic character of Christianity waned, charisma became a rare gift that the Church did not fully recognize. Should we then accept these claims of modern theology and acknowledge the charismatic character of the primitive Christianity as relative?

It seems that modern Orthodox dogmatic theology also is inclined to regard the charismatic character of ecclesial life in relative terms. Indeed, in its teaching about the sacrament of baptism it acknowledges that entrance into the Church is possible only on the basis of the charismatic gift which entails the spiritual birth of the one entering. However, it still remains but a moment in the life of a Christian and it is as if grace exhausts itself. For this reason not all members of the Church are considered "spiritual," but only those few who received the special gifts of the priesthood. What do we have then? Is this merely a coincidental affinity with the conclusions of liberal theology? Or does it mean that sometimes the point of departure for both positions was identical?

We believe that in the Church the Old Testament prophecy has been fulfilled: "And in the last days it shall be, God declares, that I will pour out my Spirit upon all flesh" (Acts 2.17). God pours out his Spirit not upon just a certain number but upon all His people. All are charismatics since all have received the Spirit as a "pledge" (*arrabôn*) of the new age to which the Church belongs while still abiding in this old age. The Church is the beginning of the "last days" (*eschatai hêmerai*).

Upon entering, the believer is set apart for ministry in the Church through the sending down of the Spirit. "The fullness of grace" (*omnis gratia*) has an absolute but not relative, a permanent but not temporary, character, for only charismatics can be the members of the Church. The gift of the Spirit that every member of the faithful receives in the sacrament of initiation is the charism of royal priesthood. In the Church there are no gifts of the Spirit without ministry and there is no ministry without gifts. Through the charisma of the royal priesthood the Christian is called to priestly ministry in the Church.

We are not aware of how extraordinary and audacious the idea of the priestly ministry of all members of the Church is. This idea could not just have arisen in the human mind. Here we are on the lofty summits of the Spirit that feeble human thought cannot attain. For this reason both those who accept this teaching and those who would gladly reject it if it were not contained in the Scriptures, do not realize that it is only in and through this idea that the "fullness of grace" (*omnis gratia*) received by the Church can be expressed. The very life of primitive Christianity was based upon the ministry of all the members of the Church. The entire ecclesial organization grew out of this concept of ministry just as the ensuing fate of this organization has been bound up with the fate of this teaching. Despite the way this teaching is viewed in modern dogmatic thought, to this day it remains the foundation of our life, its roots planted in primitive Christianity. We are accustomed to speak both profusely and frequently about the "hiatus" between the church organization of the apostolic times and the second half of the second century, after which the development of the ecclesial organization becomes more or less clear. If we were to regard the ecclesial organization from the perspective of the priestly ministry of all the members of the Church, this "hiatus" would no longer exist.

The priestly ministry of all members of the Church finds expression in the eucharistic assembly. No one could take part in the "sacred service of the Eucharist," in the words of the Pseudo-Areopagite,[1] without being appointed to the rank of priest of the Most High God. The eucharistic assembly was an assembly of the priestly people who offered sacred service to God "in Christ." Sacred service was an ecclesial ministry for the eucharistic assembly itself, was a manifestation of the Church of God in all its fullness. The Church is where Christ is, but Christ is always present in the fullness of the unity of His body in the Eucharist.

Empirically, the unity and fullness of the Church of God are expressed through the multiplicity of the local churches, each of which manifests not a part of but the fullness of the Church of God. For this reason, the multiplicity of the local churches, in empirical reality, guards the unity and fullness of the Church, that is, its catholicity. The unity of the local church itself is manifest in its one eucharistic assembly. The Church is one since it has one eucharistic assembly in which God's priestly people are gathered. Since Christ yesterday, today, and forever is one and the same, the multiplicity of the Eucharist in time does not divide the one body of Christ. In the same way, the multiplicity of eucharistic assemblies does not destroy the unity of God's Church, for in both space and time the eucharistic assembly remains one and the same. For primitive Christian consciousness the unity of the Church was not merely a dogmatic statement but a lived experience. Despite the increase of the number of local churches, the unity of the Church remained undisturbed, for they did not have different eucharistic assemblies but one and the same. Unity and fullness were not contained in the sum total of local churches nor in their confederation (which never existed), but rather in each local church.

Being one in its fullness the Church always retained its internal universality, for each local church contained in itself all remaining local churches. What was done in one church was done in all remaining ones, for everything was done within God's Church and in Christ. Due to this catholic universality, the local churches were absolutely devoid of any isolation and provincialism. No single church could separate itself from the others for it could not separate itself from Christ. All were united to one another through love. Each of the churches was loved by all and all were loved by each one of them.

The historical direction of ecclesial organization went from internal toward external universalism. Whatever aspect of the ecclesial life of the primitive Christianity we study, we must proceed from eucharistic ecclesiology without introducing into ancient ecclesial life an historically later understanding of the Church. One could defend modern ecclesial universalism as legitimate, correct, and perhaps inescapable in the conditions of our life. But one must not regard it as a primordial understanding of the Church. No surprise, then, that instead of transporting ourselves to the ecclesial life of primitive Christianity we regard it instead from the point of view of our modern understanding and perceive it in the light of our own understanding.

The Church is composed of the people God formed for himself in Christ. Viewed from this perspective, the Church is God's flock. The idea of a flock presupposes the ministry of a shepherd in the widest sense, including the ministry of administration. The opposition between the Spirit and order in modern theology stems from a false conviction that it is human will that serves as the organizing principle in the Church. Rather, it is the Spirit who serves as the guiding principle of organization and order in the Church. The beginning of the Church lies in the Spirit. Through the Spirit and in the Spirit the Church lives. The gifts of the Spirit are given not for their own sake but for ministry in the Church and for its building up. The Spirit in the Church is a principle not of anarchy but of organization. For this reason it is hard to imagine anything that would contradict the basic principles of ecclesial life as much as the hypothesis that distinguishes charismatic from non-charismatic ministries. One can admit hypotheses in science if they explain certain facts or phenomena. But a historian cannot employ hypotheses that reflect historical aberration. Such hypotheses cannot explain anything and actually create imaginary and thus unsolvable problems. Pastoral ministry is a charismatic ministry and cannot be anything else. The Church has fullness of grace (*omnis gratia*) and thus does not require the human element to govern itself. In dogmatic theology we readily acknowledge that the Church possesses the fullness of grace but we flatly refuse to recognize that in the primitive Church there were no principles other than grace. If in subsequent periods the Church employed alien principles to govern its life, we must determine when and why these came into use without elevating them to the status of norms and retrojecting them onto earlier times when the Church lived and acted through the gifts of the Spirit.

The gifts and ministries are different but the Spirit is one and the same. The same Spirit that established the ministries of apostle, prophet, and teacher established in the Church the ministry of administration. Just as these ministries' functions differed, so also did their significance. The ministry of administration was essential since the Church could not exist without it. Without this ministry there can be no eucharistic assembly and without a eucharistic assembly there can be no Church.

All of the faithful celebrate the Eucharist in the assembly but this celebration of all is manifest through one person. This is the nature of any celebration in the Church. The one who offers thanks is always one, but others concelebrate with him. The celebrant at the eucharistic assembly was the one who occupied a central place at the gathering. He "offered thanksgiving" in which all took part. He was always one and always the same but also always together with all. The people of God could neither celebrate without him nor could he celebrate without them, for not only he himself but all were priests of the Most High God.

One should not minimize the significance of place in the eucharistic assembly, in particular the central place. The significance of this place rests on the fact that Lord Jesus himself assumed it at the Last Supper. In turn when the first Eucharist was celebrated in Jerusalem this place was assumed by the apostle Peter. It is the bishop who occupies it today. Can there be any higher ministry than that of the person who assumes the place of the apostles at the eucharistic assembly? We do not grasp this today because the ancient eucharistic ecclesiology has been replaced. The ancient Church understood the significance of the central place at the Eucharist and clearly perceived the importance of the ministry of the person occupying this place. If we realized this we would be significantly closer to solving the problem of the emergence of the episcopacy. In any case we would be on the path to its resolution. It seems to me that proceeding from eucharistic ecclesiology we can affirm that the singular ministry of one presider (*proestôs*) of a local church existed from the beginning. Without him there could be no local church because without him there would be no eucharistic assembly. When Ignatius of Antioch wrote, "Wherever the bishop is, there must be an assembly of the faithful, for wherever Christ is, there is the catholic Church," he expressed in the language of his time what had existed as the pattern from the beginning.

Pierre Batiffol claimed that the history of the first two centuries of Christianity is subject to constant revision. It is in his expression only an *approximation revisable.*[2] My study is an attempt to revise the history of the primitive Christianity from the perspective of eucharistic ecclesiology. In light of this it will be shown that the basis of this life was grace and grace alone. Familiar facts then acquire new meaning and importance. A number of existing problems are thus removed but new questions arise. On the other hand, the significance of subsequent ecclesial history will appear differently because we will be viewing the Church's history in a manner radically different from that to which we were accustomed.

It is impossible for me to touch on all aspects of the ecclesial life of primitive Christianity. It is also impossible to determine the origin of all the processes taking shape in subsequent periods. My study is thus merely an effort to understand ecclesiology. Any failure is but my own and the whole ecclesiological problem will remain and need solution.

We live in an extremely difficult time. If one wished to indict our ecclesial life there would be no chance for an acquittal. Indeed everyone is guilty. History knows the periods when the disorganization of ecclesial life was no worse than in our time. There was struggle, disunity, mutual accusations, slander, and violence, but nevertheless there is a difference between the situation then and what we have now. Beneath that disorganization there was struggle over dogma. But in our time sheer human passion exposes itself in broad daylight without the protection of dogmatic debate. Our ecclesial life has reached a dead end, for the principles which penetrated it in the distant past have become obsolete and only continue to distort it. The Church is viewed as an organization subject to human legislation and, being an organization, it exists merely to serve human needs. Human will reigns within and externally human will strives to turn God's Church into a means of attaining its goals. Perhaps never before have the faithful themselves profaned the "bride of Christ" to such a degree.

A historian, a church historian in particular, does not live outside of time. If his work is for the Church he must serve the Church. Must he not then recall in his work that the Church has principles of its own, that the Church is not a human organization but a divine establishment, that it is not human will but God's will through the revelation of the Spirit that acts in it, that the Church lives and acts by the gifts of the Spirit which God does not give by measure, that "our commonwealth is in heaven, and from it we await a Savior, the Lord Jesus Christ" (Phil 3.20)? Must he not remind us, in the dullness of our everyday life, that "wherever the Church is, there is a Spirit of God, and wherever the Spirit of God is, there is the Church and the fullness of grace," that the Church is the "Church of the Holy Spirit," and therefore, abiding in the present age, it belongs to the "beginning of the last days" (*ta eschata*)?

And in the last days it shall be, God declares, that I will pour out my Spirit upon all flesh, and your sons and your daughters shall prophesy, and your young men shall see visions, and your old men shall dream dreams; yea, and on my menservants and my maidservants in those days I will pour out my Spirit; and they shall prophesy. And I will show wonders in the heaven above and signs on the earth beneath, blood, and fire, and vapor of smoke; the sun shall be turned into darkness and the moon into blood, before the day of the Lord comes, the great and manifest day. And it shall be that whoever calls on the name of the Lord shall be saved. (Acts 2.17–21)

The name of the Lord Jesus—*Kyrios Iêsous Christos.*

Chapter 1

The Royal Priesthood

---

1. Direct scriptural evidence of the priestly ministry of all the members of the Church is scarce but unambiguous enough not to require any special interpretation. The apostle Peter addresses all Christians in his epistle, saying:

> And like living stones be yourselves built (*oikodomeisthe*)[1] into a spiritual house, to be a holy priesthood, to offer spiritual sacrifices acceptable to God through Jesus Christ . . . You are a chosen race, a royal priesthood, a holy nation, God's own people, that you may declare the wonderful deeds of him who called you out of darkness into his marvelous light. Once you were no people, but now you are God's people; once you had not received mercy but now you have received mercy. (1 Peter 2.5, 9–10)

In the Book of Revelation we read:

> To him who . . . made us kings and priests (*basileis kai hiereis*)[2] to his God and Father, to him be glory and dominion for ever and ever. (1.6)

> And [you] have made us kings and priests[3] to our God and we shall reign on earth. (5.10)

> They shall be priests of God and of Christ, and they shall reign with him a thousand years. (20.6)

The Jews were God's chosen people:

> You are a people holy to the Lord your God, and the Lord has chosen you to be
> a people for his own possession, out of all the peoples that are on the face of the
> earth. (Deut 14.2)

God has formed this chosen people of the Old Testament for himself:

> The wild beasts will honor me, the jackals and the ostriches; for I give water in
> the wilderness, rivers in the desert, to give drink to my chosen people, the people
> whom I formed for myself that they might declare my praise. (Isa 43.20–21)

God has given a promise to his people:

> Now therefore, if you will obey my voice and keep my covenant, you shall be my
> own possession among all peoples; for all the earth is mine, and you shall be to me
> a kingdom of priests (LXX: *basileion hierateuma*) and a holy nation. (Ex 19.5–6)

In the New Testament, those who became this race and nation (*genos eklekton, ethnos hagion*) which the Lord has chosen and formed for himself were Christians who before were not at all a nation but who in the Church became God's people (*laos Theou*). The Church is God's people, and every faithful in the Church belongs to this people. He is *laikos*, a laic.[4] The ethnic principle, according to which ancient Israel was chosen has been surpassed and replaced by the principle of belonging to the Church: "There is neither Jew nor Greek, there is neither slave nor free, there is neither male nor female; for you are all one in Christ Jesus" (Gal 3.28). "The gifts and the call of God are irrevocable" (Rom 11.29), therefore one cannot be in the Church and not be a laic, *laikos*—a member of God's people. Every one in the Church is a laic and all together are God's people and each one is called, as a priest of God, to offer spiritual sacrifices to Him through Jesus Christ.

The priesthood in Judaism had the special character of being closed and inaccessible to the people. A boundary forever separated the priesthood from the people, a veil cut off the sanctuary from them. The royal priesthood of the whole of Israel in the Old Testament remained a promise for the future. In the present it was totally identified with the levitical priesthood to which the people of Israel in its entirety was inferior. It was a grievous crime to mingle present with future in relation to this ministry.

> Now Korah the son of Izhar, son of Kohath, son of Levi, and Dathan and
> Abi'ram the sons of Eli'ab, and On the son of Peleth, sons of Reuben, took men;

and they rose up before Moses, with a number of the people of Israel, two hundred and fifty leaders of the congregation, chosen from the assembly, well-known men; and they assembled themselves together against Moses and against Aaron, and said to them, "You have gone too far! For all the congregation are holy, every one of them, and the Lord is among them; why then do you exalt yourselves above the assembly of the Lord?" . . . And the earth opened its mouth and swallowed them up, with their households and all the men that belonged to Korah and all their goods. So they and all that belonged to them went down alive into Sheol; and the earth closed over them, and they perished from the midst of the assembly . . . And fire came forth from the Lord, and consumed the two hundred and fifty men offering the incense. (Num 16.1–35)

They rose up before Moses in the name of what the Lord said: all are God's people, the Lord is in the midst of all, all equally are members of the people and no one can set himself above God's people; therefore all will be holy and all will be priests (Ex 19.5–6). The earth opened up and the fire consumed those who rose up against Moses, but the promise remained irrevocable and it has been fulfilled in the Church. The veil was removed from the sanctuary—"and behold, the curtain of the temple was torn in two, from top to bottom" (Matt 27.51). The boundary was crossed, the gap was filled, and the entire people, the new Israel, was led into the sanctuary "by the blood of Jesus, by the new and living way which he opened for us through the curtain, that is, through his flesh . . ." (Heb 10.19–20). Through this entrance into the "temple of Christ's body" (John 2.21) the New Testament people became the royal priesthood (*basileion hierateuma*).[5] The royal priesthood became reality and the basis of the life of the Church. In the Old Testament, the temple service was restricted to the levitical priesthood, but in the New Testament, ministry in the Church, in the living tabernacle not made by hands, belongs to all the members of the Church. The people of God of the New Testament is made up of kings and priests. It is holy in its entirety, and the Lord is present in its assembly, so that it cannot be consumed by earth and destroyed by fire. The New Testament people as a whole serves God, not in the court of the Temple, but in the sanctuary itself where it is present as a whole.

You have come to Mount Zion and to the city of the living God, the heavenly Jerusalem, and to innumerable angels in festal gathering, and to the festal gathering and assembly of the first-born who are enrolled in heaven, and to a judge who is God of all, and to the spirits of just men made perfect, and to Jesus, the mediator of a new covenant. (Heb 12.22–24)

The New Israel has free access to the place the Old Testament people could not even approach.

The Old Testament priests were set apart for the service in the Temple as a tribe or clan. In the New Testament, the priesthood belongs to the whole Church. Each Christian is called to the priesthood, for no one can be baptized without having been called by God himself. "For by one Spirit we were all baptized into one body—Jews or Greeks, slaves or free—and all were made to drink of one Spirit" (1 Cor 12.13). Each member of the Church is called by God, set apart by Him as a member of the Church through the gift of the Spirit. Consequently, each member of the Church is called to life, activity, work, and ministry in the Church, for the Spirit is the principle of life and activity in the Church.[6] "God . . . has made us competent to be ministers of a new covenant, not in a written code but in the Spirit; for the written code kills, but the Spirit gives life" (2 Cor 3.6). Each one is set apart for the ministry of the royal priesthood, but they all minister as priests to God the Father, all together, for only in the Church is there a priesthood. Old Testament priesthood became a common ministry, the levitical one became the ministry of laics, for the Church is the people of God.

2. Primitive Christianity was a laic movement. Descending from the line of David, Christ did not belong to the tribe of Levi.[7] The apostles did not have any special relation to the Jerusalem Temple, for they did not belong to the levitical priesthood, either. Nor did the first Christians have any service in the Temple. For this reason they could not recreate the levitical priesthood in their community. Even if later there were some priests among them (Acts 6.7), their participation in the life of the Jerusalem church could not alter the laic character of primitive Christianity. We know that priests participated in the life of the synagogues but they did not have any leadership roles there. For Jewish consciousness the priesthood was closely connected with the Temple and without it the Temple could not exist.

Therefore even in primitive Christian thinking the emerging teaching concerning the royal priesthood must have been connected with a temple. If there is a royal priesthood, there is a temple and, conversely, if there is a temple, there must be a priesthood. The Jerusalem Temple while it was still standing could not have been this temple, even less could it be this temple after it was destroyed. When the author of the Epistle to the Hebrews was developing his teaching concerning the high priesthood of Christ, he constructed his teaching not after the image of the levitical priesthood, but "after the order of Melchizedek" (5.10), priest of the Most High God, without father or mother or genealogy (7.1–3). Both the sanctuary and the tabernacle where Christ has entered were not made by man but by the Lord (8.2). Instead of the Temple made by hands, the Christians have a temple not made by hands. Instead of bloody sacrifices they have spiritual sacrifices. The Church is "a spiritual house" (*oikos pneumatikos*), the temple in which the Christians become living stones through baptism (1 Peter 2.5).[8] As living stones of the spiritual temple they share in the high priesthood of Christ. "Since we have confidence to enter the sanctuary by the blood of Jesus, by the new and living way which he opened for us through the curtain, that is, through his flesh, and since we have a great priest over the house of God (*hierea megan epi ton oikon tou Theou*), let us draw near with a true heart . . ." (Heb 10.19–20). Therefore all the faithful, rather than just a few of them as it was in the Temple made by hands, constitute the priesthood in the spiritual house, for only priests can enter into the sanctuary. In the "spiritual house" there can be no bloody sacrifices. Rather, the priests of this house offer "spiritual sacrifices" (*pneumatikai thusiai*).[9] There is no doubt that the "spiritual sacrifices" offered through Jesus Christ (1 Peter 2.5) signify the Eucharist of which the apostle Peter was already speaking in the preceding verses.[10] Instituted at the Last Supper, the Eucharist is actualized at Pentecost. It is accomplished by the Spirit and therefore is itself spiritual. Introducing the notion of "spiritual sacrifice," the apostle Peter wished to demonstrate that the "holy priesthood" was a genuine priesthood, because for the readers of his epistle there could be no priesthood without sacrifice. But the emphasis here is not on a sacrifice as such but on the fact that it is "spiritual," corresponding to the "spiritual house" of the Christians.[11] Peter's teaching on the Church as a "spiritual house" is just another expression of the teaching of Paul on the Church as the body of Christ. Both are grounded in the primordial tradition going back to Christ himself: "He spoke of the temple of his body" (John 2.21). The idea concerning the royal priesthood of the members of the Church stems from the teaching about the Church.

3. "So I exhort the elders among you, as a fellow elder and a witness of the sufferings of Christ . . . tend the flock of God that is your charge . . . , not as domineering over possessions [of God] (*tôn klêrôn*) but by being examples to the flock" (1 Peter 5.1–3). In each local church, the Holy Spirit has set apart the presbyters (or bishops) to tend the flock of God (Acts 20.28). God's flock which the presbyters tend is their possession (*klêros*) which they have received from God.[12] God's people is one, God's flock is one, and the *klêros* is one. Belonging to God's flock, each member of the Church belongs to the possession that the presbyters tend and through them to the possession (*klêros*) of God. Thus one could say that each laic as a member of the people of God is a cleric. He is also a cleric (*klêrikos*) because the Lord took for his possession the whole people of God of which the cleric is a part. In the Old Testament the Lord took for his possession only the tribe of Israel.

> And beware lest you lift up your eyes to heaven, and when you see the sun and the moon and the stars, all the host of heaven, you be drawn away and worship them and serve them, things which the Lord your God has allotted to all the peoples under the whole heaven. But the Lord has taken you, and brought you forth out of the iron furnace, out of Egypt, to be a people of his own possession, as at this day. (Deut 4.19–20)

The whole of Israel is God's people, a people of his possession but also only a shadow of the new Israel in which the present and the future are joined together. In the strict sense of the word, God had as his possession only the tribe of Levi. "At that time the Lord set apart the tribe of Levi to carry the ark of the covenant of the Lord, to stand before the Lord to minister to him . . ." (Deut 10.8). If the entire people of Israel was set apart from all nations, the tribe of Levi was set apart from all remaining tribes and was set above the rest of the people, for the priesthood belonged to this tribe alone. In the New Testament the entire people constitutes the priesthood, therefore no part could be separated from the rest. In the New Testament, the Old Testament prophecy was fulfilled: the entire people, not just a part of it, serve in the name of the Lord. The entire New Testament people is God's possession (*klêros*) and each person within it is a cleric.[13] Just as in the course of dividing the promised land, the tribe of Levi did not receive its share of the land, so in the same way the members of the Church do not have a lasting city on earth but seek the city which is to come (Heb 13.14). Having the service of God as their possession, Christians are wholly given over to him and belong only to him. In the Old Testament the Levites were God's portion in the land and his inheritance—"they are wholly given to me from among the people of Israel" (Num 8.16). But in the New Testament the entire people of God is wholly given to God. "And you are Christ's and Christ is God's" (1 Cor 3.23). As members of the Church, Christians belong to Christ, and, through him, to God. They serve God not as a separate group but all together. As laics—members of God's people "in Christ"—they are wholly given over to God. They are clerics and as clerics (*klêrikoi*) they are all laics (*laikoi*).

4. The apostolic church did not know the separation of clerics from laics in our meaning of the words and it did not have the terms themselves in its usage. This is a basic fact of the ecclesial life in the primitive era, but it would be wrong to infer from this fact that ministry in the Church was exhausted by the notion of the priestly ministry, common for all. It was a ministry of the Church. Another fact of the life of the primitive Church was the diversity of ministries. The same Spirit by whom all were baptized into one body and of whom all were made to drink distributes particular gifts to each one "for the common good (*sympheron*)" (1 Cor 12.7), for action and service within the Church.

> And the gifts were that some should be apostles, some prophets, some evangelists, some pastors and teachers, to equip the saints for the work of ministry, for building up the body of Christ. (Eph 4.11–12)[14]

The diversity of ministries stems from the "organic" nature of the Church. Each of its members occupies in it his own position and place, proper to him alone. "God arranged the organs in the body, each one of them, as he chose" (1 Cor 12.18). In a living organism, place and position of its members depends on the functions executed by them. So in Christ's body, diverse ministries are associated with the place and position of the members. The gifts of the Spirit are not given for their own sake as a reward of some sort, but for ministry in the Church, and they are given to those who already have drunk of the Spirit. That means the common quality of having partaken of the Spirit is the foundation for the "work of ministry" because without this charismatic foundation the diversity of the Spirit's gifts would not be possible. That all the members of the Church drank of the one Spirit is manifest in their priestly ministry, for there cannot be a Spirit without action. Particular ministries are directed toward the "building up the body of Christ" (Eph 4.12). In them, various functions necessary for the common life of the whole body find their expression. For this reason common ministry in the Church presupposes a diversity of ministries and a diversity of ministries cannot exist without common ministry.

The diversity of ministries does not disrupt the unity of nature of the Church's members. Their ontological unity with each other stems from their unity "in Christ." All members possess the same nature, for they all have one and the same Spirit. "There are varieties of gifts, but the same Spirit . . ." (1 Cor 12.4). No one by his nature should put himself above others in the Church—even less above the Church—or pretend to speak for the Church in a special manner. Neither the apostles, nor the prophets, nor the teachers by themselves, nor all together, nor each in particular, constitute the Church. Both they and the others are merely members of the Church, but they are not the whole Church. Thus they cannot exist without the remaining members, for otherwise they would not be able to fulfill the functions for which God has set them apart and ordained them. The difference between a person who has a particular ministry and a person who does not have such a ministry is not ontological but functional.

This distinction would have become ontological if the Church did not have the priestly ministry common for all its members. In that case it would seem that only one part of the Church's members had a ministry while the majority did not. That would mean that the majority of members had not been given the gifts of the Spirit, for in the Church the Spirit is given for one to be active in it. The charismatic organism of the Church would then possess non-charismatic members.

> And in the last days it shall be, God declares, that I will pour out my Spirit upon all flesh, and your sons and your daughters shall prophesy, and your young men shall see visions . . . and on my menservants and my maidservants in those days I will pour out my Spirit; and they shall prophesy. (Acts 2.17–18; Joel 2.28–29)

There can be no non-charismatic members in the Church, just as there can be no members who do not minister in it. In the Church the grace of the Spirit is poured out in fullness on all of its members: "From his fullness have we all received, grace upon grace" (John 1.16). The operative difference is that those who are called for a special ministry also receive special gifts of the Spirit for their ministry in the Church. All are filled with one Spirit, but all do not have the same gifts of the Spirit. Those who have special ministries also have special gifts and those who do not perform such ministries do not. In the sacrament of marriage, the gifts of the Spirit are given to the newly wedded for their life together. Those who are not married do not possess these gifts, yet both are charismatics. Both have the grace of the Spirit.

The difference in gifts does not entail a difference in grace or its fullness. Grace is not distributed differentially. There is fullness of grace in each gift. Certainly it does not follow that all appropriate the fullness of grace in its entirety. It is the work of one's life and so each person receives that measure of grace that he or she is capable of appropriating. People cannot measure the quantity of grace which God gives without measure, but each of us knows that this measure is not always the same. The grace shines brightly in the saints, but in others it gleams little by little while never dying out. While the gifts of the Spirit are different, grace remains one and the same. But the appropriate measure of grace can be different even with the same gifts. Grace does not have levels, thus one cannot speak about higher or lower levels of grace, as does modern scholastic theology. To do so would be to divide that which God himself does not divide and to diminish the work of Christ through whom we all have received "grace upon grace." All have the same foundation in the Spirit. No one in the Church can by his nature stand higher than another, although he can fulfill a ministry that is higher than the ministries of others. Also, no one can act without or apart from the others. Even less could there be ministries in the Church that would not require the gifts of the Spirit. Wherever ministry is, there is the Spirit and wherever there is no ministry, there is no Spirit and no life.

5. Tertullian affirmed that "it is the authority of the Church and a part of the assembly of the clergy, which has established the difference between the clergy and the laity (*inter ordinem et plebem*)."[15] This would be true if we were to regard the clergy and the laics as separate groups distinct by their nature, but in reality it is not so. The conclusion presumably drawn from this statement would be inaccurate in every sense: "Accordingly, where there is no assembly of the clergy, then you yourself be the one who offers and baptizes, the priest."[16] Tertullian was tempted by the teaching concerning royal priesthood of the members of the Church, as many historically were, and he did not see that the original distinction between the clergy and the people stemmed from the distinction of ministries. In turn, the distinction of ministries was not established by the ecclesiastical authorities or a part of the clergy, but derived from the very identity of the Church herself.

The special ministry of the presider [*proestôs*] to which Tertullian refers is one of those vital functions, those manifestations of life, without which the Church cannot exist on earth as a living organism. The ministry of the presider found its expression in the eucharistic assembly. At the assembly, there were always those who presided and those who were presided over. Without this there could be no Eucharist, for by its nature it requires a presider. From the very inception of the Church the liturgical order distinguished between people and the presider.

> And on the day called Sunday, all who live in cities or in the country gather together in one place, and the memoirs of the apostles or the writings of the prophets are read, as long as time permits; then, when the reader has ceased, the president verbally instructs, and exhorts to the imitation of these good things. Then we all rise together and pray, and, as we before said, when our prayer is ended, bread and wine and water are brought, and the president in like manner offers prayers and thanksgivings, according to his ability, and the people assent, saying Amen.[17]

The presider offers the thanksgiving to which the people respond, "Amen." Among those who by their "amen" seal the thanksgiving of the presiders were not only those not endowed with special ministry but also those who performed different ministries. Among them were those whom today we call laymen; also presbyters, deacons, and teachers. All the participants of the assembly together with their presiders constituted a single people of God, the royal priesthood.

If this liturgical differentiation between presiders and people had indeed been established by ecclesiastical authorities, even in that case Tertullian would have been wrong. Establishments of that sort, based on the distinction of ministries, would be in accord with the will of God, for the will of God is for the distinction of ministries, not their confusion. Therefore Tertullian was absolutely wrong in ascribing to the laity those ministries for which they have not received the charismatic gifts: "you yourself be the one who offers and baptizes, the priest." This would be a confusion of ministries, in which case the priestly ministry of the people and its presider could not have found its expression, for it would make impossible the eucharistic assembly itself.

6. In Tertullian's time those having a special ministry of priesthood, one that took shape on the basis of the ministry of the presider, began to be called clerics. This new, narrowed-down understanding of the term *klêros* did not immediately change a common notion of *klêros* and did not create two heterogeneous strata in the ecclesial organism because the clergy did not separate itself from the people but still constituted a part of the whole assembly. Tertullian was incorrect for his own time, but he anticipated the future history of ecclesial organization. After him, empirical ecclesiastical life began to appropriate the principles of Roman law which were alien to it. The liturgical distinction between people and clerics in the narrow sense of the word turned into their separation from each other and gradually led to the appearance of two heterogeneous strata or states of being. Theological thought revived in the Church the Old Testament idea of the tabernacle, which had been replaced in the New Testament by a tabernacle not made by hands, with only one High Priest. The sword that finally cut the ecclesial body in two was the teaching on consecration. This is not a place to investigate why the idea of consecration came to permeate theological thought. When this idea began to enter theological thinking, all the members of the Church were still regarded as "consecrated" (*hierômenoi, teloumenoi*) as opposed to *anieroi, atelestoi*—i.e., those who did not belong to the Church. The mystery of initiation, by which the consecration was accomplished, was identified with the sacrament of baptism, chrismation, and Eucharist that led all who received the sacrament of baptism into a "sacred hierarchy" (*hiera diakosmêsis*).[18] Here the idea of consecration did not yet contradict the ancient teaching on the royal priesthood of God's people because the goal of consecration was initiation into the priesthood which was still understood as a "sacred people" (*tên tou hierou laou taxin*).[19] However, the ancient teaching on consecration did not remain as it had been, for the idea of consecration had its own logic. Byzantine thought concluded that it was not baptism but the sacrament of ordination that was the genuine mystery of consecration. As a result of this the majority of the "consecrated" became "non-consecrated" because they had experienced only one sacrament—baptism. Among the wide range of "the consecrated" that existed earlier there appeared lay or common people: *biôtikoi*. The "sacred hierarchy" (*hiera diakosmêsis*) was narrowed down. The laics were now excluded from it, and only clerics remained, though not all the clerics, but rather only those who belonged to the priesthood. Their distinction does not lie with ministry or their special status. These types of distinction are secondary. Their distinction is based on their distinct natures. Consecration causes a change in the nature of the consecrated person, just as baptism effects a change in the nature of the person who enters the Church. In dogmatic thinking there emerges a teaching on a "second baptism." When the Council of Trent proclaimed the impossibility of the laicization of clerics, it affirmed for Western theological consciousness the ontological distinction between clergy and laics. At the same time, the idea of consecration brought the teaching on royal priesthood to a state of lethargy. Lay people, being "non-consecrated," are alienated from the holy things (*anieroi*) and cannot draw near to the sanctuary. They cannot perform priestly service, for they lack consecration. A laic, as a member of God's people, does have the dignity of royal priesthood, which someone outside the church is lacking. In the course of history it came to be that it was not a *profanus*, an outsider, who was made "holy" (*sacer*), but on the contrary, it was "fellow citizens with the saints and members of the household of God" (*sympolitai tôn hagiôn kai oikeioi tou Theou*) (Eph 2.19), who became "outsiders"(*profani*).

7. Modern scholastic theology not only minimized the teaching on the royal priesthood but rendered it suspicious. The word of God became dangerous. In any case, it is not something appropriate to talk about. If Clement of Rome, Irenaeus of Lyons, Justin Martyr, Hippolytus of Rome, Clement of Alexandria, Origen, and finally John Chrysostom, Jerome, and the whole range of other Church fathers knew of our fears and doubts they would probably not only be utterly surprised but quite simply would not understand us at all. They would respond with the words of Irenaeus of Lyons: *omnes justi sacerdotalem habent ordinem*—"all

the righteous possess the order of the priesthood."[20] One cannot accuse Irenaeus of Lyons of being a Montanist like Tertullian, but Irenaeus, like Tertullian, professed the belief that the laics are priests. He was not afraid to say this for he knew, as did the whole early Church, that the priesthood of the laity does not undermine the ministry of bishops. He himself, more than anyone else, contributed to the development of the episcopal ministry.

What then is the problem? Why did scholastic theology turn its back on the teaching about the royal priesthood? The answer lies in this type of theology itself. More precisely, the way it raised the question made theology choose between the priesthood of the laics and the priesthood of the ecclesiastical hierarchy. "And he has made us kings and priests to his God and Father." He has made us all priests, not only the few who constitute the Church's clergy. If all are priests, how can only a few be called priests? And, on the contrary, if only some are priests, how can all be called priests? Prior to the Council of Nicea, the Church was not aware of this dilemma; nor is the Church generally, for the priesthood of God's people does not exclude the priesthood of the Church hierarchy. On the contrary, the priesthood of the Church hierarchy, as we shall see, is derived from the royal priesthood. The one priesthood cannot contradict the other, if one does not understand priesthood solely in terms of consecration, as scholastic theology does.

The idea of consecration is the product of theological speculation, not of ecclesial tradition. In spite of what is taught, ecclesial life preserves in dogma, tradition, and in its liturgical conscience the authentic teaching of the Church with respect to the people of God. At the eucharistic assembly, under the presidency of the bishop, the Church confesses the royal priesthood of its members and the diversity in the work of ministry—the variety of charismatic gifts which God himself gives "to each . . . for the common good." "Wherever the Church is, there is also the Holy Spirit, but wherever the Holy Spirit is, there is the Church and the fullness of grace" (1 Cor 12.7). The rejection of the royal priesthood of God's people, openly or in a hidden manner, is the denial of the gifts of the Spirit. Modern theology of course acknowledges that lay people receive gifts of the Spirit: in the sacraments of baptism, chrismation, repentance, and marriage. But the sphere of the Spirit's activity is thus limited to those to whom the gifts were administered in these sacraments. The gifts of the Spirit become the private property of those who receive them. Even in the sacrament of priesthood we find the same privatization of the gifts of the Spirit, for priesthood in modern Church organization does not always entail ministry. Modern theological thought, but even more so modern ecclesiastical practice, allows the gift of the Spirit received in the sacrament of ordination to remain inactive. Ministry is thus but a secondary consequence of the gift of the Spirit. Of more primary consequence is the change in the nature of the one who received the gift in the sacrament of priesthood. This is one of the instances where contemporary theological thought radically diverges from the teaching of the early Church. The gifts of the Spirit are administered for activity and the common good (*sympheron*). For this reason they are given to the Church, in the Church, and for the Church. These gifts have a dynamic nature that excludes anything static. By virtue of this fact, there can be no inactive gift of the Spirit because the Spirit is an active principle by his very nature. To deprive laics of their dignity as priests is equivalent to depriving them of the gifts of the Spirit, of which God has made them drink on the day of their baptism (1 Cor 12.13). The Church teaches that all possess the fullness of grace for the common good, but it does not teach that each one of us, in some particular moment of our life, has received gifts of the Spirit to keep us inactive, as a talent buried in the earth. In the Church we have received "grace upon grace" in order to live, to act, and to serve.

> Therefore let us be grateful for receiving a kingdom that cannot be shaken, and thus let us offer to God acceptable worship, with reverence and awe; for our God is a consuming fire. (Heb 12.28–29)

Chapter 2

The Ordination of Laics

1. In the Old Testament, physical birth determined whether someone belonged to the chosen people. Only the children of Abraham were heirs to God's promise. Despite the fact that proselytism was especially strong by the time of Christ's coming—"You traverse sea and land to make a single proselyte, and when he becomes a proselyte, you make him twice as much a child of hell as yourselves" (Matthew 23.15)—the neophytes themselves were not regarded in all respects as true members of Israel, but only their descendants. In the New Testament however, it is spiritual birth that determines if someone belongs to the Church: "Truly, truly, I say to you, unless one is born of water and the Spirit, he cannot enter the kingdom of God" (John 3.5). Beginning with the first apostolic preaching on the day of Pentecost, the sacrament of baptism by water and the Spirit is the one and only way of entering the Church, without which salvation is impossible.

The ancient church also recognized a so-called baptism by blood— (*baptisma sanguinis*)—but it was an exception from the general rule caused by especially tragic circumstances in the life of the Church in the time of persecution, when a person faced imminent death. Even this exception was conditioned by the content of the dogmatic teaching on baptism as coterminous with death. Therefore if the one who was persecuted and suffered (*martys*) and who announced himself as a Christian at the moment of suffering stayed alive, baptism by blood was eventually completed. In other words, baptism by blood substituted for the sacrament of baptism only in the time of persecution and prior to death itself—"If violence is brought against him (the catechumen) and he is killed before receiving baptism for the remission of sins, he will be justified, for he has received baptism in his own blood."[1] Only the blood shed in martyrdom for the sake of Christ's name was regarded as the sacrament of baptism.

In baptism a person dies to his previous life and is born spiritually through the Spirit as a new creation, for a new life in Church. Life in the Church is service to God through the Church and in the Church. "Receiving a kingdom that cannot be shaken, and thus let us offer to God acceptable worship (*latreuômen*), with reverence and awe" (Heb 12.28). In baptism we receive grace for the service (*latreia*) that for the author of the Epistle to the Hebrews is a priestly ministry.[2]

Like circumcision in the Old Testament, baptism by water and the Spirit is the sign that one belongs to the people of God of whom God made a "holy priesthood" (1 Peter 2.5) in the Church. "We are the true circumcision, who worship God in Spirit (*hoi Pneumati Theou latreuontes*) and glory in Christ Jesus" (Phil 3. 3). *Latreia* belongs to God's people, through which it belongs to each one of its members. Everyone in the Church is "God's minister," for it is the Church that ministers to God. *Latreia* finds its utmost expression at the eucharistic assembly that manifests the Church in all its fullness. The Eucharist is a "spiritual sacrifice" (*pneumatikê thysia*) of "reasonable worship" (*logikês latreias*). Thus the newly baptized, who has received grace for ministry in the Church, is immediately led into the eucharistic assembly to participate in the *leitourgia* of God's people.

Baptism by water and the Spirit (or, in modern terms, the sacrament of baptism and chrismation)[3] makes it possible for those who were ordained for the ministry of royal priesthood to participate in the eucharistic assembly. Baptism, chrismation and Eucharist—these are three charismatic acts through which a faithful joins the Church, becomes a member of the people of God, and abides in the Church in his status as a king and a priest.

2. The great dignity of a member of the people of God and the ministry of a laic as king and priest presupposes that he or she was ordained for this position. Every ministry in the Church presupposes God's calling and the communication of the charismatic gifts to the one called for this ministry. Without these gifts no ministry in the Church is possible. In recent times it became customary to speak of the sacrament of baptism and especially about the sacrament of chrismation as a "lay ordination."[4] The question as to whether this statement is correct depends on the meaning of "layman." It is inaccurate to regard laymen as a separate group of the members of the Church. According to modern scholastic teaching, lay people are "non-consecrated," as opposed to the "consecrated" which include all those who belong to the priesthood. As "non-consecrated," lay people do not receive any ordination and therefore the term "lay ordination" contains in itself a contradiction.

This would be accurate if the term "lay people" is understood as "laics," i.e., the members of God's people. Therefore, we should speak not of a "lay" but of a "laic" ordination.

In the earliest baptismal rite that has come down to us, the one we find in the *Apostolic Tradition* of Hippolytus of Rome, the idea of ordination can be quite clearly discerned. It is expressed in two actions.[5] The first one is the laying on of bishop's hands accompanied by the following prayer:

> Lord God, you have made them worthy to deserve the remission of sins through the laver of regeneration: make them worthy to be filled with the Holy Spirit, send your grace upon them that they may serve you in accordance with your will; for to you is glory, to the Father and the Son with the Holy Spirit in the holy Church both now and to the ages of the ages. Amen.[6]

Through the one who presides over it the Church prays that God would abundantly fill the baptized with the Holy Spirit and would send the gift of the Spirit for their ministry in the Church according to his will. Being abundantly filled with the Spirit is that state of satiety with the Spirit of which the apostle Paul spoke: "For by one Spirit we were all baptized into one body—Jews or Greeks, slaves or free—and all were made to drink of one Spirit" (1 Cor 12.13). On the basis of this charismatic state of satiety by the Spirit, they ask for the gift of the Spirit to be given to the baptized for their ministry in the Church. The *Apostolic Tradition* reflects the practice of the Roman Church at the end of the second century, but in its core this practice goes back to more ancient times, perhaps even to the apostolic era.

> Now when the apostles at Jerusalem heard that Samaria had received the word of God, they sent to them Peter and John, who came down and prayed for them that they might receive the Holy Spirit; for it had not yet fallen on any of them, but they had only been baptized in the name of the Lord Jesus. Then they laid their hands on them (*epetithesan tas cheiras ep' autous*) and they received the Holy Spirit. (Acts 8.14–17)[7]

However we might interpret this passage in Acts, in apostolic times the laying on of hands undoubtedly constituted a part of the sacrament of reception into the Church. In the ecclesial consciousness of the third century, the laying on of hands at the ordination for ministry signified the ordination for a priestly ministry. In the prayer formula, at the laying of hands on the newly baptized we find the same verb *servire* (*leitourgein*) used in the prayer formula at the ordination of a bishop. The use of one and the same verb at the laying on of hands in both instances is not coincidental. Rather this points to one and the same ministry: for one it is a high priestly ministry, for another it is a priestly ministry.[8]

The second act in the ordination of the laics, amplifying and disclosing the first, is the pouring of the holy oil that the bishop does together with the laying on of hands:[9] "I anoint you with holy oil in God the Father Almighty and Christ Jesus and the Holy Spirit." In the Old Testament only priests and kings were anointed. The ministry for which the newly baptized is ordained by prayer for the gifts of the Spirit is both royal and priestly.[10]

I have no need to examine the history of the rites of baptism and chrismation because despite all the changes that occurred, the Orthodox baptismal rite preserves to this day the idea of the ordination of the laics. It is true that the laying on of the bishop's hands has disappeared from these rites, though there are still traces that remain. The "Rite of Ablution on the eighth day" speaks of the laying on not of the bishop's but of God's mighty hand. The second prayer of the rite reads thus:

> Master, Lord our God, who through the font grants heavenly radiance to those who are baptized, who gives your newly enlightened servant rebirth through water and Spirit, and grants him forgiveness of sins both voluntary and involuntary, lay your mighty hand on him and guard him by the power of your loving kindness; preserve the pledge inviolate; and count him worthy of eternal life and your good pleasure.[11]

God imposes his mighty hand in order that the candidate might be ordained for the high calling of a member of God's people. In the prayer over the water the celebrant asks:

> Declare this water to be the water of redemption, water of sanctification, cleansing of flesh and spirit, untying of bonds, forgiveness of offences, enlightenment of soul, washing of rebirth, renewal of spirit, gift of adoption, garment of incorruption, the source of life . . . Manifest yourself, Lord, in this water, and grant that the one being baptized in it may be transformed . . . and having guarded the gift of the Holy Spirit and increased the deposit of grace, may receive the prize of his high calling (*to brabeion tês anô klêseôs*) and be numbered with the firstborn, whose names are inscribed in heaven, in you our God and Lord, Jesus Christ.

The prize of the high calling and being numbered with the firstborn inscribed in heaven is precisely the calling of the new member of God's people in his or her priestly ministry.

The anointing with holy oil has survived in the modern rite of chrismation. Today it is done by the celebrant of the sacrament of baptism and chrismation who pronounces the formula: "The seal of the gift of the Holy Spirit."[12] Contrary to the scholastic dogmatic theology which has, consciously or not, renounced the teaching concerning the priestly status of laics and thus failed to pinpoint the essence of the very sacrament that the Church celebrates,[13] the anointing is *sphragis*, the seal signifying that laics belong to God's flock, to the people of God that is the "holy priesthood."

Even in modern times, just as in antiquity, the newly baptized is clothed in white garments. We do not know when exactly this custom of clothing the newly baptized appeared. Possibly, it is this custom that is referred to already in the book of Revelation: "Who are these, clothed in white robes (*tas stolas tas leukas*), and whence have they come?" (Rev 7. 13). The custom of clothing the newly baptized in white garments was not ubiquitous until the fourth century.[14] In any case, the Church of Rome had not yet accepted this custom at the beginning of the third century. Hippolytus of Rome does not mention it in his *Apostolic Tradition*. Had this custom existed he would certainly have pointed it out, for in Hippolytus we find not a description of the rite of the entrance into the Church but an exposition of the rite itself. We find the first unquestionable testimony to the vesting of the newly baptized with Ambrose of Milan in the West,[15] and with Cyril of Jerusalem in the East. Cyril writes:

> Once you have stripped off the old garments and put on those which are spiritually white, you must be clad in white always. I am not of course saying that you must always wear white clothing on your body, but that your spiritual dress must be truly white and shining.[16]

Eusebius in *Vita Constantini* describes in detail the clothing of Constantine the Great. The author of the treatise *On Ecclesiastical Hierarchy* recounts how the clothing of the newly baptized took place:

> The priests then bring the newly baptized back to his sponsor, to the one who had brought him for introduction, and together with him they reclothe the one consecrated and bring him back once more to the hierarch. Using the most

powerful divine ointment he makes the sign of the cross on him and proclaims him ready to receive communion at the sacred initiating Eucharist.[17]

The most common term for the garment in which the newly baptized was clothed was *alba vestis* or *vestis candida* in the West, but in the East *himatia leuka, esthês lampra, stolê lampra*. Probably no later than the eighth century, the clothing was accompanied by a liturgical formula. According to the thirteenth century Sinai Euchologion, the robe in which the newly baptized is clothed is taken from the altar table: "Take the robe (*stolên*), holy and unblemished, which you brought by your hand to the altar of our Lord Jesus Christ and enter into eternal life."[18] In the contemporary rite, it is the priest who does the clothing, pronouncing the formula: "The servant of God is clothed into the robe of righteousness in the name of the Father, and of the Son and of the Holy Spirit. Amen." The custom of clothing appears less influenced by the words of St Paul: "As many of you as were baptized into Christ have put on Christ" (Gal 3. 27), as well as by the Matthean parable about those called to the marriage feast: "But when the king came in to look at the guests, he saw there a man who had no wedding garment" (Matt 22.11).[19] The one whom God has chosen and ordained for the service in the Church, is clothed into the wedding garment, without which he cannot approach the Lord's supper. The white garment was a symbol of priestly rank for each member of God's people. It is as a priest to his God that he is clothed in a special garment.[20] From the liturgical point of view, because it was practically impossible for all the faithful participants of the eucharistic assembly to clothe themselves in special garments, doubtlessly these were reserved only for members of the clergy.[21] But historically it is also doubtless that the practice of clothing in the baptismal garments was established in the Church earlier than the practice of clothing in special garments at the ordination for the priesthood.

When the teaching on the ministry of laics as kings and priests was gradually disappearing in dogmatic theology, liturgical thought continued to develop. This teaching sought to express more definitely in the rite itself not only the setting apart of the laic for priestly ministry but also as a king. Liturgical thinking clearly was inspired by the First Letter of St. Peter and also by the book of Revelation, where it says that all faithful are made "kings and priests to his God and Father."[22] On the other hand, attempts to express this teaching liturgically show how it was understood.

Very early in the West there also appeared the custom of putting on the head of a newly baptized a kind of a little cap called *linteum, chrismale, cappa,* or *mitra* to safeguard the place of anointing by the holy myron. This custom did not exist in the East, for there not only the head but different parts of the body were anointed as well. Nevertheless, in the Greek Euchologia we find references to the putting upon the head of a *koukoulion*, accompanied by the prayer with the title of the prayer for the cowl/crown (*euchê tou koukouliou* or *euchê tou diadêmatos*).[23] This prayer emphasizes setting someone apart as a king. This was expressed particularly clearly among the Copts, Armenians, Maronites, and Jacobites, who precisely "crown" the newly baptized as a king by putting on his head either a wreath of the myrtle or palm leaves or a crown. Thus in the ritual of the Syrian Jacobites we find the following prayer: *Corona, Domine, hunc servum tuum decore et gloria, sitque eius vita in bene*—"O Lord, crown this your servant with glory and honor and may his life be for good."[24] Our contemporary rite has also preserved the idea of setting someone apart as a king:

> Lord our God, who through your loving kindness have sanctified from the fullness of the font those who believe in you, bless this child here present, and let your blessing come down upon his head. As you blessed King David through Samuel the Prophet, bless too the head of your servant through the hand of me, a sinner, visiting him with your Holy Spirit, so that as he advances to mature years and to the grey hairs of old age, he may give glory to you and see the good things of Jerusalem all the days of his life. (Prayer before Tonsure)

The prayer asks that the Lord would bless the newly baptized as through prophet Samuel He blessed David as king. Although nowhere in the order of the service is it suggested that the bishop or the priest celebrating the sacrament of reception into the Church has to lay his hand upon a person, this clearly follows from the prayer itself. At the same time, this prayer also demonstrates that the concept of laic ordination has not totally vanished from the contemporary baptismal rite.[25]

The newly baptized, ordained for the ministry of king and priest, is then tonsured: "The servant of God is tonsured in the name of the Father and of the Son and of the Holy Spirit." This tonsure is absolutely the same as that of clerics and apparently came to be applied to the laics, taken from clerical ordination. The principal significance of the rite of tonsure, one of the most ancient rites in history, is to demonstrate the complete dedication of the tonsured person to the service of God. Apparently the first allusion to the tonsure of the newly baptized is found in Symeon of Thessalonica.[26] He treats this rite as an established custom which therefore must have emerged long before the fifteenth century. The tonsure of the newly baptized is the sign of their entering the ranks of clergy in the broadest sense of the term, as being numbered among those whom God himself has chosen as his own possession, and who are God's part and possession on earth.

As a priest before the God and Father, the newly baptized male infant, at the churching done after baptism, is taken inside the altar and is carried around the altar three times. In the Russian Trebnik this rite has been changed and it is said: "and he brings him inside the holy altar, if he is male." There cannot be any doubt that this change occurred under the influence of scholastic theology, which could not possibly admit that a lay person, who in the Church remains non-consecrated, would be led into the altar and carried around it, as it is done at the rite of holy orders.

Finally, according to Hippolytus of Rome, at the chrismation the bishop gives the kiss of peace to the newly baptized with the words: "The Lord be with you," to which he replies: "and with your spirit."[27] At the episcopal ordination, again according to the same testimony, Hippolytus asserts that the kiss of peace is again given to the newly ordained bishop: "When he has been made bishop let everyone offer him the kiss of peace, greeting him because he has been made worthy,"[28] i.e., worthy of episcopal ministry. The newly baptized receives a kiss of peace, for he or she also was "made worthy—*dignus effectus est*," i.e., worthy of ministry as a king and priest.

3. Tonsuring, laying on of hands, clothing and leading the baptized around the altar—these are acts constituting the sacramental rite of reception into the Church. All these aspects are present even in the contemporary rite of priestly ordination. This affinity is not coincidental. It bears witness to the fact that in liturgical consciousness, the sacrament of entrance into the Church was regarded as the sacrament of ordination for a newly baptized person. The historical sequence in which the elements of both sacraments emerged is not important. For me, however, it is important to emphasize that liturgical thought deliberately puts these elements together and thus establishes a fundamental connection between both these sacraments. The newly baptized, spiritually born in the sacrament of baptism, is ordained for service in the Church, for carrying out his calling as a member of God's people, a nation of kings and priests, so that he may keep "the garment of incorruption and the seal of the Spirit undefiled and unstained in the fearful day of Christ our God." The Spirit is a pledge (*arrabôn*) of a future age, a coming *aeon* of the Spirit which will come at the "day of the Lord." The one who preserves the "seal of the Spirit," will preserve himself on the day of the Lord which already is coming in every Eucharist in which he serves God together with all the people.

The baptismal garment is a priestly garment for the priestly ministry in the Church.

The members of the Church are members of God's people. According to authentic ecclesial thinking, being a laic means being ordained. The testimony of the liturgy, based on Scripture, is the Church's testimony. Before the idea of "consecration" cut the body of the Church in two, the setting apart of the newly baptized made them all consecrated (*teloumenoi*). That is what the author of the treatise *On Ecclesiastical Hierarchy* called the members of the Church.[29] The Church consists of those who are ordained or, to use the expression of Pseudo-Dionysius, consecrated to God for his service in the Church. That is why a laic cannot be viewed in opposition to the consecrated—*hierômenois, sacratis hominibus*—but only in opposition to the non-consecrated, *profanis, anierois*, i.e., to those who are not in the Church, who are not members of God's people. The Church does not know the first kind of opposition, for both in Scripture and in its liturgical life it bears witness that all its members are kings and priests before the God and Father. There can be no "lay people" (*biôtikoi*) in the Church, no common people, no worldly ones,[30] for the Church does not belong to this age (*aeon*), and all who entered it, having received the pledge of the Spirit while still dwelling in the present age, belong to the age to come. How could a person be non-consecrated if this is said of him or her:

> To him who conquers I will give some of the hidden manna, and I will give him a white stone, with a new name written on the stone which no one knows except him who receives it. (Rev 2.17)

Hippolytus of Rome concludes his exposition of the entrance rite into the Church with an allusion to this new name which only can be uttered at the eucharistic assembly:[31]

> He who conquers, I will make him a pillar in the temple of my God; never shall he go out of it, and I will write on him the name of my God, and the name of the city of my God, the new Jerusalem which comes down from my God out of heaven, and my own new name . . . He who conquers, I will grant him to sit with me on my throne, as I myself conquered and sat down with my Father on his throne. (Rev 3.12, 21)

This new name is the name of the Church and the name of a member of the Church.

Chapter 3

The Ministry of Laics

I. The Ministry of Laics as a Ministry of God's People

Ordained in the sacrament of baptism by water and the Spirit to be king
and priest, the newly enlightened Christian is solemnly led into the eucharistic assembly.

> But we, after we have thus washed him who has been convinced and
> has assented to our teaching, bring him to the place where those who
> are called brethren are assembled, in order that we may offer hearty
> prayers in common for ourselves and for the baptized [illuminated]
> person, and for all others in every place . . . Having ended the prayers,
> we salute one another with a kiss. There is then brought to the presi-
> dent of the brethren bread and a cup of wine mixed with water; and
> he taking them, gives praise and glory to the Father of the universe,
> through the name of the Son and of the Holy Ghost, and offers thanks
> at considerable length for our being counted worthy to receive these
> things at His hands. And when he has concluded the prayers and
> thanksgivings, all the people present express their assent by saying
> Amen . . . And when the president has given thanks, and all the people
> have expressed their assent, those who are called by us deacons give
> to each of those present to partake of the bread and wine mixed with
> water over which the thanksgiving was pronounced, and to those
> who are absent they carry away a portion.[1]

The Eucharist is the *leitourgia* celebrated by God's people gathered in
the temple of Christ's body. Therefore only one who is ordained for the

"high calling" of being a member of God's people can participate in the Eucharist. The eucharistic assembly began with the reading of the Scriptures and the homily by the presider, followed by common prayer. The catechumens were excluded not only from participation in the Eucharist but from common prayer, as well, for they did not yet have the calling of being members of God's people, the people of priests and kings. "And henceforth (after chrismation) they shall pray with all the people; they shall not pray with the people until they have performed all these things."[2] The prayer of the Church is prayer to the Father "in Christ." Whoever is not "in Christ" cannot take part in it and whoever cannot take part in it cannot participate in the Eucharist. Conversely, whoever cannot participate in the Eucharist cannot take part in the prayer of the Church. But to be "in Christ" means to offer a sacred service to his God and Father. Just as in the Old Testament "every priest stands daily in his service (*hestêken kath' hêmeran leitourgôn*)" (Heb. 10.11), thus also in the New Testament every one of the faithful in the eucharistic assembly stands before God as a liturgical minister (*leitourgos*). The whole life of the faithful is an unceasing ministry (*latreia*) to God, but in a particular way, intimately related to the ministry (*leitourgia*) at the eucharistic assembly where everything begins and ends. This is why every ministry in the Church is closely connected with the eucharistic assembly.[3]

The participation of the newly baptized in the eucharistic assembly, which completes the charismatic act of his reception into the Church, brings into the open the nature and characteristics of the ministry unto which every member of the Church is ordained. According to Hippolytus of Rome, after his ordination the newly ordained bishop presides at the eucharistic assembly for the first time.[4] This latter detail shows that the ordination is accomplished exactly for the purpose of his function as a presider. According to the same author, after his ordination a presbyter takes his place among the presbyters, being ordained in order to have "a share and inheritance with the presbyterate." Immediately after his ordination the new deacon took his place among the deacons at the episcopal celebration of the Eucharist as the bishop's assistant. We have every reason to infer that the ordination of the newly baptized for his or her ministry as king and priest also was done for the purpose of the eucharistic assembly. After the sacrament of baptism by water and the Spirit, the newly baptized "concelebrated" in the sacred ministry of the Eucharist for the first time. Since it is a liturgical action, the ministry of all the faithful in the Eucharist is just as necessary as that of the presider. This is a necessary and constitutive element of the liturgical whole, as is clear in Justin Martyr's description of the baptismal Eucharist cited above. From his indication that the communion of the faithful comes after "the president has given thanks, and all the people have expressed their assent," it follows that both are necessary at the celebration of the Eucharist. Had Justin reasoned otherwise, he could have easily omitted mentioning the people expressing "their assent." Every one of the faithful concelebrates the Eucharist together with all the rest of the people. This means that the ministry of the faithful as kings and priests is expressed in their communal service. In this everyone does not serve by himself, but together with the community. Thus the ministry of the laics no longer exists when it is no longer a communal ministry. Every one of the faithful stands before God as a *leitourgos*, but does so only when the Church is gathered *epi to auto*, i.e., when the people of God, assembled by Him, minister to Him. The common ministry of the faithful is the ministry of God's people when they act as one unified entity. In other words, the common ministry of laics is the ministry of the Church itself. From this it follows that to be in the Church means to be a member of God's people and to possess the charism of the royal priesthood, not for the sake of individual service, but for the participation in the ministry of the Church. Therefore, where there is no eucharistic assembly the faithful cannot minister as priests and kings because there is no ministry of the Church. "For by one Spirit we were all baptized into one body—Jews or Greeks, slaves or free—and all were made to drink of one Spirit" (1 Cor 12.13). Upon entering the Church each one receives the Spirit in order to serve God "in Christ" when the Church is serving God. For this reason the common ministry of the faithful does not eliminate any special ministry, for the common charism of God's people does not eliminate special charisms of particular members of the Church. The latter is the service in the Church and for the Church, and the former is the service of the Church, but the Church encompasses both one and the other.

II. Sacramental Ministry in the Church

1. According to contemporary dogmatic teaching the ministry in the Church is expressed in the three following aspects: sacramental ministry, administration, and teaching. Scholastic theological systems regard these areas of activity as the property of the ecclesiastical hierarchy. In the Roman Catholic Church only those included in the ranks of the clergy, depending on rank, can participate in these areas of ministry. The scholastic teaching of the Orthodox Church is less decisive than the Roman Catholic, and the actual life of the Orthodox Church to a certain extent contradicts this teaching. Scholastic systems of theology did all they could to suck the life out of the common ministry of God's people and disassociate it from the special ministries in the Church. The historical movement in that direction produced unfortunate results. It did not totally destroy the work of the laics' ministry in the Church but, having turned laics into "lay people" deprived of the common charism of their ministry as kings and priests, it endowed their work with the wrong intentions. The natural propensity of lay people for activity within the Church, unable to find its proper expression, often manifested itself in inappropriate forms. Being the people of the world, lay people tend to act in the Church as in the world, turning the Church from the charismatic organism into an organism bound by law. When the doctrine of the royal and priestly ministry of God's people was "forgotten," there was no possibility for lay people to act on the basis of their own charisms. Therefore the only possibility left was to act in the Church on a basis of law. That is why the lay people are allowed to minister in the areas that have no connection with the royal and priestly ministry of God's people, but rather constitute some of the special ministries bestowed on the basis of special gifts that laics do not possess.

2. According to modern scholastic teaching lay people are excluded from the area of sacramental ministry. They are the objects of the liturgy and sacraments but do not themselves perform them. Here is one of the greatest paradoxes of ecclesiastical life. Precisely those whom God has called and solemnly ordained in the Church for their ministry as kings and priests find themselves deprived of this ministry. However, this is no coincidence but came about as a strictly logical consequence of the doctrine of lay people as "non-consecrated ones," for only consecration provides access to the celebration of the mysteries. It is true though that in recent theological literature the lay people were referred to as concelebrants with a presbyter and bishop in the celebration of the sacraments. The significance of these pronouncements is obvious. This is the first and probably most significant attack on scholastic systems of theology. Yet these pronouncements are still not at all clear and definitive because for the most part their premises remain the same. They still view lay people as that part of the ecclesial body lacking consecration. How lay people actually do concelebrate the liturgy remains unclear. If expressed through some kind of dialogue between lay people and clergy during the divine service, this cannot yet be called concelebration. Still less can it be called an expression of their ministry as kings and priests. Even if one viewed this concelebration in the same terms as the concelebration of presbyters with the bishop, it would not by itself manifest the royal and priestly charism of God's people. A bishop can concelebrate with presbyters but also without them. The concelebration or its absence does not in any way change the power and effect of the liturgy that the bishop celebrates.

But can a bishop or a presbyter celebrate the divine services alone, without God's people? To answer this question, one should first determine just who actually celebrates the sacraments and divine services in the Church. For scholastic theology this is a moot question long ago resolved. Priests celebrate the mysteries, for they were ordained to do so. Likewise, lay people do not celebrate the divine services because they did not receive consecration. Despite the categorical tone of this statement one cannot be prohibited from seeking an answer to this question in Scripture and tradition. The Church responds to this inquiry with a doctrine of the priestly status of laics. If this doctrine is not a dead letter but living and active truth it means that the entire people of God are priests who celebrate all the sacraments. It would be incorrect to infer from this statement that every laic celebrates the liturgy and the sacraments individually or that a presbyter or a bishop individually, apart from others, celebrates the mysteries. The liturgy and the sacraments are celebrated by the Church and in the Church, in the assembly of the people of God. This means that the liturgy and the sacraments are celebrated in the ecclesial assembly by God's people, which includes both laics in the narrow sense of this word and the ecclesial hierarchy, all calling upon God in prayer. Every laic indeed celebrates the liturgy and the sacraments, but only together with the rest of God's people and with those who preside over them. A bishop or a presbyter, presiding over the people of God, celebrates the sacraments only together with the people without whom their role as presiders would be mere phantasy.

This communal character of celebrating the liturgy and the sacraments makes explicit the concept that in the Church it is the Church itself that accomplishes all things. According to Ignatius of Antioch, wherever the bishop is, there is the Church and, conversely, wherever the Church is, there is the bishop.[5] The bishop belongs to the Church, but the Church incorporates the bishop. There can be no Church without a bishop, but there also can be no bishop without a Church. If the bishop alone could celebrate the sacraments, he could exist without the Church, as well. If the people could celebrate the sacraments without the bishop, the Church also could exist without him. Neither the assembly of God's people nor the Church could exist without those who preside over it. That is why according to Ignatius's teaching no churchly activity can be done without the bishop. No sacrament can be celebrated without him, but not because he, as scholastic theology teaches, is the only celebrant of the sacraments, but rather because without a bishop there is no Church. Regarding the bishop as the only celebrant of the liturgy and the sacraments, scholastic theology detaches him from the Church and thus deprives him of his episcopal status. It is not a paradox but a genuine doctrine of the Church, because where there is no Church, there are no mysteries, no sacraments, and no bishop. The sacraments are not celebrated by some separate groups within the ecclesial body concocted by scholastic theology, but by the whole people of God, "without separation or division." God's people celebrate the sacraments also "without confusion," for in the one body of the Church, there are different ministries. The ministry of laics in the Church in the liturgy and the sacraments does not invalidate the ministry of those who preside over the people, because without them the ministry of laics would be unable to be expressed. More precisely, it would be left outside of the Church. Laics are concelebrants with the bishop and the presbyter, for it is in concelebration that the sacraments are performed. Laics are the bishop's concelebrants not just because they have some active role in the sacramental ministry but because they, being the priests of the most high God, actually celebrate those sacraments. Only with the concelebration of the laics can the bishop or presbyter celebrate those acts. Only a layperson who had been degraded from his priestly status (becoming non-initiated by this) is deprived of sacramental ministry. As a member of the people of God, a laic ministers together with those who preside over him. However, he ministers in a way different from the latter, who have a ministry distinct from that of the laics and special gifts of the Holy Spirit which a laic does not possess.

Therefore sacramental ministry is not only open to the laics, but the liturgy and the sacraments themselves are celebrated only when the whole people of God celebrate them, i.e., when the presiders together with the people celebrate those acts. *Habeas ergo sacerdotium, quia gens sacerdotalis es, et ideo offerre debes Deo hostiam laudis . . .*[6] The priesthood belongs to everyone, for it belongs to the Church and thus, everyone ministers when the Church ministers. The people of God, chosen by Him, are always holy just as the Church is always holy regardless of the sinfulness of some of its members. That is why the sacraments always have the grace of the Spirit and are valid. The unworthiness of particular members of the Church does not make the sacrament that the Church celebrates worthless. If unworthy members of the Church celebrate the sacrament then their unworthiness would have been reflected in their action. The "Great Church" always firmly resisted this idea, condemning the inappropriate rigorism of Novatians, Eustaphians, Donatists et al.

> If any one shall maintain, concerning a married presbyter, that it is not lawful to partake of the oblation when he offers it, let him be anathema.[7]

Defending the worthiness of all its sacraments, the Church professes its doctrine concerning their common celebration by the whole people of God. On the other hand, the teaching that a bishop or a presbyter celebrates the sacraments without the people of God or merely in the presence of the uninitiated laymen who are lacking the priestly ministry ascribes to the mysteries some magic power. Mysteries have nothing in common with magic, and primarily because the sacrosanct words uttered by a bishop or a presbyter alone, without the people—without the Church and outside of the Church—do not make mystery happen.

III. The Ministry of Laics in the Liturgy and the Sacraments

1. The historical deprivation of laics from sacramental ministry was a result of the doctrine that penetrated ecclesial consciousness. This doctrine regarded laics as non-consecrated and thus the opposite of the consecrated, namely, the clerics and in particular the hierarchy. This division came to shape the whole liturgical order of life. All aspects of the laics' priestly ministry disappeared without anyone's notice. As this ministry became obscured, the veil, like the curtain in the Old Testament, reappeared in the Church, separating holy things from the people.

The foundations of liturgical life had been formed much earlier than the time when the distinction between the consecrated and non-consecrated appeared. Nevertheless, many things in liturgical life were changed in order to adjust to this new understanding. If the laics are *biôtikoi*, that is, worldly or profane, then access to the holy things and the sanctuary must be absolutely or nearly absolutely prohibited for them. The sanctuary—the altar—begins to be segregated from the people, later on wholly shut off by means of the iconostasis.[8] Ecclesiastical authorities insisted that access to the altar was only for the consecrated, primarily the priesthood. According to Canon 69 of the Council in Trullo, "absolutely no one from amongst the laity (*en laikois*) shall be allowed to enter the holy sanctuary (*thysiastêriou*); though the emperor's majesty and authority shall in no wise be hindered from doing so, whenever he desires to offer the gifts to the Creator, in accordance with a most ancient tradition."[9] In relation to this canon, Balsamon wrote:

> By what reason does everyone who wishes enter without hindrance the divine sanctuary of the most glorious temple of our Lord Jesus Christ on the island of Chalke—I do not know . . . Make note of the present canon and by no means permit laymen to enter the holy altar of the temple. I, however, took great care in prohibiting laymen from entering the holy altar of the temple of my most holy Lady the Theotokos Hodegetria but could not succeed in that: for they say that this is an ancient custom which must not be hindered.[10]

It is striking that simple Byzantine Greeks—an *ochlos*[11] in Balsamon's estimation—indeed preserved an ancient custom whereas a highly learned Byzantine had forgotten it or did not want to remember, even though pressured to make concessions for the people. Byzantine theology was holding firmly to this canon, striving to introduce it into practice, seeing it as expressing the principle of partition between the priesthood and the people. "The altar is set apart only for the consecrated persons," wrote Zonaras in his commentary on this canon of the Council in Trullo.[12] Being more straightforward and less diplomatic than Balsamon he felt uneasy that the same canon allowed the emperor to enter the altar when he offers the gifts to God.

> Granting this privilege to the emperor, the fathers as if for their own justification adduced the mention of authority and its dignity, as if saying thus: even he, being a layman, should not be entering the altar, but for the sake of authority and its dignity, we grant to him this privilege in accordance with the original tradition of this coming from the ancient fathers.[13]

Zonaras regarded the permission for the emperor to enter the altar only an exception that confirmed the rule. Balsamon's reasoning is different. Sharing Zonaras' view that the altar is set apart for the priesthood he does not hesitate to acknowledge the archpastoral dignity of the *basileus*.

> With respect to the emperors, some, holding to the letter of this canon, contended that they should not be hindered from entering inside the altar when they wish to bring the offering to God, but they should [be hindered] when they want to come in just for veneration. I, however, do not see it this way. For the Orthodox emperors, appointing the patriarchs with the calling to the Holy Trinity and being the Lord's anointed ones, come into the holy altar uninhibited, whenever they want and also walk and make the sign of the cross with the *trikêrion* as the hierarchs. The emperors also offer catechetical instruction to the people, which is an exclusive privilege of the local hierarchs. In the nineteenth chapter of *Jewish Antiquities* by Josephus Flavius we find the following imperial signature: Tiberius Claudius, Caesar Augustus Germanicus, the greatest hierarch, consulus, second time endowed with the tribunal authority. And insofar as the reigning emperor is also God's anointed by reason of his anointing for the kingship, and Christ who is our God is also, among other things, a high priest, thus it is permissible for the emperor to be embellished with the archpastoral privileges.[14]

The typically Roman concept of the sacred seemed to be so familiar that in order to substantiate the archpastoral status of the basileus, Balsamon appeals to the fact that the Roman emperor was *pontifex maximus*. Balsamon forgot an ancient custom that was preserved in the Church but remembered the sacred tradition of Rome. Despite canon 69 of Trullo, the church had preserved the ancient custom, and the lay people, if not unconditionally allowed into the altar, are not completely prohibited from entering it.

"The altar is set apart only for the consecrated"—*to thysiastêrion monois tois hierômenois aphôristai*, due to the fact that the sanctuary is literally separated from the people. One of the most prominent Orthodox commentators on the canons, Nicodemus Milaš, thought that "from the most ancient time of the church anyone who is not part of the clergy was prohibited from entering the altar due to the mystical character of the bloodless sacrifice offered there."[15] Let us put aside the question of whether the statement concerning the antiquity of this prohibition is accurate, as well as the following comment that this is the common canon for both Eastern and Western Church. Let us ask rather, why the mystical character of the bloodless sacrifice offered in the altar can prevent the lay people from entering the altar? How is this statement an explanation? But, "I received from the Lord what I also delivered to you, that the Lord Jesus on the night when he was betrayed took bread, and when he had given thanks, he broke it, and said . . ." (1 Cor 11.23–24), and, "The cup of blessing which we bless, is it not a participation in the blood of Christ? The bread which we break, is it not a participation in the body of Christ?" (1 Cor 10.16). The apostle Paul contended that grace was given to him so that he may

> preach to the Gentiles the unsearchable riches of Christ, and to make all men see what is the plan of the mystery hidden for ages in God who created all things; that through the church the manifold wisdom of God might now be made known to the principalities and powers in the heavenly places. (Eph 3.8–10)

The manifold Wisdom of God is open to all and for this reason it is not the mystical character of the sacrifice offered in the altar that prohibits entrance to the lay people. Rather it is because the lay people are non-consecrated that they cannot approach the sanctuary and that the great mystery must be concealed from them as much as possible.

The desire to conceal the actions occurring in the altar from the non-consecrated also explains the silent reading of the sacramental prayers by the priest. That the primitive early Church practiced the silent reading of the prayers is completely out of the question, for this custom dramatically contradicts its entire liturgical practice.

> There is then brought to the president of the brethren bread and a cup of wine mixed with water; and he taking them, gives praise and glory to the Father of the universe, through the name of the Son and of the Holy Ghost, and offers thanks at considerable length for our being counted worthy to receive these things at His hands. And when he has concluded the prayers and thanksgivings, all the people present express their assent by saying Amen.[16]

When the *disciplina arcani* or "hidden discipline" appeared in the Church it was aimed at those who were not yet members. But there was nothing in the Church that was hidden from the faithful. The secret *gnosis* of which Clement of Alexandria and Origen spoke had no relevance to the liturgical acts, which were completely open to the faithful. Rather this referred to a more perfect knowledge that discloses itself gradually with the growth in perfection of each of the faithful individually. The practice of the silent recitation of the prayers entered the Church before the sixth century, for the emperor Justinian had already fought against it, prescribing in his Novella 137 that "the most holy bishops and presbyters say in a loud voice the holy anaphora to our God Jesus Christ with the Father and the Spirit."[17] It is both naïve and disrespectful to explain the silent recitation of the prayers by the negligence of presbyters and bishops who thus allegedly sought to shorten the liturgy. Even less accurate is the interpretation of the rubric *mystikôs* in the liturgical rites as mistakenly attributed to silent reading. This is a complete misinterpretation. On the contrary, the opposite is true: *mystikôs* was interpreted correctly as mysterious or mystical and for this reason the prayers began to be recited secretly to keep them from the people. The mystical character of the recited prayers must be concealed from the non-consecrated. The mystery is celebrated in secret, away from the non-consecrated and only the "mystics" are initiated into it. Is it a coincidence then that in the *Ecclesiastical Canons* the bishops are called *mystai?*[18] After many centuries passed, the content of this term, if not the term itself, was accepted.

The ancient way of receiving communion as the clergy today receive—in the sanctuary—was a privilege of all the members of the Church.

> Thus, if anyone desires to partake of the immaculate body during the service and to become one with it through participation (*hôste ei tou achrantou sômatos metaschein en tô tês synaxeos boulêtheiê kairô . . .*), he shall hold his hands in the

form of a cross and in this way approach and receive the communion of grace. But as for those who provide themselves with vessels of gold or some other material instead of their hands for the reception of the divine gift and thereby receive the immaculate communion, in no way do they have our consent since they prefer inanimate and subordinate matter to the image of God.[19]

In spite of this canon which expresses the most ancient tradition of the Church—"for as often as you eat this bread and drink the cup, you proclaim the Lord's death until he comes" (1 Cor 11.26)—attested by the entire early Christian literature beginning with Justin Martyr, at this point in time the manner of receiving the holy mysteries becomes differentiated, one for the clergy another for the laity.[20] Again Balsamon said that this distinction was not caused by "the unworthiness of the laity, but it was due to true faith, the fear of God and genuine piety."[21] This is an attempt to avoid explanation. Why did true faith, the fear of God, and genuine piety alter the ancient way of receiving communion for the laics and for the majority of the clergy? Are true faith, the fear of God, and genuine piety really virtues only for the lay people and not for those in the higher degrees of the priesthood? Certainly the explanation lies neither here nor in the purely practical reasons but rather in the view of lay people as non-consecrated.

However insignificant the changes in liturgical order, they nevertheless indicate that the ancient tradition, the teaching on the priestly dignity of all members of the Church, was broken under the pressure of the new teaching introducing the distinction between consecrated and non-consecrated. Ordinary people had kept the authentic tradition for a long time, but scholastic theology forgot or did not wish to remember it. In his commentary on a somewhat obscure canon of the Council in Trullo,[22] Balsamon says that

> Laics shall not dare to do this [to give the holy mysteries to themselves] when there is a bishop or a presbyter or a deacon present who can handle the holy things. So as some say judging from the opposite case, when neither of them is present, under a pressing need, one can freely administer to himself the divine sacraments. But I do not suppose so: for one should not admit such a boldness judging from interpretation and the opposite case.[23]

It is clear from Balsamon's interpretation of this canon that in the church life of Byzantium in his time opinions varied with respect to the content of this canon. Nevertheless, Balsamon firmly held to the view that the handling of the divine sacrament by laics is an impropriety that must be reprimanded. At the same time, his interpretation makes it clear once again that the unworthiness which caused a distinction in the manner of receiving communion did not have a moral but a sacramental and mystical origin. From the mystical or sacramental perspective only those consecrated in higher degrees of the priesthood are worthy to partake of the Mystical Supper in the manner in which Christ himself did. All others however are incapable of handling the holy mysteries. "Of your mystical supper, O Son of God, accept me today as a communicant." Every one of the faithful proclaims this before communion but at the same time laics receive communion at the moment in the liturgy which represents, according to symbolic interpretation, the appearance of the risen Christ.

2. Such are the liturgical consequences of the segregation of the people from the clergy in the Church, a separation which resulted from the teaching that laics are non-consecrated. This teaching further influenced the development of the liturgical rites. From the perspective of the outsider, these rites in their modern form have no place for lay people in liturgical worship. However, the inner core of the liturgy, especially the rites which did not suffer any significant alterations, could not have been totally obscured in the course of lay people's segregation from the clergy. This inner core still bears witness to the fact that it is the people in their entirety who celebrate the liturgy and the sacraments together with their presiders.

In this respect the sacrament of the Eucharist, the most basic of all, is especially important. Even in the modern recensions of this rite we find clear indications concerning the priestly status of God's people. To make our case more sound, we shall turn specifically to the rite which is used today rather than to the more ancient recensions.[24] In the eucharistic canon of the liturgy of John Chrysostom, the prayer of thanksgiving is the common prayer of the entire Church.

> For all these things we give thanks to you, and to your only-begotten Son and your Holy Spirit; for all the benefits that we have received, known and unknown, manifest and hidden. We thank you also for this liturgy which you have been pleased to accept from our hands, though there stand around you thousands of archangels and tens of thousands of angels . . .

Thus the entire people, gathered to offer the eucharistic sacrifice in its common worship to the God and Father of the Lord Jesus Christ, gives thanks through its presider. In the prayer that follows after this the entire Church (not a bishop or presbyter alone) prays:

With these blessed powers, Master, Lover of mankind, we also cry aloud and say: Holy are you and all-holy, you and your only-begotten Son and your Holy Spirit . . . when he had come and had fulfilled the whole dispensation for us, in the night in which he was given up, or rather gave himself up, for the life of the world . . .

In the prayer before the blessing of the holy gifts, the Holy Spirit is called upon the entire people and the gifts which are set forth:

Also we offer you this spiritual worship without shedding of blood, and we ask, pray and implore you: send down your Holy Spirit upon us and upon these gifts here set forth.

This supplication to send down the Holy Spirit "upon us" before the consummation of the mystery of body and blood makes it clear that it is not the presider alone but all the people who celebrate the mystery. The same idea is expressed even more clearly by John Chrysostom himself:

But there are occasions in which there is no difference at all between the priest and those under him; for instance, when we are to partake of the awesome mysteries; for we are all alike counted worthy of the same things: not as under the Old Testament [when] the priest ate some things and those under him others, and it was not lawful for the people to partake of those things of which the priest partook. But not so now, for before all one body is set and one cup. And in the prayers also, one may observe the people contributing much. For in behalf of the possessed, in behalf of those under penance, the prayers are made in common both by the priest and by them; and all say one prayer, the prayer replete with pity. Again when we exclude from the holy precincts those who are unable to partake of the holy table, another prayer needs to be offered, and we all alike fall upon the ground, and all alike rise up.[25] Again, in the most awesome mysteries themselves, the priest prays for the people and the people also pray for the priest; for the words, "with thy spirit," are nothing else than this. The offering of thanksgiving again is common: *for neither does he give thanks alone, but also all the people.*[26] For having first received the response, and then the assent from the people that it is "meet and right so to do," the priest begins the thanksgiving. And why do you marvel that the people also call together with the priest, when indeed even with the very Cherubim, and the powers above, they send up in common those sacred hymns?[27]

And the entire people, taking part in the blessing of the gifts, respond to the presider's words consummating the mystery with "Amen." In the modern rite this "amen" is to be pronounced by either a deacon or a priest but we have an indelible witness from the liturgical practice of the early and ancient Church that all the people pronounced it.

> There is then brought to the president of the brethren bread and a cup of wine mixed with water; and he taking them, gives praise and glory to the Father of the universe, through the name of the Son and of the Holy Spirit, and offers thanks at considerable length for our being counted worthy to receive these things at his hands. And when he has concluded the prayers and thanksgivings, all the people present express their assent by saying "Amen."[28]

Dionysius of Alexandria, in his famous letter concerning disputes about the baptism of the heretics relates the story of one of the faithful who doubted the authenticity of his baptism.

> [Being] present with those who were recently baptized, when he heard the questions and answers he came to me weeping and bewailing himself; and falling at my feet he acknowledged and protested that the baptism with which he had been baptized among the heretics was not of this character nor in any respect like this because it was full of impiety and blasphemy. And he said that his soul was now pierced with sorrow and that he had not confidence to lift his eyes to God because he had set out from those impious words and deeds. And on this account he begged that he might receive this most perfect purification, reception and grace. But I did not dare to do this; and said that his long communion with the Church was sufficient for this. For I should not dare to renew from the beginning one who had heard the giving of thanks and joined in repeating the Amen; who approached the table and stretched forth his hands to receive the blessed food; and who received it and partook for a long time of the body and blood of our Lord Jesus Christ.[29]

Two centuries later, Theodoret of Cyrus confirms the same.

> The laic, after the prayers have been proclaimed and he has responded "amen," becomes a partaker of the reward of the supplications which is in no way less than the reward of those who utters the supplications in the assembly.[30]

The mystery of body and blood is not accomplished through the priest alone but through the calling in prayer of the whole Church, the entire people of God. A bishop or presbyter presiding over the entire people of God, the invisible heavenly powers, the saints and the people that stand in the temple, all the members of the Church, living and dead—all celebrate the sacrament together. And every one of the faithful in their midst is also, together with others, a celebrant of the sacrament.

That the sacrament is celebrated by all together is even more evident in the text of St. Basil's liturgy. There, the corresponding thanksgiving prayer reads as follows:

> O Existing One, Master, Lord God, Father almighty and adorable! It is truly meet and right and befitting the magnificence of your holiness to praise you, to sing to you, to bless you, to worship you, to give thanks to you, to glorify you— the only truly existing God—and to offer to you this our reasonable worship with a contrite heart and a spirit of humility, for you have granted us the knowledge of your truth.

And further, the next prayer says:

> With these blessed powers, O Master who loves mankind, we sinners also cry aloud and say: holy are you—truly most holy—and there is no bounds to the magnificence of your holiness . . . He lived in this world and gave us commandments of salvation; releasing us from the delusions of idolatry, he brought us to knowledge of you, the true God and Father. He obtained us for *his own people, a royal priesthood, a holy nation.*[31] Having cleansed us in water, and sanctified us with the Holy Spirit, he gave himself as a ransom to death, in which we were held captive, sold under sin . . . And as memorials of his saving Passion, he has left us these things, which we have set forth, according to his command. For when he was about to go forth to his voluntary and ever-memorable and life-creating death—in the night in which he gave himself up for the life of the world—he took bread into his holy and pure hands, and having shown it to you, the God and Father, having given thanks, blessed and hallowed it, and broken it . . .

Christ has left the memorial of his saving Passion not to the priests alone but to the entire people of God—a royal priesthood, a holy chosen nation—according to the expression from the text of the liturgy itself, which, just as in the liturgy of

John Chrysostom, together with angels, archangels, the Cherubim and the Seraphim, sings the angelic triumphant hymn.

> Therefore, we also, O Master, remembering his saving Passion, and life-creating Cross, his three-day burial and resurrection from the dead, his ascension into heaven and sitting at your right hand of the God and Father, and his glorious and awesome second coming . . .

> Therefore, most holy Master, we also, your sinful and unworthy servants, whom you have permitted to serve at your holy altar not because of our own righteousness . . . we now dare to approach your holy altar and, offering to you the antitypes of the holy body and blood of your Christ, we pray you and call upon you, O Holy of holies, that by the favor of your goodness your Holy Spirit may come upon us and upon the gifts now offered, to bless, to hallow and to show . . .

All the people, being the royal priesthood, are permitted to serve at the holy altar and the Holy Spirit is called upon all the people just as in the liturgy of John Chrysostom.

> Therefore, brethren, since we have boldness to enter the sanctuary by the blood of Jesus, by the new and living way, which he opened for us through the curtain, that is, through his flesh, and since we have a great priest over the house of God, let us draw near with a true heart . . . (Heb 10.19–22)

This boldness is realized when each time at the liturgy the people of God dare to approach the holy altar. In the prayer following the blessing of the gifts all the people pray with the lips of the one who presides over them:

> And unite all of us to one another who become partakers of the one bread and cup in the communion of the Holy Spirit. Grant that none of us may partake of the holy body and blood of your Christ for judgment or condemnation.

This "us" cannot refer to the priests alone for it is not only they but all the people as well who partake of one body and one cup.

> The cup of blessing which we bless, is it not a participation in the blood of Christ? The bread which we break, is it not a participation in the body of Christ?

Because there is one bread, we who are many are one body, for we all partake of the one bread. (1 Cor 10.16–17)

O our God, the God of salvation, teach us to thank you worthily for the benefits, which you have performed for us and still perform with us. Having accepted these gifts, O our God, purify us from every defilement of flesh and spirit, and teach us how to perfect our sanctification in your fear, so that receiving a portion of your holy things with a pure conscience we may be united with the holy body and blood of your Christ. Having received them worthily, may we have Christ dwelling in our hearts, and may we become the temple of your Holy Spirit.[32]

The greatest reward—to have Christ dwelling in their hearts—cannot be a gift for the priests alone but for the entire people of God. Here also, "we" and "us" does not refer to the bishop and the priests concelebrating with him, for the ancient Church did not know [clerical] concelebration in the modern sense of the word.[33] All the people, not the presbyters alone, were bishop's concelebrants. When the prayer is uttered in the name of the presider alone, the text of the prayer leaves no doubt about that. The first person pronoun is used in the singular:

Remember, O Lord, my unworthiness also, by the multitude of your compassions, forgive my every transgression, both voluntary and involuntary. Because of my sins, do not withhold the grace of your Holy Spirit from these gifts here set forth.[34]

Celebrating the holy offering, a bishop did not separate himself from the people but counted himself as one of them. The bishop celebrated the sacrament with the people and the people celebrated with the bishop. All the liturgical prayers are common prayers, for they are the prayers of the Church and the Church is the entire people of God, not some part of it. What scholastic theology today considers the prayer of the priests alone, uttered in secret, the ecclesial thinking of the early Church regarded as a common prayer of the entire people of God.

After that we make mention of sky and earth and sea, sun and moon, stars and all creation—whether endowed with reason or not, whether seen or unseen. We recall Angels, Archangels, Virtues, Dominions, Principalities, Powers, Thrones, and the Cherubim of many faces. In effect we bid them, in the words of David: "Magnify the Lord with me." We recall also the Seraphim, whom Isaiah by the power of the Holy Spirit saw encircling God's throne. With two wings they covered the face, with two more the feet, and with two more they flew, saying: "Holy, holy, holy, the Lord Sabaoth." The reason why we utter this praise of God which the Seraphim have handed down to us is that we wish to join the heavenly hosts as they sing their hymn. Once we have sanctified ourselves with these spiritual hymns, we call upon the merciful God to send the Holy Spirit on our offerings, so that he may make the bread Christ's body, and the wine Christ's blood; for clearly whatever the Holy Spirit touches is sanctified and changed. Then, when the spiritual sacrifice—this bloodless worship—has been completed, we beg God over the sacrifice of propitiation for general peace among the churches, for the right order of the world, for the kings, for soldiers and allies, for the sick and the afflicted, and in short we all make entreaty and offer this sacrifice for all who need help.[35]

3. The common celebration of the whole people of God in the eucharistic assembly also found expression in that all together received the holy mysteries. Neither in the precise moment of communion nor in the manner of participation is the bishop with presbyters separated from the rest of the people. The thanksgiving prayer, common for all, followed the communion: "O God almighty, Father and Lord of Jesus Christ, we thank you for making us worthy of participation in your holy mysteries . . ."[36] Participation in the Eucharist for the early Christian mind was neither a duty nor an obligation, as interpreted now in ecclesiastical law, but rather a living, spontaneous expression of one's adherence to the Church. Everyone who took part in the eucharistic assembly approached the holy mysteries and it was unthinkable that some of the faithful would not receive communion. It is only in the Constantinian era that the changes begin to occur. Canon 2 of the council in Antioch and Apostolic canon 9, corresponding to the former, threatens with excommunication those who turn away from eucharistic communion.

> All who enter the church of God and hear the Holy Scriptures but do not communicate with the people in prayer or who turn away by reason of some disorder, from the holy partaking of the Eucharist are to be cast out of the Church until, after they shall have made confession and having brought forth the fruits of penance and made earnest entreaty, they shall have obtained forgiveness.[37]

> All the faithful who come in and hear the Scriptures but do not stay for the prayers and Holy Communion are to be excommunicated for causing disorder in the Church.[38]

The context of the canons makes it clear that the emphasis is upon the fact that some of the faithful who were gathering at the eucharistic assembly did not receive communion, either departing before the common prayers or refraining from the holy mysteries. That this is the meaning of the canons cited above is confirmed by Apostolic canon 8, which deals with the clerics who are present at the liturgy but do not receive communion:

> If any bishop, presbyter, or deacon or any one on the sacerdotal list, when the offering is made, does not partake of it, let him declare the cause; and if it be a reasonable one, let him be excused; but if he does not declare it, let him be excommunicated, as being a cause of offence to the people, and occasioning a suspicion against the offerer, as if he had not made the offering properly.[39]

The failing of such clerics surpasses that of the laics, for their abstaining from communion, besides being an intolerable deed, also brings suspicion upon the one who celebrates the liturgy.

That some of the faithful leave the ecclesial assembly together with the catechumens or the penitents, and that some of those present at the eucharistic assembly refrain from communion—those are the innovations that were being established in ecclesiastical practice and against which both the council in Antioch and the compiler of the Apostolic Canons were struggling. When despite these ordinances the custom of rare or relatively rare communion became entrenched in ecclesiastical practice, it then became necessary to interpret these canons in accordance with the existing practice. In twelfth century Byzantium there still was no unanimity with respect to the understanding of these canons and their indispensability for ecclesial life. In his commentary on canon 2 of the council in Antioch Zonaras wrote:

> Thus, even these fathers (of the council in Antioch) have defined that those who enter the church but do not stay in prayer and do not receive communion due to some disorder, i.e., not due to a reasonable cause, but rather without order or cause, are deprived from the Church, i.e., excommunicated and stay outside the assembly of the faithful. The fathers did not call "refraining" when one hates the divine communion and for this reason does not approach to partake, but rather when someone avoids it, maybe by reason of piety and as if out of humility of mind. For if one would refrain from holy communion out of hatred or repulsion toward it they would not be subject to excommunication only but to utter cutting off from the Church and to anathema.[40]

Aristenus holds the same opinion:

> The one who enters the church and hears the Scriptures but then neglects, exits and refrains from communion is cast away until he receives forgiveness, having shown the fruit of repentance.[41]

Both Zonaras and Aristenus indicate that in Byzantium in their time there existed an opposition to frequent communion for reasons of "piety or humility of mind." Both had to acknowledge that this opinion contradicts both Antiochene canon 2 and the Apostolic canon 9. However, in his commentary on Apostolic canon 9 Zonaras makes it clear that in his time this canon had fallen into disuse.

> This canon demands that at the celebration of the holy offering everyone would stay until the end in prayer and in holy communion. For then they demanded that laics receive communion at all times.[42]

In Balsamon we observe yet another tendency. Commenting on Apostolic canon 9 he notes its excessive strictness.

> The definition of this canon is exceedingly strict for it excommunicates those who were present in the church but did not stay until the end nor received communion.[43]

In his commentary he observes that canon 2 of the council in Antioch addresses those who depart before the end of the liturgy. He then interprets the entire canon to mean that the communion of everyone who participates in the liturgy is not called for.

> Read then what is written in the indicated Apostolic canons (in 8 and 9) and understand the present canon in accordance with those. Say then that those who turn away from communion are not the same as those who reject it or, as some have said, evade it out of piety and humility of mind—for the former should not merely be excommunicated but cast out of the Church as well as heretics and the latter deserve forgiveness by reason of piety and the fear that befits the holy things—not like those who "turn away" out of contempt and pride depart from the Church prior to holy communion and do not wait to behold the divine communion of the holy mysteries.[44]

Thus Balsamon, contrary to the opinion of Zonaras which he clearly has in mind here, deems it possible to evade communion by reason of "piety and humility of mind." Why, according to Balsamon, contempt or pride would motivate some of the faithful to depart from the assembly before the end of the liturgy remains for us unclear. Balsamon's general conclusion is as follows:

> To say that we faithful lay people and clerics who do not themselves celebrate the holy things, must each time partake of the holy mysteries and, if not, to be subject to excommunication is both inconsistent with this canon and impossible [to fulfill].[45]

Simultaneously, "staying until the end" acquires the new meaning in accordance with the present practice:

> As it seems, due to the eighth and ninth canons of the holy apostles and the present one (canon 2 of the Antiochene council), they came up with the distribution of the antidoron so that apparently those who cannot receive the holy and life-giving mysteries could also need to wait until the end of the divine service to receive the antidoron from the priest's hands for their sanctification.[46]

Nevertheless even this stipulation is taken in a limited sense.

> This definition of the mentioned canons you should relate to the liturgy alone, but not to other ecclesiastical rites. And insofar as some say: why then does not the ecumenical patriarch on the holy day of Resurrection wait until the end of the liturgy but having risen from his place departs after the Gospel?—we respond to them: this is because the divine liturgy in its proper sense takes place after the reading of the holy Gospel. Insofar as all that is sung in the holy churches to the glory of God is taken from the Old Testament or the New—for right after the beginning until the reading of the epistle they immediately sing psalms which are from the Old Testament, and after the Gospel the celebration of the bloodless sacrifice takes place—for this reason the patriarch acts rightly in departing before this celebration, not transgressing the canons. Therefore no one transgresses if he departs after the Gospel or before the Gospel, certainly if it is done for necessity or a reasonable and blameless cause.[47]

Apparently Balsamon tried to conform the early ecclesial practice, which he might have known from the *Apostolic Constitutions*, to the conditions of church life in his time. The ecclesial assembly at least until the fifth century was comprised of two parts: the first part (which might have been served separately)—*synaxis*—consisted of the singing of psalms, Scripture readings, and a homily after which the catechumens and all who did not belong to the Church were dismissed. The second part was the eucharistic assembly proper in which only faithful could participate. Allowing for the possibility of dismissal from the first part of the liturgy of his time, which to some extent was parallel to the ancient *synaxis*, Balsamon, without himself noticing it, equated the patriarch and all the rest of the faithful departing the assembly to the catechumens. So church practice suppressed the canons and the interpretation of the canons discarded their content. What constituted the very foundation of life for early, primordial Christianity became impossible to fulfill in the twelfth century. This "impossible" of Balsamon, more eloquent than his skillful reasoning, underscores the evolution that had taken place in the Christian mind. The practice of the Church in its beginning and what it was doing at this time had become mutually exclusive.

> Now to receive communion daily, thus to partake of the holy body and blood of Christ, is an excellent and advantageous practice; . . . we ourselves, of course, receive communion four times a week, on Sunday, Wednesday, Friday and Saturday, also on other days, if there is a commemoration of some saint.[48]

To this Balsamon replies: "impossible." "However, it cannot be that all the faithful would be pressed to receive communion each time they come to Church"[49]—writes Nicodemus Milaš in conclusion of his commentary on Apostolic canon 9, demonstrating his utter helplessness. The practice of both the Orthodox and Roman Catholic Churches in our time provides for nothing more than an annual communion of the laity. In reality, however, even this stipulation is not always observed.

Ecclesial practice parted ways from its origins in two different ways. On the one hand the real participation of the faithful in the Eucharist became extremely rare; on the other, the Eucharist came to be celebrated much more frequently than in the early Church. Both the first and the second aspects speak for themselves, for they both witness to the gradual erosion from the ecclesial understanding of the priestly status of laics. Originally Christians gathered for the eucharistic assembly on Sundays. Thus it was in the Roman Church at the time of Justin Martyr: "And on the day called Sunday, all who live in cities or in the country gather together to one place,"[50] which, nevertheless, did not exclude the possibility of *synaxeis* in other days of the week. One should not suppose that the first Christians, all without exceptions, gathered at the eucharistic assembly every Sunday. When Justin said that all Christians of the city and the country gathered together (*epi to auto*) on the day of the sun he did not mean to say that all the members of the Roman Church were gathered at this assembly. He noted that "to those who are absent a portion is brought by the deacons."[51] The number of those "absent" must have been considerably large. They included, first of all, the sick and elderly who could not come to the assembly, then those who could not take part in every eucharistic assembly due to their profession, and, certainly, the slaves must have been absent more frequently than others. Being totally at their masters' disposal they naturally could not attend the ecclesial gatherings regularly. Not only pagan but also even Christian slave owners created obstacles to their slaves' attending the ecclesial assemblies. The *Apostolic Constitutions* contain a direct command that the slaves must not be pressed to work on Sundays: "Let the slaves work five days but on the Sabbath-day and the Lord's day let them have leisure to go to church for instruction in piety."[52] Due to lack of evidence we are not capable of determining how many of the faithful were absent from the eucharistic assemblies. However, we have an indirect indication that the number was considerable. Despite the growth of even so prominent a church as that of Rome, until the beginning of the third century, and maybe even later, it retained a single eucharistic assembly. Thus every member could not be present at every assembly. Of the admonitions concerning attendance at the eucharistic assembly we have none or almost none coming from the first three centuries.[53] This is an indication that only a dire impossibility could be the reason for the absence of the faithful at the eucharistic assembly. This situation begins to change in the fourth century when more and more often do we encounter in the patristic literature the admonitions to the faithful to participate in the eucharistic assembly regularly.[54]

Despite the number of absentees, the eucharistic assembly in the early period was the solemn gathering of the *entire* local church, even though later subsidiary assemblies had emerged alongside the episcopal one. It could not have happened conversely, i.e., it could not have happened that Eucharist would be celebrated by itself, independently of whether all members of the church can participate in it. The Eucharist was celebrated by the Church, and that is why the eucharistic assembly took place when the entire local church participated in it. From the first statement follows another as unquestionable as the first. All who gathered *epi to auto* were eucharistic celebrants under the presidency of the bishop. The presider not only communed himself but also distributed the bread, sometimes assisted by the presbyters, while the deacons gave the chalice to the faithful. Just as today the celebrant of the liturgy cannot abstain from communion, thus in the primitive early church, all faithful participants of the eucharistic assembly could not abstain either, for it was the entire people who celebrated the Eucharist. There were no uninvolved observers "attending" the Eucharist, only participants. All who could not participate were removed from the assembly beforehand, following the homily, with deacons watching the doors so that no stranger could enter the eucharistic gathering.[55] No liturgical rites, from the most ancient to the modern, envision uninvolved observers at the eucharistic assembly. Even in the modern order of the liturgy all the prayers, whether said quietly or aloud, are proclaimed in the name of all who together with their presider celebrate the mystery of the body and blood of Christ. If the mind of the Church allowed the faithful to be merely "attending" the Eucharist, this possibility would be expressed in special prayers for them. If the Church prays for the catechumens, the penitents, the demoniacs, and the faithful participants, it would surely pray for those only "attending," and not participating, if such people existed in the early Church at all. Christian consciousness nowadays does not always realize the tragic rupture between the participation in the eucharistic prayers and the refraining from communion, whether voluntary or not.

Another tragic aspect of modern liturgical life is the transformation of the Eucharist into a "service for private needs." Modern ecclesial thinking and practice allows the liturgy to be celebrated in an empty or nearly empty church. In this respect, the practices of the Orthodox and Roman Catholic churches are practically identical.[56] The historical development of eucharistic life reveals a fatal paradox. Daily celebration of the Eucharist did not enhance the eucharistic life but rather diminished it. The practical impossibility of every member of the local church participating in the Eucharist daily led to the weakening of the need to participate even when one could be present. Daily celebration of the Eucharist strove to realize an ideal ecclesial life, namely when the entire local church gathers daily for the eucharistic assembly. This custom began in the monasteries and from there, through monastic typica, entered parish life. Here this custom could be implemented due to the obfuscation of the doctrine of the sacred ministry as the property of all the priestly people. When, instead, the teaching that saw the bishop or presbyter as the sole celebrant became more entrenched, popular participation ceased to be a necessity. Pushing the people aside from the celebration could not enhance their eucharistic life because for them it was sufficient to know the Eucharist was being celebrated in church. On the other hand, if the Eucharist could be celebrated without the people, or rather, without all the people, it could just as well be celebrated in the presence of the people. If at the Eucharist the celebrant and concelebrating clergy received communion and the people standing in the church could abstain, it follows that the people are not the concelebrants with the bishop and presbyter. The obvious inconsistency of this concept with the doctrine of the Church and Eucharist as well as with the practice of the early church cannot be mitigated by some notion of "spiritual communion," for this teaching itself is inconsistent with the doctrine concerning the Eucharist.[57] Christ instituted the sacrament of the Eucharist so that believers actually could be united with Christ in one body. If spiritual communion prevails, is there still a need for the actual reception of the body and blood of Christ? And is there still a need for the Church itself, if anyone could commune spiritually by himself? Origen and the first monastics went almost as far as this. If spiritual communion is insufficient and cannot substitute for actually receiving communion, does it not indicate how deeply the division of the church's members into the consecrated and non-consecrated had penetrated its consciousness? The actual reception of communion is thus always accessible only to the conscecrated while the non-consecrated participate spiritually in the communion of the consecrated. The actual reception of communion is only rarely accessible to lay people, the non-conscecrated, and not every time they are present at the liturgy.

Given the significance of the Eucharist for the life of the Church, the sacramental ministry of the people in the Eucharist is crucial for understanding who indeed celebrates the sacraments. All sacraments take place in the Church and are accomplished in the Church, and the eucharistic assembly is the manifestation of the Church in all its fullness. Since all the people of God are celebrants of the Eucharist, it is the people, together with their presiders, who are the celebrants of all the other sacraments.

Now let us return to what we have said above. Not only is sacramental ministry open to laics; moreover, without their participation no sacrament can be celebrated in the Church. Exercising their sacramental ministry in the Church, the people minister in a different manner from their presiders and the presiders minister in a different manner from the people, but nevertheless, everything in the Church is celebrated by their common action. "That they may all be one; even as thou, Father, art in me, and I in thee, that they also may be in us, so that the world may believe that thou hast sent me" (John 17.21).

IV. The Ministry of Laics in the Administration of the Church

1. In the holy Scriptures the people of God are called *poimnion tou Theou*—God's flock. In this flock the bishops are shepherds. Just as the shepherd goes before the flock and leads it, so the shepherds in the Church stand before the flock and lead it.

> He who enters by the door is the shepherd of the sheep. To him the gatekeeper opens; the sheep hear his voice, and he calls his own sheep by name and leads them out. When he has brought out all his own, he goes before them, and the sheep follow him, for they know his voice. (John 10.2–4)

The bishops are shepherds in a narrow sense of the word because for the whole of God's flock there is only one Shepherd—Christ. "So there shall be one flock, one shepherd" (John 10.16). Being shepherds, bishops are not ordained to be *above* the flock, but to be *within* the flock.

> Take heed to yourselves and to all the flock, in which the Holy Spirit has made you overseers, to care for the church of Lord and God which he obtained with his own blood. (Acts 20.28)

The faithful are shepherded by Christ, and only in a narrow sense of the word by their bishops, for all are Christ's sheep and are in God's flock. Bishops preside over God's flock, being themselves the sheep of this flock, just as the rest of the sheep led by Christ. If they were inferior to the flock they would not be sheep of God's flock, and thus they could not be shepherds. Being sheep of the flock they also lead the flock, having been ordained in it as shepherds, not in accordance with their own will and personal considerations but with the will of God.

> Tend the flock of God that is your charge . . . not as domineering over those in your charge but being examples to the flock. (1 Peter 5. 2–3)

One can be an example only through fulfilling God's will that leads the whole flock. Therefore, when the faithful follow their pastors it is not blind submission to their ecclesial pastors, but rather a free, creative, personal action with their co-operation and assistance. The fact that the bishops are shepherds does not hinder the personal activity of every one of the members of the Church. The distinction in the Church between those who tend and those who are tended cannot lead one to understand laics as the passive element of the ecclesial body and an object of governance by the church hierarchy. As living members of the Church the laics are active, for their activity is the expression of their life in the Church. We have seen that as laics are active in sacramental ministry, so are they in church administration. We have observed that sacramental ministry is open to them, for they minister together with their presiders. Thus church administration is also open to them, otherwise they would be merely passive. They participate in sacramental ministry by being concelebrants of the bishop and presbyter. Do they in a like manner participate in the administration by ministering together with the bishop, i.e., by governing the flock of God together with their pastors?

The activity of lay people in church administration took diverse forms in the course of church history. There were periods when this activity did not find expression anywhere, followed by the periods of renaissance in lay people's activity. Zealously protecting sacramental ministry from lay people, church authorities made concessions in the area of administration to the extent that they practically called lay people to take part in the church governance. This was the case, for example, at the Moscow Council of 1917–18, which ostensibly initiated, or rather intended to initiate, a renaissance of the Russian Church. The removal of sacramental ministry from lay people and the concessions made in their favor in the area of church administration is a historical paradox. This can only be explained by reference to the division of the members of the Church into consecrated and non-consecrated. Such a division has supplanted the fundamental distinction between those whom God has called in the Church for special ministries and those whom he did not. At the same time, for the non-consecrated it was a kind of retaliation in the area of church administration for having been deprived of their priestly status. Under the pressure of the lay people and due to some errors in the structure of church governance, the Russian ecclesiastical authorities opened church administration to lay people, bringing them into every church institution from the parish level to the local council of the Russian Church. As lay participation in the administrative institutions of the Church became normative, any questioning of it would entail an accusation of clericalism. Lay people in the meantime—at least according to the decisions of the Moscow council—became co-administrators with the clergy and in particular with the bishops. As a social organism, the Church is governed by the people through the representatives the people themselves elect. However menacing the accusation of clericalism, one should and must ask whether the fact of lay administration expresses the norm of laics' activity and of their participation in the administration of the Church.

2. To govern the Church is to exercise a special ministry in the Church that necessitates special gifts. From the beginning of the Church's historic existence, in the midst of God's people who were endowed with charismatic gifts, there were individuals whom God himself ordained for the work of administration through bestowing on them the gifts of the grace of the Holy Spirit.

> And God has appointed in the church first apostles, second prophets, third teachers, then workers of miracles, then healers, helpers, administrators (*kybernêseis*), speakers in various kinds of tongues. (1 Cor 12.28)

> And his gifts were that some should be apostles, some prophets, some evangelists, some pastors (*poimenas*) and teachers. (Eph 4.11)

Only the one who has received the gift of administration can govern the people of God. The most ancient prayer for the ordination of a presbyter, which was preserved in the *Apostolic Tradition* of Hippolytus of Rome, says:

> God and Father of our Lord Jesus Christ, look upon your servant and impart the Spirit of grace and counsel of presbyterate so that he might assist and guide your people with a pure heart (*kybernan ton laon sou en kathara kardia*).[58]

If administration is a special gift bestowed upon those whom God has specifically called for this ministry, the people of God do not have this gift. The entire people of God are called to the ministry of priesthood, for everyone entering the Church is ordained for this ministry through bestowing of the charismatic gifts of royal priesthood. Without this gift the laics would not be able to be *leitourgoi*. Without this gift the presiders of the people of God would not be able to exercise their priesthood as well. Administration belongs only to those specifically called for this, rather than to all the people who did not receive the gifts of administration. And without charismatic gifts there is not and there cannot be any ministry in the Church. The bishop "it is who is entrusted with the people of the Lord, and of whom will be required the account of their soul."[59] The bishop is entrusted with God's people, for he is called and ordained by God for the ministry of administration and therefore is the one who governs the people of God as a pastor. No one else is entrusted with God's people, and therefore no one else could govern them. The people do not govern themselves, but their pastors do on the basis of the work of ministry that God himself has established. Not having a charism of administration, laics cannot be co-administrators with the bishop just as they cannot govern themselves by themselves. They are not the bishop's co-ministers in the area of administration. "The bishop it is who is entrusted with the people of God," living and active members of the Church. Thus the bishop's governance of God's people does not rule out the activity of laics. However, this activity is of a very different nature than the activity of bishops. Activity in the Church equals ministry and ministry presupposes a corresponding charism, for there can be no ministry in the Church without the gifts of the Spirit.

Not having the gift of administration, the "people of the Lord" have a gift of discernment and examination which is a special kind of ministry not entrusted to particular members of the Church but rather to all the people of God, i.e., to all the members of the Church in their common action. "Let two or three prophets speak, and let the others discern what is said (*hoi alloi diakrinetôsan*)" (1 Cor 14.29). "Test everything; hold fast what is good (*panta de dokimazete, to kalon katechete*)" (1 Thess 5.21). The people have discernment and examination (*diakrisis* and *dokimasia*) concerning everything being done in the Church. The bishop together with presbyters does not govern the people of God in his own name. Neither does he govern them on the basis of law as the one who received his power from the people or through the people. Rather he governs the people in God's name, as the one ordained by God for the ministry of governance. Having the charism of discernment and examination the people witness that everything done in the Church under the guidance of the pastors is done in accordance with the will of God revealed by the Holy Spirit. In the early church all ecclesial acts, such as the celebration of the mysteries, the reception of the catechumens and penitents into the Church, excommunication, and so forth, involved the people's participation. In the early church the people's testimony concerning the revelation of God's will had the character of "consensus" with what was about to happen in the Church and their reception of what was accomplished as corresponding to God's will. It would be a mistake to suppose that the people gave their consent as a result of a vote, just as it is a custom in the popular assemblies of the Greek cities—*poleôn*—or in the representative institutions nowadays. The consent and reception by the people did not mean that the people expressed their own private opinion or wish concerning one or another ecclesial act. The ecclesial authority in the person of the bishops were not bound by the will of the laics, just as the people were not bound by the will of their presiders. Neither the will of laics nor the will of bishops is *per se* sufficient for the action in the Church. The Church lives and acts not by the will of man, but by the will of God. Consent and reception were the witness of the Church through the witness of the people that the presiders act and govern in agreement with the will of God.

The history of the early church prior to Constantine the Great indicates that both those aspects were a living and active factor of ecclesial life. We can recall here the remarkable words of Cyprian of Carthage: "From the outset of my episcopacy I have set as a rule to do nothing using my own discretion without your (presbyters) counsel and the consent of the people."[60] One should not suppose that the examination and consent of the people necessarily preceded each action of the bishop. The ministry of the bishop is examined and attested by the people at his ordination. "Let the bishop be ordained as we appointed above, being without sin having been elected by all the people."[61] In the ordination prayer, this election of the bishop by that local church for which he is being ordained is regarded as an election by God himself. "Father, you know the heart; grant that your servant whom you have chosen for oversight (episcopacy) should shepherd your [holy] flock . . ."[62] Hence one must have naturally presumed that the bishop elected by God himself with the gift of administration acts in accordance with God's will. The examination and consent of the people could have been latent. In many instances it silently accompanied actions of the bishop and showed itself in subsequent ecclesial reception of what the bishop has done. Therefore one should not overestimate Cyprian's indication that he did not undertake anything without the counsel of the presbyters and the consent of the people (*sine consilio vestro et sine consensu plebis*). "Nothing—*nihil*" should be understood in the sense of nothing important. Indeed, the epistles of Cyprian witness to us that the people took part in all important and significant moments of the ecclesial life of the church of Carthage. This especially concerns questions that caused debate and divergence of opinion. Thus it was, for instance, with the question of the reception of the lapsed during persecution back into the Church. We know how steadfastly Cyprian resisted making any decisions in this question while the persecution was still going on and there was no possibility to discuss this question at the assembly of the church. We observe the same thing at the ordination of clerics. Recalling Cyprian's words, we could have said that indeed as a general rule no ordination for ecclesial service took place without the people's consent. With regard to exceptional circumstances caused by the persecution, when Cyprian was pressed to do ordinations outside of the ecclesial assembly he deemed it necessary each time to justify his actions. In his epistle to the presbyters, deacons, and all the people of his church concerning his ordination in exile of Aurelius as a reader without preliminary consent of the people and the presbyters, Cyprian wrote:

> At the ordination of the cleric we are accustomed to ask for your counsel and to discuss with you the behavior and dignity of each person. But there is no need to await a testimony from men when God himself has preordained his judgment.[63]

In another epistle, he wrote:

> Know then that I have made Saturus a reader and Optatus, the confessor, a sub-deacon. With common consent we already had made them part of the clergy, having entrusted the reading to Saturus on Easter day and again when with the teacher-presbyters we were carefully examining readers—in appointing Optatus from among the readers to be a teacher of the catechumens, examining, first of all, whether he has the appropriate qualities for those in preparation for clerical office. Thus, nothing new has been done by me in your absence. However what had been begun by common assent has in urgent necessity been accomplished.[64]

Cyprian's letters do nothing else than ask the people of the Church to confirm what their bishop has done. Cyprian's stance was not exceptional for the ecclesial life of that period. The situation in the Roman Church was the same. Cornelius of Rome relates the fact that Novatus was ordained at the bishop's special request in a letter.

> His (Novatus's) ordination took place not only against the will of the clergy but also many laymen as well, for it was not fitting to promote to any ecclesial degree one who was baptized by sprinkling in his bed while ill as was the case with Novatus. But the bishop petitioned to allow him to ordain only this person.[65]

Regardless of some radical change that already had taken place at the time of Cyprian, the life of the Church still preserved its solid unity, as before. "Now there are varieties of gifts, but the same Spirit; and there are varieties of service, but the same Lord" (1 Cor 12.4–5). The gift of witnessing and the gift of the ministry of governance are different, but "there are varieties of working, but it is the same God who inspires them all in every one" (1 Cor 12.6). The same God and the same Spirit inspire both the ministry of people's examination and the ministry of presiding, which presuppose the agreement of the people with their presiders. This agreement does not have human characteristics but is founded upon the charismatic nature of everything that occurs in the Church. For what takes place in the Church is done by the Church according to God's will. For church administration as well as sacramental ministry there must be the unity of God's people with the presiders which Ignatius of Antioch stressed so often in his letters: "Now do each of you join in this choir, that [you could always be] harmoniously in concord."[66] Both the bishop charged with administration and the rest of the people serving

God together in fulfillment of his will in the Church constitute this symphony to which Ignatius refers. The people whom God has ordained for the ministry of kings and priests give their consent to what occurs in the Church, by this action witnessing to the will of God that works in the Church. The people do not govern in the Church, for they do not have a charism of administration; rather the will of God reigns, for it has provided the grace of the royal priesthood.

The *consensus* of the people for what occurs in the Church indicates that the presiders act in the midst of the people, rather than separately from them. The people could approve only what was known to them. In the early Church all administration, just as the whole life of the Church, was public. Everything began and ended at the ecclesial assembly. The early Church left for all times the image of the unity of the ecclesial body in which all together and each one in particular live and act not according to their own will but according to God's. The bishop does not govern the people in separation from them but in the midst of the flock in which (*en hô*) he is ordained (Acts 20.28). The bishop does not govern the people as a passive body. Rather, they are active, having full knowledge of what is being done in the Church and themselves witnessing to the will of God. This is a permanent norm for laic activity in church administration. The people of God do not govern themselves in the ecclesial assembly, which has no authority in itself. It is incapable of making any act of the Church necessary or valid. It cannot create any ministry for itself and is unable to appoint for these ministries the people whom they find appropriate. If this were the case, every local church in the early period of Christian history would have had charismatic ministers. However, as we know, not every church had prophets. The *Didache* clearly shows that the prophet can frequently be missing from a local church.[67] Although this document represents the early Montanist period,[68] its witness can be applied in some degree to the primitive Church. The people of God do not govern themselves through their bishop as their chosen and ordained delegate, nor do they participate in episcopal administration through representatives. In the Church there can be neither delegates nor representatives of the people, for the source of power of the ecclesial assembly (where everything is accomplished) is not found in the assembly itself but stems from its witnessing to God's will revealed in the Church. God's people are ruled by God through the bishop whom He has ordained to fulfill his will. For this reason, in sacramental ministry as well as in that of administration, a bishop cannot be without the people, just as the people cannot be without their bishop. Having been ordained in and for the Church the bishop cannot rule God's people without their participation. Otherwise his ministry of governance would cease being charismatic and ecclesial and would become merely a legal procedure.

Legal norms cannot be applied to the Church because the Church is a charismatic organism.

Beginning with the era of Constantine, the Church becomes a body governed by law in the eyes of Roman state authorities. It is quite natural, but in turn, the Church recognizes the law as indispensable for itself. This was the step that inevitably led to destruction of the primordial concordance or symphony between the people and bishop. The bishop becomes a high official and prince of the Church whose subjects are the people and clergy. Both the consent of the people and their reception of the bishop's acts were then out of the question. Laics were deprived of any activity, and church organization did not provide any expression of this activity. Nevertheless the ancient foundations of ecclesial life could not have been once and for all destroyed. Ecclesial reception continued to play, at least sporadically, not an unimportant role in the course of the whole history of Byzantium. Without the possibility of a proper expression, this reception took a chaotic form of protest and opposition to the ecclesiastical or state authorities. Nevertheless, both the former and the latter had to take it into consideration. Just before the very fall of Byzantium the people refused to accept the solemn decisions of the council in Florence. "Do not quench the Spirit, do not despise prophesying" (1 Thess 5.19–20). No matter how despised became the gift of the prophecy the Church received on Pentecost, the norm of the charismatic activity of the laics persevered in the depths of the ecclesial consciousness.

3. Christianity came to Rus' when the legal norms had become definitively entrenched in the Byzantine Church. The legal norms in ecclesial life came from Byzantium to the Russian Church together with Christianity, but the ancient traditions maintained in the Byzantine Church came over as well. In Rus', given the weakness of legal consciousness and the lack of firm ecclesial traditions, this process took quite a peculiar form. The activity of the laics was preserved even in medieval Rus', often taking abnormal forms. It is sufficient to remember the distortions in parish life against which the Stoglav/Hundred Chapters council hopelessly struggled. This kind of lay activity in parish life, based on the founders' law, has nothing to do with the ancient norm of laic activity in the church administration. This distorted type of popular activity disappears completely during the Synodal period in Russian church history. The distortions were radically corrected by eradicating any activity of the people. The entire life of the Church was organized on a juridical basis and the Church itself became a state institution. The bishop and the people were separated by a wall that could not have been overcome even with a good will of some bishops. The Moscow council of 1917–18 tried to overcome this partition by reviving the activity of the people in the Church. However, legal norms had entered so deeply into the mind of the church that in implementing its reforms it was the legal norms that guided the Moscow council. Thus this council unwillingly furthered the period of the Russian Church which it intended to terminate.

The evaluation of the entire work of the Moscow council is beyond the scope of the present study. Yet it is necessary to tackle the measures of the council aimed at reviving the activity of lay people in the Church. The council called the lay people into administration—in contradistinction to the ancient standard which it could not restore without reforming the whole ecclesial structure. Rather the council was guided by the principle of representation, positing the lay people as the co-governors together with the bishops. The highest ecclesiastical body—the local council of the Russian Church—includes apart from the bishops representatives of all ecclesiastical groups including lay people. The bishops remained at the head of diocesan administration but they were supplanted with institutions together with which they had to govern the diocese and which thereby circumscribed the bishops' legal power. By this act the council not only *de facto*, but also *de jure* (which never happened in Byzantium) recognized that the bishop's authority has a juridical nature. Just as during the Synodal period the entire church administration is founded on a juridical basis: the bishops with juridical authority on the one hand and on the other—the institutions affiliated with the bishop and based on the principle of representation. These institutions, central as well as diocesan, include laypeople as the representatives of laypeople, just as the clerics represent clerics and monastics represent monastics. Lay representatives rule the diocese jointly with the bishop just as at the local council they share with the bishops the higher authority standing above all ranks in the Russian Church.

The principle of representation, introduced by the Moscow council of 1917–18 into the system of church administration destroyed the unity of the ecclesial body and proclaimed its partition a norm. It authoritatively acknowledged that in the Church there are diverse groups with diverse interests. The Moscow council failed to see that the principle of representation, as a principle based on law, cannot have any application in the Church. The bishop does not represent his diocese and cannot act as its representative. He is at the head of the diocese, presiding over it and acting in the name of the Church constantly accompanied by the people's consent and by their subsequent reception. The Church acts through the bishop by means of consent and reception. A cleric or a layman can act in the Church merely in his own name or in the name of the group he represents. Surely, if the Church is a legal body with diverse groups within it such as the episcopacy, clergy, monastics, and lay people, then from the legal perspective each group can have its representatives. Nonetheless the question remains: how through the representatives of distinct groups could one hear the voice of the Church? The sum of particular groups within the Church does not make the living body of the Church. God's will disclosed itself in the Church rather than in the conglomeration of the representatives from particular groups. However paradoxical this is, according to the design of the Moscow council, the people of God—*laos tou Theou*—do not have a part in the governance. Calling the lay people as co-administrators with the bishop is not equivalent to the participation of God's people in the administration. Rather, what this accomplishes is nothing but creating public servants and ecclesiastical institutions. The majority of these institutions were newly established by the Moscow council but some were transplanted from the Synodal period, naturally with corresponding changes. There is no substantial difference between the consistory and the diocesan council—both the former and the latter are legal institutions—while there is a difference in the scope of privileges. The individuals elected by lay people share the governance in the Russian Church with the parish priest, the diocesan bishop, and the Holy Synod.

The fact that the lay people were called to govern still does not lay aside the question of the basis on which they govern the Church. In the Church, how can the common election of lay representatives endow them with the ministry of governance and the grace for this ministry? The indirect election of the diocesan council and of the central institutions cannot guarantee that what happens is an ecclesial act, because election cannot bestow any charismatic gifts. If the lay elected representatives do not possess the gifts of governance how could they govern the Church? The most striking thing is that this question is never posed at all. Is that not a retaliation for the reign of law in the modern ecclesial organization? Given this scheme of administration, is there any place for grace in the Church? Surely the Moscow council did not deny the bishops their charismatic gifts of administration. However, having set the laity whom general opinion views as non-consecrated on the same plane with the bishops, the council thereby recognized that the charismatic gifts are to a certain extent unnecessary for governing the Church. In any case, those governing in the charismatic organism of the Church are deprived of grace. They are laicized in the negative sense of the word. This is the dead end to which law has led ecclesial thinking. Ultimately it does not matter for the people of the Church whether the bishop rules by himself or with lay representatives. It does not matter because the people do not fulfill their ministry in the field of administration, the ministry to which God has called them—the ministry of witness. The people cannot pass this ministry onto their representatives, for grace cannot be transferred to someone else. These representatives cannot express the consent of the people or their reception of the bishop's acts, for both consent and reception belong to all the people rather than to its representatives. In fact, the structure of the administration established by the Moscow council has no place either for the people's consent or for ecclesial reception. If the former can be observed, with certain reservations, in parish organization it totally disappears in the structure of diocesan and central administration. None of the contemporary bishops could repeat the words of Cyprian, namely, setting for themselves as a rule to do nothing without the counsel of the presbyters and the consent of the people, for they cannot fulfill it in the contemporary ecclesial organization. On the other hand, all ecclesial acts thus remain without ecclesial reception. Certainly one can assume that the decisions of a local council can be appealed at an ecumenical council; however, in modern conditions it is practically impossible. Moreover, the appeal to an ecumenical council cannot replace ecclesial reception since these are unrelated phenomena. The appeal has a juridical nature, whereas ecclesial reception has a charismatic one. An appeal puts a certain decision into question before a higher authority capable of reviewing the appeals. A new decision on the case being appealed does not constitute its ecclesial reception, for everything remains on the juridical plane. Given the conditions of modern church life, the separatism and nationalism of local churches, if the decisions of the local council of one church were to await confirmation by other churches, it would be perceived by that church as subverting its autocephalous status. Nor does the reception of the decisions of the diocesan assembly exist. The act of reception could have proceeded from other dioceses of the Russian Church, but even this act would be perceived as an undue intervention of one diocese in the affairs of another. The appeal to the central authority concerning the diocesan assembly also cannot count as its reception, any more than appealing to an ecumenical council. If in church organization consent and reception by the people of the Church does not exist, the activity of laics in church administration does not exist either.

The Moscow council assembled in an extremely difficult time and its members displayed enormous churchly courage. The Moscow council thus serves as an example that even with the best intentions Church reform cannot actually take place unless it leads the Church out from under the aegis of law, for the law is anything but a creative principle in the Church. The Russian Church was still waiting for reform in the beginning of the twentieth century, as it had been in the beginning of the eighteenth century. The reform that it was waiting for was the one that would have liberated the Church from law, or in any case would have weakened the legal principle in the life of the Church. As the Russian state in that time of its history demanded the strengthening of juridical norms in its life, so the Moscow council strengthened juridical principles in the Russian Church. Ecclesial consciousness did not comprehend that law, being a vital necessity for the life of the state, cannot be applied to the life of the Church without subverting the foundations upon which this life rests. Any Church reform must take into account not only the current historical period but also the principles of ecclesial life that cannot be subordinated to principles alien to the Church. However sublime and perfect the democratic principles which the Moscow council had introduced into church government, they have no place in the Church, for the Church is not a democracy but the people of God whom God himself has chosen and ordained for the service. The activity of the people has nothing in common with elective or representative principles, but originates from charismatic gifts. The people of God cannot jointly govern with those who were endowed with the gifts of the Holy Spirit and called to govern in the house of God. This is our conclusion from the experience of the Moscow council and this conclusion corresponds to the ancient norm of the Church.

V. The Ministry of Laics in the Field of Teaching

1. The third field of activity in the Church is teaching. According to the canon 64 of the council in Trullo:

> It does not befit a layman to dispute or teach publicly (*dêmosia*), thus claiming for himself authority to teach, but he should yield to the order appointed by the Lord, and to open his ears to those who have received the grace to teach, and be taught by them divine things.[69]

The commentary to the twelfth chapter of 1 Corinthians by Gregory the Theologian, which the fathers of the council cite in their canon, served as a basis for this canon. The canon says:

> For in one Church God has made "different members," according to the word of the Apostle: and Gregory the Theologian, wisely interpreting this passage, commends the order in vogue with them saying: "This order brethren we revere, this we guard. Let this one be the ear; that one the tongue, the hand or any other member. Let this one teach, but let that one learn." And a little further on: "Learning in docility and abounding in cheerfulness, and ministering with alacrity,

we shall not all be the tongue which is the more active member, not all of us Apostles, not all prophets, nor shall we all interpret." And again: "Why do you make yourself a shepherd when you are a sheep? Why become the head when you are a foot? Why do you try to be a commander when you are enrolled in the number of the soldiers?" And elsewhere: "Wisdom orders, Be not swift in words; nor compare yourself with the rich, being poor; nor seek to be wiser than the wise."[70]

Teaching is a charismatic service; therefore, only those who received the grace of the teaching word can teach in the Church. On this basis, i.e., on the basis of St. Paul's teaching on the work of ministry, the council in Trullo banned the laics from exercising this ministry. Laics cannot teach, because they do not possess the charism of teaching.

Prohibiting the laics to teach publicly (*olêmosia*), the council in Trullo was continuing the ancient tradition of the Church. However, it was continuing this tradition in the conditions of its time. "And his gifts were that some should be pastors and teachers ..." (Eph 4.11). From the apostolic times, in the Church, there were *didaskaloi* as the bearers of a special charismatic ministry.[71] It is difficult for us to determine with precision in what their ministry consisted, but it did not rule out teaching done by the presiders both in the churches that had *didaskaloi* and also in the churches that did not have such ministers. From very early on, if not from the very beginning, preaching constituted a part of the ministry of a bishop. We have a direct indication concerning this fact in Justin Martyr. In his *Apology*, he reports that "thereafter, when the reader ceases to read, the presider, by means of the word, instructs and admonishes to imitate those beautiful things."[72] If this was true for the Roman Church, even more likely this was the case for other churches. Justin Martyr was one of the early *didaskaloi* of whom we know. Whether he had any opportunity to teach in the ecclesial assembly, we do not know. Even if he did, there was also the presider of one church present who was likewise a preacher. In the third century, there develops a tendency to attribute the function of teaching in the ecclesial assembly exclusively to the bishops and to remove from this position the ancient *didaskaloi* who were still extant in some places. From this period, we know the conflict that arose between Origen and his bishop, Demetrius of Alexandria. Origen's preaching in church upon the request of two Palestinian bishops—Alexander of Jerusalem and Theoctist of Caesarea—caused vigorous protest on the part of Demetrius of Alexandria. In their letter to Demetrius, the Palestinian bishops justified Origen's action and their own request to him to preach in their churches.

He has stated in his letter that such a thing was never heard of before, neither has hitherto taken place, that laymen should preach in the presence of bishops. I know not how he comes to say what is plainly untrue. For whenever persons able to instruct the brethren are found, they are exhorted by the holy bishops to preach to the people. Thus in Laranda, Euelpis by Neon; and in Iconium, Paulinus by Celsus; and in Synada, Theodorus by Atticus, our blessed brethren. And probably this has been done in other places unknown to us.[73]

Frequently voiced opinion claims that this incident in the life of Origen attests to the ancient tradition of the Church that teaching was a special charismatic ministry[74] which was thus banned to those not charismatically called to this ministry. The conflict of Demetrius of Alexandria with the Palestinian bishops who lived in the same period was in fact a conflict of different eras. Demetrius did not at all forbid Origen to preach privately, but in his point of view teaching in church was an exclusive prerogative of the hierarchical ministry. Demetrius could not have been ignorant of the existence of *didaskaloi*, for Clement of Alexandria often mentions them. Origen himself was a *didaskalos* who was not barred by Demetrius from expounding his teaching, with the exception of teaching in the ecclesial assembly and particularly in the bishop's presence. The Church of Alexandria had a lesser need for the preaching of *didaskaloi* in churches than did other churches, for in Alexandria, due to some peculiarities of church organization, the presbyters at a very early point received an opportunity to preach in ecclesial assemblies. While in Alexandria Origen did not claim this right for he did not number himself among the hierarchy, considering however the ministry of *didaskaloi* to be higher than all other ministries. The Palestinian bishops were aware of another more ancient tradition that permitted the *didaskaloi* to teach in the ecclesial assembly. In order to smooth out the brewing conflict, the Palestinian bishops ordained Origen a presbyter, perhaps following his own advice. It was an extremely unfortunate move. On the one hand, Origen's ordination was a breaking of the church discipline, for it was celebrated neither with consent nor with any knowledge of his bishop. On the other hand, Origen's presbyterial title did not give him a right to preach in church, for in the Alexandria of his time not every presbyter possessed a ministry of teaching, but only those who stood at the head of particular churches. The Palestinian bishops were not totally right when they pointed out to Demetrius that the Church allowed laics to preach in the ecclesial assembly, because the early Church allowed to teach in the ecclesial assembly only those laics who were called to the ministry of *didaskaloi*. Whether the bishops were intentionally imprecise remains unclear. The clash of two eras represented by Demetrius and the Palestinian bishops turned out not in the favor of the latter. The conflict that we are talking about did not have consequences in history: Demetrius's opinion prevailed and the idea that firmly took root in ecclesial thinking was that teaching belonged to the hierarchy; thus the laics, as before, could not "utter a word in the presence of the people." This point of view was shared by the council in Trullo that forbade the laics to teach the people. The stance of the council in Trullo is beyond any argument, for the laics, being ordained as kings and priests, do not receive the gifts of the teachers.

2. Canon 64 of Trullo does not define who possesses the "grace of the teaching word." Apparently, this definition was outside of the scope determined by the council's fathers, but it is beyond any doubt that it is the bishops, as the presiders of the churches, whom they primarily, if not exclusively, had in mind. Canon 19 of the same council states that "It behooves those who preside over the churches every day but especially on the Lord's day, to teach all the clergy and people words of piety." In the time of the council in Trullo the bishops exclusively presided over the churches rather than presbyters, the rectors of the parishes, as is the case in contemporary ecclesiastical structure. The reservation of the teaching function to the presiders alone ruled out the possibility of teaching by other members of the clergy. Their teaching status was completely ignored by the council. They, just as laics, had to receive instruction from the bishop. In the actual life of the Church the presbyters had an opportunity to preach in church "in the presence of the people," and the fathers of Trullo could not have been ignorant of this fact. However, this fact did not in any way diminish the significance of the definitive statement of the Trullan council that the teaching belongs to the bishops. Presbyters preached in churches with the knowledge and permission of the bishop, which by far has not always found understanding with the people, as the incident with Augustine shows.[75] In Byzantium, the opinion was established on the basis of the prescription of the council in Trullo that teaching belonged to bishops alone. "Observe from the present canon,—Balsamon pointed out,—that only bishops are given a right to teach the people."[76] According to the opinion of Balsamon, even the clerics in holy orders do not by themselves have a right to teach in church unless the bishop would specially ordain them to do so.

> Perhaps, someone would ask,—wrote Balsamon,—if the canon (64 of Trullo) prohibits laics from teaching in the presence of the people or discussing the subjects of the Church, must it be prohibited to monks and clerics as well in the same way as to laics or not? Insofar as the right to teach belongs only to the hi-

erarchs and to those assigned for this [teaching] whoever breaks this canonical requirement would, it seems to me, be subject to sanction. For that is why for having written or spoken imprecisely about the Gospel saying "My Father is greater than I," many monks and clerics suffered punishment.[77]

Being ordained to be a teacher, as referred to here, is not an ordination to a special charismatic ministry, but rather a simple commission. "Only the hierarchs and those whom the hierarchs commission to teach,—repeats Balsamon,—are given right to teach the people of God and to interpret the dogmas by the grace of the All-Holy Spirit."[78] Not having an opportunity to fulfill their teaching function in person, the bishops chose from among their clerics those they considered to be "teachers" and commissioned them to teach in church. These appointed teachers did not teach in their own name but in that of the bishop who commissioned them. "Only bishops are given the right to teach the people,—Balsamon points out,— and the teachers (didaskaloi) teach after the right that belongs to the patriarch . . . That is why when the current patriarch dies they cannot teach anymore."[79] Constantinopolitan didaskaloi, appointed by the patriarch, did not teach in their own name but in the patriarch's. The patriarch, appointing teachers to this ministry, delegated to them his own right to teach and for this reason when the patriarch died they had to cease teaching until the new patriarch delegated to them his own rights. This act of delegating of which Balsamon spoke belongs to the realm of law.

It is in and through the juridical norm that Balsamon found a compromise between the doctrine that ascribes the teaching to the bishops as the presiders of the churches and the practice of his time that allowed other clerics to teach. If teaching is a charismatic ministry it cannot be delegated, just as no one can delegate the gifts of the Holy Spirit that God bestows upon his chosen ones for the service in the Church. The gifts of the Holy Spirit do not fall into the realm of law and therefore cannot be transferred in a juridical manner. The juridical norm is a phenomenon foreign to the Church, and its incompatibility with the Church is manifested each time one tries to base the life of the Church on a juridical foundation. In the fourth or fifth centuries one hardly thought of delegating the privilege of teaching when admitting presbyters to preach in churches at the eucharistic assembly. The memory concerning didaskaloi, the bearers of the teaching ministry, was still living in the ecclesial mind. At that time, to admit some presbyters to teaching in the ecclesial assemblies meant to recognize in them a dignity of teacher, and so it was equivalent to their being set apart for this ministry. Certainly, Balsamon did not deny the charismatic nature of teaching, nor does theology nowadays.

If he spoke of the possibility of delegating instruction he based this juridical norm on a teaching that regarded clerics as consecrated. A bishop could delegate some of his prerogatives to clerics, i.e., every cleric by virtue of his consecration is capable to act in the Church and therefore he can be commissioned by a bishop for certain acts. The teaching that divided the members of the Church into consecrated and non-consecrated replaced the fundamental teaching of the Church concerning the work of ministry based on a variety of the gifts of the Spirit. "All these are inspired by one and the same Spirit, who apportions to each one individually as he wills" (1 Cor 12.11). Commissioning some of the clerics to do certain acts, the bishop himself distributes the ministries in the Church, but in a juridical rather than a charismatic manner, delegating some of his prerogatives. This act of delegating has distinct limits. It occurs within a group of people who received consecration. For this reason the laics, being non-consecrated, are incapable of receiving the prerogative of teaching in the Church.

For Balsamon as well as for ecclesiastical writers of the following era, the office of a teacher is inaccessible to laics. The point of view expounded during the late Middle Ages agreed with the original teaching of the Church, but this agreement is a mere appearance, undermined by the deep divergence in basic principles of ecclesial life: the principle of grace and the principle of law. Modern theology has not yet wholly absorbed the teaching advocated by Balsamon, although we find some of its traits in the theological doctrines that regard the presbyters as bishop's delegates. According to modern teaching, instruction in the Church belongs to the members of the ecclesiastical hierarchy alone. With the permission of the ecclesiastical authority, this prerogative is sometimes expanded to include all members of the clergy. As a general rule lay people are completely excluded from the teaching office in the Church, but in practice are sometimes admitted against all the ancient tradition of the Church and its centuries-old practice. The admission of lay people to teaching is such a rare instance that it may be easily ignored, especially since the scholastic theology is unable to give any substantial dogmatic or canonical reasons to justify this practice. Until the special ministry of teacher is restored in the Church in the conditions of contemporary Church life, none but the bishop and presbyter are called to teach, for only they have received the gifts of the Holy Spirit in the sacrament of holy orders that cannot be delegated.

3. When instruction takes place, the people are taught by the *didaskaloi*, and whoever did not receive the charism of instruction cannot, together with *didaskaloi*, take part in the instruction of others. The one who has "to open his ears to those who have received the grace to teach" cannot be a teacher.

The people listen to the teachers and receive instruction from their *didaskaloi*, but at the same time they listen as the bearers of their royal and priestly dignity. That they listen to the teachers does not mean that they remain passive in the process of instruction. Just as in the area of administration, the people possess the right of examination and witness with respect to the instruction which is being offered to them.[80] The office of a teacher, as a special ministry, is dedicated to the instruction of God's people. The "teacher" does not instruct God's people in his own name but rather in the name of the Church, not expounding his own teaching, but the Church's. "Even if we, or an angel from heaven, should preach to you a gospel contrary to that which we preached to you, let him be accursed" (Gal 1.8). The office of the teacher aims at disclosing what is deposited in the Church. In the proper sense of the word, there is only one Teacher and Instructor in the Church— Christ—and the ecclesiastical *didaskaloi* are called teachers in a relative sense.[81] For this reason the people of the Church who bear the charism of examination also must witness whether the teaching expounded by the *didaskaloi* agrees with that of the Church. The testimony of the people is the judgment of the Church rather than a judgment of some of its members. Therefore just as the teaching itself, this judgment is not "man's" nor is it "from man" (Gal 1.11–12: *kata anthrôpon, para anthrôpou*) but from God. In most cases the witness of the Church accompanies the teaching of the *didaskaloi* silently, i.e., the *didaskalos* himself was examined by the people of God beforehand. In disputed cases the witness of one local church concerning the teaching expounded by its *didaskaloi* becomes subject to reception by other churches. The history of the Church is full of examples of when the people's reception was decisive for the victory of orthodoxy over heresy. It suffices to recall that Athanasius the Great, after enduring tribulations, would hardly have come out of the Arian controversy victorious without the support of the people and their ecclesial reception of his teaching.

In the ecclesial life of our time, reception cannot find its expression. Consequently there is no place for the people's examination of the teaching with which they are instructed. The examination of the teachers and judgment concerning the teaching imparted by them has passed over to the ecclesiastical hierarchy and, in the more important cases, to synods and councils. The question of the basis upon which the authority of the councils rests is one of the most complicated theological problems. We are not going to analyze this question here, for it requires special investigation. However we resolve this question, one thesis always remains beyond any dispute. The decisions of the council are binding only when they express the decision of the Church. Decisions of this kind cannot be made without the Church or outside the Church, thus it cannot be made without the people of God, i.e., without its witness concerning the will of God that has been revealed through this decision. If the decision of the council lacks the reception of the Church it remains a *theologoumenon*, a matter of theological opinion. Being a voice of the Church, the decisions of the council can be accepted as final only after their reception by the Church. By itself this statement is so indisputable that it does not even need to be proved. If we give up this thesis, we would lose the only criterion by which the ecclesial mind discerns a true decision of the council from a false one. Again, Church history is full of examples of councils that were technically sound but were rejected by the Church. In the present time synods or councils of the local churches hardly ever discuss any doctrines but when, as an exception, they do discuss doctrinal questions, the decisions of these councils have only legal force at their disposal, as the bodies with the higher juridical authority in local churches. These decisions are binding in terms of Church discipline but their judgments cannot claim truthfulness in the ecclesial manner, for these decisions remain without reception by the Church. It is not the fault of any particular ecclesiastical figures, but rather the fault of the whole system. For founded on the legal principle which penetrates areas where it has no place, the charismatic character of the judgments is inevitably transformed into a legal one. For this reason the system of ecclesiastical organization based on law would rather recognize in lay people a right to teach in Church than acknowledge in them the charism that naturally belongs to the people of God—the examination and witness to the will of God.

4. The office of the teacher does not belong to laics. They are not able to teach in the ecclesial assembly and to instruct the people of God. However, the lack of the gifts for teaching that characterizes laics does not rule out the fact that laics as members of God's people can have their own individual views and privately express their own opinions. Even Balsamon and Zonaras did not deny the lay people this right, on the basis of the definition of the Trullan council that prohibited only public teaching (*dêmosia*) for lay people.

> It is well said in addition: "publicly," for if some intelligent man is asked privately on some dogmatic subject or any other matter that benefits the soul, he would not be subject to punishment, if he gives an answer, guided by his own reasoning.[82]

> But, whoever is asked privately, he is not forbidden to reply and to teach the inquirer.[83]

In our time this private instruction raises the question concerning scientific study and in particular freedom in theological research. Theological science does not directly relate to the ministry of teaching in the Church and therefore cannot be considered a special ministry. It is open to every laic. However, it does not follow that scientific theological research is deprived of grace. In the Church as a charismatic organism everything works by grace. Theological study remains within the Church and while the theological student remains in the status of a laic—it is a charismatic ministry. Just as every work done in the Church, scientific theological study is a responsible work, for everything is done before the face of Christ. Every laic is responsible for his life and his work in the Church: "If any one destroys God's temple, God will destroy him. For God's temple is holy, and that temple you are" (1 Cor 3.17). This is the highest responsibility that there can be—not to destroy God's temple and it does not deprive any laic of his freedom of thought, as a gift of God. "Where the Spirit of the Lord is, there is freedom" (2 Cor 3.17). The Spirit of the Lord is in the Church and freedom is in the Church, not the freedom of slaves—"you are no longer a slave but a son" (Gal 4.7)—not a juridical or a political freedom but that of the sons of God, freedom in love or as a gift of perfect love. "There is no fear in love, but perfect love casts out fear" (1 John 4.18). In the Church freedom abides, for in the Church perfect love abides. "And you will know the truth, and the truth will make you free" (John 8.32). The content of freedom is something positive: it is truth. In the Church love, freedom, and truth are identical: freedom stems from love and contains truth. The breach of freedom would signify the impoverishment of love and the fear of truth. In their love for truth the children of the Church do not know fear in expressing their own opinions, however disputable. "For there must be factions (*haireseis*) among you in order that those who are genuine among you may be recognized" (1 Cor 11.19). Freedom ensures creativity in the Church which can never fail while the Spirit of the Lord abides in it. Prophecy does not cease in the Church, not a Montanist "new prophecy," but rather the prophetic spirit that the Church received on the day of Pentecost. To tread on the freedom of theological research would signify distrust in the prophetic spirit or a deliberate quenching of this spirit. The Church protects the freedom of theological research for the aim of this research is truth. "If what you heard from the beginning abides in you, then you will abide in the Son and in the Father" (1 John 2.24). To keep ancient tradition in the Church means to keep the truth. The aim of theological research is to disclose and know the original tradition that remains in the Church unchanged, though often overshadowed by the temporary and transient. The controversy that theological research may cause is a sign of the unceasing creative spirit of God's people, and the charism of discernment is expressed in this. Theological work is a charismatic endeavor but it is also human activity and as such is subject to error. One can indeed fail to attain the truth, the goal of theological study. The divergence of opinion that theological research may cause is part of the process of the discernment of the truth by the people of God. The truth will be manifest in divergence and thus the discernment or judgment of the people of God is not "censorship" (*censura*). "If I have spoken wrongly, bear witness to the wrong; but if I have spoken rightly, why do you strike me?" (John 18.23). These words of Christ should always remain the standard for the Church's attitude toward theological research. The judgment of the Church comes only following the process of discernment and that can be, and usually is, rather lengthy. As an ecclesial act this judgment is subject to ecclesial reception. Just as in relation to the office of teaching, the Church's judgment concerning theological research cannot be juridical. In this judgment, as well as in every ecclesial act, lies the revelation of the will of God. Therefore, it is not the work of a human "forum" but rather of God's judgment. Ecclesial reception must verify this revelation. Therefore, when the Church judges concerning theological research it judges whether the sole aim of theological research, the truth, was attained. If the truth is not attained it means that this theological research remains outside of the Church, that it is built on the foundation other "than that which is laid, which is Jesus Christ" (1 Cor 3.11).

––––––––

The people of God live in the Church as its living members. Their life is their action, their unceasing service in the Church, beginning with their entrance into the Church and their ordination as kings and priests there. If the Church had a field of activity banned for the people of God it would mean that in the Church there is an extra-ecclesial sphere, for the Church is the people of God gathered by God in Christ. Or it would mean that the people of God have ceased to be the people of God.

The ministry of laics as members of the Church is not expressed in different spheres of activity in the same way. The ministry of laics is most intensely expressed in worship. Laics as a whole concelebrate with those who preside over them. It is the entire people of God that worships in the Church whose head is Christ.

> We have such a high priest, one who is seated at the right hand of the throne of the Majesty in heaven, a minister in the sanctuary and the true tent which is set up not by man but by the Lord. (Heb 8.1–2)

It is the Church itself in the person of its High Priest that worships.

In the sphere of administration and teaching the people of God is governed and instructed by those ordained for these ministries. In these spheres laics can neither govern nor teach jointly with those who govern or instruct them. The prerogative of the people in these spheres is examination, expressed through *consensus* and ecclesial reception. Examination is the testimony of the people of God to the fact that the rulers and teachers whom God has ordained do in fact rule and teach according to the will of God and that the gifts of the Holy Spirit that they have received abide in them. Pastors and teachers do not rule and teach in their own name or in the name of the people that has authorized them, but Christ himself rules and teaches through them as the one Shepherd of one flock. In all of the three main spheres of activity in the Church, Christ worships, rules, and instructs through the gifts of the Spirit that God has poured upon the ministers of the Church.

Modern dogmatic theology and ecclesiastical law construe the participation of the people in the life of the Church through opposing principles. Liturgical worship is ascribed to the ecclesial hierarchy alone, while the lay people are deprived of any role. Yet the lay people are admitted to the administration as co-administrators with the bishop. And the ministry of teaching is ascribed to individuals who do not possess the gift of teaching. Modern scholastic theology can see no significance in the fact that the variety of ministries is conditioned by the variety of the gifts of the Holy Spirit and that only one who received the gifts of the Holy Spirit can fulfill the ministry that corresponds to a certain gift. Scholastic theology and ecclesiastical law in particular proceed from the thesis that the ecclesiastical hierarchy possesses the fullness of privileges. The hierarchy retains certain of these and the rest it delegates or transfers to others. Naturally the juridical principle in the Church had to create its own logical and coherent system and organization, based on law. However, such a system and organization, as we should openly acknowledge, do not reflect in most cases the organization that is inherent in the Church. The course of Church history has diverged from its beginnings. Our time, however, is not yet the end of time.

Chapter 4

The Work of Ministry

I. Special Ministries

1. Life in the Church, to which every one of the faithful is called, is unceasing ministry through the Church to God and to the Church. "Whoever would be first among you must be slave of all. For the Son of man also came not to be served (*diakonêsthênai*) but to serve (*diakonêsai*), and to give his life as a ransom for many" (Mark 10.44–45). This was a new principle previously unknown to human society, and Christ made it the foundation of the Church's life.[1] In the Church, life and ministry are the same because the Spirit, by whom and in whom the Church lives, is the basis of all its activity. Wherever the Spirit is, there is life, also work and ministry. The entire teaching of St. Paul on the "work of ministry" was based on this commandment of Christ. All the people of God who minister to God as kings and priests are called to the work of ministry. "Let us offer to God acceptable worship, with reverence and awe; for our God is a consuming fire" (Heb 12.28–29). Therefore there is no one who is a laic, a member of God's chosen people and not a minister of God. Every laic set apart for a priestly calling receives the gift of the Spirit in order to participate in the ministry of the Church. The gift of the Spirit is given to each one separately,[2] yet not for a separate but rather for the communal ministry done by the Church. The common ministry of all is a communal ministry of all the members of the Church maintaining "the unity of the Spirit in the bond of peace" (Eph 4.3). This ministry reveals the communal life of the Church, and through this ministry is manifest the life of all its members. Without this ministry there is no life in the Church. For without this ministry there can be no eucharistic assembly in which every one of the faithful is a celebrant (*leitourgos*) and every one ministers to God under the lead of the presider.

Through the communication of the gift of the Spirit everyone in the Church is ordained for the ministry of kings and priests. But the same Spirit, by whom all were baptized distributes particular gifts to each person (*idia hekastô*) for the ministry in the Church as he wills. All the members of the body of Christ, participating in the common ministry of the Church, fulfill in the Church their particular functions. Union with Christ in his body is union with all the members of his body. Each person is given a particular gift for ministering to all. Each person ministers to all and all minister to each person. "As each has received a gift (*charisma*), employ it for one another, as good stewards of God's varied grace (*poikilês charitos Theou*)" (1 Peter 4.10).

> To one is given through the Spirit the utterance of wisdom, and to another the utterance of knowledge according to the same Spirit, to another faith by the same Spirit, to another gifts of healing by the one Spirit, to another the working of miracles, to another prophecy, to another the ability to distinguish between spirits, to another various kinds of tongues, to another the interpretation of tongues. All these are inspired by one and the same Spirit, who apportions to each one individually as he wills. (1 Cor 12. 8–11)

As the gift of royal and priestly ministry, the gifts of God's varied grace are given to each one separately, but, again, not for someone's separate ministry, but for the communal ministry of God's people. This is a common ministry of the people, based not on one gift, but on many gifts. The ministry of the people to God is simultaneously expressed through their ministry to the Church.

The variety of the gifts of the Spirit not only creates the common ministry of God's people but also the special ministries fulfilled not by all but by a few.

> And his gifts were that some should be apostles, some prophets, some evangelists, some pastors and teachers, to equip the saints for the work of ministry (*eis ergon diakonias*), for building up the body of Christ (*eis oikodomên tou sômatos tou Christou*). (Eph 4.11–12)

Not everyone is set apart for building up the body of Christ, only those God has specially called for this ministry. All being priests, God ordains some for the apostolic ministry, some for the ministries of prophets, pastors, and teachers. The Church is where the Spirit works, whose gifts God distributes, as it is pleasing to him, to each individual. Only those who are in the Church can be called to a particular ministry, but to be in the Church means to belong to God's people and to serve God as king and priest. The ministry of "building up the body of Christ" is possible only when one participates in the ministry of the entire Church. The one who does not possess the ministry of king and priest cannot have a particular ministry, for this would place him outside the sphere of the Spirit's work.

Every ministry presupposes a particular gift of the Spirit especially bestowed. The interdependent relationship between the gifts of the Spirit and ministries lays the ground for the structure of the Church as the body of Christ. The relationship stems from the principle of the work of ministry established by Christ himself after the image of his own ministry. Everyone in the Church is charismatic, for each receives the gifts, but the gift received depends on the ministry to which one is called. However, it does not follow that the one who is called to a particular ministry can possess only one gift. In the early church an apostle could have the gift of prophecy, the gift of healing, and the gift of teaching, all the time remaining an apostle. The prophet could have the gift of tongues and the gift of powers. The presider of a local church could have the gift of prophecy, and so forth. In the person of St. Paul we find a classic example of a person who possessed many gifts. Paul considered himself an apostle of Christ rather than a prophet or a teacher, so he remained an apostle in ecclesial understanding. Those having particular ministries were ordained in the Church rather than outside of or above the Church. Therefore they did not cease to be in God's flock and continued to fulfill the common ministry with all the people. God ordained for particular ministries those whom he himself called without depriving them of other gifts, if this was pleasing to him. However, the ministry to which God personally called a person remained his or her basic ministry which was acknowledged and witnessed by the Church.

2. Several times throughout his epistles, St. Paul gave lists of various ministries. In his epistle to the Corinthians he wrote:

> And God has appointed in the church first apostles, second prophets, third teachers, then workers of miracles, then healers, helpers, administrators, speakers in various kinds of tongues. Are all apostles? Are all prophets? Are all teachers? Do all work miracles? Do all possess gifts of healing? Do all speak with tongues? Do all interpret? (1 Cor 12.28–30)

In his epistle to the Ephesians, he said: "And his gifts were that some should be apostles, some prophets, some evangelists, some pastors and teachers" (Eph 4.11). His indication from the epistle to the Romans relates to the same subject:

> Having gifts that differ according to the grace given to us, let us use them: if prophecy, in proportion to our faith (*kata tên analogian tês pisteôs*); if service (*eite diakonian*), in serving; he who teaches, in his teaching; he who exhorts (*ho parakalôn*), in his exhortation; he who contributes (*ho metadidous*), in liberality; he who gives aid (*ho proistamenos*), with zeal; he who does acts of mercy (*ho eleôn*), with cheerfulness. Let love be genuine . . . (Rom 12. 6–9)[3]

Finally, one should add to these the excerpt from the epistle to the Corinthians, cited above, where he lists various gifts of the Spirit.

By enumerating various ministries St. Paul did not mean to give an exhaustive list. Even if he wanted to he could not have given a complete list, for the ministries in his time were still *in statu nascendi*. Apart from that, the epistles were not specialized treatises in ecclesiology. Their intention was conditioned by the state of the churches which Paul was addressing. Paul tackled one or another ecclesiological question as far as it related to his goal. The goal of the epistle to the Romans and especially of the epistle to the Corinthians was to preserve the unity of these churches which apparently were under the peril of division into groups in Rome or into factions in Corinth. Those who possessed individual gifts of the Spirit had set themselves off against both those who did not have individual gifts and those who had other kinds of gifts. They ignored other members of the Church or set themselves above the Church or, in the end, considered no one but themselves to be the Church. This destroyed the unity of the local church, not only with respect to its integrity but even more with respect to the distinction of many members within this integrity. In a local church, there is no single member who could manage without another member, whatever their place within the body. Life in the Church is life in the Spirit (*en pneumati*) (Rom 8.9). All were baptized by the same Spirit into one body and all were given to drink of the same Spirit. The same Spirit by whom we enter the Church and in whom we abide while being in the Church distributes the gifts to each person individually. These gifts are not given for their own sake but in the Church for its ministry. The Church's integrity is of "the one," i.e., of Christ in his body. However, the body is not made of one but of many members. Neither the distinction of the gifts nor the ministries disrupt the ontological unity of all members of the Church, for their distinction within the body is not ontological but functional. However significant the functions fulfilled by the members ordained for the ministry, these members alone do not make up the Church. "Are all apostles? Are all prophets? Are all teachers?" (1 Cor 12.29) Both the first and the second as well as the third are just members of Christ's body, but not the whole body. By their nature they are the same, for they all have one and the same Spirit through whom they become members of the body of Christ. They differ from one another only by their ministry, based on the gifts of the same Spirit. By his own nature no one can place himself over another in the Church; even less can he place himself over the Church. "There is one body and one Spirit . . . one Lord, one faith, one baptism, one God and Father of us all . . ." (Eph 4.4–6). Therefore, "there are varieties of gifts . . . and there are varieties of service . . . and there are varieties of working, but it is the same God who inspires them all in every one" (1 Cor 12.4–6).

3. In all lists of gifts and ministries given by St. Paul there is no mention of the charism of priesthood or its ministries or the individuals endowed with these.[4] It is impossible to think it is by coincidence that St. Paul each time failed to mention this ministry, for it is one of the major ones and he could not have forgotten about it. Does it follow from this that the ministry of priesthood did not yet exist at the time of St. Paul? This supposition is in total conflict with everything that we know of this time. Prayer and the glorification of God constituted the inner life of the first Christians. The Eucharist was the foundation of their ecclesial life and the sacrament of the Church to which all other ministries were related. St. Paul himself in his epistle to the Corinthians expounds the teaching concerning the gifts of the Spirit right after mentioning the Eucharist.

If we still suppose that St. Paul "forgot" to mention the ministry of priesthood, how can we explain the fact that all the writers of the New Testament are equally forgetful? Priesthood existed in apostolic times, occupying, just as in all subsequent periods, the preeminent place among other ministries. And if it existed, according to the teaching of St. Paul, the respective charism existed as well. "And like living stones be yourselves built into a spiritual house, to be a holy priesthood, to offer spiritual sacrifices acceptable to God through Jesus Christ" (1 Peter 2.5). This is the ministry of God's people gathered by God "in Christ," through which the ministry of the Church as a whole is manifested. God did not ordain just certain persons in the Church, but his entire people so that they would offer him "spiritual sacrifices." When the Church worships God, all are priests and all have a priestly charism. This is why St. Paul in laying out the teaching on the difference of ministries and the gifts of the Spirit did not need to speak of the ministry bestowed on all the faithful. We find him mentioning the ministry of priesthood not in the lists of gifts and ministries but in his teaching on baptism. "For by one Spirit we were all baptized into one body—Jews or Greeks, slaves or free—and all were made to drink of one Spirit (*kai pantes hen Pneuma epotisthêmen*)" (1 Cor 12.13). Baptism incorporates the charism of priesthood through which all the faithful serve God at the eucharistic assembly. Although the charism of priesthood is bestowed upon each one of the faithful in the Church, there is but one priesthood as there is one baptism, and one Church, into which we are baptized, as there is one people of God gathered "in Christ."

It is necessary to mention one more peculiarity of St. Paul's lists of ministries. As bearers of a particular ministry, apostles are mentioned twice in his lists (1 Cor 12.28 and Eph 4.11), but nowhere is there mention of the apostolic charism. Just as it is unlikely that St. Paul simply forgot to mention the ministry of priesthood so it is as unlikely that he could forget to mention the charism of apostleship.[5] One can hardly admit that this omission is motivated by the fact that St. Paul was laying out his teaching on the "work of ministry," adapting it to the local churches, and for this reason did not need to mention the ministries that had a universal character.[6] As we will see below, such differentiation of ministries does not have much ground. If St. Paul was guided by this motive he would not have included apostleship in the list of ministries (1 Cor 12.28 and Eph 4.11). Does it follow from his omission of the apostolic charism that St. Paul regarded apostleship as an institution, and for this reason, having mentioned the apostles, did not talk about the apostolic charism? Even this is unlikely, because for St. Paul no ministry could exist in the Church without the respective charism. It is more correct to seek the explanation in the fact that for St. Paul the apostleship that existed in his time was an unusual and exceptional phenomenon.[7] He could not fail to mention the apostles among the individuals endowed with particular ministries with regard to the importance of the ministry that they fulfilled. But could he include the charism of apostleship in the list of the gifts of the Spirit that can be bestowed upon *each and every one* of the people? The charism of apostleship cannot be bestowed upon everyone in the Church, but was given once to a certain group of individuals. For this reason the apostolic charism is not included among the gifts of the Spirit continually given in the Church. In Paul's time the beginning of apostleship was already history.

4. The discovery of the document called *Teaching of the Twelve Apostles* (The *Didache*) was a turning point in the teaching on ministries in the early Church. After its discovery the opinion that took root in theological research claimed that this document shed light upon the previously nearly unknown institution of charismatics. While not sharing the general enthusiasm for this document, we nevertheless are not inclined to reject its historical testimony. On the other hand, we are also not inclined to overestimate its significance, particularly compared with the testimony of the apostolic epistles whose historical value is incomparably higher than that of the *Didache*.

Combining the data from the New Testament writings and the *Didache*, theological scholarship beginning with Adolf Harnack became convinced that in the primitive era there existed two primary types of organization in the Church: on the one hand, the so-called charismatic institution; and on the other, a secular organization managing the affairs of a particular local church.[8] The first type consisted of the individuals possessing their ministries by virtue of the charism received directly from God, major representatives of which were apostles, prophets, and teachers. Possessing a charism of ministry from God, every charismatic, whether apostle, prophet, or teacher, was free from connection to any ecclesial community. He was not ordained for his ministry by this particular community and was not dependent on it. He did not belong to it and for the most part did not have a fixed church location or residence, fulfilling his ministry out of free inspiration. In contradistinction to charismatics, presbyter-bishops and deacons who constituted the secular organization were ordained by the community itself, were also dependent on it, and fulfilled their ministry exclusively within the limits of that local church which elected them.

First of all, one has to note that in the apostolic epistles we do not find this opposition of two types of organization. Neither could anyone point to any serious vestiges of struggle between them. Moreover, we do not find this in the *Didache*. Of the "charismatics" we find only an apostle who appears in the *Didache* as an extremely pale and nearly lifeless figure, most likely a traveling preacher, whereas prophets and teachers can choose one of the churches as their permanent location. When they appear as travelers, their activity is not limited to one local church only but spreads to many other churches. They come to these churches as it were ready-made and that is why there is no indication in the *Didache* how these persons are ordained. The bishop and deacon are the individuals who stay in the church permanently, and the compiler of the *Didache* indicates the manner of their ordination. Given all this differentiation, no opposition is found between bishops and deacons, on the one hand, and the "charismatics" on the other. The status of a bishop—and we are almost exclusively referred to the liturgy—is defined by the fact that he fulfills the ministry of a prophet in his absence. The bishop shines with the reflected light of the prophet and to a certain extent stands as his deputy. The *Didache* does not establish an opposition between prophet and bishop. Rather it seeks to put prophet and teacher—and the former in particular—in the foreground of ecclesial life.

The basic thesis at which theological scholarship arrives regarding "charismatics" is not determined by data found in the Scriptures but by the teaching concerning the Church. The latter is conceived from the universal perspective as some kind of pure spiritual entity that exists alongside and independently of the local churches. With respect to the universal church, a local church is mostly regarded either as a community or, in the best instance as a "fragment" (*Splitter*) of the universal church or finally as *pars pro toto.*[9] This universalist conception of the Church suggests that alongside the offices that each local church creates to serve its local needs there exist certain individuals whose ministry is not bound by the limits of a local church and is not attached to it but relates to the Church as a whole. This hypothesis comes about as nearly an axiom for modern theological thought, but we do not find it either in the apostolic or in the ancient church. For this period in the history of ecclesiological thought the differentiation between local churches and the Church as *Gesamtkirche* did not yet exist. All the fullness of the Church of God was present in each of the local churches.[10] According to the expression of Ignatius of Antioch, the local church was a "catholic" church. The ecclesiology of the New Testament as well as that of Ignatius of Antioch was a eucharistic ecclesiology that excluded any thought that the Church can be divided into parts.[11]

In light of this conception of the Church, any separation between the ministry of bishop-presbyters and deacons and the ministry of prophets and apostles appears to be totally artificial and foreign to the character of life in the primitive Christianity. The ministry of a bishop-presbyter as well as the ministry of a prophet were attached to the Church itself rather than to a community alone. It did not matter that the bishop fulfilled his ministry within the limits of one local church whereas the prophet might not have been bound by these limits. The bishop ordained in the local church is not ordained in this church only but in the Church of God in Christ that is present in the church for which he is ordained. The close connection of the bishop with the local church in no way diminishes the catholic nature of episcopal activity for, due to the catholicity of every local church, whatever is done in one local church is not done in this church only but in the Church of God and thus in all of the local churches as well. Similarly the nature of the prophet's activity was ecclesial and catholic, for it always took place in some of the local churches but not in the Church in some general sense. Whatever the prophet accomplished outside of the local church did not have an ecclesial nature, for outside of the local church the Church of God in Christ did not exist.

5. According to the *Didache,* the apostles, prophets, and teachers were not customarily attached to one local church as were the bishops-presbyters and deacons. Also, an apostle or a prophet who stayed in the local church for more than two days was a false prophet.[12] The apostolic writings show no awareness of such a demand. Due to the basic character of his work the apostle was a traveling evangelist. Nevertheless, nowhere in the apostolic writings do we find indications that he could not stay in one or another church for a longer period. According to a church tradition that had emerged quite early, the apostles stayed in Jerusalem for twelve years after Pentecost.[13] Whether this number is correct does not matter, for the prolonged stay of the apostles in Jerusalem remains beyond any doubt. St. Paul never limited his stay in the local churches to any specific period of time. His apostolic ministry was not only to create new local churches but involved existing ones as well.

The itinerant character of the prophets' activity also is not intentionally emphasized in the apostolic writings. The text of 1 Corinthians clearly presupposes that prophets have a permanent residence with the local church.[14] With even more certitude we can deduce that the teachers mostly fulfilled their ministry within the limits of a local church.

On the other hand, the permanent residence of bishops-presbyters in one specific local church where they were ordained did not rule out the possibility in the apostolic or sub-apostolic age that they could fulfill some temporary mission in another church or churches.

> Then it seemed good to the apostles and the elders, with the whole church, to choose men from among them and send them to Antioch with Paul and Barnabas. They sent Judas called Barsabbas, and Silas, leading men among the brethren. (Acts 15.22)

Clearly, the term "leading men among the brethren" (*andras hêgoumenous en tois adelphois*) indicates that Judas and Silas belonged to the rank of presbyters in the church of Jerusalem.[15] The church of Rome according to the epistle of Clement of Rome sent to the church in Corinth "faithful and prudent men who have lived among us without blame from youth to old age, and they shall be witnesses among us."[16] Who these "witnesses" (*martyres*) were we do not know, however it is most probable that they were presbyters of the church in Rome. According to the *Ecclesiastical Canons* the church that does not have twelve adult members for the election of a bishop must turn to another church which should send three men. Although again we do not know exactly who they were, it is most probable that they were presbyters and that one of them could have been a bishop.[17] In the beginning of the third century it became customary for neighboring bishops to gather to ordain a bishop for the widowed church.[18] The bishop-presbyter at some point could have found himself traveling as an apostle or a prophet. A prophet and a teacher could have been permanently residing within one specific church while a bishop-presbyter could have been entrusted with a temporary mission outside of his own church.

Therefore, we ought to ask whether the suggestion based on the *Didache*—that the traveling character of the charismatics' activity was one of their distinctive traits as opposed to presbyters-bishops—originates in a misunderstanding. Can we give preference to the witness of the *Didache* before that of the New Testament writings? Even if we do not consider the *Didache* as an early Montanist document, it undoubtedly reflects the life of small churches that existed somewhere on the borders of the Roman empire. Certainly the question is not whether the ministry of the apostles and prophets was predominantly vagrant. The question really is whether it is true that apostles, prophets, and teachers as opposed to presbyter-bishops and deacons did not actually belong to any local church but belonged to the universal Church, and for this reason were welcomed everywhere as transitory guests.

We know very little concerning the life of the primitive church, and many of its aspects remain obscure for us. Hence we are bound to create one or another hypothesis concerning those aspects. Would it not then be more accurate to suppose that apostles, prophets, and teachers, as well as presbyters-bishops and deacons and all the rest of the faithful, were all members of one concrete local church? For original ecclesial consciousness, the Church manifested itself in the empirical life of the local churches. This is the rule of Church life in empirical existence. Why then do we have to suppose that this rule was broken for a small group of Christians, however special their place in the life of the Church, and that these individuals were thus placed into an extra-ecclesial territory? Belonging to the Church is determined by one's belonging to one specific eucharistic assembly. Entrance into the Church is accomplished through entering a eucharistic assembly. Acceptance into the Church always took place in a local church and for this reason was always a specific church. Nowadays we have lost to a large extent this sense of concreteness, for due to the church organization of our time acceptance into the Church became for us an abstract notion. It affected our choice of expression as well. If in the early church one was accepted into the church of Rome, of Antioch, or of Corinth, i.e., into the Church of God abiding in Rome, Corinth, or Antioch, today we cannot say that one is accepted into such and such parish or diocese. We prefer to speak about acceptance into the Russian, Greek, or Syrian church, or even at its best, into the orthodox church. The very idea of the Russian Church or of a national church in general is largely a phantom concept denoting the predominant nationality of the church while in truth there cannot be any special Russian or

Greek church, but only one Church of God in Christ. In this second instance, the acceptance into the orthodox church becomes an abstract notion and nothing but an acceptance into the Church in a general sense. But there never was a eucharistic assembly of the Church that existed in a general sense, as there is no such thing today. Rather, there are eucharistic assemblies of local churches. Each of them individually and all of them together were and still are one and the same eucharistic assembly, and therefore they all are one and the same Church of God. In order to share by virtue of communion of love in the eucharistic assemblies of all local churches one has to be a member of one of these assemblies, for it is only through one of the assemblies that the doors of all other assemblies are opened.

How then could an apostle or a prophet take part in the eucharistic assembly of some local church not being a member of any local church in particular? Not having any precise information we can still propose legitimate conjectures which nevertheless would be adequate to the spirit of the age about which we are talking. However, the hypothesis that apostles, prophets, and teachers were not members of any particular church is inadequate precisely given the lifestyle of the original and early Church. This hypothesis proceeds from an *a priori* concept of universal church and universal ministries that existed in it. There is no factual data to support this hypothesis except for the fact that a prophet or a teacher while fulfilling his ministry very frequently moved from one church to another. But must this exclude membership in a particular church, replacing it with a membership in the Church in a general sense? "Now in the church at Antioch (*kata tên ousan ekklêsian*) there were prophets and teachers" (Acts 13.1). Should we think then that it was merely by coincidence that the prophets and teachers were at that time at the church of Antioch, or, as the writer of the Acts says, at the Church that abides in Antioch? Even the compiler of the *Didache*, as we have seen, admitted that a prophet could choose one of the local churches for his permanent place of residence. What this could only mean is that the prophets and teachers that stayed at this church permanently, became the members of that church. Therefore we should understand Luke's testimony that among the members of the church of Antioch there were individuals who fulfilled in this church the ministry of prophets and teachers. One can hardly doubt that the prophets referred to in 1 Corinthians were also members of the church at Corinth endowed with the prophetic ministry. Can we not then legitimately make a more general supposition that the apostles, prophets, and teachers were always permanent members of one particular church and that their travels throughout different churches constituted a mission with which they were entrusted by their local church?

Now in these days prophets came down from Jerusalem to Antioch. And one of them named Agabus stood up and foretold by the Spirit that there would be a great famine over all the world; and this took place in the days of Claudius. And the disciples determined, every one according to his ability, to send relief to the brethren who lived in Judea. (Acts 11.27–29)

Did they come down merely on their own initiative or did the church of Jerusalem take part in their sending, having given them a special mission? If we keep in mind that the coming of the prophets to Antioch resulted in the decision of the church of Antioch to send relief to the brethren in Judea, the evident conclusion is that they had a specific commission from the church of Jerusalem, where they were members. By reporting that they had come from Jerusalem, Luke had indicated that they were members of the church of Jerusalem. The same fact is supported by another testimony of Luke:

While they [prophets and teachers] were worshiping the Lord (*leitourgountôn de autôn tô Kyriô*) and fasting, the Holy Spirit said, "Set apart for me Barnabas and Saul for the work to which I have called them." Then after fasting and praying they laid their hands on them and sent them off. (Acts 13.2–3)

If Saul and Barnabas, on the basis of the revelation of the Spirit, were sent by the church of Antioch where they were members, can we not legitimately argue that both prophets and teachers were also sent by that local church, where they were members, so that the other churches as well could receive "upbuilding and encouragement and consolation" (1 Cor 14.3)?

A local church, entrusting a prophet or a teacher with a missionary task, could not act on its own initiative but only on the basis of revelation. Therefore the bestowal of a missionary task upon "charismatics" always had a double nature. On the one hand, acting on the basis of revelation received in the Church, a prophet departed from his own church to other churches. On the other, a local church bestowed upon a prophet a missionary task to minister to other churches. "Then after fourteen years I went up again to Jerusalem with Barnabas, taking Titus along with me. I went up by revelation" (Gal 2.1–2). St. Paul regarded his journey to Jerusalem as a fulfilling of a special mission which the Spirit had laid upon him. However, this is but one aspect of this mission. St. Paul was going to Jerusalem on the basis of revelation (*kata apokalypsin*), given to the Church through him or through some other prophet. Every revelation is tested by the Church. Upon accepting it as a true manifestation of the divine will, the church acts in accordance with the received revelation. This is another aspect of Paul's mission described in Acts.

> But some men came down from Judea and were teaching the brethren, "Unless you are circumcised according to the custom of Moses, you cannot be saved." And when Paul and Barnabas had no small dissension and debate with them, Paul and Barnabas and some of the others were appointed to go up to Jerusalem to the apostles and the elders about this question. (Acts 15.1–2)

As a historian of the primitive church, Luke naturally takes into account the aspect of the ecclesial act as related to the activity of the local church.[19]

If the local church entrusted a prophet, teacher, or even an apostle such as Paul with a missionary task, it could act in this way only with respect to its own members. For this reason we can legitimately claim with maximal probability that prophets and teachers were, as it was pointed out, members of one particular local church, just as the presbyter-bishops and the rest of the faithful. Even the Twelve were not an exception in this respect. Originally, they constituted a nucleus of the church in Jerusalem, remaining a part of this church even when it rapidly increased in number and other local churches began to emerge alongside it. In spite of generally exceptional status of the Twelve, the church of Jerusalem entrusted them with certain missions, as for instance at the baptism of Samaritans (Acts 8.14). They reported back to the church of Jerusalem on their activity, as did St. Peter at the baptism of Cornelius's household (Acts 10). Whether they continued to count themselves as members of the church of Jerusalem when they dispersed from Jerusalem we do not know. However, it is beyond any doubt that their adherence to the Church had a concrete character of adherence to one particular local church. This church could change, as the story of Aquila and Priscilla shows, if the personal or ecclesial circumstances so demanded. This change could take place exactly because the adherence to the Church always actualized through the local church. The universal scope of the ministry of the Twelve did not entail their membership in a universal Church and did not envision a universalistic concept of the Church. It is in the *Didache* that we find the first traits of such universalistic understanding of the Church and of an abstract adherence to it. One cannot build anything upon this fact. In this respect, just as with other things, the *Didache* shows the peculiarities that we find nowhere else. If it occurred in practice that prophets did not reckon themselves as bound by any form of adherence to the Church, it was not the norm, but an abuse of the norm, which precisely was one of the reasons why the special ministry of the prophets had ceased to exist.

6. If "charismatics" were members of a specific local church in the same manner as the bishop-presbyters, this resolves the problem concerning distinct manners of their ordination, the point which modern theological scholarship stresses so much. Should we take as some kind of axiom the idea that "charismatics" fulfilled their ministry guided by their inner inspiration, whereas bishops were ordained or appointed by the local church itself? We would point out once again, without restating what already has been said, that both the first and the second fulfilled their own ministry in the catholic Church. In this respect there is no distinction at all between prophets and teachers on the one hand, and bishops and deacons on the other. The question remains, whether the Church did in fact ordain only bishop-presbyters, while all other "charismatics" fulfilled their ministry without any ecclesial ordination. The latter possibility became so much grounded in the mind of scholars that we have ceased to understand that this question is impossible as such, being in direct contradiction with the doctrine concerning the Church.

Before investigating this question we should clarify the meaning of ordination shared by the Church itself. Ordination for ministry is an ecclesial act, thus it cannot signify an appointment to a certain position done by the ecclesiastical authority or an ecclesiastical assembly. If, as it was from ancient times or nowadays, one or a number of bishops ordain bishops, presbyters, and deacons, this does not mean that they, by virtue of the authority they possess, ordain by themselves or together with the people of the Church those to whom they wish to entrust these ministries, accompanying this ordination with the prayer that asks the Holy Spirit to be sent upon them. If the common mind in the Church today understands ordination in such a way, this indicates that the authentic meaning of this act has been lost. It is the divine, not the human, will that is active in the Church, even if this man be a bishop endowed with grace for his service in the Church. The divine will cannot depend on the human will or be subject to it. God sends the gifts of the Holy Spirit not upon those chosen by the bishops or the people of the Church but upon those whom He himself chooses. The bishop has the grace to celebrate the sacrament of ordination, but this does not mean that he manages the gifts of the Holy Spirit. Even to a lesser extent does it mean, as scholastic theology claims, that at the ordination of the presbyters and other clerics the bishop passes on to them the gifts of the Holy Spirit, and for this reason in the ordination of a bishop, several bishops must participate, for a single bishop cannot pass onto another person the grace equal to the one he already possesses. This dogmatic statement also clearly shows a total misunderstanding of the sacrament of ordination. On his own a bishop cannot pass anything from his own grace to anyone either the charismatic gifts for the episcopal ministry or even the gift for the ministry of a reader. Grace is not something to be passed from one to another and the bishop is not the one who has a depository of grace in order to distribute it to anyone he wills.[20] Grace is a living gift of the Spirit who dwells in the Church. Therefore the idea of the depository of grace is a self-contradiction. In the Church God himself ordains people for particular ministries just as God ordains everyone called into the Church to his ministry of king and priest. "And God has appointed (*etheto*) in the church . . ." (1 Cor 12.28), "and he ordained some to be apostles . . ." (Eph 4.11). Neither a bishop nor a council of bishops nor the people of the Church, but God himself, ordains apostles, prophets, teachers, and pastors. God ordains these individuals for the ministry in and not outside of the Church, and for this reason the ordination which is from God is accomplished within the Church and with the participation of the Church. "Take heed to yourselves and to all the flock, in which the Holy Spirit has made you overseers (*en hô hymas to Pneuma to hagion etheto episkopous*), to care for the church of God which he obtained with his own blood" (Acts 20.28). In his address to the presbyters of Ephesus, St. Paul reminded them that God himself ordained them as bishops, those whom St. Paul had appointed. "And when they had appointed elders for them in every church, with prayer and fasting they [Paul and Barnabas] committed them to the Lord in whom they believed" (Acts 14.23). Apostles appointed to the presbyterate those whom God had chosen. Both in apostolic times and afterward those who were ordained for ministry in the Church were the people whom God had chosen.

In the New Testament, God's election or appointment is expressed through the term *procheirizomai*. Having appeared to Paul, Christ says to him:

> Rise and stand upon your feet; for I have appeared to you for this purpose, to appoint you (*procheirizasthai se*) to serve and bear witness to the things in which you have seen me and to those in which I will appear to you. (Acts 26.16)

Ananias also tells Paul concerning this election by God:

> "Brother Saul, receive your sight." And in that very hour I received my sight and saw him. And he said, "The God of our fathers appointed you (*procheirisato se*) to know his will, to see the Just One and to hear a voice from his mouth." (Acts 22.13–14)

In the same way as with St. Paul, God chooses every one of his ministers in the Church. The ancient church testifies to this its conviction through the words of the ordination prayer: "You who know our hearts, Father, grant that your servant whom you have chosen for oversight, should shepherd your holy flock and should serve before you as your high priest . . ."[21] The *Epitome* uses the expression *hon exelexô*, "whom you have chosen"[22]—just as in Acts 1.24: "and they prayed and said, 'Lord, who knowest the hearts of all men, show which one of these two thou hast chosen (*hon exelexô*).'" The verb *eklegomai* expresses the same notion of election as the verb *procheirizomai*. The same concept of election by God has been fully preserved in the ordination rites used today. After laying his hands upon the ordinand the bishop exclaims:

> The grace divine which always heals what is infirm and completes what is lacking ordains (*procheirizetai*) N., the most devout . . . , as . . . (the rank to which he is being ordained): let us therefore pray for him, that the grace of the All-Holy Spirit may come upon him.

Thus the bishop calls the whole church gathered at the eucharistic assembly to pray for sending down the grace of the Holy Spirit upon that man whom the Spirit himself has "ordained," i.e., has elected, appointed, or put forward for an ecclesial ministry.

The election by God, manifest through the ordinations of the bishop, presbyter, and deacon, does not exclude a possibility of their election by the Church itself. "Let the bishop be ordained, having been elected by all the people."[23] Election by the local church is one of the ways to discover God's will, for it is not the one who is pleasing to the people that is elected but the one who was already appointed by God for ministry. The election was the people's testimony concerning the will of God revealed in the Church and at the same time the expression of their consent to the ordination of this particular person who was elected, in fulfillment of God's will, for this ministry. Therefore in the act of ordination the election by the people possesses but a functional meaning. Through this election it is revealed that this person has been appointed by God.

> And the twelve summoned the multitude of the disciples (*to plêthos tôn mathêtôn*) and said, "It is not right that we should give up preaching the word of God to serve tables. Therefore, brethren, pick out (*episkepsasthe*) from among you seven men of good repute, full of the Spirit (*plêreis pneumatos*) and of wisdom, whom we may appoint to this duty." (Acts 6.2–3)

The election of the seven by the church of Jerusalem aimed at finding in the midst of it the people "full of the Spirit," i.e., those whom God has already appointed for

this ministry. However if God's will is revealed apart from the election it would become unnecessary. Both election by the people and revelation concerning God's
appointment are accomplished within the Church, for both have the goal of designating the person chosen by God for the ministry in the Church. That God had
appointed St. Paul was revealed to him by Christ himself and thereafter announced by Ananias, but it was also disclosed to the Church through prophetic
revelation. "The Holy Spirit said, 'Set apart for me Barnabas and Saul for the work
(*eis to ergon*) to which I have called them (*ho proskeklêmai autous*)'" (Acts 13.2).
The church of Antioch, fulfilling God's will given through prophetic revelation,
set apart or separated from its midst Barnabas and Saul as those whom God has
called for the "work of ministry." The divine calling revealed to the Church, attested and accepted by the Church, was accompanied by the setting apart of
those designated for ministry from the rest of its members. This designation for
the ministry was a first step in the act of ordination and was understood as a disclosure by the Church of the choice made by God. Human will must yield to divine will because in the Church there is no place for the former as something
self-subsistent and independent of the divine will. For this reason the mind of the
Church firmly resisted any other ways of designating individuals for ministry,
particularly those where human will predominated. Already during Origen's time
in Alexandria there apparently was a tendency to hand hierarchical ministry down
as an inheritance. It is in connection to this that Origen utters his bitter words:
*Propinquis agrorum et praediorum relinquatur haereditas: gubernatio populi illi tra-
datur, quem Deus elegerit . . .*[24] Church history knows too many instances when
this rule was transgressed. The ones set apart for the ministry in the Church were
not those whom God elected but those whom human will in one way or another
set apart. Origen perceived this inconsistency as a tragedy. His tragic sense was
enhanced by his view of the Church as nearly a Church of the saints. For Origen
those who are set apart for the ministry in an unworthy manner were "imposters"
(*simulatores*).[25] Human will can set apart these individuals for the ministry, but it
is unable to make true ministers out of them.

Setting apart for ministry merely designated individuals whom God has
chosen for it, but did not initiate their ministry. Rather the ministry begins when
God sends down charismatic gifts for the ministry upon his chosen ones. Both
the election and sending down of the gifts for the ministry to the chosen one are
done in the Church. For this reason setting apart is usually followed by the laying
of hands upon the person chosen for ministry. "Then after fasting and praying
they laid their hands on them and sent them off" (Acts 13.3). From the earliest
times in the history of the Church at ordinations the laying on of hands marked

the moment when by the prayer of the Church the charismatic gifts are sent down upon the one who is set apart for the ministry by the will of God. In the ordination prayer, the gifts are asked for the one who is chosen by God. "Father, you who know the hearts of all, grant that your servant whom you have chosen for oversight . . ."[26] God sends down the gifts to the one whom he has chosen.

Finally, the third step of ordination is the acknowledgment by the Church of what was accomplished in it. This is the acknowledgment that the person is worthy of his ministry, the one whom the Church has set apart for the ministry and for whom the Church was praying and asking that the charismatic gifts be sent down. Like the two preceding steps, the acknowledgment too has a charismatic nature. It is a witness to the Spirit dwelling within the Church and to the Spirit's gifts sent down upon it. At the same time, this acknowledgment is the witness of the Church to the one now called to begin his ministry in the Church. The acknowledgment is a final step and a witness of the Church. It encompasses everything the preceding steps contained. Testifying to the sending down of the gifts of the Spirit, the Church bears witness to the election made by God. Bearing witness that the ordained person has begun the ministry to which the Church admitted him, the Church also bears witness that God has elected him and sent down the gifts of the Spirit upon him. In the Church there is no ministry without gifts of the Spirit, but also there are no gifts without ministry. Acknowledgment by the Church testifies to both: to the gifts of the Spirit and the ministry. In the New Testament we do not find clear indications of this aspect of ordination but it is attested by the examination entrusted to the people of God. In the early church this element was extremely important and to a large degree shaped the current form of episcopal ordination. The people's acknowledgment of the newly ordained bishop is attested in Hippolytus' *Apostolic Tradition*, which prescribes that after the bishop's ordination all the people should give him a kiss of peace because he "has been made worthy" (*quia dignus effectus est*).[27] The worthiness of the episcopal ordinand does not reside in him alone but in his election by God, and in the sending down of the Spirit's gifts upon him. The kiss of peace was a seal concluding the act of ordination which initiated the ministry. The purpose for which the bishop was ordained in the Church was the eucharistic assembly, and that is why immediately following the ordination he celebrated the Eucharist. To this day the liturgical rite of ordination preserved the acknowledgment in the form of *axios* ("worthy") which at that time was acclaimed by the people, but now by the bishop who performs the ordination, and by the clergy and the choir.

The acknowledgment of an ordination in the Church is a catholic act. It signifies that the ordination being done by the local church is not done by the local church alone but by the Church of God. Hence reception by the remaining churches accompanies the acknowledgment by the local church. Every local church as a Church of God appropriates as its own action everything that takes place in other churches. Thus every church in principle bears witness to the fact that the ordination conforms to the will of God. Cyprian of Carthage tells us that the ordination of Cornelius of Rome was received by the bishops of the whole world.[28] In Cyprian's language this meant that the ordination was received or witnessed to by all the churches. The reception by the local churches does not add anything to the acknowledgment of the ordination in the local church where it took place, but reveals the catholic nature of the entire act of ordination. That is why this reception does not constitute a separate action in the act of ordination but is included in its acknowledgment.

Our analysis of the main aspects of the sacrament of holy orders allows us to see what it means to be ordained for ministry. Ordination is a definite ecclesial act in which the Church singles out the moment when the person whom God has called to the ministry (and who received the gifts of the Holy Spirit) begins his ministry. Ordination is an act by which the Church, in fulfillment of the divine will, calls and admits to the ministry those who were already ordained by God. All three aspects of ordination indicated above are directed toward the goal present in the rite of ordination itself. These aspects are present in every ordination but their meaning can change or, more precisely, the degree in which the local church is really involved in those aspects can change. This is the cause of the difference in the form which ordination to different ecclesial ministries takes. The major flaw of scholastic theology as well as of theologians in general lies in that they recognize just one form of ordination, considering it to be the one and only, thereby rejecting all other forms of ordination. More precisely, scholastic theology concentrates on one form of ordination, disregarding all other forms. This tendency stands out especially clearly in the question of the ordination of so-called "charismatics." The form of their ordination was not the one which is recognized now as the one and only form of ordination. Hence comes the conclusion that unlike bishop-presbyters and deacons, "charismatics" were not ordained at all. The majority of theologians derive their conclusions from the form by means of which bishops-presbyters are ordained, in particular, from their election by the local church. Apostles, prophets, and teachers were not elected by the local church. Thus theologians assert that they were not ordained, and if not ordained by a local church they must be independent from it. This entire argument contains one accurate statement, namely that the "charismatics" were not elected, but one cannot conclude from this that they were not ordained.

Among many the ministries that existed in the primitive church, there was the ministry of bishop-presbyters. This ministry was an absolute necessity for the empirical existence of a local church and thus from the very beginning it was entrusted to the local church itself.

> Our apostles also knew through our Lord Jesus Christ that there would be strife for the title of bishop (*epi tou onomatos tês episkopês*). Therefore since they had received perfect foreknowledge they appointed those who have been already mentioned, and afterwards added a rule (*epinomên*) that, should they fall asleep, other approved men should succeed to their ministry (*leitourgian*).[29]

In these words of Clement of Rome we find a genuine apostolic tradition stipulating that the ministry of bishop-presbyters must not cease in the local churches. In fulfillment of divine will the apostles, preaching the gospel of Christ, in all places ordained the first fruits of the faithful to be bishops and deacons.[30] In fulfillment of the same divine will they decided that the care of this ministry would be entrusted to the local churches which had to ordain the successors of those who had died. This rule (*epinomê*) is preserved in the Church today. From apostolic times every local church ordained for itself bishops, presbyters, and deacons, as well as all other members of the clergy whose offices emerged later. These ordinations, done by the local church, contained all of the three aspects: (1) the election of the individuals designated for these ministries; (2) their ordination and the calling in prayer to send down the gifts of the Holy Spirit; (3) the acknowledgment by the local church that the ordination had been made effective through grace. In all these aspects the role and significance of the local church in ordaining its own pastors is clearly and distinctively emphasized. It is the church itself that elects them. It is the church itself that ordains them. It is the church itself that bears witness and acknowledges the ordination it has done. That throughout history these aspects, particularly the first and the third, experienced some change, is not of much significance to us.

For the thinking of the primitive Church, the election by the Church meant the election by all the people. Clement himself spoke about this, pointing out that the bishops are ordained "with the consent of the whole church" (*suneudokêsasês tês ekklêsias pasês*),[31] which entailed their election by the same church. The earliest liturgical rite of episcopal ordination, preserved by Hippolytus in his *Apostolic Tradition*, states: "Let the bishop be ordained, having been elected by all the people."[32] The *Didache* points to the same thing, urging the faithful: "Therefore, then, choose and ordain bishops and deacons." (*Cheirotonêsate oun heautois episkopous kai di-*

akonous.)[33] We saw above that Cyprian did not consider it possible to perform any ordination without the consent of the people. He spoke of Cornelius of Rome that the latter was made a bishop "by God and the judgment of his Christ, and with the witness of all the clergy and of the people who had elected him" (*de Dei et Christi eius iudicio, de clericorum paene omnium testimonio, de plebis quae tunc adfuit suffragio*).[34] However the same Cyprian tells us of a certain change that was in progress during his time:

> You must diligently observe and keep the practice delivered from divine tradition and apostolic observance which is also maintained among us and throughout almost all the provinces; that for the proper celebration of ordinations all the neighbouring bishops of the same province should assemble with that people for which a prelate is ordained. And the bishop should be chosen (*episcopus deligatur*) in the presence of the people who have most fully known the life of each one, and have looked into the doings of each one as respects his habitual conduct.[35]

This is a language of a different age and Cyprian was aware of it, pointing out that the custom he described is observed "mostly in the provinces" (*fere per prouincias*). According to this canon election belonged to the bishops, the people being present. After law penetrated the church, beginning with the Nicaean era, the people are gradually deprived of the right to elect their own pastors. This prerogative is ascribed either to the council of bishops or to the authority of a single bishop. Nevertheless, the idea that the person designated by a council or a bishop is elected by God does not altogether disappear from dogmatic thinking and, as we have seen, liturgical rites continue to witness to this fact. At the time when juridical principles penetrated the Church and effected the deprivation of election by the people, the third aspect of ordination—the witness of the people—lost its meaning. The people's testimony enters a state of lethargy where it remains until this day, for when the church is organized on the basis of juridical principles, there is no place for the consent of the people, nor for ecclesial reception. Scholastic theology focused all its attention on the second step, the laying on of hands with the prayer that calls for the gifts of the Holy Spirit. The charismatic nature of clerical ordination, of the first degrees of priesthood in particular, is still preserved in the church. And the church both in antiquity and today takes care that its pastoral ministry continues without interruption. The ordination of individuals for pastoral ministries constitutes a classic form of ordination, which, as we have already said, the ecclesial mind had perceived as the one and only form.

Apart from the ministries under the care of a local church that assured these were not interrupted, there existed other ministries outside the concern of the local church. Those ministries did not constitute a vital necessity for the church's empirical existence or for pastoral ministry. Among these were the ministries of prophets, evangelists, and teachers.[36] However important these ministries might be in themselves they were not a necessity such as the ministry of bishops-presbyters for already existing churches. These ministries might have existed in these churches, but they equally well might not have existed. The care for these ministries did not burden the local churches. The individuals were directly selected and called by God for their ministry, rather than elected by local churches. However, if they were not elected by these churches, would it mean that the local churches did not participate at all when they were ordained? The absence of election does not necessarily entail the absence of other elements of ordination. Those who were called to special ministries were not members of the Church in some general sense but were members of a concrete local church in whose eucharistic assembly they participated. They were set apart from the midst of the local church for ministry in this or another local church. For this reason, this setting apart could not have taken place without any involvement on the church's part. Just as with everything in the Church, the setting apart of those called by God for a special ministry was done on the basis of revelation of the Spirit, which replaced the first step of ordination, i.e., the election. This setting apart was usually followed by a laying on of hands with a prayer, asking to send down the gifts of the Spirit upon the one designated for the ministry. The laying on of hands was accompanied by the subsequent witness of the local church concerning the ordination that has happened. St. Paul himself gives us an example of such an ordination. Set apart before he was born and called by Christ—"when he who had set me apart before I was born, and had called me through his grace, was pleased to reveal his Son in me"—after a prophecy concerning his call at the assembly of the Antiochian church, he was set apart by this church for the work to which he was called. "Then after fasting and praying they laid their hands on them and sent them off" (Acts 13.3). This ordination accomplished within a local church gave a start to Paul's apostolic ministry. In the mind of the Antiochian church, this ordination was not unlike the ordination of Barnabas that took place at the same time as Paul's. If Barnabas indeed presided over the church of Antioch, his ordination is even more remarkable than Paul's. Sending them off, the church of Antioch witnessed to its own submission to God's will, as well as to the ordination that has happened. Just as with an episcopal ordination, the ordination of Paul and Barnabas was done by virtue of a "good will" of the whole church. If Paul was indeed ordained to his ministry by a local church, it is hardly possible to hold that evangelists could start their ministry by themselves, without any involvement on the part of local churches. Apparently, the *didascaloi* were ordained in a similar manner.

In contrast to the ordination of bishop-presbyters, election by a local church was not present in the ordination of evangelists and teachers. However important election might be by itself, it does not exhaust the whole act of ordination. Election is necessary when the care for the continuation of a ministry is entrusted to the local church. As we have seen already, election was meant to make known the will of God. When the will of God was revealed by other means than by election, this aspect is left out from the act of ordination, but not the ordination itself. We have a number of examples when even at the election of bishops the revelation of the will of God was decisive in the choice of a candidate for the episcopal office. It would suffice to remember the election of Ambrose of Milan.

Do we have a right to assert that the act of ecclesial ordination sustains the same power and significance even when not only the election by a local church is lacking, but also the rite of laying of hands upon those who are called? To the best of our knowledge, the prophets were not elected by a local church, nor was the laying on of hands performed upon them. Undoubtedly, neither election nor laying on of hands were applied to the individuals called to the ministries of powers and healing, tongues and others, mentioned by St. Paul (1 Cor 12.28). Does it follow from here that these ministries were totally "free" of control in the sense implied by theological scholarship today? Prophets were not elected, for the continuation of the prophetic ministry was outside the concern of the local churches. Some of the churches could have had no special prophetic ministry (which, however, does not entail that this church did not have a prophetic charism) and other churches could have had a few prophets. The laying on of hands was not done for them, for the beginning of their ministry did not depend on the common manifestation of the church's good will. The prophet was elected and called by God himself, who communicated to him the prophetic charism directly, without any involvement on the part of the local church. Nevertheless, it would be absolutely inaccurate and contrary to the entire spirit of the ecclesial life of early Christianity to hold that prophetic ministry was "free" of control, i.e., that the prophet, feeling in himself the prophetic charism, fulfilled his ministry independently of the local church. If it was so, it would mean that prophetic ministry was inferior to the Church. The prophet is chosen and called by God, who bestows charismatic gifts upon him. But the call and the communication of the gifts of the Spirit take place in the Church and for the service of the Church. Without electing or laying hands on them, a local church participates in their ordination by acknowledging them as prophets. Without this acknowledgment it would be impossible for a prophet to fulfill his ministry, for it was up to a decision of an ecclesial assembly in the person of its presider, whether to allow a prophet to prophesy or not. The Church attends to the prophetic word when the Church is aware that it is a prophet who speaks this word to the Church. This awareness is manifested in the Church as the acknowledgment of a prophet as prophet. Just as in relation to all remaining ministries, this acknowledgment is not juridical. Acknowledgment is a witness of the Church that the prophet was given a prophetic charism. It is a discernment of God's will, its disclosure and submission to it, and this is precisely what it means for the local church to ordain a prophet. For the ordination of a prophet there is no need for election or laying on of hands, for God's election and bestowal of charismatic gifts is manifest in the very ministry of a prophet. Therefore the ordination of a prophet by a local church consists only of a witness concerning the divine will that has been revealed and the acknowledgment of a prophet in his status as a prophet. In and through this action the one whom God has called and to whom he has communicated charismatic gifts for his ministry is ordained for this ministry in the Church. Through acknowledgment, a local church ordains to the prophetic ministry for itself one of its members who is also a member of its eucharistic assembly. Aside from ministering to itself, a church can commission a prophet to minister to other churches. Probably it is in this case that the commissioning of a prophet involved laying on of hands and prayer. However, this was not an addition to the ordination for prophetic ministry since the latter already took place, but was a new ordination for an additional ministry.

Thus everyone who has a special ministry in the church is ordained by the Church. Depending on the type of ministry ordinations may take different forms. In some instances ordination includes all three elements: election by the church, laying on of hands, and the Church's witness to the sending down of the charismatic gifts for the ministry. In other cases, it comprised only two elements: laying on of hands and an acknowledgment. Finally, in a few instances there was only the witness of the Church. But in all these instances the ordination sustains its authentic meaning and true sense: the Church entrusts a ministry to the individuals whom God himself has chosen and upon whom he has bestowed the charismatic gifts. All three elements are equally important and are present, in one or another way, in every type of ordination. The extent to which the local church is involved may vary, but this involvement cannot be reduced to nothing, i.e., it cannot be the case in the life of the Church that a local church does not in any way participate in the ordination of individuals designated for special ministries. In every type of ordination there always exists the acknowledgment of the ordination on the part of the church. If there is none, not only has there not been an ordination, but there is no ministry, for no ministry exists or can exist outside of the local church. Consequently there cannot be individuals whom the church did not ordain. Any ministry in which a local church is not involved is inferior to the Church, and individuals who fulfill such ministries are indeed "free" from control of the local church, for they do not belong to those who fulfill the "work of ministry." Only individuals ordained by the Church can exercise in it ministries and only a person whom God has called and who received from God the gifts of the Holy Spirit can be ordained. Despite the divergence in the form of ordination there is no essential difference between different types of ordinations. A teacher and a prophet is likewise an individual ordained by the church, as is a bishop-presbyter.

7. Coming back to the previously stated question on the essential distinction between those whom theological scholarship calls "charismatics" and, on the other hand, presbyter-bishops and deacons, we have to acknowledge that this is a phantom distinction based on a misunderstanding. Every ministry in the Church is based upon a charism and, therefore, every one endowed with the ministry is a charismatic, just as, in general, is every member of the Church, for upon entrance into the Church, every one receives the gifts of the royal priesthood. To consider possible the existence in the Church of some type of ministry for which the gifts of the Spirit are not given, would mean to allow the possibility of existence within the Church of a territory deprived of grace. This possibility, in turn, by necessity makes us question the charismatic nature of the Church. As a bearer of charismatic ministry every charismatic is ordained by, in, and for the Church. However, the Church ordains only those who are chosen and called by God. Thus from this perspective no distinction can exist between the ministry of an apostle, prophet, or teacher on the one hand and the ministry of a bishop-presbyter and deacon on the other. The Church as a community does not create any ministries, because the Church as a community does not exist. It does not create, as theological scholars assert, apostolic and prophetic ministries and it also does not create episcopal ministry. It is God who creates ministries for the catholic church which in the fullness of its unity abides in each of the local churches. All individuals who have special ministries exercise them in the Church, for which reason a local church admits to the ministry only those whom it acknowledges as ecclesial ministers. By virtue of this fact all charismatics depend on a local church and at the same time are free from its control. For in the Church, as a charismatic organism, all ministries depend

on the gifts of the Spirit which God distributes as he finds pleasing. "All these are inspired by one and the Spirit, who apportions to each one individually as he wills" (1 Cor 12.11).

II. The Apostle

1. In the eyes of St. Paul, the apostle occupied the first place among those endowed with special ministries.[37] This shows, on the one hand, that apostles were ranked together with other individuals whom God has ordained in the Church and on the other hand it points to the exceptional status of the apostles. This status, at least for Paul, had no connection to the apostle's own individuality. "And from those who were reputed to be something (what they were makes no difference to me; God shows no partiality)—those, I say, who were of repute added nothing to me" (Gal 2.6)[38] for "neither he who plants nor he who waters is anything, but only God who gives the growth" (1 Cor 3.7). The exceptional status of the apostles in the life of the Church was determined by their ministry. The faithful are "built (*epoikodomêthentes*) upon the foundation of the apostles and prophets, Christ Jesus himself being the cornerstone" (Eph 2.20).[39] Ecclesial consciousness expressed this idea in the formula: "the apostolic church."

Like everyone who held ministries in the primitive church, the apostles were ordained by God. However, this ordination was a singular one and could not have been repeated. This peculiarity of apostolic ministry is evident in the writings of Paul, where, as it was pointed out before,[40] the gift of apostleship is not reckoned among the gifts that God could bestow upon everyone. God bestowed this gift upon the people whom he chose for this ministry and to these this ministry was also limited in its entirety. If the charism of apostleship is not bestowed anymore thus the apostolic ministry in the Church cannot be repeated.[41]

The unique character of the apostolic ministry entailed the idea of fixed boundaries for the circle of those fulfilling this apostolic ministry. "For I think that God has exhibited us apostles as last of all (*tous apostolous eschatous*), like men sentenced to death . . ." (1 Cor 4.9). In the same epistle, Paul restates the same thought, in a slightly changed form: "Last of all (*eschaton de pantôn*), as to one untimely born (*ektrômati*), he appeared also to me" (15.8). Paul considered himself as the last of the apostles: after him the boundaries of the apostolic circle were closed.[42] It is upon Paul that the gift of apostleship—"according to the grace of God given to me" (*kata tên charin*)—was bestowed for the last time. It does not matter that in Paul's mind, as in the mind of all first Christians, the second coming of Christ was to find some, if not all, of the apostles still living. The essence of the apostolic ministry is not conditioned by the interval between the resurrection and the Parousia, but is conditioned by the content of the ministry.[43]

2. If the apostolic circle is limited, then by whom? This question is subject to much debate. It is hardly possible to determine who exactly belonged to it. In order to attempt to answer this question even approximately, we first need to clarify the concept of the apostolic ministry itself, and this is still the subject of great debate. Do we really have, as often claimed, two different concepts of apostleship: one of Paul and the other of the church in Jerusalem, the first concept being charismatic, the second institutional?

> So one of the men who have accompanied us during all the time that the Lord Jesus went in and out among us, beginning from the baptism of John until the day when he was taken up from us—one of these men must become with us a witness to his resurrection. (Acts 1. 21–22)

It would be very strange to regard the words of Peter in the Acts of the Apostles as defining the ministry of the apostles as it was understood in the church of Jerusalem. If it were so, Luke, precisely by including these words in the Acts, would exclude Paul from the rank of the apostles. We can say with assurance that Luke would never do this, for nowhere did he ever doubt Paul's apostleship. Moreover, the church of Jerusalem—the Twelve, to be precise—also did not reject Paul's claim for apostleship, which it might have done if such a notion of apostleship had existed in this church at all. Paul himself never claimed and could not claim that he was with Christ beginning from Jesus' baptism by John until the Ascension. He openly professed that he was "the least of the apostles (*ho elachistos tôn apostolôn*), unfit to be called an apostle, because ... [he] persecuted the church of God" (1 Cor 15.9). Can one suppose then that St. Paul, putting forward his claim for apostleship, had deliberately changed the original concept, having invested it,[44] wholly or for the most part, with charismatic characteristics?

> But by the grace of God I am what I am, and his grace toward me was not in vain. On the contrary, I worked harder than any of them, though it was not I, but the grace of God which is with me. (1 Cor 15.10)

Paul was a man of tradition before his conversion to Christ; thus he remained even after his conversion. He received the tradition which Christ has imparted to him:

> But rise and stand upon your feet; for I have appeared to you for this purpose, to appoint you to serve and bear witness to the things in which you have seen me and to those in which I will appear to you. (Acts 26.16)

Through this imparting of the tradition he became its bearer: "Whether then it was I or they, so we preach and so you believed" (1 Cor 15.11). Paul did not alter the original concept of the apostleship which was already a tradition in his time. He did not need to do that. Luke could easily insert the words of Peter without risk of undermining Paul's apostleship, for these words had nothing to do with its definition. Peter had spoken them in the context of Matthias's election in place of Judas. This election was aimed at filling the rank of the Twelve whom Christ has chosen during his earthly life. Election was done at the time when the Twelve were awaiting the Spirit—"He charged them not to depart from Jerusalem, but to wait for the promise of the Father, which, he said, 'you heard from me'" (Acts 1.4). The election of Matthias was an action that, in a way, was a continuation of Christ's earthly life. Naturally only one who had remained with the rest of the disciples all this time, beginning from the baptism of John, could be numbered among the Twelve. At that point, the Twelve were not yet apostles in the strict sense of this term. This last comment requires some explanation.[45]

3. The Twelve were established by Christ, but they were not yet apostles during his earthly lifetime. "Follow me and I will *make (poiêsô)* you fishers of men" (Mark 1.17). They were "preordained" by Christ in order to be apostles. The temporary mission that Christ has conferred on them (Mark 6. 7 and parallel passages) was not identical with their ministry following the Pentecost.

> But you shall receive power when the Holy Spirit has come upon you; and *you shall* be my witnesses in Jerusalem and in all Judea and Samaria and to the end of the earth. (Acts 1.8)

The mention of the power proceeding from the Spirit reveals the pneumatological basis of the apostleship and, in turn, the ecclesiological nature of the apostolic ministry. The Church is the locus of the Spirit's activity so the power proceeding from the Spirit can be acquired only within the Church. Thus the apostolic ministry could have existed only from the beginning of the Church's existence,[46] for without the Church, the apostolic ministry would make no sense. The Eucharist was instituted by Christ at his Last Supper with the Twelve, but they actually celebrated it on the day of the descent of the Spirit. The promise that Christ gave concerning the Church (Matt 16.18) was fulfilled in the eucharistic assembly of the Twelve. The Church, where they at that moment became apostles, has become actualized in them.[47] This is the most significant moment in the history of the Church, and it is connected with the Twelve.

The ecclesiological nature of the apostolic ministry solves the dilemma of whether its character is charismatic or institutional. Everything in the Church is established by or stems from the will of God, and is established upon this will because everything that is established exists in the Church and, just as the Church itself, is established in and through the Spirit.[48] The apostleship is established at the same time as the Church, for it exists when it is incorporated into the Church. On the day of Pentecost the Twelve, chosen and established by Christ during his earthly life, became apostles *dia tês charitos*, that is, through his grace. But Paul also became an apostle *dia tês charitos*, being appointed in advance for the apostolic ministry just as the Twelve.

> But when he who had set me apart (*aphorisas me*) before I was born, and had called me (*kalesas*) through his grace, was pleased to reveal his Son in me, in order that I might preach him among the Gentiles .... (Gal 1.15–16)

To set someone apart means to appoint him in advance: "And he said, 'The God of our fathers appointed you in advance (*proecheirisato se*) to know his will . . .'" (Acts 22.14; cf. 26.16). Perhaps in Paul's thinking his being set apart before he was born was identical with the appointment of the Twelve and did not differ in any way from their setting apart. Paul knew that the Lord who had chosen and called the Twelve had chosen and called him too. Being first appointed to the apostolic ministry, both the Twelve and Paul received the apostolic charism. Here another dilemma is solved, namely the argument that for Paul, only that person is an apostle who has received the Spirit, whereas for Luke, the Spirit is received by those who already are the apostles.[49] In the Church the gifts of the Spirit are granted to those whom God has chosen for the ministry. Charism and ministry are mutually interconnected. The gift is bestowed for ministry and therefore there is no ministry without gift, but likewise no gift without ministry. It is through the Spirit that the ministry God has established is actualized and continues to be established by God every time the gift of the Spirit is bestowed.

4. Rejecting the testimony of Acts 1.21–22 as having nothing to do with the definition of apostleship, we find the same understanding of it both with Paul and with the Twelve. The apostle is the one appointed by God to whom the Risen

One had appeared, whom he had directly called and to whom he had granted the power of the Spirit. All these aspects, definitive for the understanding of the apostleship, are equally present both with Paul and with the Twelve. "Am I not free? Am I not an apostle? Have I not seen Jesus our Lord? Are not you my workmanship in the Lord?" (1 Cor 9.1) These words of Paul are particularly significant due to their apologetic character: "This is my defense to those who would examine me" (v. 3). The same connection between the apostleship and the appearances of Christ is also evident in 1 Cor 15.1–11. "For I delivered to you as of first importance what I also received . . ." (v. 3). From this follows the exposition of the "tradition" concerning the death, burial, resurrection, and apparitions of Christ. Paul's gospel ends with the establishment of the apostolic office. Christ appeared last to Paul, and that is why he is "the least of the apostles." By means of this apparition Paul came to be ranked with the apostles to whom Christ appeared earlier and who were apostles before Paul (Gal 1.17).

Not all who saw the risen Christ, but only those whom he specifically called to this ministry, became his apostles.[50]

> But you shall receive power when the Holy Spirit has come upon you; and you shall be my witnesses in Jerusalem and in all Judea and Sama'ria and to the end of the earth. (Acts 1.8)

This indication of Luke finds affinity with Christ's commandment in Matthew: "Go therefore and make disciples of all nations, baptizing them in the name of the Father and of the Son and of the Holy Spirit" (Matt 28.19). Finally, here is the most important witness, the witness of John.

> Jesus said to them again, "Peace be with you. As the Father has sent me, even so I send you." And when he had said this, he breathed on them, and said to them, "Receive the Holy Spirit." (John 20.21–22)[51]

As for Paul, his apostleship fully derives from his encounter with the Lord at the road to Damascus. "For I have appeared to you for this purpose, to appoint you to serve and bear witness" (Acts 26.16). Paul specifically insisted that he was an apostle "not from men nor through man, but through Jesus Christ" (Gal 1.1)[52] just as were the Twelve. Chronologically he was the last of the apostles but he was not inferior to the rest of them in anything, for whatever the Twelve as apostles had, Paul had too. "And from those who were reputed to be something—what they were makes no difference to me" (Gal 2.6). Having been called to apostolic service Paul did not become one of the Twelve, just as the Twelve, having become apostles, did not stop being the Twelve. Paul had everything that the rest of the apostles had, but he did not have what the Twelve had. Through them the Church was brought into existence and they were the bearers of its primordial tradition. Paul became a bearer of the tradition, too, when it was imparted to him, but at that point it was the tradition of which the Twelve were the bearers. The Twelve's recognition of Paul's working for the gospel was for him a witness that he was not "running or had run in vain" (Gal 2.2).

The third aspect of the concept of apostleship is inseparably tied to the first two. Those called to the apostolic ministry became apostles "through grace" (*dia charitos*). No apostolic ministry can exist without power from on high, for no ministry can exist without grace. If the moment in Paul's life when the call took place can be disputed, it is certain that it took place in the Church (*en tê ekklêsia*), for the power of the Spirit could have been administered only in the Church. We saw that it was in the Church that the apostleship of the Twelve was actualized. The difference between Paul and the Twelve was that the apostleship of the latter was actualized at the moment when the Church was brought into existence through them. The Church was not brought into existence through Paul. However, this distinction does not relate to their apostleship but to their status as the Twelve. Both the Twelve and Paul received the power of the Spirit, by means of which they became apostles. Thus the manifestation of the Spirit is a "sign" of apostleship both for Paul and for the Twelve.

> The signs of an apostle (*ta men sêmeia tou apostolou*) were performed among you in all patience, with signs and wonders and mighty works (*en pasê hypomonê, sêmeiois kai terasin kai dynamesin*). (2 Cor 12.12)

The same statement can also be applied to the rest of the apostles: "Many signs and wonders (*sêmeia kai terata*) were done among the people by the hands of the apostles" (Acts 5.12). Signs done by the apostles were of the same nature as the signs of Christ:[53] "If it is by the finger of God that I cast out demons, then the kingdom of God has come upon you" (Luke 11.20).

> And Jesus answered them, "Go and tell John what you hear and see: the blind receive their sight and the lame walk, lepers are cleansed and the deaf hear, and the dead are raised up, and the poor have good news preached to them." (Matt 11.4–5)

Signs and wonders accompanying the apostolic preaching bore witness of the salvation that has come in Christ.

5. The apostles were witnesses to this salvation in Christ: "You shall be my witnesses" (*kai esesthe mou martyres*). They are witnesses of Christ's resurrection clothed with a power of the Spirit (1 Cor 15.14). Here again we find full affinity in the understanding of apostleship by Paul and by the Twelve. "This Jesus God raised up, and of that we all are witnesses" (*hou pantes hêmeis esmen martyres*) (Acts 2.32). This is a central idea of St. Peter's first sermon and is constantly reiterated: "[You] killed the Author of life, whom God raised from the dead; to this we are witnesses" (3.15). "And with great power the apostles gave their testimony to the resurrection of the Lord Jesus" (4.33). "The God of our fathers raised Jesus whom you killed by hanging him on a tree . . . And we are witnesses to these things, and so is the Holy Spirit" (5.30, 32; cf. 10.40–41). The apostle Paul spoke of the same thing, joining his voice with the rest of the apostles: "We are even found to be misrepresenting God (*pseudomartyres tou Theou*), because we testified of God that he raised Christ, whom he did not raise" (1 Cor 15.15). To bear witness to the resurrection of Christ means to bear witness to the historical Jesus because only under this condition can the resurrection have a salvific effect. The resurrection of Christ completed his earthly life beginning with his birth and extending to Golgotha, thus encompassing all his life. The testimony of the apostles bore witness to a historical event.[54]

The apostles were the witnesses of Christ in Jerusalem, Judea, Samaria, and to the ends of the earth. That is why their witness comes together with the mission of the preaching of the gospel. For

> every one who calls upon the name of the Lord will be saved. But how are men to call upon him in whom they have not believed? And how are they to believe in him of whom they have never heard? And how are they to hear without a preacher? And how can men preach unless they are sent? (Rom 10.13–15)

Paul knew that the preaching of the gospel was his life's work (Gal 1.15–16). As an apostle to the Gentiles he sought to carry the word of Christ from one end of the Roman universe to the other (Rom 15.19–24). But the preaching of the gospel was the life work of other apostles, too, even though we know very little of them. Having stayed for some time after the Pentecost in Jerusalem, where they witnessed of Christ's resurrection to the Jews, the apostles departed from this city in order to give testimony to Christ in other places. The segregation of the apostolic mission between the Twelve and Paul was a temporary one.[55]

> James and Cephas and John, who were reputed to be pillars, gave to me and Barnabas the right hand of fellowship, that we should go to the Gentiles and they to the circumcised. (Gal 2.9)

It marked but one stage of their joint mission which was a continuation of Christ's own mission—"as the Father has sent me, even so I send you." However, the gospel that the apostles brought was not their gospel, but it was the gospel "in Christ."[56]

The gospel "in Christ" was the gospel of the Church. Christ cannot be separated from the Church, just as the Church cannot be separated from Christ. That is why from its very beginning the apostolic mission had an ecclesial character. Its goal was not an individual conversion but the "building up of the body of Christ." The apostolic mission began in the Church, for there could be no apostleship without the Church. The mission itself, however, was aimed at building up of multiple local churches. It was not a building up of different churches but of the "Church of God in Christ" because the eucharistic assembly of each local church was identical to the first eucharistic assembly where through the Twelve the Church was brought into existence. Establishing eucharistic assemblies, the apostles were building up the local churches. That is why the churches founded by the apostles were the "seal of their apostleship." "If to others I am not an apostle, at least I am to you; for you are the seal (*sphragis*) of my apostleship in the Lord" (1 Cor 9.2; cf. 2 Cor 3.2). "You . . . in the Lord" are not individual Christians but the entire church of Corinth founded by Paul. We find the same idea in the following words of Paul: "For Christ did not send me to baptize but to preach the gospel" (1 Cor 1.17). Paul preached the gospel in Corinth to build up the church there whose first members he had baptized. The baptism of the rest was no longer his doing, but was entrusted to the church he had founded.

6. The concept of apostleship as shown in the New Testament implies that it cannot be applied to an indefinite number of people.[57] The circle of the apostles is limited only to those who were witnesses of the risen Lord and received from him a mission that cannot be handed down to anyone else. Returning to the question formulated above, namely, who belonged to the apostolic circle, we now are able to answer with assurance that the Twelve and Paul were the apostles. Who else except for them was an apostle? The response to this question largely depends on an interpretation of 1 Cor 15.3–8; however, this passage from Paul's writings remains the most difficult and debatable until this day.

> For I delivered to you as of first importance what I also received, that Christ died for our sins in accordance with the scriptures, that . . . he appeared to Cephas, then to the twelve. Then he appeared to more than five hundred brethren at one time, most of whom are still alive, though some have fallen asleep. Then he appeared to James, then to all the apostles. Last of all, as to one untimely born, he appeared also to me.[58]

It cannot be ignored that in this excerpt Paul was not specifically expounding the teaching concerning the apostleship or its establishment, though he does mention the latter issue. In chapter 15, he brought to the memory of Corinthians his "gospel," the pinnacle of which was the resurrection of Christ. He enumerated the witnesses to Christ's resurrection, the majority of whom were still alive in the time when Paul was writing his epistle. Therefore only a part of the appearances of the Risen One which Paul described had any relation to the establishment of the apostleship. This conclusion follows from the fact that, having mentioned the appearance of Christ to him, Paul points out that he is least of the apostles. We can attempt to establish which particular appearances had connections with apostleship in Paul's mind. Thus on the basis of symmetrical relationship between verses 5 and 7, we could reason that James was also an apostle. That means, the Twelve of verse 5 are not identical with "all the apostles" in verse 7, the conclusion to which the majority of the interpreters are inclined.[59] However, this does not follow directly from the text, being only our conclusion. We could assume equally well that the Twelve of verse 5 are totally identified with "all the apostles."[60] The indication that Christ appeared to "*all* the apostles" does not oblige us to include James. Rather, this comment may be pointing out that Christ did not appear to all the apostles, what Paul does not mention.[61]

Thus, 1 Cor 15.3–8 does not provide us with anything new except what we have already established, namely that it was Paul and the Twelve who belonged to the apostles. Concerning James, the brother of the Lord, we can find some confirmation for his being numbered among the apostles in Gal. 1.19: "But I saw none of the apostles except James the Lord's brother." The Greek text allows a possibility for another translation, which would mean the following: except for Peter, Paul did not see any of the apostles in Jerusalem, but in addition he saw James, the brother of the Lord.[62] This interpretation is most probable, for in Acts James does not appear as an apostle but rather as the senior presider of the Jerusalem church. At any rate, we do not know anything about his apostolic activity.

There is even more uncertainty with respect to the co-workers of Paul. We should mention here in the first place Barnabas, who played a significant role in Paul's life and also enjoyed a great authority in the Jerusalem church. But was he an apostle? 1 Cor 9.5–6 does not give an answer with respect to his apostleship, for the right to have with oneself "a sister believer as wife" (*adelphên gynaika*) and to receive financial assistance from local churches did not belong to the apostles exclusively. A single passage that could be seen as speaking in favor of Barnabas's apostleship is Acts 14.14, but we cannot rely on Luke's precision in rendering of the terminology.[63] Paul nowhere called his closest associates Timothy and Titus apostles. 1 Thessalonians cannot serve as proof that Paul considered Timothy an apostle. Also, it is still unclear whether Paul enumerated among the apostles Andronicus and Junia (Junias) whom he mentions in Rom 16.7: "Greet Andronicus and Junias . . . who are of note among the apostles (*episêmoi en tois apostolois*), and they were in Christ before me (*hoi kai pro emou gegonan en Christô*)." The Greek text *episêmoi en tois apostolois* allows for two ways of translation: "who are of note among the apostles" as it is in the current translation or "who are noted by, or known to the apostles."[64] The latter translation seems more plausible, especially if we consider "Iounia" a female name. The New Testament has completely no knowledge of female apostles. Besides, Paul's text gives some ground for considering them, having believed in Christ after Pentecost just as Paul himself did and thus their recognition as apostles by the Twelve is most improbable. In more concrete terms Paul seems to number Apollos among the apostles: "For I think that God has exhibited us apostles as last of all" (*hêmas tous apostolous eschatous*) (1 Cor 4.9). But it is almost certain that "us" is used here as a figure of speech. We could hardly apply to Apollos everything that Paul says in verses 9–13. Thus, we come to our previous conclusion that the Twelve and Paul alone could be with assurance enumerated among the apostles. With respect to other people, there is such an uncertainty that it seems preferable not to include those among the apostles. But even if some of them were considered apostles, the apostolic circle still remains closed.[65]

If the circle of the apostles could easily have been enlarged in the days of Paul, then it is unclear why Paul's apostleship met with so much objection on the part of Judaizing Christians. Undoubtedly the church in Jerusalem held the view that apart from the Twelve there could not be any apostles of Christ equal in honor with them, for the apostleship cannot be passed through man. Paul himself attests to this view in his epistle to the Galatians: "Paul an apostle—not from men nor through man, but through Jesus Christ . . ." (1.1).

The apostolic ministry could not come through the Twelve despite all their authority, for in that case apostleship would come through man. Paul was in full agreement with the church of Jerusalem on this issue. If he is an apostle, that is only because he became such "through Jesus Christ and God the Father" (*dia Iêsou Christou kai Theou Patros*). This was an extraordinary event. Only once in history the circle of the apostles opened to receive Paul, in order to close again afterwards. The whole first chapter of the Epistle to the Galatians was written in order to demonstrate that the extraordinary nature of Paul's apostleship was part of the plan of God's economy. That is why his appointment was identical to the election of the Twelve.

7. Fixed membership in the community of the apostles implies that, as was shown above, upon their death their ministry, as a whole, had ceased. If prior to Pentecost the Twelve could elect someone to fill Judas's place, after Pentecost the place of James son of Zebedee was left unfilled. Sensing the imminence of death, Paul did not pass to anyone his ministry in its entirety. However we would regard the commissions given by Paul to Timothy and Titus, which we will address later, there is no ground for the view that Paul regarded them as his successors continuing his ministry in its fullness. If Paul indeed passed onto them his ministry, then he would not be an apostle, for the ministry of the Twelve as apostles remained without any successors. The Church's understanding bears witness to the fact that since post-apostolic times the Church no longer had apostles. The Church was founded upon the apostles and this foundation is unique. Confessing that the Church is an apostolic Church we confess that the ministry of the apostles cannot be repeated or passed on to successors. Nevertheless the apostolic work of ministry is continued within the Church. Their ministry was to actualize the variety of the local churches in empirical reality. When this variety was actualized, the apostles had been fulfilling the ministry of presider which cannot cease in the Church. This ministry had its beginning with the apostles and, through the apostles, this ministry has passed on to individuals who in the post-apostolic era received the special designation of bishops.

III. The Evangelist

1. In the list of ministries in Eph 4.11, the evangelist is mentioned after the apostle and prophet.[66] From this it follows that Paul saw a difference between apostle and evangelist. The New Testament writings name only two evangelists—Philip, one of

the seven (Acts 21.8) and Timothy (2 Tim 4.5), one of Paul's closest associates—but apparently the general number of evangelists was significant (Phil 4.3; 2 Cor 8.18; Col 1.7, 4.12). As the very term *euaggelistês* indicates, this ministry was the preaching of the gospel. St. Paul pointed out that God called him in order that he might preach his Son among the Gentiles (Gal 1.16). Elsewhere he says that Christ did not send him "to baptize, but to preach the gospel" (1 Cor 1.17). Like the rest of the apostles, Paul was an apostle and an evangelist at the same time, but not all evangelists were apostles. On this ground we can state that one of the functions of the apostleship was a special ministry of evangelist. This is the first distinction which we are able to make. But there was also a distinction in the very "preaching" of apostles and evangelists. The preaching of the apostles, as we saw already, aimed not at individual conversion to Christianity, but at the "building up" of the local churches, whereas the preaching of the evangelists apparently aimed at individual conversion. Its support was in the existing local churches. Therefore their ministry could take place within the churches, aimed at increasing their number and confirming their members in faith. It also happened that they accomplished this ministry outside of these churches. In that case their work was completed by apostles who were building up from converts a local church. We find support for this view in Acts 8.5–17.

> But when they believed Philip as he preached the good news about the kingdom of God and the name of Jesus Christ, they were baptized, both men and women . . . Now when the apostles at Jerusalem heard that Samaria had received the word of God, they sent to them Peter and John. (vv. 12–14)

Somewhat later we find the same Philip in the church of Caesarea where, it seems, he resided permanently (Acts 21.8). The term "evangelist" which Luke applies to him could have had a double meaning. Perhaps by using this term Luke might be pointing to the previous activity of Philip, thus specifying the Philip about which he was talking. Or else he could have wanted to note that Philip, permanently residing in Caesarea, continued his ministry as evangelist in the church of Caesarea. It is possible that he also presided over this church, but it is a risky assumption that the term "evangelist" was used to refer to the presiders of the churches. The ministries of evangelist and presider were different ministries, but they could have been combined when fulfilled by one and the same person.

2. In the post-apostolic era evangelists succeeded the apostles in the ministry of gospel preaching. Perhaps it is in this sense that Paul was speaking of them as of those who "occupied the first place among the successors of the apostles."[67] Somewhat further on, Eusebius describes the work of these "evangelists" in the following way:

> For indeed most of the disciples of that time, animated by the divine word with a more ardent love for philosophy, had already fulfilled the command of the Savior, and had distributed their goods to the needy. Then starting out upon long journeys they performed the office of evangelists, being filled with the desire to preach Christ to those who had not yet heard the word of faith, and to deliver to them the divine Gospels. And when they had only laid the foundations of the faith in foreign places, they appointed others as pastors, and entrusted them with the nurture of those that had recently been brought in, while they themselves went on again to other countries and nations . . . But . . . it is impossible for us to enumerate the names of all that became shepherds or evangelists who in the churches throughout the world immediately succeeded the apostles (*hosoi pote kata tên prôtên tôn apostolôn diadochên en tais kata tên oikoumenên ekklêsiais*) . . .[68]

Eusebius provides the same image of the evangelists' ministry in conjunction with describing the work of Pantenus:

> They say that he displayed such zeal for the divine Word that he was appointed as a herald of the Gospel of Christ to the nations in the East and was sent as far as India. For indeed there were still many evangelists of the Word who sought earnestly to use their inspired zeal, after the examples of the apostles, for the increase and building up of the divine Word. Pantenus was one of these and is said to have gone to India. It is reported that among persons there who knew of Christ, he found the Gospel according to Matthew, which had anticipated his own arrival.[69]

This second generation of evangelists was different from the first. They acted in the name of existing churches which became mother churches to those the evangelists founded. Apparently, from Eusebius's description, in most cases the evangelists presided over the local churches. They preached the gospel and, like the apostles, ordained the first fruits of the faithful to be pastors.

Perhaps it is these evangelists that the compiler of the *Didache* had in mind when he designated them "apostles," doing this to preserve the impression of the apostolic origin of his work.

IV. The Prophet

1. The image of the prophet as one who carried out one of the New Testament ministries is discerned clearly enough in the epistles of St. Paul.[70] Prophets are the people whom God has called and ordained for a special ministry in the Church by communicating to them the prophetic charism. Their ministry was to proclaim in the Church the will of God according to which the Church lives and acts. The importance of the prophetic ministry can be discerned from the fact that in the lists of ministries cited by Paul, the prophet has the second place. In the eyes of St. Paul the prophetic gift was one of the highest manifestations of the Spirit in the Church. In the words of the apostle, the faithful were built upon the foundation of the apostles and prophets (Eph 2.20). The mystery of God's economy, of which Paul was a minister, was revealed to apostles and prophets (Eph 3.5).[71]

In apostolic times there were apparently several prophets in the church of Corinth. "Let two or three prophets speak . . ." (1 Cor 14.29). However, it was not the local churches who took care of the prophetic ministry, and thus it could happen, as indeed it did, that a local church could lack prophets completely. A local church could be without a prophet, but it could not be without the prophetic charism, for the gift of prophecy was essential for its life. "Now I want you all to speak in tongues, but even more to prophesy" (1 Cor 14.5). For St. Paul prophecy was a common ministry of the people, or more precisely, the ministry of the Church itself. Many could possess the gift of prophecy without being specially called to prophetic ministry. "Having gifts that differ according to the grace given to us, let us use them: if prophecy, in proportion to our faith" (Rom 12.6). Whether or not these words of Paul, which are difficult for us to interpret, refer to the prophetic ministry of all the people (as John Chrysostom thought), from these words it nevertheless follows that a prophetic revelation may be given in the Church even to a person who is not a prophet, i.e., to a person who is not endowed with this special ministry.[72] Eusebius cites Miltiades' writing against the Montanists where he says that "the apostle thought it necessary that the prophetic gift should continue in all the Church until the final coming."[73]

2. As a revelation of God's will given in the Church, prophecy is concerned with what happens in the Church.

> Now in the church at Antioch there were prophets and teachers . . . While they were worshiping the Lord and fasting, the Holy Spirit said, "Set apart for me Barnabas and Saul for the work to which I have called them." (Acts 13.1–2)

The revelation of the Spirit about which Luke is talking was concerned with Paul's apostolic mission, for which he was chosen from his mother's womb.

> This charge I commit to you, Timothy, my son, in accordance with the prophetic utterances (*prophêteias*) which pointed to you, that inspired by them you may wage the good warfare. (1 Tim 1.18)

The "charge" (*paraggelia*) committed to Timothy, is based on prophetic utterances concerning him. Apparently this charge dealt with the future activity of Timothy in case of Paul's death. However, the ministry which Timothy exercised in Paul's time was also bestowed upon him in accordance with prophetic utterance. "Do not neglect the gift you have, which was given you by prophetic utterance (*dia prophêteias*) when the council of elders laid their hands upon you" (1 Tim 4.14).[74]

> Now in these days prophets came down from Jerusalem to Antioch. And one of them named Agabus stood up and foretold by the Spirit (*esêmainen dia tou Pneumatos*) that there would be a great famine over all the world; and this took place in the days of Claudius. (Acts 11.27–28)

Prophetic utterance about the famine also had direct relevance to the life of the church. In fulfillment of the will revealed through this prophecy "the disciples determined, every one according to his ability, to send relief to the brethren who lived in Judea" (Acts 11.29). Prophecy also had relevance for the plan of God concerning the Church. The mystery of Christ (*to mystêrion tou Christou*)[75] that "he might create in himself one new man in place of the two, so making peace, and might reconcile us both to God in one body" (Eph 2.15–16) was revealed by the Spirit to the apostles and the prophets (Eph 3.5). The goal to which Paul committed himself was revealed to the Church by means of prophecy (Eph 3.3).

In relation to this the question arises whether prophecy as a revelation of God's will is related to what we today call dogmatic truths. This question, concerning the essence of prophetic ministry can be stated in a more generic way. Was the prophetic ministry a continuing revelation of new truths of the faith? We do not find any trace of such a question in the apostolic writings. "The mystery of Christ" (Eph 3.4) was not a new revelation but was already present in the economy of God, fulfilled in Christ through the Church. The age (*aeon*) of the Spirit, in which the Church already abides is not an *aeon* of new revelation. "He (i.e. the Spirit) will glorify me for he will take what is mine and declare it to you" (John 16.14). He "will teach you all things, and bring to your remembrance all that I have said to you" (John 14.26), but "the word which you hear is not mine but the Father's who sent me" (v. 24). For St. Paul, his teaching was not *his own*, but one in which he merely handed down what he had earlier received: "For I received from the Lord what I also delivered to you ..." (1 Cor 11.23), "for I delivered to you as of first importance what I also received ..." (1 Cor 15.3). The gospel he preached was the gospel preached by the apostles before him. "Whether it was I or they, so we preach and so you believed." (15.11) The tradition into which Paul was incorporated could not have been opposed to the Spirit, for the tradition itself is built in the Church by the Spirit. Therefore the teaching received from the Lord himself and handed down to the Church must remain without change. Prophetic revelation cannot change what the Lord himself has revealed, neither can it add what the original revelation did not contain. "But even if we, or an angel from heaven, should preach to you a gospel contrary to that which we preached to you, let him be accursed." (Gal 1.8) Drawing his proclamation from the Lord, the Spirit cannot proclaim what the Lord's teaching did not contain. Despite all the reverence that surrounds prophetic ministry in the *Didache*, it stands on the same ground as Paul: "whosoever then comes and teaches you all these things said before, receive him" (*hos an oun elthôn didaxê hymas tauta panta ta proeirêmena, dexasthe auton*).[76] Was not the opposition to Montanism caused partly by the fact that the "new prophecy" introduced the kind of principles which did not correspond to the ecclesial tradition? We are unaware of anything that would distinguish Montanism from orthodox teaching, but the firm stipulation on the part of the Eastern churches to receive Montanists into the Church through baptism suggests that Montanism was not all in good order. *The Shepherd of Hermas* very distinctly belonged to the prophetic literature, but it did not contain any dogmatic revelation. In relation to the reception of sinners back into communion, Hermas expounded the teaching that had been upheld in the Church. It was not a new teaching but the application of an ancient teaching to the realities of ecclesial life in the age when the work was written. For the "Great Church" prophecy had to do with life and action in the Church rather than with the teaching of the faith. The idea of a new revelation undermined the tradition of the Church by introducing a totally foreign concept of progress in revelation unknown till then. It was a heresy about the Church for it put prophecy outside the Church. The Church was ceasing to be a locus of the activity of the Spirit because, according to Montanism, the Spirit became incarnate in particular individuals in a special way.

3. Prophetic utterance provides for the faithful upbuilding, encouragement, and consolation (1 Cor 14.3) for such is always God's will for the members of the

Church. Here the ministry of the prophet finds affinity with the ministry of the teacher. The prophet instructs the church through the revelation of the Spirit, and therefore every prophet is to some extent a teacher. A question that should be raised here is whether ecstasy is a necessary part of prophetic inspiration. Most if not all of the Montanist prophets were marked by an extreme level of ecstasy. Was this ecstasy their own idiosyncrasy or did they just intensify what already took place in the "Great Church"? The anonymous anti-Montanist writer cited by Eusebius regarded the ecstatic state of Montanist prophets as one of the faults of the movement, asserting that a true prophet never loses control of his spiritual capabilities. Thus, he says:

> When Gratus was proconsul of Asia, a recent convert, Montanus by name, through his unquenchable desire for leadership, gave the adversary opportunity against him. And he was beside himself, and suddenly in a sort of frenzy and ecstasy, he raved, and began to babble and utter strange things, prophesying in a manner contrary to the constant custom of the Church handed down by tradition from the beginning.[77]

Miltiades, according to Eusebius, also tried to prove that "a prophet ought not to speak in ecstasy."[78] Miltiades himself wrote:

> But the false prophet falls into an ecstasy in which he is without shame or fear. Beginning with purposed ignorance, he passes on, as has been stated, to involuntary madness of soul. They cannot show that one of the old or one of the new prophets was thus carried away in spirit. Neither can they boast of Agabus, or Judas, or Silas, or the daughters of Philip, or Ammia in Philadelphia, or Quadratus, or any others not belonging to them.[79]

Possibly these witnesses contain some degree of exaggeration with respect to Montanist prophets, as well as to the statement that the New Testament prophets did not speak in ecstasy. We are not absolutely certain that the prophets whom St. Paul mentioned ever spoke in ecstasy. However, St. Paul himself did not count the ecstatic state as a necessary attribute of prophetic utterance. Contrasting prophecy with speaking in tongues (*glossolalia*), he gave preference to the former.

> He who prophesies speaks to men for their upbuilding and encouragement and consolation. He who speaks in tongues edifies himself, but he who prophesies edifies the Church. (1 Cor 14.3–4)

According to Paul, prophetic speech did not require interpretation whereas the one who spoke in tongues could bring good to the church only when he himself explained what he had uttered. Thus for Paul the prophetic charism did not render the prophetic utterance incomprehensible and the prophet did not lose control of himself.[80]

> What am I to do? I will pray with the spirit and I will pray with the mind also; I will sing with the spirit and I will sing with the mind also. Otherwise, if you bless with the spirit, how can anyone in the position of an outsider say the "Amen" to your thanksgiving when he does not know what you are saying? (1 Cor 14.15–16)

It was thus not so much ecstasy by itself but the ecstasy of the Montanist prophets, close to madness, that was a novelty, naturally causing opposition because it did not find affinity with the general ecclesial tradition. The roots of Montanist ecstasy are not found in the Church but rather in pagan cults.[81]

4. The charism of prophesy was connected with the charism of "judgment and discernment of the spirits" belonging to the people of God.[82] "Let two or three prophets speak, and let the others judge (*diakrinetôsan*) what is said" (1 Cor 14.29; cf. 1 John 4.1). Prophecy is directly followed by judging. Prophetic revelation is subject to investigation, to testing aimed at making clear whether the divine will was indeed revealed. "Do not quench the Spirit, do not despise prophesying, but test everything (*panta de dokimazete*); hold fast what is good, abstain from every form of evil" (1 Thess 5.19–22). The Church in the second century held fast to this rule. The same anti-Montanist writer whom we have already cited, said:

> Some of those who heard his spurious utterances at that time were indignant, and they rebuked him as one that was possessed, and that was under the control of a demon, and was led by a deceitful spirit, and was distracting the multitude; and they forbade him to talk, remembering the distinction drawn by the Lord and his warning to guard watchfully against the coming of false prophets. But others imagining themselves possessed of the Holy Spirit and of a prophetic gift, were elated and not a little puffed up; and forgetting the distinction of the Lord, they challenged the mad and insidious and seducing spirit.[83]

Judgment is testing that belongs to the Church, for only the Church can judge what is done in it. It is not the divine will that is tested. There can be no judgment about it. Rather what is tested is whether this prophecy is indeed a revelation of the divine will, i.e., whether this prophecy is indeed a prophecy. The Church listens to the prophetic word, judges and tests it, and only upon that testing does the word of a prophet become a prophecy. Therefore the prophecy consists in the words of a prophet tested by the Church. The prophecy belongs to the Church, being revealed to it and for it. Apart from the Church there can be no true prophecy, for apart from the Church there can be no judging and testing of the prophetic word. The word of a prophet uttered outside of the Church ceases to be a prophecy and the prophet himself becomes a false prophet, for the prophecy is an ecclesial ministry and it is accomplished in the Church itself. As Hermas says in *The Shepherd*,

> When the man who has the divine Spirit comes into a meeting of righteous who have the faith of the divine Spirit, and intercession is made to God from the assembly then the angel of the prophetic spirit rests on him and fills the man, and the man, being filled with the Holy Spirit, speaks to the congregation as the Lord wills. Thus, then, the Spirit of the Godhead will be plain. Such, then, is the power of the Lord concerning the Spirit of the Godhead. Listen now, concerning the spirit which is earthly, empty, has no power and is foolish. In the first place, that man who seems to have a spirit exalts himself and wishes to have the first place, and he is instantly impudent and shameless and talkative, and lives in great luxury and in many other deceits, and accepts rewards for his prophecy, and if he does not receive them he does not prophesy. Is it then possible for a divine Spirit to accept rewards and prophesy? It is not possible for a prophet of God to do this, but the spirit of such prophets is of the earth. Next, on no account does he come near to an assembly of the righteous but shuns them. But he cleaves to the double-minded and empty and prophesizes to them in a corner and deceives them by empty speech about everything according to their lusts, for he is also answering the empty. For an empty vessel which is put with others that are empty is not broken, but they match one another. But when he comes into a meeting full of the righteous who have a spirit of the Godhead and intercession is made by them, that man is made empty, and the earthly spirit flees from him in fear, and that man is made dumb and is altogether broken up, being able to say nothing ... So also the prophets who are empty, when they come to the spirits of the just are found out to be such as when they came. You have the life of both kinds of prophets.[84]

Thus the word of the prophet spoken in the Church and recognized by the Church serves for learning and encouragement (1 Cor 14.31). But if it is said outside of the Church it does not instruct or encourage anyone, being just a human word.

The compiler of the *Didache* does not provide a thorough description of prophetic ministry, perhaps assuming that it was well-known to all the faithful. His perception of prophetic ministry mostly agrees with the apostolic writings but at the same time differs in some details. Like Hermas, he is fully aware of true and false prophets being there and he gives characteristics by which the faithful can judge whether the prophet is true. The prophet who came to a local church was to be tested in order to discover whether he is true or false. The first teaches only the things contained in the *Didache* itself.[85] This first requirement of the true prophet is apparently reminiscent of the words of St. Paul: "But even if we, or an angel from heaven, should preach to you a gospel contrary to that which we preached to you, let him be accursed" (Gal 1.8), since the *Didache* itself does not contain any specific doctrine, only moral instruction that does not bear any distinctly Christian characteristics.[86] Besides, the prophet must not only teach the truth; he himself must do what he teaches.[87] He must be a moral exemplar to the faithful—that is why he must "behave like the Lord" (*tous tropous Kyriou*).[88] The false prophet must not be received by the local church, but the true one must be received and honored as the Lord himself would be. Therefore, "While a prophet is speaking in the spirit you must not test or examine him" (*kai panta prophêtên lalounta en pneumati ou peirasete oude diakrineite*).[89] This statement directly contradicts St. Paul, who urged the subjecting of every prophetic utterance to judgment. "Let others discern" (*hoi alloi diakrinetôsan*)—but "you do not judge" (*oude diakrineite*). This change in the treatment of the prophetic word suggests a rupture in the ecclesial understanding of prophetic ministry, making it possible for a prophet to prophesy outside of the eucharistic assembly. For St. Paul, prophetic revelation is given through an ecclesial prophet, but for the compiler of the *Didache*, it is given to a prophet almost independently from the church. For St. Paul it is the Church that fulfills the will of God; for the author of the *Didache*, the prophetic revelation must be fulfilled in and of itself, while the prophet can demand that whatever was revealed to him must be fulfilled. The compiler of the *Didache* is already expounding the Montanist view. In the debate concerning the authority to remit sins, Montanism claimed that this power belongs to a prophet rather than to a bishop. This view was shared by the confessors who demanded that Cyprian reconcile the lapsed and receive back into the Church those whom they granted remission of sins. Both positions were digressions from the original view. The revelation of the will of God through a prophet was necessary in order to be received back into the Church, but the prophet himself did not have any authority to remit sins. Montanism was indeed a "new prophecy" and the fight against it was wholly legitimate and natural, even though it led to the shunning of any kind of prophecy, not only the "new" one.

Another peculiarity of prophetic ministry according to the *Didache* is that its compiler proclaims the prophet to be a high priest: "for they are your high priests" (*autoi gar eisin hoi archiereis hymôn*).[90] We shall return to the idea of high priesthood later, but here we shall note only those aspects which have relevance to prophetic ministry. One cannot uphold the point of view that the compiler of the *Didache* inserted the concept of the prophets' high priestly status in order to vindicate the practice of offering the first fruits to the prophet in the eyes of the faithful. According to the *Didache* the prophet indeed accomplishes the high priestly ministry. The text permits the prophets to "give thanks" (*eucharistein*) as long as they desire.[91] With respect to chapters 9 and 10 of the *Didache*, doubts still persist as to whether they describe a eucharistic assembly or *agape* meals. Even if they deal with *agape* meals (we personally are more inclined to think that they deal with the Eucharist) to permit the prophet to "give thanks" means to ascribe to him the functions of the presider which in the "Great Church" were executed by the bishop. Having been separated from the Eucharist proper, *agape* meals, especially in the East, were still gatherings of the entire local church to the Lord's Supper, where naturally the bishop presided. Only in the beginning of the third century in the West, particularly in the Roman church, did it become possible to celebrate private *agape* meals either in the presence of one particular member of the clergy or even without him. However, we cannot date the appearance of the *Didache* to that time, especially as the emergence of such private *agape* meals in the East must be attributed to the beginning of the Nicaean period.[92] "Thanksgiving" at the *agape* meals, as well as at the eucharistic assembly, belonged to the bishop. If the *Didache* indeed ascribes this right to the prophet, it thus appropriates to him the functions of the presider. These functions mainly included the offering of the Eucharist. Having stated that the Eucharist must be celebrated on the "Lord's day" and that the sacrifice must be pure, the compiler immediately turns to the instructions concerning the election of bishops and deacons. He thereby acknowledges that in his time the bishop was a regular eucharistic celebrant, but only in the absence of the prophet, "for they also," adds the author of the *Didache*, "minister to you the ministry of the prophets and teachers."[93] The bishop as a eucharistic celebrant with some kind of dependent relation upon the prophet is not regarded as a high priest. In the absence of the prophet the faithful must render the first fruits not personally to the bishop but through the bishop and deacons to the poor.

Apart from the fact that the sacerdotal character of the prophetic activity was unknown to Paul, the treatment of this aspect of prophetic ministry in the *Didache* is truly exceptional among the whole body of Christian literature of which we are aware. In this body of writings we do not find even a trace of the idea concerning the prophets as high priests. When the concept of high priesthood took shape in ecclesial thinking, it was decisively and resolutely associated with the bishop rather than with the prophet. Nowhere do the prophet or the *didaskalos* stand as rivals to the bishops in the area of liturgical worship. Neither Clement of Alexandria nor Origen ever claim from the bishop the presidency at the eucharistic assembly, even though for Origen the *didaskalos* did indeed represent the "spiritual" hierarchy. In apostolic and post-apostolic time perhaps there were not a few instances when the prophet executed the ministry of the one who presides over a community. The first indication concerning this fact we find in Acts, which recount that after the council in Jerusalem,

> then it seemed good to the apostles and the elders, with the whole church, to choose men from among them and send them to Antioch with Paul and Barnabas. They sent Judas called Barsabbas, and Silas, leading men among the brethren (*andras hêgoumenous en tois adelphois*). (Acts 15.22)

It is later reported concerning these men that they themselves were prophets (Acts 15.32). This means that Judas and Silas as prophets were ordained presbyters by the church in Jerusalem. Given the enormous respect ascribed to the prophets they were favored candidates for the office of presbyter-bishop. Hermas in his *Shepherd* reprimands the prophets who seek to have the "first seats" (*proto-kathedrian*) in an ecclesial assembly.[94] It could mean of course that prophets, given their status in the church, desired to have the first seats when the church was gathering. However, it is probably more correct to regard this fact as indicating that prophets struggled to get ordained as presbyters, seeking by that to acquire the presidency in the ecclesial assembly.[95] Hermas also recounts that the "old lady," despite his protest, commanded him to sit on her left before the presbyters. Hermas was not a presbyter, neither did he consider himself to be one. Thus his sitting before the presbyters signified only an honorary place. In both cases the prophetic ministry was either combined with the presbyterial or it just had an honorary place in the ecclesial assembly, but it did not incorporate any other ministry, much less the high priestly one, as it does in the *Didache*.[96] In the early church the conjunction of ministries was a usual phenomenon, but was merely a conjunction, not a mixing which would go against the will of God that established various works of ministry in the Church. To some extent we still are perplexed at how the concept of the high priesthood of the prophet emerged and what were the ways by which it managed to penetrate into the milieu from which the *Didache* originated. If we keep the traditional dating of this text, this peculiarity cannot be explained, as it is unfathomable; likewise the fact that this concept had no influence on ecclesial thinking. The only milieu that could produce this concept were Montanist circles, but in this case we would have to attribute the emergence of the *Didache* to a much later date. Therefore we cannot consider the concept of the high priesthood of the prophet as characteristic for prophetic ministry. Prophetic ministry essentially did not incorporate the high priestly ministry. At the same time, the prophetic and high priestly ministry could be conjoined if a prophet was elected to preside over a local church.

5. In this connection we have to note in passing one more detail. The concept of the high priestly status of the prophet must have initiated changes in the concept of the Church. As we shall see later, it was always the one who presided over the local church who was the high priest. As a high priest in the local church, he was the high priest of the Church of God. The prophet as high priest must have found himself in an opposite situation. As a high priest of the universal Church he was a high priest of any local church that he visited. This cut the prophet off from that local church of which he was a member and introduced the idea of the universal Church existing independently of the local church. "As this broken bread was scattered upon the mountains but was brought together and became one, so let thy Church be gathered together from the ends of the earth into thy kingdom."[97] "Gather it together from the four winds."[98] This is not the language of St. Paul, at least not entirely. The Church that is spoken about here is not a local church in which the Church of God abides in its fullness, but the Church that encompasses all local churches scattered throughout the world. How this universal Church relates to the local church remains unclear from the text. Later the idea of the universal church will be put forward especially forcefully by Origen and will become most fully developed by Cyprian of Carthage. The sources for the idea of the universal church have not been fully discovered but it is almost without doubt that the compiler of the *Didache* has drawn it from Judaic consciousness. The eucharistic understanding of the Church gives way to the concept of the Church as the gathering of God's people, the new Israel in the sense found in the Old Testament. The high priesthood of the prophet pertains to the universal church comprised of the local churches. Thus the local church can temporarily prove to be without the high priest and to have a bishop as the prophet's deputy. However, this does not deprive the universal church of a high priest. If we put aside the Gnostic literature we could affirm without any particular risk that the *Didache* is the first text establishing, albeit rather vaguely, the idea of universal church.

"He who prophesies speaks to men for their upbuilding and encouragement and consolation." (1 Cor 14.3) Thus the prophetic ministry directs its purpose to the already existing local churches. As the revelation of God's will in accordance with which the Church lives and acts, prophecy ministers to the Church built upon the foundation of the apostles. In this lies its distinction from the apostolic ministry though the latter may be joined with the charism of prophecy. Nevertheless an apostle who possesses the prophetic charism remains an apostle rather than becoming a prophet, whereas, conversely, a prophet called to apostleship ceases to be a prophet if he actually fulfills the ministry of apostle. The prophetic ministry, while being directed at local churches, must not necessarily be a traveling ministry, as was already said above. The prophet primarily ministers to one local church which, however, can entrust him with a mission of ministering to other churches. As the prophetic ministry gradually ceases to exist, prophets became figures more and more rarely seen in local churches and their activity became increasingly characterized as a traveling ministry.

V. The Teacher

1. Teachers (*didaskaloi*) were the third group of people having a special ministry found in the primitive church. St. Paul mentions them as also does the *Didache*, but in neither instance is their ministry defined with precision. The church history of the second and third centuries has left us with some images of *didaskaloi*, of whom Clement of Alexandria and Origen are the most renowned. However, all of them represent pinnacles of Christian thought; therefore it is hard to draw from their example the impression of a common *didaskalos*.

Whether the ministry of Christian *didaskaloi* had any connection with the ministry of the Old Testament scribes and teachers is not particularly significant.[99] The need for a Christian teacher must have arisen from the very outset of the church's formation. If the view that in later history the office of *didaskalos* was transformed into the office of reader is correct, it was not the reading only, but also the living word that constituted the major responsibility of the ancient *didaskalos*. While a prophet spoke to the people "for their upbuilding and encouragement and consolation" through the revelation of the will of God, a teacher also spoke for their upbuilding and consolation through laying out the teaching of the faith. As Clement of Alexandria said, "for us, the gnostic alone is the one who, having grown old in the Scriptures, maintains apostolic and ecclesiastic orthodoxy in doctrines (*tôn dogmatôn*)."[100] For Clement, the true gnostic is near to being *didaskalos* for he cannot keep his vision of Scripture to himself, but "teaches the churches" (*ecclesias docet*).[101] The *didaskalos* instructed the church through disclosing the truths of faith contained in the Tradition and in Scripture.[102] If not all then most of the *didaskaloi* were the learned theologians of the ancient church representing the scholarly theology that is in the Church's service. The first works of Christian literature such as the *Letter of Barnabas*, the *Letter of Clement of Rome*, et al., were authored by the *didaskaloi*. They considered it their duty not only to instruct the church but also to defend it before pagans and the political authority of Rome. In opposition to the pagan schools they opened their own schools where they taught not only the catechumens but also the faithful who desired to know God's Word.[103] The Church valued the work of the *didaskaloi* very highly, making sure to preserve their writings. The author of the *Letter of Barnabas* does not even dare to call the ministry of *didaskalos* his own. For him the *didaskalos* is the inspired teacher possessing the charism of *gnosis* by which he acquires the higher knowledge that Christ passed on to his disciples. Faithfulness to this knowledge and teaching constitutes a distinctive feature of the true gnostic and teacher. In the concluding chapters of the *Letter to Diognetus*, which, as it is thought, were written by Pantenus, the great founder of the Alexandrian school,[104] the following is said:

> My speech is not strange, nor my inquiry unreasonable, but as a disciple of apostles I am becoming a teacher of the heathen. I administer worthily that which has been handed down to those who are becoming disciples of the truth. For who that has been properly taught, and has become a lover of the word does not seek to learn plainly the things which have been clearly shown by the word to disciples, to whom the Word appeared and revealed them? . . . For in all things which we were moved by the will of him who commands us to speak with pain, we become sharers with you through love of the things revealed to us.[105]

In opposition to false gnosis, the true teaching of the *didaskalos* contains only that which was handed down by Christ. In these words from the *Letter to Diognetus* one can feel already an inkling of suspicion toward *didaskaloi* who apparently were accused of making innovations. Alongside respect that surrounded true *didaskaloi*, there was a slow rise of mistrust, directed against *gnosis* in general. The primitive church knew not only false prophets, but false teachers as well. We find first warnings against them in the Pastoral epistles. On the one hand, the words that we find in them resonated with both true and false *gnosis:* "And what you have heard from me before many witnesses entrust to faithful men who will be able to teach others also" (2 Tim 2.2). But, on the other hand,

> there are many insubordinate men, empty talkers and deceivers, especially the circumcision party; they must be silenced, since they are upsetting whole families by teaching for base gain what they have no right to teach (Titus 1.10–11),

for "by rejecting conscience, certain persons have made shipwreck of their faith" (1 Tim 1.19). The *Didache* speaks of false teachers and Hermas in his *Shepherd* cautions the faithful against those who "introduced strange doctrines and corrupted the servants of God."[106] If Irenaeus, while treating as nonsensical the questions of what God did before the creation of the world,[107] or how God gave birth to his Son,[108] did not ultimately deny the *gnosis*, especially with respect to the economy of salvation,[109] Tertullian firmly asserted that there is nothing in common between Athens and Jerusalem, Academia and the Church.[110] The currents directed against *gnosis* were so strong that Clement of Alexandria had to address the problem of faith and *gnosis*, which has never found a proper resolution in the Church. He said:

> Some who think themselves naturally gifted, do not wish to touch either philosophy or logic; nay more, they do not wish to learn natural science. They demand bare faith alone, as if they wished, without bestowing any care on the vine, straightway to gather clusters from the first.[111]

The synthesis of faith and knowledge to which both Clement of Alexandria and Origen were striving was not received by the ecclesial thinking of their time. Nevertheless, Celsus certainly was exaggerating when he claimed that "the church is an assembly of the ignorant led by dull priests, animals as the women and children whom they instruct."[112] Origen resolutely rejected this accusation, although he himself suffered from the narrow-mindedness of the Christians of his time. The Church cherished knowledge and loved its *didaskaloi*.

Teaching was a special ministry, but the charism of teaching, more often than other charisms, could be combined with other ministries.[113] To some degree, the charism of teaching was part of prophetic ministry. It also, as we shall see later, might have been joined with the ministry of the one who presides. Moreover, to one or another degree, the charism of teaching belonged to all, or nearly all members of the church, for everyone must instruct each other: "therefore encourage one another and build one another up" (1 Thess 5.11).

2. In the first letter to the Corinthians St. Paul enumerates the following gifts as well: the powers (working miracles), healings, and various tongues. The first two gifts are self-explanatory. *Glossolalia* or "speaking in tongues" provoked a number of scholarly works but still remains not fully clear to us. For us, however, this question is not significant and therefore it suffices just to indicate this gift that the apostolic church had. Must we consider the ones who possessed these gifts as having special ministries as did apostles, prophets, and teachers? To some extent the question is without an answer or, more precisely, the answer could be both positive and negative. Prophecy was a special ministry, but even those who did not have this ministry could have the gift of prophecy. It is entirely possible to admit that those who had the gifts of powers or healing fulfilled a special ministry when God especially called them to it through the Church. However, these gifts might have been joined with other ministries or might have shown themselves forth only in special circumstances. In the same epistle St. Paul speaks about the word of wisdom, the word of knowledge, about faith, the gifts of healing and of miracles, about prophecy, the discernment of the spirits, about various tongues and their interpretation. However we interpret this passage from the letter to the Corinthians (12.8–10), faith as a gift was never a special ministry.

Finally, in his letter to the Ephesians St. Paul speaks about pastoral ministry, in the letter to the Corinthians about the gift of administration and assistance, but in the letter to the Romans about the ministry of those who preside (*proistamenoi*). The ministries of pastors and assistants were special ministries, on the same level as the ministries of the apostles, prophets, and teachers.

Chapter 5

"Those Who Preside in the Lord"

I. "All Things Should Be Done Decently and in Order"

Theologians have firmly adhered to the view that primitive Christianity, at least outside Palestine, existed in a state of charismatic anarchy. The end of charismatic anarchy signified the end of a charismatic period and the beginning of firm and definitive organization of church life. This external organization emerges on the basis of episcopal authority that did not exist during the charismatic period, or at least in the way it appeared at the end of the second century.[1] As often happens, the most problematic statements are the ones most trusted, hence the thesis concerning charismatic anarchy received universal acclamation. No solid evidence has been given in support of this thesis with one exception: the abundance and rich variety of charismatic gifts which had no parallel in any subsequent period. In this respect, one should point to another claim that at first glance appears indisputable. It proceeds from the presupposition that St. Paul, the major figure in primitive Christianity, believing the Parousia to be imminent, did not intend to provide the churches he founded with a solid organization. Founding the churches, he limited himself to giving some indispensable guidelines for church life in order that these churches might persist until the second coming of Christ.[2] This line of reasoning leaves the organization of church life in total dependence on the personal good intentions of St. Paul or lack thereof. It fails to notice that the principles of ecclesial life, such as they appeared in primitive Christianity and still today, were not random, but rather derived from the very nature of the Church. Christians living at the time when the book of Acts was written were well aware that it was not for them to know the times or seasons of Christ's coming. Thus the projected length of the Church's existence could not have affected the organization of the local churches. Even if the churches had but one day to exist, their ecclesial life had to be "organized," since, as we will see, none of the churches could exist a single day without a person to preside over it. Therefore it is unclear how and why the abundance of charismatic gifts could lead to anarchy or their disappearance to solid church organization. If the charismatic era banned legalism from the Church it does not follow from this that there could exist a church organization not based on principles of law. If the Church in the course of history appropriated the principles of law and built its actual external structure on this foundation, it does not mean that the Church became deprived of charismatic gifts. The Holy Spirit lives in the church of our times just as in the primitive church. Charismatic gifts are still sent down in the church of our time just as in the apostolic age. The charismatic age did not end but continues to exist within the Church even though it now takes a different form. The end of the charismatic age would signify the end of the Church's very existence, for the Church was and still is a charismatic organism.

"All things should be done decently and in order" (1 Cor 14.40) because "God is not a God of confusion, but of peace" (1 Cor 14.33). The Apostle's admonition completely destroys any claim concerning the charismatic anarchy of primitive Christianity. Wherever there is rank, structure, or order (*taxis*) no anarchy can exist. That is why it is surprising how that view—that primitive Christianity lived in the state of anarchy—managed to appear at all. If the abundance and rich variety of gifts caused some defects in the church life of that age, it was primarily, even exclusively, due to the overly ecstatic state of some members of the Church. We have no right to extrapolate the image of life in the Corinthian church onto other churches founded by St. Paul. The ecstatic state of the first Christians was not an exclusive feature of those times. We find it in the time when according to almost universal conviction the church had passed through its anarchic stage and entered a period of organization. Montanism could not have spread so quickly and taken control over such an enormous number of churches had it not had any ground in the life of the church. An extreme ecstatic mindset revealed itself not only in Montanism but in the "Great Church" as well,[3] represented not by prophets but by the bishops. As for flaws in the life of the church, one sort gave way to another in the course of history. With the end of the "charismatic period" flaws did not disappear but became more intense as the organizing principle evolved into formalism and bureaucracy. Did the church's defects move Tertullian to embrace

Montanism despite his legalistic frame of mind? Inspiration was leaving the church and its everyday life was becoming dim and pale. But the strengthening of church hierarchy brought its own defects. Tertullian noted with bitter irony that the apostles founded the churches only so that bishops could exploit church incomes, carefully guarding themselves from any trouble with Roman authorities,[4] or could create fasting periods in their own churches for their own personal profit.[5] Origen's *Philippics* exceed even Tertullian's sarcasm and bitterness. In their pride bishops go beyond the evil rulers of the nations surrounding themselves with guards as kings do. Further he says, "We render ourselves fearful and inaccessible, especially to the poor. So we treat those who petition or ask us about something as not even the tyrants and most cruel of rulers treat their suppliants. Thus it is, at any rate, in many esteemed churches and especially those in bigger cities . . ."[6] In the search for the faded prophetic inspiration, the Roman lawyer sought the "pious women" through whom he expected to receive a revelation, while Origen sought resolution of the tragic conditions of life in the teaching about the heavenly church.

Can we compare the defects St. Paul spoke about in his letter to the Corinthians with the distortions of church life at the time when ecclesiastical law was already firmly established? Scenes of outrageous violence at the Council of Ephesus in 449 were not commonplace in ecclesiastical life, but violence and coercion in all possible forms were regular at almost every council. The flaws of the life of the church were indelible, but to justify the argument for the anarchy of early Christianity one has to lose any sense of historical objectivity. If an extremely ecstatic mindset was the norm for ecclesial life, why would St. Paul, the most gifted charismatic of all, establish a *taxis*, a structure and order for the life of the church, order which for him derived from God himself because God is not the God of disorder or anarchy, but the God of peace? Here St. Paul expressed the basic intuition of the life of the church, a life whose order rests upon the revelation of God's will. If revelation creates anarchy, this principle should have come from God himself, who thus becomes the god of disorder, but not the God of peace. Organization does not come into church life in the second century as a *deus ex machina*, but dates from the earliest period. From the very beginning local churches appear to us as orderly and structured. This is not contradicted by the fact that the life of early Christianity was in a stage of fluctuation. Local churches were in their initial stages. They were just beginning to understand the shape their empirical organization would take. Here all kinds of misunderstandings and deviations from the established order were possible. Nevertheless the basic principles of organization appear to be the same everywhere because the empirical multiplicity of local churches reveals the unity of the Church of God. "Thus it is in all the churches of the saints" (1 Cor 14.33).[7] These basic principles were not imposed by St. Paul from outside but came from the very structure and order of the Church itself. This order is repeated in every church because the fullness of the Church abides in every church, identical at all ages of the historical existence of the churches. St. Paul knew better than anyone else that it is the will of God, not of man, that acts in the Church, not even the will of the charismatically gifted as he himself was.

II. The Presider

1. The very name of the Church,[8] which we find from the earliest time of its existence, implies the notion of an organized congregation of people rather than a mob or a crowd that defies any order or structure. The term "church" could not have been accepted by the Christian mind if the ecclesial life of the early church was guided by anarchy and a lack of any authority. The contents of this term were quite strictly defined, so much so as to exclude any ambiguity with respect to its meaning. The Church is *ekklêsia* because it is the assembly of God's people in Christ rather than a random mob or a gathering of Christians who came together by chance. What manifests the Church as a gathering in Christ is the eucharistic assembly, because Christ is present there. The last commandment that Christ gave to the apostles before his passion—"do this in remembrance of me" (1 Cor 11.24)— could not refer to random gatherings of his followers, but to the new people of God with whom He made a New Covenant in the blood of his Son. ("This cup is the new covenant in my blood.") This new people is gathered with Christ for eucharistic celebration just as the apostles gathered with Christ at the Last Supper. Wherever there is a eucharistic assembly there is the Church, because Christ is present there. There can be no Church without the eucharistic assembly, just as there can be no eucharistic assembly that does not manifest the fullness and unity of the Church. Thus the structure and order of the Church originate in the eucharistic assembly, the foundation of the Church's entire organization.

As the assembly of God's people, the Church cannot exist without one or several persons who stand before God on its behalf. Without someone to preside, the church assembly would turn into a disorderly mass. As there can be no eucharistic assembly without the ministry of presiders, so there can be no Church without this ministry, either. However, the ministry of presiders also cannot exist without eucharistic assembly, for in the absence or outside of eucharistic assembly the presiders have no one over whom they may preside. This means that wherever the local church appears, there the ministry of presiders is established. From this follows one of the fundamental principles of eucharistic ecclesiology: no local church can exist without the ministry of presiders. Therefore the presider is an empirical, outward sign of the catholic church. Due to this character of presidential ministry, this ministry becomes absolutely necessary for the empirical existence of every local church. This leads us to the conclusion that not only did the special ministry of presiders exist in the early era, but no church could exist without this ministry. If in the early church, as was shown above, there was no essential difference between the ministries of "charismatics" and the ministry of presbyters-bishops, the difference still existed with respect to the degree of importance of these ministries for the existence of a local church. A local church did and could exist without prophets, teachers, and bearers of various charisms—powers, healings, diverse tongues, but the local church could not exist even for a time without the ministry of their presiders. For this reason, the care for this ministry was entrusted to the local church itself, as it saw to its own existence.

The ministry of God's people as kings and priests found its expression at the eucharistic assembly. Every participant of the assembly ministered as a priest to his God and Father, not on his own, however, but together with all the people and by necessity with his presiders. In this ministry the presiders as members of God's people did not differ from the rest of the people. They served as priests together with all the people and therefore, like all the rest, they could not serve on their own. However, the eucharistic assembly could not take place without presiders and consequently the Church could not exist without them, either. This was the content of their ministry and in this they were different from other members of the Church. The charism of presidency belongs only to those whom God had especially called and ordained for this ministry. It was not the charism of priesthood, which God has granted to every member of the Church, but the charism of presidency that distinguished presiders from the rest of the Church. The eucharistic assembly is the assembly of the royal priesthood under the presidency of one of this priesthood who has the charism to preside. Such a structure of eucharistic assembly leaves aside the question concerning degrees of priesthood in the early church. All were priests and no special priesthood existed at that point. If one neglects this essential characteristic of early Christianity one would misunderstand the ecclesial life of this time, just as one would if one thought that the presiders, who shared in the priesthood with all the members of the Church, alone were the celebrants of the mysteries in the Church. The main hindrance to our proper understanding does not lie in the teaching of the Church, since the Church, as we saw, still professes the royal priesthood of all its members. Rather, our main hindrance lies in the scholastic textbooks of theology whose authors feared this teaching. They thought it might undermine the doctrine concerning hierarchy in the Church. In some cases, the illusion of the alleged danger of Protestantism resulted not in a genuine overcoming of it but in the unnoticed penetration of Protestant ideas into scholastic teaching. Indeed, if the idea of a bishop as presider whose status derives from the royal priesthood of all members of the Church is absolutely indispensable for the very existence of local churches, it is difficult to grasp how it could in any way undermine the role of episcopal ministry. For the church, a bishop as presider is an ontological necessity. His ministry is not a product of a historical development of the church organization. Rather it derives from the very foundations of the Church and thus using modern theological language, its origin is divine. This ontological character of episcopal ministry hardly stands in opposition to the ministry of royal priesthood, a ministry which a bishop shares with the remaining members of the Church. Moreover, this royal priesthood precisely generates its ontological character, because without the people of God no Church can exist. In affirming the priestly status of the bishop and denying it to all the members of the Church, scholastic theology brings the Church back toward the Old Covenant and undermines the New, made in the blood of Christ. As a result, the concept of the Church itself becomes diluted and approaches the Protestant understanding of it.[9]

2. The eucharistic assembly as the Church's self-manifestation was itself the focus of ecclesial life in every local church. At the assembly new members were received into the Church, individuals with special gifts were ordained for their ministries, unworthy members were cast out, and upon their repentance received back into communion. There all questions concerning the life of the local church were resolved on, both those which concerned the church as a whole and those with respect to its individual members. Nothing could happen in the church outside or apart from the assembly gathered "all together and at same time" (*epi to auto*) which itself could not exist without its presider. Thus from the very beginning nothing could be accomplished in the local church without or apart from the person or persons who presided over the church. As such they were keepers of structure and order in every local church because without those elements the assembly gathered *epi to auto* would turn into a disorderly mass of gathered Christians. In other words, the presiders were the bearers of the administrative function without which no order or structure in churches can exist.

This function of the presiders was not limited to implementation of the decisions of the ecclesial assembly. The eucharistic assembly was not merely an actual gathering of the members of this one local church, but was an assembly of the Church in all its fullness as an assembly of God's people in Christ. Therefore the actions of the local church do not have a merely local and communal character. Rather they are ecclesial and catholic as an accomplishment of God's will, active in the Church. Everything was accomplished at the ecclesial assembly but not in accordance with the desire or will of an individual or of its presiders. The source of authority of the ecclesial assembly did not reside in the assembly itself but in that it bore witness to the revealed will of God, since only this is significant in and for the Church. The ecclesial assembly is the place where God's will is revealed, while it is the people of the Church who examine the revelation and attest to its truthfulness. Once received, such revealed testimony is to be followed by the presiders. Consequently, the reason why the administration became associated with the presidency and became part of their ministry was that the examination and attesting of a revelation took place at the eucharistic assembly led by the presiders. Through their administration, structure and order were preserved in the ecclesial body, for this was the purpose of their administration, while structure and order proceeded from the will of God: "God is not a God of confusion but of peace." Presiders fulfilled the will of God revealed in the Church. For this reason they could not be officials whose offices were made up by a local church, but rather they were charismatics whom God ordained for their ministry in order to exercise his will.[10] Hence, administration exercised by the presiders fulfilled and followed God's will and had a charismatic character.

Administration, the keeping of divinely established order and structure in ecclesial life, also involves another more interior aspect, namely the administering of human souls on their way to God (2 Cor 10.8). Administration is *oikodomê*, the building up of the faithful. Ordained by God to be at the head of His people, the presiders led the people, fulfilling the will of God revealed to this people, to which the presiders themselves belonged. The will of God was binding for them above all, for they stood at the head of the people before God. Fulfilling the will of God, they became an example for God's people (1 Peter 5.3) by means of which they governed the people, leading them on the "way of life" common for all (2 Cor 6.4).[11] That is why in the Church administration is a pastoral ministry and those who administer the house of God are pastors (1 Tim 3.5). "He who enters by the door is the shepherd of the sheep ... When he has brought out all his own, he goes before them, and the sheep follow him, for they know his voice": (John 10.2, 4). As Christ is the one shepherd for the whole flock, in the same way presiders [*predstoiateli*] are its shepherds, for they stand at the head [*predstoiat*] of Christ's flock before God and lead this flock fulfilling God's will. Pastoral service signifies care—

both for all of the people and for its individual members in order that the will of God might be fulfilled in all. Pastoral service, at the same time, stands as both the guarding of structure and order in ecclesial life and as the guarding of every individual member of the church lest none of Christ's sheep be lost. Therefore pastoral service is identical with administration, which in turn is identical with the presidency, for in the Church, the presidency is a pastoral service. Both one and the other is a dynamic leadership on the way to God before whom the pastors stand [*predstoiat*] together with the people. In this lies the distinction between administration in the church and outside in empirical societies.

3. In the first letter he wrote, St. Paul makes note of those who preside over the church: "We beseech you, brethren, to respect those who labor among you and preside over you in the Lord and admonish you" (*eidenai tous kopiôntas en hymin kai proistamenous hymôn en Kyriô kai nouthetountas hymas*) (1 Thess 5.12).[12] Not even a year had passed since the church in Thessaloniki was founded, but St. Paul was already addressing it with a letter. To suggest that it is during this time that the ministry of presider emerged in the church which he founded is not only difficult but utterly impossible. St. Paul speaks about presiders as individuals whom the Thessalonians knew well enough. He asks that they be respected (*eidenai*) and highly esteemed in love because of their work (v. 13). This is not a way to refer to the people who more or less accidentally emerge or set themselves apart from the midst of the church members after Paul's departure from Thessaloniki, and whom he could not have known or knew not well enough. These were the people whom Paul himself had ordained for the work of ministry through divine calling. They were *proistamenoi en Kyriô*: those who preside in the midst of God's people gathered in Christ. They labored[13] in the midst of these people, furthering the work of Paul himself, in order that Christ may be imprinted in the hearts of all. They instruct, teach, and admonish every one of the faithful and all the faithful together, as St. Paul did, "warning (*nouthetountes*) everyone and teaching (*didaskontes*) everyone in all wisdom, that we may present every person mature in Christ Jesus" (Col 1.28). In this their work of ministry corresponded to that of St Paul himself, who also labored in the Lord: "For this I toil (*kopiô*), striving with all the energy which he mightily inspires within me" (Col 1.29). The Lord granted them the charism as he granted the special grace to St. Paul:

> By the grace of God I am what I am, and his grace toward me was not in vain. On the contrary, I worked (*ekopiasa*) harder than any of them (the apostles), though it was not I, but the grace of God which is with me. (1 Cor 15.10).

The formation of a local church came about with the establishment of the ministry of the presiders, for without them there could be no eucharistic assembly for which the people are gathered in the Lord (*en Kyriô*). Their presidency is an administration of the church in fulfillment of God's will. This is a gift of leading God's people who with love and through the love of their leaders follow them. Hence, all the faithful in return for the love of its presiders, must "esteem them very highly in love because of their work" (1 Thess 5.13).

St. Paul speaks concerning the presiders of the church in his letter to the Corinthians:

> And God has appointed in the church first apostles, second prophets, third teachers, then workers of miracles, then healers, helpers, administrators, speakers in various kinds of tongues. (1 Cor 12.28)

There is no basis for arguing that the first half of this verse deals with the people who had a definite ministry in the church whereas the second half merely enumerates the gifts which were not yet associated with certain individuals but manifested themselves only sporadically.[14] Both the first and second parts of this verse deal with those who had specific ministries in the church on the basis of special gifts of the Spirit.[15] Otherwise the second part of verse 28 would be an unnecessary repetition of verses 8–10 of the same chapter. We have noted above that the same list lacks any reference to the charism of apostleship.[16] If the absence of reference to the apostolic charism is explained by the fact that the apostolic ministry cannot be repeated in the life of the Church, the same explanation cannot be applied to the ministry of administration. Not only can it be repeated—it cannot possibly cease to exist in the Church. The gifts listed in verses 8–10 are given to all the people for common ministry. The ministry of administration belongs to the individuals specially called for it. By its own nature this ministry cannot belong to all the people and be a ministry common to all. The people do not share this ministry with the individuals who are called to it, and therefore the charism of administration is out of place with the *charismata* that belong to all the people. This specific charism of the ministry of administration brings it closer to the apostolic ministry. The latter pertained to an enclosed circle of ministers, thus the ministry of administration also pertains just to certain individuals, continuing to some degree the ministry which was to remain irrepeatable in history.

But to a greater extent than other ministries, that of administration cannot be exercised without the people. Wherever the ministry of administration is in place, there are the people, and, conversely, wherever the people are, the ministry of administration is in place. For this reason the individuals who possessed ministries could not have considered themselves above the rest of the churches' members, nor could they isolate themselves into a separate group. When St. Paul again in verses 29–30 enumerated the individuals endowed with special ministries, he had in mind only those people in the churches who considered themselves higher than others and who in one way or another were setting themselves apart from others. Among them we do not find the people endowed with the ministry of administration, and there could not have been any of this kind because such could not function without the rest of the church members.

We do not know and we will never know why in 1 Corinthians St. Paul designated people who had the ministry of administration not through mentioning them by proper name but through specifying the ministry which they fulfilled. There is no doubt however that these individuals were exercising the same ministry as "those who labor among you, preside over you and admonish you," from the letter to Thessalonians.

The ministry of presidency was not an invention of St. Paul existing only in the churches he founded. It was God's work in the Church of God. Presidency existed everywhere where there was a eucharistic assembly and therefore wherever the Church was present. St. Paul spoke about presiders in his letter to the Roman church which he had not founded. He exposed the teaching concerning the work of ministry to the Romans in the same terms as he did to the Corinthians. Enumerating ministries and charismata, he exhorted presiders to preside with zeal (*ho proistamenos en spoudê*) (12.8)[17] The church of Rome, just as the churches in Thessaloniki, Corinth, and elsewhere could not exist without presiders. Whoever was to found the local churches had to ordain presiders in them, for the ministry of presidency was absolutely necessary for the existence of those churches.

That is why we encounter such people not only in the Gentile churches but also in the mother of all churches, in Jerusalem. The writer of the Acts recounts that at the "apostolic council" the Jerusalem church had elected a delegation to be sent to Antioch which included both Judas and Silas, "leading men among the brethren" (*andras hêgoumenous en tois adelphois*) (Acts 15.22). The term *hêgoumenos* is not encountered in the Pauline letters with the exception of the letter to the Hebrews. This allows for speculation that this term was specific for the Palestinian churches and the churches dominated by Jewish Christians. In its original meaning, customary for the Septuagint, this term had the same semantics as the term *proistamenos. Hêgoumenos* is a person who leads the others and is followed by those whom he is leading.[18] This is the same figure as a presider of Paul's letters to Thessalonians and Romans. Quite remarkably this term is also found in the letter to the Hebrews: "Greet all your leaders and all the saints" (*aspasasthe pantas tous hêgoumenous hêmôn kai pantas tous hagious*) (Heb 13.24). The greeting addressed to the *hêgoumenoi* and all the saints at the end of the letter is the greeting to the whole church. That the *hêgoumenoi* are mentioned alongside the rest of the church members indicates that these *hêgoumenoi* are none other than those who preside above the rest of the saints. Hence it is clear why the author of the Hebrews demanded obedience to the *hêgoumenoi:* "Obey your leaders (*peithesthe tois hêgoumenois hymôn*) and submit to them; for they are keeping watch over your souls, as men who will have to give account" (Heb 13.17). The terms "to respect" (*eidenai*) and "to obey" (*peithesthai*) express almost the identical notion, for respect was not merely a rendering of the signs of honor but also an obedience, a following after those to whom the respect is given. And conversely, in the Church those who were obeyed were also respected rather than feared. The letters to the Thessalonians and the Hebrews prescribe the identical attitude toward the figures whom the first of them calls presiders and the second *hêgoumenoi*. At the same time the author of Hebrews reminds the faithful of those presiders who were already dead: "Remember your leaders (*hêgoumenôn hymôn*), those who spoke to you the word of God; consider the outcome of their life, and imitate their faith" (Heb 13.7). Obedience to the living and remembrance of the dead who still remain a model for the living—this attitude can be offered to none others but the presiders of the church. If the letter to the Hebrews has its origin in the church of Rome,[19] its compiler was using the term then current in this church. Both the *Letter of Clement* and *The Shepherd of Hermas* attest to the use of the term *hêgoumenoi* in the church of Rome.[20] Initially it appears that the church of Rome accepted the term *hêgoumenos* to designate their presiders. The word could already have been imported there by Palestinian Jews in the time when it had not yet been supplanted in Jerusalem by the term "presbyters."[21] We have to note that for determining the nature of the ministry of *hêgoumenoi*, the origin of the term is not significant for us. Its origin is not important—but what is important is the fact that the term *hêgoumenos* designated the same figure whom St. Paul called presider.[22]

The absence of the term *hêgoumenos* in Paul's letters does not support the argument that this term was unknown to him. Paul was well aware of the conditions of church life in Jerusalem. He was no less aware of church life in Rome. On the other hand it is quite difficult to imagine that the term *hêgoumenos* was in use in the churches founded by Paul. Luke gives an unambiguous witness to the fact that Paul was ordaining presbyters in the churches that he founded (Acts 14.23). We will see later that this testimony should not be neglected. On this basis we should suppose that to some degree Paul was distancing himself from this term.

He could have been avoiding the use of *hêgoumenos* in the Gentile churches because for the Gentile mind this term implied the idea of state-based authority and therefore was based on a different principle than that of love, which was at the basis of presiders' activity.[23] This danger did not exist for the Jews because for them a *hêgoumenos* could denote a leader as pastor.[24] Indeed, the pastoral status of *hêgoumenoi* is clearly discerned in the letter to the Hebrews. They must care for the soul of each of the faithful for they will have to give an account for these souls before God (13.17). They lead the faithful like a shepherd leads his sheep. They have to be examples to the faithful which the faithful then have to imitate (13.7). Here we find almost a word-for-word parallel with 1 Peter: "Tend the flock of God that is your charge, . . . not as domineering over those in your charge but being examples to the flock" (5.2–3). Therefore, there is no doubt that the pastors about whom Paul speaks in his letter to the Ephesians ("And his gifts were that some should be apostles, . . . some pastors and teachers"; 4.11),[25] are identical with those named *hêgoumenoi* in the letter to the Hebrews.

There is one detail in the activity of *hêgoumenoi* which seems to be lacking when we look at the presiders of St. Paul. They are designated as those who preach the Word of God (*hoitines elalêsan hymin ton logon tou Theou*) (13.7).[26] In this detail they find affinity with *didaskaloi*. This detail indicates that at the time of the letter to the Hebrews the ministry of *hêgoumenoi* also encompassed teaching.[27] Were Paul's presiders indeed lacking this aspect in their ministry? We saw above that the presiders from the letter to the Thessalonians labored in the midst of the faithful (*kopiôntas*, 1 Thess 5.12) as did Paul himself preaching the Word of God. In this respect they continued his work. The ministry of *didaskaloi* did not only allow for the presiders to assume a teaching role where the *didaskaloi* were not present but also allowed them to teach where they were present.[28] The management of God's household (1 Tim 3.5 and 15) with which the presiders were entrusted was exercised through God's Word. As those who managed God's household, *hêgoumenoi* and pastors must have been a model for the faithful to imitate. In order to be a model (*typos*) of the faith one has to uphold the true doctrine himself.

As presiders, *hêgoumenoi* and pastors could not uphold the true faith for themselves only. They had to uphold it for all the faithful over whom they presided at the ecclesial assembly, for only then could the faithful imitate them. But to uphold the faith for others means to guard it. That is why from the very beginning the presiders were the guardians of the doctrine entrusted to the Church as to the "pillar and foundation of the truth" (1 Tim 3.15). The treasury of faith was handed over to the Church and further by the ecclesial assembly to the presiders.

Precisely because of this they had to safeguard the right faith of God's people, of whom they were shepherds.

The presiders were guarding this "treasury of faith" at the ecclesial assembly, i.e., they were not guarding it on their own but together with God's people. For whatever is entrusted to the Church,[29] is guarded by none other than the Church itself. Therefore the ecclesial assembly with its presiders, i.e., the whole people of God, was responsible for the faith upheld by a local church as well as for the doctrine offered to the people. At the examination of prophetic revelation and of the teaching done by *didaskaloi,* the people followed their presiders so that in fact it was the presiders who were ultimately responsible for the correct faith. We do not know who were the angels of the churches from the book of Revelation. The only convincing argument questions their identification as prophets, for prophets, not being presiders of the churches, could not bear the responsibility for the correctness of faith upheld by the churches. Most likely the angels of Revelation were the personifications of local churches which manifested themselves at ecclesial assemblies under the guidance of presiders.[30] For this reason, we can rightfully attribute everything that is said there concerning ecclesial assembly to the presiders themselves.

> To the angel of the church in Ephesus write: ". . . I have this against you, that you have abandoned the love you had at first. Remember then from what you have fallen, repent and do the works you did at first. If not, I will come to you and remove your lampstand from its place, unless you repent. Yet this you have, you hate the works of the Nicolaitans, which I also hate." (Rev 2.1–6)

> And to the angel of the church in Thyatira write: ". . . I have this against you, that you tolerate the woman Jezebel, who calls herself a prophetess and is teaching and beguiling my servants to practice immorality and to eat food sacrificed to idols." (Rev 2.18–20)

> And to the angel of the church in Pergamum write: ". . . I have a few things against you: you have some there who hold the teaching of Balaam, who taught Balak to put a stumbling block before the sons of Israel, that they might eat food sacrificed to idols and practice immorality. So you also have some who hold the teaching of the Nicolaitans which I hate." (Rev 2.12–15)

The ecclesial assembly is guilty before God, for it has permitted the false prophets to teach and to mislead the servants of God. St. Paul tried to convince the church in Corinth not to forbid speaking in tongues (1 Cor 14.39) and the church in Thessaloniki not to despise prophesying (1 Thess 5.20). The book of Revelation, however, accuses the "angel of the church in Thyatira" of permitting a false prophetess to prophesy in the church. The authority to prohibit (*kôlyein*) and to permit (*aphienai*) belonged to the ecclesial assembly through its presiders.[31] Hence it is clear that while Paul's letters were addressed to the churches of Corinth and of Thessaloniki, that is, to the ecclesial assemblies where these letters must have been read, it was the presiders who had the authority to carry out the instructions of the apostle. This guardianship over the "treasury of faith" was the expression of presiders' pastoral service.

Instruction in correct faith, the treasury of which was entrusted to the church, could have been a creative force only when the correct faith which was upheld found its expression in a correct way of life. Faith must have its expression in life, as life must correspond with faith. Care for the faith is disclosed at the same time as care for the way of life of each and every person in the church. The angel of the church in Thyatira was guilty of permitting the false prophetess to prophesy in the ecclesial assembly and corrupt the faithful, leading them from the way of life to death. Both in faith and in life the presiders had to be models for the faithful in order to lead them on the way of life, being truly ahead of, not behind, those on whose behalf they stand [*predstoiat*] before God. With presiders, the charism of love, the highest gift according to St. Paul, had to find its fullest expression. Active love cannot treat any human soul with indifference, overlooking his or her needs, either spiritual or material. If the ministry of "assistants" was a special ministry, distinguished from the ministry of presiders, the latter, being at the head of eucharistic assembly, had in their care the supervision over the gifts which the faithful brought to the Eucharist. The presiders were entrusted with the treasury of faith as well as with the treasury of love. The supervision over the latter was a function of the ministry of presidency as a pastoral service. However, the presidency arose from supervising and distributing the treasury of love. Pastoral service encompassed teaching without which the keeping of correct faith and correct way of life is impossible.

By watching over the life of each and every one in the church, the ministry of presidency expressed an active love, but it was not able to overshadow or replace the ecclesial assembly because this ministry itself originated from the assembly and in the assembly found its expression. Without the assembly the presidency would be pointless, and active love could be cast out of the church's boundaries. This ministry would be pointless, for without an assembly a presider would cease to be a presider. His ministry would be cast out of the church because it could not be accompanied by the testimony of the people of the Church witnessing to the will of God that has been fulfilled. This testimony could not have been delegated to presiders and been made part of their ministry because it was the testimony of the Church concerning that which was accomplished in it. The fullness of the Church is manifested in the eucharistic assembly, rather than in its individual members or a group of members. For this reason, no one can be a substitute for the voice of the ecclesial assembly for no one can speak in the name of the Church except for the Church itself.

Presidency at the eucharistic assembly, pastoral service as governing the entire people of God as well as each of its members, teaching as supervising and keeping the "treasury of faith" and care for the "treasury of love"—this is the substance of the ministry of presiders in the New Testament writings. What in our time the Church possesses in the figure of its bishops and what it continued to possess in the course of its entire history was already present in the apostolic times. All these functions were in the possession of the Church's first presiders, ordained by the apostles.

III. Bishop-Presbyters of the New Testament Writings

1. In the New Testament alongside such terms as "presider," "pastor," and *hēgoumenos* we find two more, namely "presbyter" and "bishop." These terms survived in the church as designations of the hierarchical ministry, whereas the former terms, while still kept in use in some ways, lost their ancient meaning. The entire burden of the problem concerning the origins of hierarchical ministry in the Church falls on these terms, more precisely on the ministries that they designate. The question concerning the origins of the episcopate and the presbyterate remains unsolved in theological scholarship until this day. One theory replaces another, one sometimes being proven wrong, one sometimes supplementing another. In the chaos of opinions and hypotheses, the solution to the question constantly evades us and probably it will never become absolutely clear. In this chaos the traditional point of view of the Church is sometimes resolutely rejected, but also finds unexpected support. Purged of everything added to it in the course of the centuries by scholastic theology, this tradition must not be regarded as a subject for critique but rather as a grounding point of any investigation concerning the episcopate or presbyterate. This tradition does not just reveal some teaching that had emerged at a certain moment in the Church's historical being, but rather the Church's very memory concerning itself. As long as the Church remembers itself, it remembers the existence of bishop-presbyters in it.

The investigation of the historical development of the episcopate and presbyterate goes beyond the scope of the present work. We are not interested in how and in what way the present doctrine of church hierarchy emerged, but rather in what types of presbyteral and episcopal ministry existed in the primitive church, types from which, as from a nutshell, the present ministry of bishops and presbyters emerged. Our task is to encompass, as far as possible, the diversity of ministries in the primitive church and we cannot bypass the figures to whom the New Testament writings assign the name of presbyters and bishops.

The existence of two different titles—bishop and presbyter—does not by itself mean that these titles refer to different individuals. We have already come to the conclusion that in the primitive church those who presided over local churches were called pastors and *hêgoumenoi. Proistamenoi, hêgoumenoi,* and *poimenes* were the same persons who fulfilled one and the same ministry. Did the titles "presbyter" and "bishop" denote different persons who had different ministries, or the same persons who had one and the same ministry? This is the question, we have to solve in the first place. Apart from resolving this question, we also have to clarify the relation of individuals designated with the titles "bishop" and "presbyter" to the presiders of the churches. These two questions are interconnected. If we come to the conclusion that presbyters and bishops were different persons, then they—or at least one of them—naturally have to be distinguished from the presiders of the churches. If, however, bishop and presbyter signified one and the same person, this person could be identical with the presider of the church. If this is so, the entire problem amounts to a clarification of terms, as long as the essence of the ministry of presiders has been made clear for us above.

2. Several times in the New Testament we come across the title of "bishop" designating individuals who had a special ministry in the apostolic church. There are four specific texts where this title is found, excepting 1 Peter 2.25—"For you were straying like sheep, but have now returned to the Pastor and Bishop of your souls" (*epi ton Poimena kai Episkopon tôn psychôn hymôn*)—where the title "bishop" does not refer to a person who has a special ministry in the Church. As concerns the rest of the texts, their analysis leaves no doubt that the title "bishop" and "presbyter" denote one and the same person. The evidence of Acts 20.17, 18, 28 is the most decisive in this respect:

> And from Miletus he (i.e., Paul) sent to Ephesus and called to him the presbyters
> of the church (*tous presbyterous tês ekklêsias*). And when they came to him, he
> said to them: ". . . Take heed to yourselves and to all the flock, in which the Holy
> Spirit has made you bishops (*etheto episkopous*), to care for the church of the
> Lord and God which he obtained with his own blood."

Paul addresses the assembled presbyters of Ephesus, calling them bishops. These
are the same individuals whom Luke calls "presbyters" of the church, but St. Paul
calls "bishops." Consequently Luke appears to have accurately rendered Paul's
discourse, otherwise he would not change the designation "presbyters," which
he himself preferred above all other titles, to the term "bishops." At the same time
St. Paul never used the title "presbyter" anywhere except for the Pastoral letters.
No other interpretation of this text is possible without doing direct violence to it.
Irenaeus of Lyons partly employs it when he interprets this text in the following
way: "In Miletus thus were gathered bishops and presbyters who were from Ephesus and from the remaining nearby cities" (*in Mileto enim convocatis episcopis et
presbyteris, qui erant ab Epheso et a reliquis proximis civitatibus*).[32] Having learned
from the text that the same persons are called presbyters and bishops, he was dis-
turbed by the multiplicity of bishops in one city. Therefore Irenaeus makes it look
as if St. Paul had gathered around himself bishops and presbyters of Ephesus and
its neighboring cities, but addressed his discourse, cited in Luke's text, to the bishops only. We should hardly dwell on this interpretation, which is not in the least
degree endorsed by the text cited above.

The argument that in the New Testament the terms "bishop" and "presbyter" are synonymous is supported by the letter to Titus:

> This is why I left you in Crete, that you might amend what was defective, and
> appoint presbyters (*presbyterous*) in every town as I directed you, if any man is
> blameless, the husband of one wife, and his children are believers and not open
> to the charge of being profligate or insubordinate. For a bishop (*ton episkopon*), as
> God's steward, must be blameless; he must not be arrogant or quick-tempered
> or a drunkard or violent or greedy for gain. (1.5–7)

Titus was left in Crete so that he might ordain presbyters. With respect to their
ordination he received instruction that these were men without reproach who
should be ordained presbyters, because it was the bishop who must be a man
without reproach. Put differently, bishop and presbyter are synonymous terms

which apply to one and the same person. There is no reason to suppose that the text cited above deals with two different figures: first, with presbyters and the requirements set for them, and then with bishops and what is required of the latter. This supposition contradicts the text itself, since the verses 6 and 7 are connected by the conjunction *gar*. Just as it was in Acts, here too we find in the same text different terms designating one and the same person. If in Acts, as we saw above, this is explained by the fact that one term was used by Luke, and the other by Paul, this diversity of terms in the letter to Titus remains a mystery at least until the New Testament exegesis will decisively answer the issues relating to the letter itself.[33]

The text of the letter to Timothy is much less concrete, lacking a juxtaposition of the terms "bishop" and "presbyter":

> The saying is sure: If any one aspires to the office of bishop, he desires a noble task. Now (*oun*—consequently, due to this, therefore) a bishop must be above reproach, the husband of one wife, temperate, sensible, dignified, hospitable, an apt teacher . . . Deacons likewise must be serious, not double-tongued, not addicted to much wine, not greedy for gain. (1 Tim 3.1–8)

Episcopacy is a solemn task and therefore the bishop must answer to certain requirements entirely consistent with those set forth for the presbyter in the letter to Titus. On the basis of this consistency we suggest that the "bishop" from the letter to Timothy is synonymous with the presbyter. This conclusion is further bolstered by the fact that in the third chapter of 1 Timothy, "presbyter" is not mentioned at all and, after dealing with the bishop, the author of the letter immediately turns to the deacon.[34] Besides, one cannot rule out the possibility that the "episcopacy" in the first verse of the third chapter of the letter does not mean the office of a bishop, but an office in a general sense, such as we find in Acts 1.20 ("His office/episcopacy let another take").[35] Therefore, it can be applied not only to the bishop's but also to the deacon's ministry. In this case the meaning of the text would be as follows: the one who aspires to the church office desires a noble task, but since church office is a demanding one not everyone can be ordained as bishop or deacon but only the person who corresponds to a number of requirements.

The last text where "bishop" is mentioned without juxtaposition with presbyters is the inscription of the letter to Philippians: "Paul and Timothy, servants of Christ Jesus, to all the saints in Christ Jesus who are at Philippi, with the bishops and deacons . . ." (1.1). This is the only inscription among Paul's letters where he mentions bishops and deacons. On this basis, can we infer that this text is dealing with bishops as those who have a special ministry distinct from the ministry of presbyters? This possibility is almost completely excluded. Indeed, if the bishops in this letter are thought to be distinct from presbyters, how did St. Paul fail to mention the latter? Did he forget about them, which is utterly incredible; or were there no presbyters in Philippi? The latter suggestion does not hold, for Luke asserts that during his first travels Paul ordained presbyters everywhere in the churches he founded (Acts 14.23). One can hardly imagine that St. Paul departed from his custom and during his second journey did not ordain presbyters, but presbyters as well as bishops, or the bishops only. Even if the second suggestion is true, the bishops of the second journey are the figures which are completely identical with the presbyters of his first trip. But if he was ordaining both bishops and presbyters, the same question remains. Why did he not mention presbyters in the letter to Philippians? Can one possibly think that St. Paul did it on purpose, meaning to express special gratitude to bishops and deacons?[36] The care which the Philippians showed for St. Paul could not have been exclusively an accomplishment of bishops and deacons, but of the entire church including, in the first place, the presbyters. Besides, the most important aspect is that the letter was not addressed to separate groups of members of the church in Philippi, but to the church itself. The formula St. Paul used in this letter is consistent with the formulae found in other letters. The faithful with their presiders comprise the Church of God which abides in Philippi. Therefore the bishops from the letter to Philippians are identical with the presbyters mentioned by Luke. Here, obviously, the difference is of the terms, rather than of the people designated by those terms.[37] Paul remained faithful to himself, avoiding the use of the title "presbyter." We must add to all this discussion that an attempt to ground the hypothesis concerning the existence of bishops distinct from presbyters on the evidence from the letter to Philippians does not reach its goal. It was already obvious for Jerome that the multiplicity of bishops in Philippi cannot account for the emergence of monarchical episcopate. "Surely, in one city, there cannot be many to be called bishops. But since at that time they used also to call those same bishops presbyters, therefore, [here] the same persons are mentioned indifferently, either as bishops, or as presbyters."[38]

3. If the analysis of the New Testament has led us to conclude that the same persons were denoted by the titles "bishop" and "presbyter," this does not yet answer the question concerning the essence of their ministry. We have already raised this question above, as well as the question of the relation of these individuals to the presiders of the church. The crucial evidence to resolve these questions comes from Luke's passage (Acts 14.23), the significance of which has been generally under-estimated: "And when they had ordained presbyters for them in every church (*cheirotonêsantes de autois kat'ekklêsian presbyterous*), with prayer and fasting they committed them to the Lord in whom they believed." We must not limit the meaning of this witness by the churches to which these words directly refer. There is no ground for suggesting that special conditions obtained in Iconia, Lystra, and Pisidian Antioch, due to which St. Paul deemed it necessary to ordain *presbyters* to these churches. No such special circumstances were in place or, more precisely, the same conditions existed in every church which was formed at that time. Not only in Iconia, Lystra, or Antioch, but wherever the churches were emerging, presbyters were ordained. The beginning of the presbyterial ministry coincides with the formation of local churches. Therefore their ministry was necessary for the existence of a local church. What primarily concerned Paul was the ordination of presbyters in the churches which he founded rather than the ordination of prophets or teachers. Without the latter two a local church could exist, but it could not survive without presbyters. "This is why I left you in Crete, that you might amend what was defective, and appoint elders in every town" (Titus 1.5). Without presbyters the church would be defective and only the appointment of presbyters completes the work of proclaiming the Word of God, whose goal was the formation of a church. We already know that the only ministry without which no church could exist—for no eucharistic assembly could exist without it too—was the ministry of presidency. In the assembly of God's people, there must be those who would preside over these people and therefore, the first concern upon the formation of the churches was the ordination of these men. That is why the presbyters whom St. Paul ordained to the newly formed churches were the presiders of these churches. The ministry of presbyters consisted of presidency and so did the ministry of bishops.

This conclusion made on the basis of Lucan testimony concerning the ministry of presbyter-bishops is also supported by other indications in the New Testament. In his discourse with the presbyters, St. Paul said: "Take heed to yourselves and to all the flock in which the Holy Spirit has made you bishops, to shepherd the church of the Lord and God" (Acts 20.28). The Holy Spirit had ordained presbyter-bishops in the flock (*en hô . . . etheto episkopous*) to shepherd (*poimanein*) the Church of Christ—therefore, he had ordained them to be pastors (*poimenes*). We have already seen that the ministry of presiders was pastoral and was so closely intertwined with the pastoral service that presiders were called pastors/shepherds. Equally clearly, the First Letter of Peter presents the pastoral ministry as the presbyters' ministry: "So I exhort the elders among you, as a co-presbyter and a witness of the sufferings of Christ . . . tend the flock of God that is your charge" (5.1–2). In the letter to Timothy, the presbyters, some of them, anyway, are openly called "presiding": "Let the presbyters who rule well be considered worthy of double honor" (1 Tim 5.17). These "presiding presbyters" (*proestôtes presbyteroi*) are the *proistamenoi* ("presiders") of the letter to Thessalonians.[39] Lastly, the presbyters of the church in Jerusalem, according to Luke's narrative, were presiders or "leaders" (*hêgoumenoi*). They occupy a prominent position in the church, taking part in every important moment of its life. At the "Jerusalem council," they act alongside the apostles. The letter to the church in Antioch is composed in their name as well as in the name of the apostles and all the brethren. There is no doubt that Judas and Silas, whom we mentioned already, were presbyters (Acts 15.22–23). The next day upon his second arrival to Jerusalem St. Paul goes to James, where the presbyters were assembled (Acts 21.18). Even if not all presbyters were *hêgoumenoi*, all *hêgoumenoi* were presbyters.

4. Stemming from the eucharistic assembly and having its foundation in the latter, the presidency was a unique ministry which was not itself internally divided into any degrees. Any such division has no ground in the New Testament and contradicts the essence of the eucharistic assembly. At the assembly of the royal priesthood which is the people of God, there must have always been those who presided over this priesthood, sharing the same priesthood with the rest of the people. Division of the ministry of presidency into degrees could have been made possible only on the basis of a special priesthood of which the bishop represented a highest degree, while the presbyters were a second degree. However, this special priesthood did not exist in the early church. It is impossible to build the division of presidency into degrees on another principle, which is another evidence in favor of the view that the terms "bishop" and "presbyter" are synonymous and refer to one and the same ministry. If we raise the question of whether the New Testament presbyter-bishops were presbyters or bishops, are we not transposing into the apostolic times a ministry which did not yet exist at that point and which fully formed only in the third century? The New Testament bishop-presbyters were neither today's presbyters nor modern bishops, because neither the first nor the second existed at that time. Likewise unfounded is the attempt to present the New Testament bishops as presbyters in a later understanding of the term and to consider apostles or their vicars rather than presbyters as the bishops. In recent times this point of view was advocated with an unexpected vigor by Roman Catholic scholars, even though as a matter of fact this view is not a novelty and was known in the early church. Both in ancient times and in ours this view proceeds from dogmatic presuppositions rather than from the witness of the New Testament and historical evidence. According to this view, in the apostolic times neither of the local churches founded by the apostle Paul had bishops; rather, the apostle Paul himself—or one of his legates—was the only pastor of this enormous "diocese" which he had acquired through his labor of preaching the gospel. All churches of this "diocese" were served by deacons and governed by the council of elders which were called at the same time either as bishops, or as presbyters. While still alive St. Paul commissioned his closest co-workers to govern some of the churches. The addressees of the Pastoral letters, Timothy and Titus, were such apostolic legates. Like St. Paul himself, they also were real bishops who upon the death of the apostle, had, just like others, to take upon themselves the full governance of all the churches.[40] We find an organization of this kind among the Palestinian churches at one time headed by James. If this hypothesis appears to salvage a dogmatic thesis concerning the existence of three ranks of the church hierarchy from the very beginnings of the Church, this theory at the same time significantly undermines the apostolic succession of the episcopate. If the apostles or their legates or vicars headed a number of the churches as their only bishops, how did the successors of the apostles and of their co-workers receive the title of bishops, applied at the time to the presbyters, rather than keeping the title of apostles? If we leave aside this terminological issue, we are left with another more crucial question relating to the transition from apostolate to episcopate. The apostles did not govern one local church but a number of churches. Consequently their successors could have been only such bishops who also governed a number of churches, i.e., either future metropolitans or patriarchs. To pursue this idea logically to the end, the bishop-presbyters of the apostolic times would not have been able to rise to the level of real bishops but would remain a second rank in the church hierarchy. But if they indeed rose to the level of bishops, as contemporary dogmatic theology contends, how could it happen and when did it happen? How in turn were they capable of becoming the successors of the apostles?[41] Those presbyter-bishops who together with deacons were governing the churches in the apostolic times did not have the apostolic succession. Would it not be logical to arrive at an idea that only a bishop of all the churches or several such bishops are the successors of the apostles? As a matter of fact, we find the tendency to think in this way in the West as well as in the East, even though expressed to a different extent and with a varying success at its realization. However, this tendency did not eradicate the idea of the common apostolic succession applied to all bishops. At the same time, the tradition of the Church shows an exceptional consensus in ascribing the apostolic succession to all of the bishops rather than just to particular ones.

Surely the doctrine concerning apostolic succession of all bishops could not be a final argument against the hypothesis of the apostles as bishops because it needs supporting evidence itself. Still, this doctrine remains one of the major arguments against this hypothesis, especially if taken in conjunction with other arguments which we find in the New Testament. We have so few historical facts relating to primitive Christianity at our disposal, but even those that we have do not witness in favor of this theory. From the very beginning local churches appear as quite independent bodies. The apostles' relation to the churches they founded was unique, as was the ministry of the Twelve in general. It was not succeeded by anyone in its fullness and it was not handed over to anyone—neither while the apostles were alive nor after their death. However, even given this stipulation, the apostles' relation to the churches they founded was not as it would be seen in the theory that presents apostles as first bishops. As a "master builder" (*architektôn*) (1 Cor 3.10) of local churches the apostle Paul enjoyed a special authority and had an exceptional influence upon the life of these churches. The faithful of these churches were his children with whom he was in travail until Christ was formed in them (Gal 4.19).

Nevertheless one cannot infer from his letters that he regarded himself as some authority above the churches. He was not above the local churches but within them, and that is why he always acted in the name of the church. He does not act in his own name but in the name of the church of Corinth when he excommunicates its adulterous member:

> For though absent in body I am present in spirit, and as if present, I have already pronounced judgment in the name of the Lord Jesus on the man who has done such a thing. When you are assembled, and my spirit is present, with the power of our Lord Jesus . . . (1 Cor 5.3–4)

Desiring another excommunicated person to be received back, he does not give orders but encourages the Corinthian Christians to show compassion to the one who sinned. ("So you should rather turn to forgive and comfort him . . ." [2 Cor 2.7].) He exhorted the Corinthians: "Examine yourselves, to see whether you are holding to your faith. Test yourselves. Do you not realize that Jesus Christ is in you?—unless indeed you fail to meet the test!" (2 Cor 13.5) He presents his apostleship, his life's work handed to him by Christ, for the examination and judgment of the ecclesial assembly. "You desire proof that Christ is speaking in me" (2 Cor 13.3). One who would stand above the church could not have written in this manner, even less could he succumb to defending himself with respect to the work of preaching the gospel as St. Paul did in his letter to Galatians. The words of Paul, usually cited as evidence in favor of the kind of authority the apostles enjoyed over the churches, have a completely different meaning than this interpretation of authority. "What do you wish? Shall I come to you with a rod, or with love in a spirit of gentleness?" (1 Cor 4.21)[42] The one who possesses power can use it at any time through his representatives. The apostle Paul could have used this power in his letter, which, however, bears witness to the opposite. The apostle indeed had power (*tên exousian*) but such power about which he himself wrote:

> I write this while I am away from you, in order that when I come I may not have to be severe in my use of the authority which the Lord has given me for building up and not for tearing down. (2 Cor 13.10)

This is the authority for building up the house of God. It is present within the church rather than standing above it. This is the shepherd's rod from within the flock rather than above the flock. Therefore St. Paul could use this power only from within the local church, himself being situated within it, rather than outside of it. St. Paul did not have power over the churches because no such kind of power existed. The power over the local church would be power over the eucharistic assembly and consequently over the body of Christ.

Another even more striking example demonstrating the lack of authority above the churches in the apostolic times is the Third Letter of the apostle John. However the issues concerning the authenticity of this letter are resolved, this writing in any case dates to the time immediately adjacent to the apostolic era. If this letter belongs to St. John it bears witness to the fact that he, just like St. Paul, did not have authority over the church that he founded. Not being present in the church in person he could not alter the decision promulgated under the presidency of Diotrephus. He writes in the same terms as St. Paul wrote to the Corinthians:

> So if I come, I will bring up what he is doing, prating against me with evil words. And not content with that, he refuses himself to welcome the brethren, and also stops those who want to welcome them and puts them out of the church. (3 John 1.10)

His authority is localized in the church, not above the church, and therefore his authority is the authority of the church itself. However, if this letter does not belong to the apostle John it does not in any way alter the conclusions we made. It was written by an individual who enjoys authority in the church likely founded by him, but his authority does not turn into a power over this church.

The theory that apostles had authority over the churches they founded came as a result of a later theological speculation. Modern dogmatic theology, Orthodox as well as Roman Catholic, regards the right of bishops to celebrate the sacrament of ordination as a basic distinction between the ministries of bishop and presbyter. The right to ordain implies and expresses the juridical power of the bishop. The bishop performs the ordination within that part of the universal church directly subject to him. This understanding reflects ecclesial organization that begins to take shape in the fourth century, but not the original ecclesial organization. Contending that in the primitive church it was the apostles themselves who performed ordinations, the proponents of the "apostle-bishops" theory argue that after the apostles this prerogative was passed on to their successors. There is no indisputable evidence in support of this contention, but even if it were accurate the act of ordination nevertheless did not comprise the essence of the episcopal ministry in the second century. Ignatius of Antioch tells nothing about the prerogative to ordain in his letters. From his silence we might infer that this aspect did not constitute the essence of episcopal ministry. For Ignatius the bishop is the only presider of the local church. As such he alone presides at the eucharistic assembly and therefore the Eucharist is valid only when celebrated by the bishop. For Ignatius the center of gravity was situated in the Eucharist. Whoever presided at the eucharistic assembly performed all liturgical actions. The theology of later periods transferred the center of gravity from the eucharist to the sacrament of ordination. Indeed, the apostles performed ordinations, but this action of theirs did not derive from their alleged authority over the churches they founded but rather from their ministry of building up local churches.

If the apostles themselves did not have any juridical power over the churches, even less could they pass this kind of power to their successors. In connection to this we have to return to the question of whether Timothy and Titus were indeed the successors of the apostles or at least were destined by Paul to succeed him. If there might be some doubt with respect to Timothy there cannot be any with respect to Titus. The mission which Titus received from Paul was a temporary one (Titus 3.12). The proponents of the "apostle-bishops" theory view Timothy and Titus as Paul's successors on the basis of the fact that the Pastoral letters were written during the period immediately preceding Paul's death, for one cannot draw that conclusion from the simple fact of Paul assigning them that task. Paul had been assigning various tasks to his collaborators without yet having his own death in mind. Thus it was with a certain task that he sent Timothy to the Thessalonians:

> Therefore when we could bear it no longer, we were willing to be left behind at Athens alone, and we sent Timothy, our brother and God's servant in the gospel of Christ, to establish you in your faith and to exhort you. (1 Thess 3.1–2)

This same Timothy was sent by Paul to Corinth: "When Timothy comes, see that you put him at ease among you, for he is doing the work of the Lord, as I am." (1 Cor 16.10) We know from Paul's letters that he has been also assigning his tasks to other people, including Titus (2 Cor 8.6–23). Nobody considers Timothy, Titus, or Tychicus to be Paul's future successors in this period of his life. Even if Timothy and Titus were Paul's legates or vicars, one in Ephesus and the other in Crete, why do we not know anything of Paul's other successors in other church districts? Generally, church tradition did not preserve any names of the apostolic plenipotentiaries who would receive from the apostles their ministry and would be dated to the transitionary period between the apostolate and episcopate, if such a period existed at all.

There is only one statement which we can still maintain out of this whole theory concerning the apostles as the first bishops. It is this, that the ministry which the New Testament bishops fulfilled was not entirely the same as the ministry of the bishops of later period, just as their presbyterate was not the same as the ministry of the presbyters of later period. In the primitive church the ministry of presidency was one as the eucharistic assembly was one and as the Church was one. No ministry of administration existed outside of the local churches and within the local church itself this ministry was not subdivided into any kind of ranks.

IV. Origin and Meaning of the Terms "Presbyter" and "Bishop"

1. In the course of the formation of the basic structure of ecclesial organization, the existence of different terms designating the ministry of presidency is a natural and legitimate phenomenon. We find similar terminological instability even with reference to the proper title of members of the Church. The New Testament provides us with a number of such designations: the beloved, saints, the saints who were called, sanctified in Christ, holy and faithful brethren in Christ, disciples and, finally, Christians. All these terms are synonyms in the sense that they refer to one and the same group of people. Nevertheless, each of these terms underlines and expresses one particular aspect of their position in the Church.

The designation of the presiders as "pastors" does not cause any confusion or raise any difficult questions. Pastoral service constitutes the essence of the ministry of presidency, as well as of the ministry of administration, and points at the very nature of the administration in the Church. The term *hegoumenoi* carries the sense identical with the terms "presbyter" and "bishop" and unites in itself the concepts of pastorship and of presidency. Designating one and the same group of people having the same ministry, do the terms "presbyter" and "bishop" reveal the essence of the presidency? Or does the argument that different terms were used in different churches suffice for the explanation of how these terms emerged? Certainly, one could suppose that the term "presbyter" was used in the churches dominated by Jewish Christians whereas the term "bishop" was accepted by Gentile Christians.[43] This supposition would have been somewhat plausible if we were absolutely certain about the origin of the term "presbyter" in the Palestinian churches, which we are not. Besides, one has to note that no strict delimitation existed between the churches comprised of Jews and the ones comprised of Gentiles. It is not possible to determine a precise ratio of Jews and Gentiles in the churches founded by St. Paul. It is quite risky to follow in this direction up to the point of claiming that the term "bishop" had appeared for the first time in Philippi, where the Jewish colony was very small in number and hence the Gentiles comprised the nucleus of the original church.[44] Even if this supposition were correct, despite the lack of undisputable evidence it cannot substantiate the claim that the term "bishop" originated in Philippi. It is unlikely that Philippians would risk introducing in their church a new term which did not exist in other churches. The church in Philippi was founded by St. Paul, hence the initiative in this respect could belong to none other than St. Paul himself. However, he could as well have initiated its usage in other churches which he founded earlier than the church in Philippi.

On the other hand, as we have seen, St. Paul never uses the terms "bishop" or "presbyter" in his letters with the exception of the letter to Philippians, the Pastoral letters being a special case. But undoubtedly he was aware of both terms, as his discourse with the Ephesian presbyters shows.[45] Luke mainly employs the term "presbyter" but also cites the term "bishop" in the same discourse of St. Paul. Therefore, it does not seem possible to answer the question concerning the place where the terms "bishop" and "presbyter" originated if we follow these lines of reasoning. We can only remark with some degree of probability that the term "presbyter" was more widespread in the primitive church than the term "bishop." However, that does not give us anything by which to solve the above mentioned issue.

Whether the term "presbyter" discloses the essence of the ministry of presidency can be only partially resolved. There was nothing specifically Christian in the term "presbyter." The council of elders was the most widely spread form of communal governance in the ancient world. By the time of the beginnings of Christianity the council of elders was at the head of every Jewish community. In Palestinian communities, the members of this council bore the designation *zeqenim*, but with the diaspora Jews it seems that only in extreme cases did the members of the council bear the designation *presbyteroi*.[46] The appropriation of the title "presbyters" for the presiders of the churches cannot be considered a mechanical repetition of the Jewish institution of *zeqenim*. More likely, this appropriation was motivated by general conditions of life in antiquity. Every local church had a differentiation of its members into young and old, according to their age, as well as according to the time of their entrance into the church. Due to their position, the oldest members, *presbytai* (Titus 2.2) or *presbyteroi* (1 Tim 5.1), not having any specific ministry, enjoyed a greater respect and honor than younger members of the church. However, to speak of some "charisma of eldership" in the early church would be an exaggeration.[47] By itself the title "elder" was an honorary one: "Yet for love's sake I prefer to appeal to you—I, Paul, an elder (*presbytês*) and now a prisoner also for Christ Jesus" (Philem 1.9). Here "elder" refers mainly to the apostle Paul's age, for which sake alone he could count on being respected and his request fulfilled. The apostle John applies the same title to himself in his two letters: "the elder to the elect lady and her children . . ." (2 Jn 1.1), "the elder to the beloved Gaius, whom I love in the truth" (3 Jn 1.1). As the eldest members they occupied honorary seats at the eucharistic assembly, which in turn even more elevated their honorary status in the church. In a wide sense of the word they were "the first seated" (*prôtokathedritai*).[48] It was from their midst, as the eldest and according to the time of their membership in the Church, that the presiders were ordained. Clement of Rome testifies that the apostles, preaching across the lands and cities, ordained the first fruits of the faithful to be bishops and deacons.[49] Being ordained to be presiders they did not cease to be presbyters, i.e., the eldest members of a local church. They did not lose their former titles because their ministry could not deprive them of their former status in the church or segregate them from the rest of the eldest members, as it did not segregate them from the rest of the church members. They occupied a place among the eldest members but at the head of everyone, as presiders of a local church. Thus they were *prôtokathedritai* in a special sense. Thus the title "presbyters" did not at first encompass the presiders of the churches only, but also all of the eldest members of the churches. When there appeared a need to narrow the term more precisely, either other terms were used or the term "presbyter" was supplanted with the adjective *kathestamenoi*.[50] The term *presbyteroi kathestamenoi* could not have caused confusion, for the presbyter who has been set apart could have only been a presider of the church. The phenomenon that we observe in the case of the term "bishop" is of a totally analogous character. When bishops came to be distinguished out of the midst of presbyters as the persons with a special ministry they continued for some time to be called presbyters. However, to distinguish them from other presbyters, when necessary their generic designation "presbyters" was supplanted with an indication to their apostolic lineage. As time passed, the term "presbyter" was narrowed, designating only those who had a ministry of presidency and later, when the special ministry of bishops emerged, only those who possessed a second degree of priesthood. Taken in this particular sense, the term "presbyter" precisely denotes the ministry of those who bear this title.

2. The term "bishop" causes much more difficulty. Its philological and even semantic analysis hardly provides anything to determine the Christian sense of this term. It was a common term in antiquity, designating individuals who had very diverse ministries in Greek communities. It is often used in the Septuagint, also, to designate various individuals. It is a risky endeavor to build a theory of the origin of the episcopate on the basis of one or another non-Christian meaning of the term "bishop," and it can lead to apparent misunderstanding like Hutch's theory.[51] There is no doubt, however, that among different meanings of the term "bishop" was one which allowed this title to be applied to Christ: "For you were straying like sheep, but have now returned to the Shepherd and Guardian (*Episkopon*) of your souls" (1 Peter 2.25).[52] Christ is the Shepherd of his sheep in his Church. At the same time, he is Guardian/Bishop of his sheep. We can readily admit that here the title "bishop" is synonymous with the title "shepherd," but this suggestion does not rule out the possibility that the title "bishop" is an extension of the notion of pastorship, designating more distinctly one aspect of pastoral activity. The only meaning of the word "bishop" in the above text may be the original one: a keeper or guardian. Pastoral service, as we have pointed out, is not only to lead the flock but also to care for every member of the flock entrusted to the pastor's leadership.

> I will seek the lost, and I will bring back the strayed, and I will bind up the crippled, and I will strengthen the weak, and the fat and the strong I will watch over; I will feed them in justice.

Thus speaks the divine Shepherd in Ezekiel 34.16. As Shepherd, Christ keeps and guards his sheep and therefore he is the bishop of his sheep. Guard and care, as functions of pastoral service, are such significant aspects that they can be isolated from this notion and endowed with a special name.[53] The bishop is a pastor fulfilling the ministry entrusted to him in its fullness, and the pastor is a bishop, for there can be no pastor who would not have cared for his sheep. The legend about the apostle John, preserved by Clement of Alexandria, speaks of John committing a certain young man to the presbyter of the church.

> The presbyter taking home the youth committed to him, reared, kept, cherished, and finally baptized him. After this he relaxed his stricter care and watchfulness, with the idea that in putting upon him the seal of the Lord he had given him a perfect protection. But some youths of his own age, idle and dissolute, and accustomed to evil practices, corrupted him when he was thus prematurely freed from restraint. At first they enticed him by costly entertainments; then, when they went forth at night for robbery, they took him with them, and finally they demanded that he should unite with them in some greater crime . . . Time passed and some necessity having arisen, they sent for John. But he, when he had set in order the other matters on account of which he had come, said, "Come, O bishop, restore to us the deposit which both I and Christ committed to thee, the church, over which thou presidest, being witness." But the bishop was at first confounded, thinking that he was falsely charged in regard to money which he had not received, and he could neither believe the accusation respecting what he had not, nor could he disbelieve John. But when he said, "I demand the young man and the soul of the brother," the old man, groaning deeply and at the same time bursting into tears, said, "He is dead." "How and what kind of death?" "He is dead to God," he said; "for he turned wicked and abandoned, and at last a robber. And now, instead of the church, he haunts the mountain with a band like himself."[54]

What the bishop could not do, the apostle did himself. Despite his old age he went up to the mountains and returned to the church the soul that the bishop had lost. Every member of the church is entrusted to the church and through it, to the presider, for this soul the presider has to give account before God. Origen said,

> You who preside over the church are the eye of Christ's body, so that you may especially keep an eye on everything, examine everything, and even foresee things about to come. You are a pastor, you see the lambs of the Lord unaware of

danger to be carried to precipices and suspended over steep places. Do you not run? Do you not call them back? Do you not at least restrain them with your voice and deter them with a shout of reproof?[55]

Every soul is a deposit given by the Lord to the presider in the view of the church which he has to guard and preserve.[56] In certain circumstances when the task of guarding overrides other pastoral tasks, the title "bishop" can become predominant.

The connection between pastoral service and episcopacy, which we have established on the basis of 1 Peter 2.25, is also to be discerned in Acts 20.28: "Take heed to yourselves and to all the flock in which the Holy Spirit has made you overseers, to care for the Church of God which he obtained with his own blood." Here, just as in the letter of Peter, the Church appears as the flock of God which Christ had obtained for himself. The apostle Paul reminds the presbyters whom he summoned that they were made bishops in the flock in order to tend the flock. In other words, he brings to the attention of Christian pastors their episcopal duties. In his subsequent words to the Ephesian pastors, Paul makes this aspect of pastoral service, a special episcopal task, even more concrete: "I know that after my departure fierce wolves will come in among you, not sparing the flock" (20.29). Presbyters as pastors must keep, preserve, and oversee in order that Christ's disciples, the sheep of his flock, would not be snatched by wolves. The guarding of the sheep from the fierce wolves who do not spare the flock constitutes the essence of episcopal ministry, closely linked with the guarding of the truths of faith which apostles have entrusted to the local churches. If faith is not preserved, the sheep likewise are lost for the flock of Christ.

In the words of Paul's discourse in Ephesus, the essence of episcopal ministry is revealed with utmost clarity as a function of pastoral service. Another aspect revealed with equal clarity is the affinity between this ministry and the ministry of presidency. The title "bishop" emphasizes that aspect of presider's ministry which concerns the guarding of the right faith and through it the guarding of all sheep of Christ's flock. For this reason the presiders as bishops are responsible for diversions from the faith if such occur in the local churches they lead. The witness of the book of Revelation on this issue is in full agreement with that of the apostle Paul.[57] In connection to this one might present a theory which, however, cannot be verified. The title "bishop" emerged later than any other titles applied to the presiders. More exactly, it emerged when in the churches the danger of false teachings became distinct, a danger which did not exist from the very beginning. The more outspoken this danger, the more clearly defined became the pastors' activity aimed at guarding doctrine. It is possible that concern for the right faith in the churches he founded began to alarm St. Paul, particularly during his journey to Jerusalem and at the time when he was in chains. Sensing that the end of his life was approaching, he began to reflect more on the future of the churches he founded. This thought must have been particularly tormenting for him since the danger of false teaching had increased notably. Hence, he naturally wanted to bring to the attention of those who preside over the churches the fact that the guarding of the teaching—episcopacy—constitutes one of the main tasks of their pastoral activity. This is what he points out to the presbyters gathered with him in Miletus by calling them bishops. Being aware of how significant the ministry of presidency was and the role presiders play in the life of local churches, Paul feared that they themselves might betray the task of guarding the right doctrine and would themselves become a cause of false teachings. "From among your own selves will arise men speaking perverse things, to draw away the disciples after them" (Acts 20.30). In his letter to the Philippians, written when he was already in chains, Paul mentions bishops, something he never did in his letters before. It is customarily said that the church in Philippi was in a fine state, but even given this assumption it cannot be excluded that St. Paul was burdened by the care of safe-guarding this church from false teachings of any kind. He openly writes to Philip-pians: "Look out for the dogs, look out for the evil-workers, look out for those who mutilate the flesh" (Phil 3.2). Thus there were people, perhaps not within the church but wandering around as wolves, not sparing the flock. He writes to them with tears concerning the enemies of the cross of Christ: "For many, of whom I have often told you and now tell you even with tears, live as enemies of the cross of Christ" (3.18). If we may propose a theory about why Paul in the letter to Philip-pians made note of the bishops, we must conclude that he did not do so merely in order to emphasize his gratitude to the bishops for the assistance given to him, but rather in order to focus the attention of the faithful upon the importance of the presiders' ministry and the attention of the presiders themselves upon the aspect of their activity that was becoming more and more significant. Perhaps here we can find an answer to the question why in the post-apostolic times the title "bishop" becomes a predominant and later an exclusive title applied to one of the presiders. The Church was entering the path of a hard and bloody struggle for existence against the Roman authorities and a no less severe struggle with the false teachings which threatened to destroy the work of apostolic preaching from within.

Therefore as a synonym of presider and pastor, the title "bishop" revealed to the faithful that function of the ministry of presidency which was steadily acquiring special significance. These are just different names for one and the same ministry appearing in the Church from the moment of its inception and without which no local church could exist. However, each one of these titles partially discloses the essence of this ministry. In post-apostolic times those who preside over the churches revealed themselves as guardians and keepers of the right doctrine which the apostles handed down to the churches. The presidency and episcopacy are fully coterminous, for at the eucharistic assembly it is the bishops who preside, together with the people of God, offering a service to the one God and Father.

V. The Ministry of Assistance

1. All ministries were connected with each other, for each one was grounded in the charismatic gifts. The variety of gifts produced the variety of ministries but there was "the same Lord and . . . it is the same God who inspires them all in every one" (1 Cor 12.5–6). One ministry completed another and all of them were to some degree interwoven with the ministry of presidency. But the ministry which was most intimately connected with presidency was the ministry of assistance (*antilêmpsis*).[58] This ministry was necessary for the existence of the local church, but this necessity was of a different kind than the necessity for the ministry of presidency. No local church could exist without a presider, for without him the eucharistic assembly could not take place. But wherever the eucharistic assembly took place, there the ministry of assistance must have been found. The foundation of ecclesial life is love that finds its fullest expression in the eucharistic assembly, which is the manifestation of the Church in its fullness. Love is the common charism of the entire people of God and without love no ministry in the Church is possible. Without love any ministry is a "clanging cymbal" or "noisy gong," for without love one gains nothing. That is why love is a "more excellent way." "So faith, hope, love abide, these three; but the greatest of these is love" (*meizôn de toutôn hê agapê*) (1 Cor 13.13). If any activity without love is nothing, love cannot exist without its active expression. "Love is patient and kind, . . . rejoices in the right, love bears all things, believes all things, hopes all things, endures all things" (1 Cor 13.4–7). Every member of the church must express actively his charism of love in all his or her action in the Church, for there is no life in the Church without love. The love that is characteristic of the Church finds in such assistance its manifestation, so that this function becomes a special ministry in the Church. Not neglecting an active love of one member of the Church to another, assistance is not a common ministry of all but rather a ministry of some through whom the love of all is manifest. In the early church individual charity either did not exist at all or in a very limited way. Instead, every member of the Church offered his gift of love to the eucharistic assembly. Out of these offerings a "treasury of love" was collected from which in turn the means for the work of assistance were taken. "If one member suffers, all suffer together" (1 Cor 12.26). This suffering was alleviated by the action of all through the one who was entrusted with the special ministry of assistance. For this reason, the charism of assistance was not among the gifts which were given to everyone—rather, it was given only to those who exercised this ministry.[59]

2. The ministry of assistance appeared in the Church quite early. It would be more precise to say that it appeared with the first eucharistic assembly. We have indisputable evidence that it was already present in the Jerusalem church in the early period of its existence. "Daily distribution to widows," mentioned in the sixth chapter of Acts, was one of the functions of this ministry. From Luke's narrative it clearly follows that the daily distribution to widows as well as the entire ministry of assistance was in firm connection with the eucharistic assembly. On the other hand, the same Luke again testifies that the "treasury of love" was managed by the apostles at first and then by presbyters (4.35; 11.30; 21.18). Whether the "seven" were future deacons or presbyters[60] one thing is certain. Rendering assistance was part of their ministry. If we accept the first assumption, the ministry of assistance becomes a separate ministry of specially ordained people. If, however, we stay with the second assumption, this ministry becomes connected to the ministry of presidency. But both in one and the other case it is bound up with the ministry of these individuals at the eucharistic assembly.[61]

In Paul's writings the ministry of assistance is presented no less clearly. He mentions this ministry in the list of ministries in the letter to Corinthians (1 Cor 12.28) and also in Romans (12.8). With respect to the latter some doubt may persist about whether Paul speaks here concerning a common charism of love or concerning a special ministry of assistance. The ministry of assistance is most distinctly presented in the inscription of the letter to Philippians: "Paul and Timothy, servants of Christ Jesus, to all the saints in Christ Jesus who are at Philippi, with the bishops and deacons" (*syn episkopois kai diakonois*). Here for the first time we encounter the term *diakonos* in its technical meaning. Deacons, mentioned alongside bishops, could not have been any other than the individuals referred to in the Pastoral letters. Also, Clement of Rome directly points out, in accordance with the Pastoral letters, that the apostles ordained deacons out of the first-fruits of the faithful.

What was the ministry that the deacons exercised on the basis of the letter to Philippians? The letter itself does not provide any indication, but the term "deacon" itself allows us to make the assumption that they fulfilled a "service" at the eucharistic assembly. They were "servants" at the assembly alongside those who presided. Ignatius of Antioch witnesses to this.[62] In the first centuries of church history, diaconal ministry suffered the least amount of change; thus Ignatius's witness can be extended to apostolic times as well. As "servants" at the bishop's side at the eucharistic assembly, which was the expression of love, deacons exercise this ministry of assistance not only with respect to material but spiritual needs as well. They took an active part in gathering the "treasury of love," accepting the offerings from the faithful. It was also they who from this treasury provided help for anyone in need. A reference to the ministry of assistance is found in the Pastoral letters (1 Tim 3.8–10) and in a negative form the same is spoken about in *The Shepherd of Hermas*: "[The stones] with spots are ministers (*diakonoi*) who ministered amiss, and devoured the living of widows and orphans, and made gain for themselves from the ministry which they had received to administer."[63] Nevertheless, the treasury of love was still administered by those who presided over the churches. They could not relinquish it, for their ministry of presidency was the most complete expression of love. For this reason very soon, if not from the very beginning, deacons became executors of the bishop's decisions in the area of assistance. This function was enhanced by their becoming the bishop's liturgical assistants. The dependence of diaconal ministry on the ministry of presidency evolved into the deacons themselves being dependent on the bishops. According to the *Apostolic Tradition* of Hippolytus of Rome the bishop alone lays hands upon a deacon at his ordination, for the latter is not ordained to be a priest but to be a bishop's servant in order to do whatever the bishop commands.[64]

3. Assistance was a charismatic ministry fulfilled by those who received special charismatic gifts. Stemming immediately from the eucharistic assembly, this ministry was found in all churches. Thus the churches had responsibility to take care that this ministry did not terminate in them. Deacons, like presiders, were ordained for their ministry by local churches from those chosen by God. The compiler of the *Didache* instructs the faithful to ordain bishops and deacons for themselves.[65] We find the description of diaconal ordination already in Hippolytus of Rome.

Given the nature of this activity, the ministry of deacons required a great deal of energy. From the third century on, in a number of canonical texts, the deacons are characterized as the eyes, ears, and hands of the bishops.[66] They watch over all things and report everything to him. The *Apostolic Tradition* directs the deacon to be always at his bishop's disposal. He must report to him all sick persons so that the bishop could come and visit them.[67] Given such mobility it is hard to imagine that deacons would be selected from the eldest members of the church. The deacon's activity required full command of his physical and spiritual powers as well as a number of moral qualities such as impartiality, unselfishness, and honesty. Thus the deacons were probably selected from the most respected members of the church, if not the eldest by age, then by faith, i.e., from the first-fruits of the faithful, as Clement of Rome said. If before their ordination they were not numbered among the presbyters, after ordination, at least in some churches, the deacons were included in the presbyterial college. The *Ecclesiastical Canons* provide some ground for this suggestion. There it is said that the number of presbyters must be even, in accordance with the indication in the book of Revelation; but at the same time it is prescribed that they not be two but three in number. A. Harnack supposed a copyist's error but the slip of such kind is hardly possible.[68] According to this text, at the ecclesial assembly half of the presbyters must be on the bishop's right and the other half on his left. If we pay attention to this note it would be clear why the text speaks about three presbyters on the bishop's right, because there were three deacons on the bishop's left. It follows that the compiler of the *Ecclesiastical Canons* numbered the deacons together with the presbyters. From a later period we have some evidence that deacons were included into the presbyterial college, but we have no certain proof that this was the case in all churches. At any rate, we have no ground to think that when deacons were chosen from among the presbyters broadly understood that they lost their honorary title. This is another proof of terminological instability in the early church which only gradually begins to wane.

Chapter 6

"The One Who
Offers Thanksgiving"

I. The Problem of the Origin of Bishop-Presbyters

1. And lo, a throne stood in heaven, with one seated on the throne! And he who sat there appeared like jasper and carnelian, and round the throne was a rainbow that looked like an emerald. Round the throne were twenty-four thrones, and seated on the thrones were twenty-four elders, clad in white garments, with golden crowns upon their heads. (Rev 4.2–4)

This vision of St. John the Theologian [in the Book of Revelation] brings to us the image of a eucharistic assembly.[1] From the very beginning at the eucharistic assembly a certain order was established in which the participants were placed in accordance with their status in the church. The witness to this is the letter of James, where it is shown that the order and arrangement of the assembly was sometimes violated in favor of worldly human interests.

For if a man with gold rings and in fine clothing comes into your assembly, and a poor man in shabby clothing also comes in, and you pay attention to the one who wears the fine clothing and say, "Have a seat here, please," while you say to the poor man, "Stand there," or, "Sit at my feet," have you not made distinctions among yourselves, and become judges with evil thoughts? (2.2–4)

If everyone at the eucharistic assembly occupied his own place it is more likely that the presbyters had certain places of their own which must have been in front of everybody else, since it was they, and nobody else, who presided over the churches.[2] The thrones of the elder-presbyters in Revelation correspond to the seats of the presbyters who presided over the eucharistic assembly. Then to what element in the eucharistic assembly does the throne of the One Who sat in the middle correspond? For Ignatius of Antioch this place belonged to a bishop, and after Ignatius's time it was the bishop who always took this place. This is also attested by the official record describing the confiscation of church property, indicated in the footnotes, as well as by all ancient liturgical rites. Is the same true for the apostolic times? At that time there were no bishops such as we find in Ignatius; rather, there were bishop-presbyters. However, this answer cannot be an absolutely exhaustive response to the question raised. We cannot disregard the fact that a central place at the eucharistic assembly existed from the very beginning, and that someone assumed it. Without this central place, the eucharistic assembly could not exist, and consequently without the figure that occupied this place, it could not exist as well. The single objection against this proposition is the alleged anarchy that characterized the churches in the apostolic times. But we have seen already that the anarchical character ascribed to the churches is a phantasy which finds no basis in the actual ecclesial situation of the apostolic times. However, the question still remains: Who *did* assume this central place? Was it a prophet, or a teacher, or one of bishop-presbyters, or, finally, one of the church members who did not even possess any special ministry? With a remarkable consensus the church tradition associates the origin of the episcopate with the apostolic times. Should we disregard this tradition? If perchance we accept it, should we follow scholastic theology in accepting, in spite of our own knowledge, that the episcopal ministry that is traced back to the apostolic times was essentially identical with the ministry established in the third or fourth century, let alone with what it contains today? Put otherwise, the still pending question is whether in the apostolic times there existed a predecessor of the bishop or whether such a figure existed at all. The answer to the question of who in the apostolic times assumed a central place at the eucharistic assembly depends on this.

2. In approximately the second half of the second century we find in the majority, if not in all the local churches, bishops who have a ministry that is distinct from the presbyters. If to the bishops the title "presbyters" is still applied, the latter are no longer called bishops, as it was the case in the apostolic times. In a local church, there is only one bishop. If we turn to general church history, we will not find there any abrupt changes in any area of the church life, especially in the area concerned with the church organization. If reforms of such a sort were ever imposed upon church life, they were usually accompanied by a fierce struggle. Changes in the life of the church happen slowly and imperceptibly to ordinary consciousness. The changes that take place in the course of this process can be very significant but in their starting point they necessarily have a foundation in the past. Nothing new was created in the church *ex abrupto*, rather, anything new was based in the preceding tradition. If in the second half of the second century we observe the existence of a monarchical episcopate in local churches, we have to ask how it could have been founded, accepted, and become a basis of the ecclesial organization if prior to this time it did not exist. It would have been an unprecedented revolution in church life. If this revolution indeed had taken place, undoubtedly some evidence of the struggle which accompanied it would also have come down to us. No such evidence exists except for some hints at the rivalry between bishops and prophets where the prophets rather than the bishops were championing innovation. Likewise, we do not find any traces of struggles between presbyters and bishops, if again we exclude some controversy between the former and the latter in Alexandria, and, it seems, only there. Therefore we have to admit that the episcopate which we discover in the second century must have had its nucleus in the preceding period, i.e., in apostolic times. Where must we search for this nucleus?

The New Testament presbyter-bishops were neither bishops nor presbyters but bishop-presbyters and nothing else. However important it is to clarify their position in the original local churches, it is even more important to clarify their origins in those churches. Traditional scholastic teaching that the three-rank hierarchy was established by Christ himself is a dogmatic statement grown out of theological speculation which has no connection with the historical fabric of the church life. Indeed, it has no need to have this connection. This position cannot be proven with historical evidence. It is more correct to say, as do some Roman Catholic theologians, that the church hierarchy is divinely established. This is more accurate, since while this statement cannot be proven historically, neither can it be disproved. Nevertheless, this theological axiom does not remove the question of when the church hierarchy came into existence. Both axioms can be accurate, if understood ecclesiologically. However, it is precisely our theological thought nowadays that has separated most of the issues from ecclesiology. Hence, the question of the origins of the ministry of presbyter-bishops remains without answer.

Attempts to explain the emergence of the bishop-presbyter's ministry through a borrowing from Jewish or pagan institutions have been futile.[3] Early Christianity possessed such a creative force that it could create within itself anything that it needed. Surely, one can attempt to disintegrate Christianity, like a composite chemical body, into its constituent elements, but such analysis does not bring us closer to an understanding of Christianity, for it leaves us nothing with which to deal. Any analogies between Christianity and what we find in the pagan or Jewish worlds are nearly always dubious. For the most part, these are based on evidence coming from the Christian era. Even if in some instances we can assert with certainty that what we find in the Christian era had already existed, we never can be sure in what form and with what content. If we acknowledge the influence of the ancient non-Christian world upon the Christian world, we also have to acknowledge the influence in the opposite direction, for osmosis can never go in one direction only. Given that we cannot always be certain about the dating of some of the texts, we can never be sure about the direction in which the borrowing proceeded. Christianity found a niche for itself in the Judeo-Christian world to which it was unwillingly trying to adjust. There is no doubt that this world exerted some influence on Christian thought, but this influence was external, not intrinsic. Most importantly, it was not significant enough to serve as an explanation for the form and content of Christianity. This is also true with respect to the church's organization. If the very concept of the Church is a mere secondary phenomenon, then the organization of the Church is also a result of the mutual influence of different factors, none of which were grounded in the teaching of Christ.[4] In its naked form this point of view is absolutely unacceptable for us today. Yet in its latent and mitigated form it still continues to determine the process of our research. Not only can the Church not be called a phenomenon secondary to Christ, it cannot even be called a primary one. Whoever says "the Church" says "Christ," and whoever says "Christ" says "the Church." That is why there is no understanding of Christ and consequently no understanding of Christianity in all its fullness apart from the ecclesiological approach. We cannot regard a single aspect of Christian life apart from the Church, for not a single manifestation of Christianity ever existed apart from the Church. The form of early Christian life as presented to us from the scarce evidence we possess is totally conditioned by the image of the Church. There is no doubt that the terms "presbyter" and "bishop" were borrowed by Christians from the contemporary world. But the fact that these terms were borrowed does not mean that the respective institutions defined by these terms were borrowed as well. We are well aware that in apostolic times there existed among the Christians those designated by the terms "presbyter-bishops" or even "bishops and presbyters." However, no inquiry into the terms themselves is capable of elucidating the place these individuals occupied in the Christian life of that age. These individuals existed in the local churches and for the local churches. Thus it is only from within the Church itself that we are able to determine the place that they occupied and the functions that they fulfilled for the local churches. This does not mean that we have to introduce in an arbitrary fashion any *a priori* concepts or theological formulae which did not exist at that time. But this does mean that we find ourselves on the same ground from which these concepts and formulae have grown and developed. We are legitimate in completing the lack of our historical evidence by the evidence the Church provides for us. This approach in no way diminishes the historical value and objectivity of our research in the area of early Christianity, for the Church itself is a fact of history.

II. Jewish and Christian *Chabûrah*

In fulfillment of the promise given to the Twelve (Matt 16.18) Christ founded the Church by instituting the Eucharist at the Last Supper.[5] The Last Supper was not the only meal Christ had with his disciples, but it was the last meal of his earthly life.[6] "And he said to them, 'I have earnestly desired to eat this Passover with you before I suffer; for I tell you I shall not eat it until it is fulfilled in the kingdom of God'" (Lk 22.15–16). In the course of his earthly life Christ had numerous meals with his disciples and participated in the meals to which he was invited. "The Son of man came eating and drinking, and they say, 'Behold, a glutton and a drunkard, a friend of tax collectors and sinners!'" (Matt 11.19). We know what great significance meals on Sabbaths and feasts had in the life of the Jews. No pious Jew, whatever rank he might occupy or how poor he might be, could violate the general law regarding meals. These meals brought all the family together and all the members of the family participated in them. We do not know anything about Christ's family meals in the course of his earthly ministry. In these years of Christ's life he was constantly accompanied by his Twelve, whose institution was one of the first acts in his ministry.[7] From the beginning until the night at Gethsemane they were with him and lived a common life with him. For his sake they left everything behind and followed him.[8]

> Peter began to say to him, "Lo, we have left everything and followed you." Jesus said, "Truly, I say to you, there is no one who has left house or brothers or sisters or mother or father or children or lands, for my sake and for the gospel . . ." (Mk 10.28–29)

These words of Christ refer primarily to the Church but at the same time they define the manner in which the Twelve were related to Christ. Christ confirms the words of Peter, who in the name of the Twelve witnessed that they left everything behind and followed him. Due to this fact the disciples' following after Christ was an exceptional event and differed from the ordinary manner in which disciples followed a rabbi. Christ accepted from others the title of *rabbi* and even applied it to himself (Matt 26.18). But he had no school and was not brought up "at the feet" of some renowned rabbi of that time, as was the apostle Paul (Acts 22.3). He was not appointed as rabbis were and did not receive through human succession the spirit of Moses, for Christ was higher than the Torah. He opposed to the Law his own *I*: "You have heard that it was said to the men of old . . . But I say to you . . ." (Matt 5). Having followed him, his disciples formed a fraternity which was unique by its internal content while by its external form it was similar to other fraternities that existed at that time among the Jews. The fraternities of this kind bore the name of *chabûrah*, plural *chabûrôth*, deriving from the word *chaber*, meaning "friend."[9] Common upbringing in the Law and charity were the goals of such fraternities. The fraternities found their fullest expression at meals organized by the members on Sabbaths or feast days. The ritual of these meals coincided with the ritual of household meals. The fraternity itself was a household of a sort or a family built upon the principles of friendship which bound all of its members. The senior member of the fraternity took upon himself the role of the head of the household. Jewish meals had a religious character. Sabbath and festal meals were sacred rites. The "thanksgiving" over bread and over wine, an essential part of these meals, was always done by one person. At household meals it was the master of the house who "offered thanksgiving." In *chabûrah*, it was the one who presided over the fraternity. The liturgical functions of the one who "offered thanksgiving" derived from his status in the family or in the fraternity, not conversely, for neither he nor the members of fraternity usually belonged to the priesthood.

One can certainly argue against the existence of *chabûrôth* in the time of Christ's earthly life. One can doubt that Christ and his disciples indeed formed such a fraternity, but all this argument would amount to controversy about how this fraternity was named rather than about the fact that the fraternity of Christ and his disciples really existed. Finally, one could eliminate this issue altogether and regard Christ individually. But to take such point of view would mean to eliminate the whole of evangelical history. Beyond any doubt, Christ had meals with his disciples where he was the one who "offered thanksgiving."

Established at the Last Supper, the Church was actualized on the day of Pentecost,[10] when the meal of the disciples became a eucharistic assembly. Christ's fraternity on earth did not cease to exist with the end of his earthly life. In the course of his earthly life Christ was always present with his disciples, but after the descent of the Spirit, they came to be "in Christ." Christ's fraternity, his *chabûrah*, became the Church. In this Christian *chabûrah* it was the *disciples* who would break the bread and bless the cup. The bread which they broke is the bread which Christ broke at the Last Supper, and the cup which they blessed is the cup which Christ blessed. "For as often as you eat this bread (*ton arton touton*) and drink this cup (*to potêrion*), you proclaim the Lord's death until he comes" (1 Cor 11.26). The Eucharist that the disciples celebrated until he comes is the continuing of the last evening meal of Christ. As he was present with the disciples at the Last Supper, so he is present with the disciples at the eucharistic assembly in the eucharistic gifts. "This is my body . . . This cup is the new covenant in my blood" (1 Cor 11.24–25). In the Eucharist that the Church celebrates, Christ is present in the fullness and unity of his body, and through the eucharistic gifts his disciples come to be "in Christ." In the eucharistic assembly the Church as the body of Christ is realized in all its fullness.

The Church was actualized at the first eucharistic assembly. We do not possess a full description of the eucharistic assembly in the New Testament. We do not even have any indication of *who* in fact presided at the eucharistic assembly in apostolic times. Merely on the basis of one remark (Acts 20.11) we know that it was Paul who presided at the eucharistic assembly in Troas, but the Acts are silent on the issue of who presided at the Eucharist before and after Paul. This is not a unique instance when texts do not provide us with what we could have expected. However sad it is for us, we have to admit that this kind of omission on the part of the New Testament writers is absolutely natural. In most instances this omission concerns the aspects which were quite clear to their contemporaries but have become most cryptic for us. Any one of the faithful who took part in the eucharistic assembly was acquainted with its procedure. Thus not only Paul but even Luke, in spite of the historical characteristics of his work, fails to mention anything about it. Touching upon the very first moments in the history of the church in Jerusalem, only fleetingly does Luke mention the "breaking of bread," leaving the modern reader somewhat puzzled as to what he is talking about. Luke fails to mention how the first eucharistic assemblies proceeded or who stood at the head of them. He certainly might not have known that, for he did not witness the first days of the Jerusalem church and the sources which he used may not have contained this information. However, he knew how the Eucharist was celebrated in the time he was writing and he might have included this in the first chapters of the Acts. It is precisely because he, like all of his contemporaries, knew how it was celebrated that he did not speak about it but dwelled rather on such aspects as the sharing of possessions, which did not exist in the churches outside of Palestine.[11] We are capable of filling in this blind spot from the evidence of our sources. Surely not to the extent that Luke's contemporaries did, but in some respects we know how the Eucharist was celebrated in the church of Jerusalem. The first eucharistic assembly on the day of Pentecost was an exact repetition of Christ's Last Supper. There cannot be any doubt or hesitation on this point. The "Lord's Supper" was done in exactly the same way that the Lord himself did in the course of his earthly life. The only question, although the most essential one, is, who at the eucharistic assembly occupied the place Christ did at the Last Supper? While there can be some doubt about who stood at the head of eucharistic assembly in the churches founded by Paul, prophets, *didaskaloi*, or other individuals, there can be no such doubt about the first eucharistic assembly. At that point in the life of the Jerusalem church it had no prophets or teachers, but it had the Twelve who became apostles, and probably a very small group of disciples. The earthly fellowship with Christ did not cease to exist. The apostles continued to view their fellowship as the continuation of Christ's *chabûrah*, which became the Church. Only Peter, whom Christ was preparing for this role, could be the senior member of this fellowship. Due to this it was he and none other from the midst of the apostles who at the eucharistic assembly took the same place which Christ took at the Last Supper. He was the first who "offered thanksgiving" at the first eucharistic assembly. He was the one who "offered thanksgiving" when the Church of God in Christ was actualized for the first time. The rest of the apostles took the places which they occupied at the Last Supper.

The first eucharistic assembly was definitive for the organization of the Church. The eucharistic assembly is the ecclesiological continuation of the Last Supper. Just as the Last Supper is one and unique, so also the eucharistic assembly is one and unique. In space and time there exists not a multiplicity of eucharistic assemblies but a single one, identical with the first eucharistic assembly headed by Peter. Therefore the ecclesiastical organization, also being established at the first eucharistic assembly, remains in its core unique and unshaken. The apostle Peter was not a super-apostle who would have stood above the apostles and also consequently above the Church. Next to him stood other apostles who were as much the apostles as he was. He was merely the first one or the senior among them and consequently he could not be without them because otherwise he would have ceased to be the senior among the apostles. It is precisely due to this status of his that he became the one who "offered thanksgiving" at the first eucharistic assembly. By this it was immediately determined that the one who "offered thanksgiving" at the eucharistic assembly was always the same person, just as it used to be at Jewish household meals and the *chabûrah* meals. At the same time it was determined that the same person stands at the head of the local church. Peter became the head of the church in Jerusalem, but presiding in it belonged not to him only, but to all the apostles who together with him occupied the first places at the eucharistic assembly. Even with the scarce evidence that Luke provides, the position of St. Peter in the Jerusalem church is very clear. He pronounced the first homily at the descent of the Spirit. Even when he speaks out alone he speaks not in his own name but in the name of the apostles as the first or the senior presider of the Jerusalem church. In the first period of the church's existence in Jerusalem the ministry of administration in the broadest sense of the term did not belong to St. Peter only, but to all the apostles.

The position of St. Peter and of the rest of the apostles in the Jerusalem church answers the question which we have not yet raised, but which is pending nevertheless. We have stated above that in the early local churches there were several presiders rather than one. This is naturally bound to cause some confusion. The early churches were so few in number and administration in them was not as complicated an issue as it became later. It could easily have been done by one presider. If there were few of them this was only because it was "as in all the churches of the saints" (*hôs en pasais tais ekklêsiais tôn hagiôn*) (1 Cor 14.33). Thus it was from the very beginning in the church of Jerusalem. And it was so there because it was that way at the first eucharistic assembly, having been established by the Lord who during his earthly life chose the Twelve rather than one. In the Church of God in Christ there must be only one who "offers thanksgiving," but there must be several who "preside in the Lord."

III. The "Seven" of the Jerusalem Church and Their Ministry

1. The actualization of the Church in Jerusalem was at the same time the building up of the local Jerusalem church. Empirically the Church of God is not realized through one local church but through the plurality of them. The goal of the apostolic ministry was the building up (*oikodomê*) of this plurality of local churches. "It is not right (*ouk areston estin*) that we should give up preaching the word of God to serve tables (*diakonein trapezais*)" (Acts 6.2). Peter's words here were spoken in the name of the Twelve. The moment must have been coming in the life of the Jerusalem church when the apostles had to relinquish their administrative role in it, for its "building up" was complete. When did it happen in this church, and did it happen immediately or was it a gradual process? Only with Luke, the historian of the early church, can we seek an answer to this question. Unfortunately, his meager evidence and somewhat imprecise chronology make our task extremely difficult.[12]

Luke tells about the apostolic institution of the "seven" but relates nothing concerning the institution of the presbyterial ministry which makes an unexpected appearance in Acts 11.30. Why did Luke deem it necessary to provide information concerning the establishment of the "seven," usually considered to be the predecessors of future deacons, and why was he silent about the establishment of presbyters? We are not capable of answering this question. The only suggestion which one could make is that Luke did not so much intend to relate the story concerning the institution of the "seven," but to mark some point of transition in the history of the Jerusalem church.

It is entirely obvious from Luke's narrative that, before the institution of the "seven," the "serving of the tables" (*diakonia trapezais*) was exercised by the apostles themselves.[13] This is witnessed by Peter's words, cited above. According to Luke's testimony the decision of the apostles to appoint seven men to serve the tables was caused by the murmuring of the Hellenists,[14] "because their widows were neglected in the daily distribution" (*en tê diakonia tê kathêmerinê*) (Acts 6.1). From these remarks of Luke, does it follow that *diakonia trapezais* and *diakonia katêmerinê* were identical?[15] It is hard to give a categorical answer to this question because in the New Testament the term *diakonia* encompassed various ministries starting with the ministry of the apostles. We can outline a more or less probable answer after trying to define the meaning of "serving the tables." In this attempt we must proceed from the concept of eucharistic assembly.

At Jewish meals, both family meals and the meals of *chabûrah*, there used to be a person who served at the meal, especially if the participants were reclining. In the wealthy households a specially designated person such as a servant or a slave was the one who served. But more regularly it was the youngest participant who served at the meal. At the meals which Christ had with his disciples it was probably the apostle John, the youngest of the Twelve, but at the Last Supper Christ himself was the one "who served." "For which is the greater, one who sits at table, or one who serves (*ho diakonôn*)? Is it not the one who sits at table? But I am among you as one who serves (*ho diakonôn*)." (Lk 22.27; cf. Mk 10.45) It would be utterly incorrect to limit Christ's "serving" to the washing of the feet, not related by the Synoptics. At the Last Supper Christ was indeed "the one who serves," the role previously exercised by John. Being faithful to the Teacher's word: "Whoever would be great among you must be your servant (*diakonos*)" (Mk 10.43), the apostles served at the eucharistic assembly. The rapid growth of the church in Jerusalem required several servants at the Eucharist. Apparently soon enough this service of the tables became additionally complicated with the distribution of aid to widows and poor members of the church. This distribution was connected to the eucharistic assembly and consequently to the "service of the tables," for the eucharistic assembly was both a meal and a "treasury of love." The offerings of the faithful formed special funds intended for constant aid to the poor members of the church. Luke indicates that the distribution to the widows occurred every day. It is hard to say with certainty what this meant. At any rate, one must not think that the eucharistic assembly occurred on a daily basis. We have every reason to suppose that it took place on the "first day of the week." The *agape* meals, distinct from the eucharistic assembly, did not yet exist in Jerusalem at that time. Therefore we should take the Lucan reference to "daily distribution" either in the sense of widows receiving their aid every day or in the sense of different widows, one after another, receiving their aid for the whole week.[16] Hence the "service of the tables" was not identical with the "daily distribution."

It follows from Luke's narrative that "daily distribution" was at least one of the reasons why the apostles decided to commit the service of the tables to specially appointed people. Luke testifies that a murmur arose among the Hellenists against the Jews that their widows were neglected at "daily distribution." The verbal form *paretheôrounto* indicates that the murmur of Hellenists was a more or less usual occurrence. For us, the very fact of their dissatisfaction is more important than the question that we cannot answer, namely why the "neglect" of the Hellenist widows could take place. Luke connects this event with the increase in the number of the disciples: "In these days when the disciples were increasing in number . . ." The only explanation to this connection is that the disciples were increasing by means of the indigent inhabitants of Jerusalem. If it was so, the increase in number had changed the original composition of the Jerusalem church. Its basic background consisted of Galileans who after the first homilies were joined by a large number of Hellenists. Considering themselves to be a more privileged part of the church, the Jerusalemites could have demanded special treatment at the "daily distribution," and this demand might have caused some opposition from the Hellenists. There is no ground for seeking in the Lucan narrative what is not expressed directly and to regard it as a hidden expression of a doctrinal conflict between Jews and Hellenists in the church of Jerusalem.[17] But nevertheless it is admissible for us to think that it was the usual split between Hellenists and Jews within Judaism itself that was underlying the disquiet about the distribution of aid. To what extent the apostles themselves were a reason for disquiet on the

Hellenists' part, we are unable to tell. It is possible that the apostles did not always distribute the aid themselves, but entrusted some members of the church in Jerusalem to do it in their name who, probably, gave more attention to the Jewish widows, than to the Hellenist ones. In any case, the dissatisfaction was a fact, and the apostles acknowledged it; but to say that they acknowledged the dissatisfaction of Hellenists as well-founded,[18] would be a rather risky assumption.[19]

At the suggestion of the apostles, the Jerusalem church[20] elected seven men "of good repute, full of Spirit and of wisdom" (Acts 6.3). Luke reports to us the names of the "seven," one of whom was a proselyte and the names of the others were of Greek origin. For this reason one can never be sure that all of them were Hellenists, since Palestinian Jews just as the diaspora Jews very often took Greek or Latin names.[21] But if they indeed were Hellenists, it means that at the time of the election of the "seven" the Hellenists were still a dominant force in the church of Jerusalem while the Jerusalemites, as we pointed out above, were a rather new element in it. Perhaps it is more accurate to suggest that the "seven" included, with the exception of the proselyte Nicolaus, both Jews and Hellenists.[22] In connection to this we should point at verse 7, where Luke again mentions the increase of the disciples in number, indicating that Jewish priests happened to be among them for the first time. If verse 7 is indeed in its right place, then it does not indicate the strengthening of the Hellenistic current in the Jerusalem church after the appointment of the "seven," but its weakening, which further on led to the predomination of the Jewish current.[23]

The "seven" were ordained to "serve the tables," which included the "daily distribution" of aid. Thus their ministry closely resembles that of deacons. The church tradition does not have a very stable position with respect to the connection between the ministry of deacons and the ministry of the "seven." If the West insists on this connection,[24] in the East the council of Trullo solemnly rejected it,[25] citing the commentary of John Chrysostom which stated that the church of Jerusalem, at the time when the "seven" were ordained, did not have the rank of deacons nor of priests and bishops but only the apostles.[26] This remark of John Chrysostom is absolutely correct if we take it as referring to the time before the ordination of the "seven." Until this moment the church in Jerusalem had only apostles, but after that ordination apart from the apostles, it came to have also the "seven." In order to elucidate the status of the "seven" in the church itself we need to turn again to eucharistic assembly. The "daily distribution" was a function of a larger "ministry at the meals" that took place at the eucharistic assembly. The apostles committed to the "seven" their own ministry, which they originally fulfilled in the church of Jerusalem. Did the apostles commit the whole of their ministry or just a portion of it?

What were the places that the "seven" began to occupy at the eucharistic assembly? This second question is bound up with the first, for one's place at the eucharistic assembly depended on the ministry that one fulfilled in the church, just as conversely one's ministry in the church depended on the place which one occupied at the eucharistic assembly. These two questions are extremely important for understanding the ecclesial organization of the apostolic times and in particular for defining the status of the "seven" in the Jerusalem church.

2. Providing the narrative on the institution of the "seven" Luke fails to mention anything on the institution of the presbyters. But also according to him all churches had presbyters in the time of Paul. Their ordination in the churches that Paul founded was not a novelty but was already based on church tradition (Acts 14.23). The Pastoral letters of Paul, referring to the bishops-presbyters, leave the same impression. When and by whom were the presbyters instituted? The New Testament seems not to give us any indication in this respect. The first indication that can shed some light upon the origin of the presbyterial ministry is only found in the age when the special episcopal ministry begins to take shape, namely in the letters of Ignatius.

> See that you all follow the bishop, as Jesus Christ follows the Father, and the presbytery as the apostles. And reverence the deacons as the command of God.[27]

> Be zealous to do all things in harmony with God, with the bishop presiding in the place of God and the presbyters in the place of the council of the apostles, and the deacons, who are most dear to me, entrusted with the service (*diakonian*) of Jesus Christ . . .[28]

> Let all respect the deacons as Jesus Christ, even as the bishop is also a type of the Father, and the presbyters as the council of God and the college of apostles.[29]

Not once have scholars paid attention to these excerpts from the letters of Ignatius but they have underestimated their significance, mainly utilizing them as a proof that Ignatius did not know the doctrine of the apostolic succession of bishops. Meanwhile, these excerpts are extremely important regardless of whether Ignatius knew the doctrine of apostolic succession. We must not forget that from the very beginning the church of Antioch had strong ties with the church of Jerusalem. Palestinian traditions penetrated it at quite an early stage. They became more intense with the fall of Jerusalem, as not a few Palestinian Christians emigrated to Antioch. If there were any place where they would know fully about the first days of the Jerusalem church, it would be the church of Antioch. Taking this into consideration, we have to give the words of Ignatius the status of historical evidence.

The excerpts from the letters of Ignatius cited above should be read in the context of the eucharistic assembly. At the assembly the bishop occupied the central place, surrounded by the seats of the presbyters, while deacons fulfilled the ministry of Christ. In his description, did Ignatius have in mind the eucharistic assembly of the church in Jerusalem or the Last Supper? Probably both, since he was certainly aware that the first eucharistic assemblies of the Jerusalem church exactly repeated the order of the Last Supper. An indication of this is Ignatius's stating that deacons are entrusted with the service (*diakonian*) of Christ. It is clear that he could not have thought that the deacons were to fulfill the earthly ministry of Christ. Deacons at the eucharistic assembly exercised the same ministry which Christ put on himself at the Last Supper. They were "servants" at the assembly. That is what Ignatius meant in his exhortation to revere deacons as "the command of God" (*hôs Theou entolên*),[30] having in mind the command of Christ (Mk 10.43). The presbyters in turn as a college (*hôs syndesmon*) occupied the seats of the apostles at the eucharistic assembly. Where did the presbyters first assume the seats of the apostles? It could have happened only in the church of Jerusalem. Ignatius was thinking of its first eucharistic assemblies which were the type of the Last Supper. At these assemblies the apostles were seated around the apostle Peter, who "offered thanksgiving." Ignatius bears witness to the fact that at some point in its history the apostles' seats were taken by presbyters. This circumstance must be our starting point in the question on the origin of presbyters, especially since the ministries in the early church were always matched to certain places at the eucharistic assembly.

3. Coming back to Acts again, first of all we have to ask whether this text has any evidence that would confirm the conclusion made on the basis of the evidence from the letters of Ignatius. The first excerpt from Acts which we can cite in support of our theory is the following one:

> And the disciples determined, every one according to his ability, to send relief (*eis diakonian pempsai*) to the brethren who lived in Judea; and they did so, sending it to the elders by the hand of Barnabas and Saul. (11.29–30)[31]

According to Luke's testimony, the church of Antioch sent the aid that it had gathered to the presbyters, not to the apostles, as we might have expected on the basis of 4.36–37: "Thus Joseph who was surnamed by the apostles Barnabas . . . sold a field which belonged to him, and brought the money and laid it at the apostles' feet." The means of support were initially in the hands of the apostles. This, as we have seen, derived from the place that they took at the eucharistic assembly. Acts 4.37 confirms the evidence of 6.2, which speaks about the "service of the tables." Why did Barnabas and Saul not put what they had gathered in the church of Antioch "at the apostles' feet"? The simplest answer is that there were no apostles at that time in Jerusalem, but this answer is a theory which can hardly be supported by the evidence in Acts. When did Paul and Barnabas come to Jerusalem? Was it before or after the persecution of Herod spoken about in chapter 12? The question remains unanswered. When did the famine which Luke attributes to the reign of the emperor Claudius really take place? If it indeed happened under this emperor it was in the years 47–49, while Herod Agrippas I, apparently the one spoken about in the twelfth chapter, died in 44 AD. Almost all the chronological dating of Luke is dubious.[32] From Luke's indication in 12.17, the apostle Peter left Jerusalem during the persecution of Agrippas. But we see Peter again with other apostles at the time of the "Apostolic council." It is more likely to suggest that, as it seems to follow from Luke's text, Peter and some of the apostles were at Jerusalem when Paul and Barnabas arrived there. Even if they were not, this does not change anything. In both cases the presbyters referred to in Acts 11.30 were fulfilling the ministry which the apostles exercised before. It is inevitable that we have to make a connection with what Luke relates in 6.2.

The second excerpt from Acts which we can adduce in favor of our suggestion is the following: "When we had come to Jerusalem, the brethren received us gladly. On the following day Paul went in with us to James; and all the presbyters were present" (21.17–18). This excerpt confirms what Luke said in 11.30. Acts 6.2, 11.30, and 21.17–18 are all connected with each other. This connection indicates that the institution of the "seven" is not a random episode unrelated to Luke's ensuing narrative. However the sending of aid to the presbyters which Luke mentions in 11.30 was not random event caused by some special circumstances. Rather it was bound up with the ministry of presbyters.[33] Having originated before the time to which Acts 11.30 is referring, the ministry of presbyters is presented here as a permanent one. At the time of Paul's arrival in Jerusalem with the collection from the churches (chapter 21) the apostles had long since been absent. There can be no doubt that the presbyters received from the apostles their entire ministry in the church of Jerusalem after the latter's final departure from the city.

Thus Ignatius's remarks about presbyters correspond with the remarks found in Acts. The difference lies in a difference of approach toward the presbyterate. Luke regarded the presbyters from the perspective of their ministry in the church of Jerusalem while Ignatius indicated the place they occupied at the eucharistic assembly. We must not forget, however, that a place at the eucharistic assembly always corresponded with a ministry, while the ministry was expressed by means of a place which the person took at the assembly.

4. Can we establish when the ministry of presbyters in the Jerusalem church emerged? It has been pointed out above that Luke's chronology is quite vague and at times erroneous. The restoration of the chronological sequence of events in Acts is a daunting and hardly feasible task, unless we resort to restructuring the whole Lucan material.[34] Such attempts are always dubious and arbitrary. We do not have to take upon ourselves this entire task. It will suffice if we just try to pinpoint major stages in the development of the church organization in Jerusalem.

When the apostles instituted the office of the "seven" they committed to them the "service of the tables" which they previously fulfilled. What exactly did Luke mean by the "service of the tables"? We saw above that the "daily distribution" to the widows was among its functions, but it was merely one of the functions. If we were able to define this "service of the tables," we would know exactly the place the "seven" took at the eucharistic assembly. Luke gives no indication for us in this question, so we inevitably have to resort to one hypothesis or another. Until the institution of the "seven," the apostles occupied first places at the eucharistic assembly. Using later terminology, they were "in the first seats" (*prôtokathedritai*), while the apostle Peter as the one who "offered thanksgiving" took the place in the center. If the "seven" were "servants" at the meals, in the narrow sense of the word, the order of the eucharistic assembly should not have suffered changes. All of the apostles would have remained in their seats while the "seven" must have taken the seats positioned directly after the apostolic ones. As this hypothesis stands, the "seven" would have fulfilled, to a certain degree, a future diaconal ministry. This hypothesis possesses a great degree of probability, since the institution of the "servants" at the tables would have restored the normal order of Jewish meals. However, the transmission by the apostles of a portion of their ministry created the possibility that in certain circumstances their whole ministry might be transmitted to other individuals. Those same "seven" would have been such individuals and therefore initially not only would they have been future deacons but future presbyters as well.[35] After the killing of Stephen the "seven" were pressed to depart from Jerusalem. Luke reports that "they were all (*pantes*) scattered throughout the region of Judea and Samaria, except the apostles" (8.1). We have no grounds for questioning this statement. The dispersion of Christians from Jerusalem did not happen right after the killing of Stephen but came as a result of persecution, which followed the killing and is described in verse 3 of the same chapter. There is no need to correct the text of Luke in the sense that "all" in this passage does not refer to all members of the church in Jerusalem, but merely to Hellenist Christians. We have no ground to think that Jewish authorities treated the Jewish Christians somehow differently than Hellenist Christians. The trial of Stephen revealed the Christian attitude toward the Law and the temple, which without doubt was not a personal opinion of Stephen or of a group of Hellenist Christians, but rather was shared by all members of the Jerusalem church. Neither was the speech of Stephen a manifestation of his Hellenism. We do not find the opinions voiced by Stephen in Hellenistic Judaism. Since the discovery of the Qumran documents we have known that the adherents of this sect expressed an attitude toward the temple identical to Stephen's. Leaving aside the question of the influence of the Qumran doctrines on Stephen, we have reason rather to think that his views were based on the teaching of Christ himself. The fact that the apostles, according to Luke's report, stayed in Jerusalem, is not hard to believe. They could have easily remained unnoticed in Jerusalem when it was abandoned by all other members of the Jerusalem church.

The persecution was a short-term one and the Jerusalem Christians returned to the city. At the same time, apparently, the departure of the "seven" was final, for they probably did not consider it safe to stay in Jerusalem. Again, their refusal to return to Jerusalem was not connected to their "Hellenism" but rather to the status which Stephen and the rest of the "seven" had in the Jerusalem church. Upon the return of Christians to the city the apostles could have easily decided not to restore the ministry of the "seven" and to assume again the "service of the tables" themselves. But certainly they also could have appointed new individuals in place of the "seven" who left Jerusalem. Here we are in the realm of speculation, for Luke tells nothing about it. If the latter hypothesis is correct, the institution of the apostles must be dated to the time the apostles themselves dispersed from Jerusalem after the "Apostolic Council." James the brother of the Lord took the place of Peter, the place of the one who "offered thanksgiving," while the individuals who received the designation of presbyters took the rest of the apostles' seats. It seems that in accordance with Luke's testimony (12.17) this should have happened immediately after the killing of St. James and the release of Peter from chains. But in that case we have to admit that chapter 15 is not in its proper place and that its place must be somewhere between chapters 8 and 12. We have indicated above that this way of resolving different problems in the text is highly doubtful. Besides, it is hard to imagine that the apostles would not take care in advance that normal life would continue in case of their departure from Jerusalem. However, Luke reports that Peter asked that a message be sent to James concerning his release from prison and his departure. This might have meant that Peter was bestowing his ministry on James, i.e., that he passed onto him the place of the one who "offers thanksgiving" at the eucharistic assembly, while James himself ordained presbyters in place of other apostles. It might seem possible, if this manner of passing on the ministries in private were indeed permitted in the early church.

If the dispersion of apostles occurred after the council of Jerusalem, the difficulties indicated above are in part eliminated. Leaving Jerusalem, the apostles took care of those who would continue their ministry in the church there which, upon the apostles' proposal, (cf. 6.2) could have elected James in place of the one who "offers thanksgiving" and the presbyters in place of the other apostles. The most serious objection to this theory is that it necessitates that we acknowledge that the institution of presbyters occurred in the churches founded by Paul in accordance with Luke's testimony (14.23) rather than in the church of Jerusalem, or else that the presbyters were first instituted by Barnabas in the church of Antioch. Both suggestions are highly unlikely, for both Paul and Barnabas were men of tradition and would hardly have introduced in their churches something that had no foundation in the church of Jerusalem.

5. We can propose one more theory concerning the date of the origin of presbyters. Establishing the ministry of the "seven," the apostles conceded to them their own places at the eucharistic assembly. This means that the apostles fully passed onto them their ministry in the church of Jerusalem. This theory does not raise any serious objections. Certainly one may refer to the fact that even after the institution of the "seven," the apostles stayed for some time in the church of Jerusalem and therefore it is unlikely that they had passed on their leadership in it to other people. We have to note that even having passed on their original ministry in the Jerusalem church to the "seven," they did not cease to be the apostles and continued to enjoy an exceptional position in it. Without doubt they had influence upon the affairs of the Jerusalem church, especially on those concerned with the issues of Christian mission among the Jews and Gentiles. At the "Apostolic council" Peter's opinion was one of the decisive factors. The very fact that the apostles ceased to be immediate leaders of the church in Jerusalem cannot be viewed as unique. Not once were the apostles in such a position in the course of their activity. The evidence of Acts does not in any way contradict this supposition. Rather, the general impression with which Luke's narrative leaves us speaks in favor of the view that upon the institution of the "seven" the apostles ceased to play the role in the Jerusalem church which they had before. Undoubtedly it was not Peter but James who presided at the "Apostolic council."

On the other hand, this theory is more attractive than the first one since it explains the apostles' decision to institute the "seven," not only relying on the outside circumstances of the life of the church, but also on the task of the apostolic ministry itself. The "building up" of the church in Jerusalem was finished. The apostles were facing the task of preaching the word of God, i.e., of the "building up" of other local churches. They could not dedicate themselves in permanent ministry to only one local church, even if it was the Jerusalem church, and neglect the ministry of God's word. These reasons could motivate the apostles to pass on in full measure their ministry to specially ordained persons, in this case the "seven." Putting together various data provided in Acts we can easily ascertain that this decision was followed by the energetic activity of the apostles outside of Jerusalem, whereas activity within the city itself, including preaching, was transferred to the "seven." Passing on the "service of the tables" to the "seven," the apostles passed on to them the presiding in the Jerusalem church, for the service of the tables derived from their status as presiders. The "seven" were the presiders of the church in Jerusalem, i.e., they were "presbyters" who at the same time fulfilled the ministry of deacons. This eliminates the question of why Luke noted the institution of the "seven" but kept silence concerning the institution of presbyters. Understood in this way the institution of the "seven" was not only a turning point in the history of the church in Jerusalem, but also the beginning of a veritable ecclesial organization.[36]

Were the "seven" ever called presbyters? If they were, Luke would directly point to this fact. With respect to the designation of the "seven" we could suggest a theory which, however, we do not insist upon. Very soon, if not immediately, the presiders in Jerusalem received the title *hêgoumenoi*.[37] This term reflected their actual status and the commandment of Christ: "Whoever would be great among you must be the slave of all" (Mk 10.43). The "seven," being presiders, were servants at the eucharistic assembly, hence, they were "deacons." It is this title that Luke probably had in mind while calling Judas and Silas "leading men among the brethren" (*hêgoumenous en tois adelphois*) (Acts 15.22). If this term did not designate the presiders of the Jerusalem church, its meaning remains obscure. Perhaps this term was present in the sources which Luke relied upon for compiling his book of Acts. In its meaning this term was fully identical with the term "presbyter." With respect to the very term "presbyter" in Acts, it seems that instead of the term *hêgoumenos* common in Palestine, Luke merely employed the term used in the churches outside of Palestine and which was more accessible to the readers of his book. In other words, we are ready to argue that, contrary to an almost common perception, the term "presbyter" did not originate in Palestine, but rather in the Pauline churches or, possibly, in Antioch.

Since in instituting the "seven" the apostles ceased to preside in this church, so also the apostle Peter apparently conceded his place as the one "who offers thanksgiving," for this position was bound up with the presiding status of the apostles in the church of Jerusalem. His later successor was James, the brother of the Lord.[38] But was he the one "who offers thanksgiving" at the time when the "seven" had been instituted? We doubt that. Luke mentions him for the first time in 12.17. Besides, only one of the presiders could "offer thanksgiving," but we do not find James's name among the "seven." Therefore the only person who could "offer thanksgiving" at this time was Stephen. We do not have another alternative. Stephen's activity upon his election as one of the "seven," his preaching, arrest, and his speech before the Sanhedrin are so much reminiscent of the first steps of the activity of the apostle Peter.

The killing of Stephen and the dispersion of the rest of the "seven" put before the apostles the task of restoring the disrupted organization of the Jerusalem church. Probably the new *hêgoumenoi*, like the "seven," were elected by the whole church at the suggestion of the apostles. Among them they elected James, the brother of the Lord, as the one who took the first position and consequently became the one who "offered thanksgiving." When St. Peter, upon his miraculous delivery from prison, orders others to report to "James and the brethren" about his release and departure (12.17), this obviates the fact that even at that time James was already the first presider of the church. The brethren mentioned together with James could have been the *hêgoumenoi* of the church in Jerusalem.[39] Apparently Peter's departure from Palestine was final. Probably he headed from there to Antioch or, perhaps, through Antioch to Rome.

6. Both theories concerning the time of emergence of *hegoumenoi* in the Jerusalem church are equally plausible, but as we have indicated above, we prefer the second hypothesis. It agrees more closely with the evidence of Acts, but apart from this, it stands out as an excellent working hypothesis. If we accept this theory, the institution of presbyters falls in the period prior to the beginning of Paul's missionary activity and the foundation of the church in Antioch. "Building up" the local churches, Paul and Barnabas were exactly recreating in them the order that already existed in the church of Jerusalem. This order was already hallowed by the church tradition and was associated with the name of the apostles. Founding churches, Paul and Barnabas were appointing presbyters (14.23). Luke's indication about them appointing presbyters refers to their return journey. For this reason, we have liberty to assume that Paul and Barnabas were initially appointing only the one who "offers thanksgiving" due to the small quantity of members in the churches they have founded. Further, as the churches were getting somewhat stronger, they appointed also other presbyters. They preferred the term "presbyters" to the term *hêgoumenoi* because the latter could give cause to misunderstanding among the former pagans.[40] Besides, the appointees to the presbyterate were indeed the senior members of the churches Paul and Barnabas have founded. In the light of our interpretation of 14.23, we can find an explanation to Paul's commission which we encounter in the letter to Titus. "This is why I left you in Crete, that you might amend what was defective, and appoint presbyters in every town as I directed you" (1.5). This passage deals with the appointing of presiders, with the exception of the leading one, the one who "offers thanksgiving," who was appointed by the apostle Paul himself. The order of the eucharistic assembly which took shape in Jerusalem was transposed into the Gentile world and easily took roots there, because the life conditions of the Graeco-Roman world not only failed to be an obstacle to it, but even proved to be favorable.

7. We could summarize our answer to the question concerning the origin of presbyterate which we stated in the beginning of this chapter in the following way. The presbyterial ministry grew out of the order of first eucharistic assemblies which in turn went back to the order of the Savior's Last Supper. The presbyterate was established by the apostles when the task of "building up" the Jerusalem church was complete. They received from the apostles their ministry of presiding in the church of Jerusalem and by means of this reception they began to occupy at the eucharistic assembly the places which were reserved after the apostles themselves. That is why Ignatius of Antioch had all grounds to consider the presbyters at the eucharistic assembly as representing the "college of the apostles." From the apostles they received the ministry of presiding, but they did not appropriate the apostolic ministry. This was quite clear for Ignatius, who nowhere spoke of presbyters as the successors of the apostles. Through the "building up" of the local churches by the apostles the ministry of presiding emerged, for it was essential for the eucharistic assembly. For the first time this ministry was actualized by the apostles, who celebrated the first Eucharist. This was not a confusion of ministries, for at that time the Church did not have any prophets or teachers or presbyters, but only had the apostles. This is how this ministry could have been passed on to

the presbyters, in the Church and through the Church. Nevertheless the starting point of the ministry was with the apostles. They were the first presiders of the first local church. Through this transmission of the ministry of presiding, the presbyters took the apostles' seats at the eucharistic assembly; not only in the eucharistic assembly of the church in Jerusalem, but at every eucharistic assembly the presbyters continued to take the seats of the apostles.

8. The first eucharistic assembly not only effected the actualization of the presiders' ministry, it also singled out the first or the senior from their midst. He was singled out in the person of St. Peter, who was the chief apostle, and as their leader he assumed the place of the one who "offers thanksgiving." It was not a special ministry but a function of the presiders' ministry which belonged to all the apostles. This function of the presiders' ministry was not accidental in the sense that it did not matter whether it existed or not. No eucharistic assembly could exist without the one who "offers thanksgiving" because without "thanksgiving," there is no Eucharist. Wherever there was a eucharistic assembly there also was the one who "offers thanksgiving," the first or senior of the presbyters. Just as St. Peter in his function as the one who "offers thanksgiving" did not in any way differ from other apostles, so also the chief presbyter in the function of his ministry did not differ from other presbyters. The difference was in the place at the eucharistic assembly through which the ministry of presiding was actualized.

The eucharistic assembly, celebrated for the first time in Jerusalem, was repeated in every local church, since all eucharistic assemblies no matter where and when they occur are identical by their nature and hence are identical with the first eucharistic assembly. Cephas, Paul, Apollos, or anybody else founding the local churches instituted there the presiders' ministry, which necessarily included the one who "offers thanksgiving." Therefore, it is not surprising to us that the New Testament writings say nothing of a senior presbyter or a senior bishop. There was no need for this, for it was absolutely clear to everybody that among the presbyters there was always the senior or the chief presider. The apostle Paul did not need to speak of it, either, when he was enumerating special ministries in the Church, for the chief presbyter did not possess a charism in any way different from the charism of other presbyters. In his letters Paul sought to eliminate the flaws which were visible in the church life of his time. He was trying to establish an orderly fulfillment of the prophetic ministry, persuading the faithful that God is not a God of confusion but of peace (1 Cor 14.33). But he did not have to convince the faithful that they had to "come together into the Church" in order to share in the "Lord's Supper." They were baptized into "one body," i.e., they had entered the Church to participate in the eucharistic assembly. They were aware that without this participation there is no life in the Church. But they also knew that Eucharist is "thanksgiving" and that "thanksgiving" cannot happen without the one who offers it. One aspect is bound up with the other. If there was a Eucharist, there was also the one who "offers thanksgiving."

IV. Evidence from Early Christian Literature concerning the Senior Presbyter

1. Is the existence of the senior presbyter a mere speculation? In a certain sense it is, for nothing in the New Testament necessitates us to accept the existence of the chief presbyter. However, this speculation would become an obvious reality if we proceed from the nature of the Church. We are faced with the dilemma: either we have to consider the existence of the chief presbyter a speculation and thus to acknowledge the existence of the Church as speculative, or we have to consider the Church a reality and henceforth to acknowledge the existence of the chief presbyter as historically self-evident. In a historical study we are fully entitled to proceed from the nature of the organism with which we are dealing. At any rate, this is not the same thing as proceeding from the *a priori* presuppositions. In many cases, such a method is the only one left if any positive evidence is lacking. But this method can be legitimate even when this evidence is present, for it enables us to make a better use of the material that we possess.[41] If we accept the fact that the chief presbyter existed then we are able to recover some indications in the New Testament which would confirm that the chief presbyter indeed existed. If we choose not to proceed from this fact, these details will either entirely evade our attention or we will ascribe to them entirely different sense and meaning.

We must assign the primary significance to the evidence which we find in Luke concerning the figure of James. We saw above that the place which James, the brother of the Lord, began to occupy in the church of Jerusalem was the same place that initially was occupied by the apostle Peter. At least initially James could not have had more authority than St. Peter. James stood at the head of the church in Jerusalem and for this reason he occupied the place of the one who "offers thanksgiving" at the eucharistic assembly. Acts says nothing of this latter function of James, just as other New Testament texts are silent about it, but otherwise James's role is presented quite clearly. It was James who presided at the Apostolic

Council, not the apostle Peter who at this council was defending either his own work among the Gentiles or Paul's work of "preaching the gospel." At the end of the session James summarized the debates and put forward the resolution. His speech was decisive for the question of whether the Law was mandatory for the Gentile Christians. Upon his release from chains under Herod, Peter asked to report the event to James and the brethren, the latter apparently being the presbyters (Acts 12.17). In his letter to the Galatians St. Paul relates that on his first visit to Jerusalem he saw the apostle Peter and no one else except James, the brother of the Lord (1.19). That is, he saw two men, one of whom was at the head of the apostles while the other was the head of the local church in Jerusalem. During his last visit in Jerusalem before his imprisonment, on the next day after his arrival, Paul went to see James, at whose place all the presbyters were gathered. They all together suggested to him to make purification in accordance with the Law (Acts 21.18–26). In the same letter to the Galatians St. Paul tells about the arrival of messengers from James (2.12). Everywhere James is presented as the chief figure of the Jerusalem church, but nowhere does he act on his own, but either together with the presbyters or with the whole church. His role fully corresponds to the role of St. Peter when he, in the first period of the existence of the church in Jerusalem, stood at the head of this church. If James could not have had more authority in Jerusalem than St. Peter had, the presbyters who were constantly around James could not have had less authority than the rest of the apostles, for they took their places at the eucharistic assembly. Just as the apostles together with Peter stood at the head of the church, so also James together with the presbyters stood at the head of the church in Jerusalem after them. Just as Peter was among the apostles, James was the chief or senior presbyter among other presbyters. He did not differ from them in his ministry, but by the fact that he assumed the central place at the eucharistic assembly. His personal authority as the Lord's brother added to his authority as the one who "offers thanksgiving." One should not exaggerate the existing dynastic tendencies in the church of Jerusalem, but without doubt the blood relationship with the Lord had put James in a special position.[42] His status in the church of Jerusalem could have been both more and less significant than that of the other senior presbyters in their churches. It could have been more significant, because he was the Lord's brother and for this reason could not have been compared with any other senior presbyter. But it was less significant than the apostles' status when they and especially St. Peter were in Jerusalem. James had less authority than the apostles, but the apostles recognized the primacy of James in the Jerusalem church. He was its senior presider; not the only one, but merely the first among others.

Did he bear the title of bishop? This is unlikely. A church tradition considers James to be the first bishop of Jerusalem, but this tradition is unreliable. It probably emerges in the second half of the second century when the title bishop began to be applied to the chief presbyters, since at that time the bishops were the ones who presided over the local churches. This transposition of the term is natural, especially since there existed a succession of ministry between chief presbyters and bishops. In the end, the whole issue is about ministry, not about terminology. The church tradition confirms the testimony of Acts that James stood at the head of the church in Jerusalem as its chief or senior presbyter.[43] But if the church of Jerusalem had the chief or senior presbyter, other local churches must have had one as well.

2. Indeed, the Third Letter of John testifies that the chief or the senior presbyters existed in the churches outside of Palestine. Naturally, if we do not presuppose the existence of the chief presbyter, the figure of Diotrephes would be seen in a completely different light. The letter does not state directly that Diotrephes was a senior presbyter in his church, but some details speak for themselves. In the letter Diotrephes is called the one "who likes to put himself first" (*ho philoprôteuôn*). This term means that Diotrephes did not only consider himself to be, but that he indeed was, the first among the members of the church. If there is a reproach in the words of the Elder it refers not to the primacy itself, as if he could consider it wrong, but to the issue that for Diotrephes his primacy turned out to be a human passion and hence it acquired an improper character.[44] The Elder accuses him of refusing to acknowledge his authority (*ouk epidechetai hêmas*, verse 9), i.e., that Diotrephes does not read his letters in the church and not only refuses to accept the traveling brethren but casts out of the church those who in fact accept them. By this he violates the obligation of hospitality which befits every Christian, and especially a presbyter (1 Tim 3.2). His authority in the church where he was a presider was so great that he could dare to stand in open opposition to the Elder and to criticize his instructions. His orders were obeyed by almost every one of the church members. We should not think that Diotrephes acted on his own. Rather he acted in the ecclesial assembly and with its consent. This appears clear from the fact that the Elder was unable to undertake anything against Diotrephes while being outside of the church which he was leading; but upon his visit to the church, the Elder would bring up in the same ecclesial assembly "what he is doing, prating against me with evil words . . ." (v. 10; cf. 1 Cor 5.3–5). This incapacity of the Elder is explained by the fact that he did not have any power over the local churches. This power he exercised while he was within the church itself.

The Elder, in accusing Diotrephes of refusal to accept the brethren who come from him, certainly did not mean to undermine the right of a local church to refuse hospitality to a person who spreads a suspicious doctrine, which right it exercised through its senior member. In the Second Letter of John we find a positive statement to this effect: "If anyone comes to you and does not bring this doctrine, do not receive him into the house or give him any greeting" (v. 10). The presiders of the church, as we have seen, were entrusted with responsibility of safeguarding the true faith. The Elder could not refuse this right to Diotrephes. His error, against which the Elder struggled, consisted in using the authority that belonged to him and that was not disputed by the Elder, against the Elder himself.

Another figure who stands out in the Third Letter of John is Gaius. The Elder commends him for what he does for the brethren and strangers while remaining loyal to him. As we have pointed out, the obligation of hospitality was incumbent upon the presbyters. Thus there can be hardly any doubt that Gaius was a presbyter and most likely a senior one in some neighboring church. The third person mentioned in the letter, namely Demetrius, apparently either had been a presbyter of Diotrephes' church who had courage to stand up against him or perhaps was a presider of some other church.

Among the three people indicated in the letter, Diotrephes and Gaius are those whom we call "chief or senior presbyters."[45] We should not be surprised that the other presbyters of their churches are not mentioned in the letter alongside these two figures. It is a wholly incredible admission that each of these churches was governed by one person without any presbyters. If this were so, this person could not have been named the "first" (*prôteuôn*). Diotrephes as well as Gaius was the first among presbyters and therefore he occupied the central place at the eucharistic assembly. The silence concerning the presbyters does not mean that these did not exist, just as the silence of the New Testament concerning the senior presbyter cannot be regarded as evidence that the latter did not exist. The structure of local churches outside of Palestine formed in the shape which it had taken from the very beginning in Jerusalem, where all the apostles presided over the church alongside St. Peter. We do not know whether the churches mentioned in the letters had, in addition to presbyters, prophets and teachers also, just as we do not know who were the brethren whom Diotrephes refused to accept. Even if they were indeed traveling "charismatics," there is hardly any basis for reading the letter as reflective of the conflict between the solidifying church hierarchy and "charismatics." We have to note another peculiar feature of 3 John. Neither heretics nor heresies are ever mentioned in it. John does not accuse Diotrephes of heresy[46] but merely of an inimical attitude toward him.

So if I come, I will bring up what he is doing, prating against me with evil words. And not content with that, he refuses himself to welcome the brethren, and also stops those who want to welcome them and puts them out of the church. (v. 10)

The goal in writing this letter was apparently to exhort Gaius not to follow Diotrephes' example: "Beloved, do not imitate evil, but imitate good" (v. 11). Good and evil here refer to what was indicated in the preceding verse, namely the attitude of Diotrephes to the Elder and the conduct of the former within the church where he was the first member. It does not matter for us whether Diotrephes ascribed to himself a larger authority than that for which he was entitled. It rather matters for us that the existence of a senior presbyter in local churches is established as a fact.

Could we extrapolate this fact to the other churches? It would be implausible to suggest that the situation of the churches in Asia was different from other churches, particularly dealing with a question as important as that of ecclesial structure. There was much more uniformity in the apostolic times than in the subsequent period. The foundations of ecclesial organization were the same in all the churches, for they proceeded from the very essence of the Church. They were formed in the church of Jerusalem at the time of its first eucharistic assembly and were repeated in every local church, for the eucharistic assembly remains always the same throughout space and time. Empirical factors had insignificant influence. At any rate, they did not overshadow the ecclesiological framework of the processes. If deviations existed, they were insignificant and dealt with the details, not basics. It suffices to recall the amazement which Irenaeus of Lyons expresses at the fact that all the churches, different from each other by language and ethnicity, everywhere keep the same faith, same customs, and same structure.[47] We have not only the right, but even the obligation, to draw general conclusions from the fact preserved in the letter of John.

3. We could have hoped to get some evidence concerning the churches in Europe from the letter of Clement of Rome. It stands on a verge of the apostolic era and still reflects it in many respects. The importance of this letter for us could have been even greater since it speaks of the churches of Rome and Corinth. If not exactly in Clement's time, then very soon after him the church of Rome began to enjoy primacy in the common family of local churches. Its organization became the paradigm for other churches. The church of Corinth was St. Paul's favorite child and it played a significant role in the history of the church. Unfortunately, the letter of Clement does not give clear and unambiguous evidence concerning the existence of the chief presbyter who always occupied a central place at the eucharistic assembly. However, this letter cannot be used to argue against the existence of senior presbyter either. One of the difficulties in using this text consists of Clement's somewhat uncertain terminology. Given Clement's legalistic mind this terminological uncertainty appears strange. In all probability the explanation lies in the fact that the terms designating the individuals endowed with the ministry of presiding in the church of Corinth did not coincide with the terms used in the church of Rome.[48] It was noted above that for awhile the church of Rome remained loyal to the archaic terminology of the Jerusalem church while the church of Corinth, founded by Paul, accepted terminology of much later origin. Naturally, Clement had this diversity in mind when he was writing to Corinth.

In his letter we encounter the following terms: *episkopos, presbyteros, hêgoumenos, proêgoumenos* and *diakonos*. All these designations appear in various conjunctions, but nowhere is the bishop mentioned together with a presbyter or with a *hêgoumenos*. As far as the terms *hêgoumenos* and "presbyter," they are found together in the expressions where the term "presbyter" does not have a specific ecclesial meaning but rather designates the senior members of the church as opposed to its younger members.[49] In turn, the terms "bishop" and "deacon" are found used together. Clement refers to these terms when he lays out the story of their origin. He indicates that the apostles, preaching the gospel, were appointing the first-fruits of the faithful to be bishops and deacons.[50] At the same time they have added an injunction that upon the death of the bishops they have ordained, others must undertake their ministry. Hence it is unjust to remove from their position those who fulfill their ministry without reproach. "Blessed are those presbyters who finished their course before now . . . for they have now no fear that any shall move them from the place appointed to them."[51] That the presbyters are identical with the bishops is presented quite clearly. The terms "bishop" and "presbyter" do not designate different, but the same, figures. A curious detail is that Clement used the term "bishop" when he was referring to apostolic times and replaced it with the term "presbyter" when he turned to his own time. It is much more difficult to pinpoint the difference between the terms *hêgoumenoi* and *proêgoumenoi*. If the term *hêgoumenoi* designated generally those who occupied an official position, i.e., both presbyters and deacons, the term *proêgoumenos* referred to the presbyters only.[52] But if *hêgoumenoi* signified presbyters, then *proêgoumenos* must have meant the senior or the first among them in every church. It is impossible to establish which of the two definitions is more accurate. Whether we accept one or another theory, *proêgoumenos* and *hêgoumenoi* either wholly or partially become identical with presbyters. The analysis of various loci from the letter of Clement, where the different terms designating those who have the presider's ministry are found, cannot do anything but establish the identity of these terms. The churches of Rome and Corinth had chief or senior presbyters, because each of these churches had a eucharistic assembly. However, we are unable to prove this fact if we base ourselves on Clement's terminology.

Another difficulty, and the major one in using Clement's letters for our purposes, is that we do not know precisely what happened in Corinth. Once in his letter, Clement remarks that, because of one or two people, the revolt against the presbyters was taking place (*di' hen ê duo prosôpa stasiazein pros tous presbyterous*).[53] The letter does not give clear indication of the reasons the revolt occurred or who these people were. We should abandon attempts to answer these questions as obviously hopeless. It is not as important for us as the very fact of "revolt" against the presbyters. What was it about? To take Clement's own words, it is unjust to remove from the ministry those who fulfill this ministry without reproach, for the bishops are ordained by the apostles or other individuals with a good will of the church. Hence it seems beyond any doubt that the "revolt" was expressed in wanting to depose the presbyters (or have deposed them already from the ministry). More precisely, we do not know whether only one or several presbyters were deposed. Indeed, one wonders whether we can be sure, as it is commonly held, that it was several presbyters who were deposed, arguing so on the basis of Clement's words that the revolt against the presbyters had occurred. The "revolt" could have happened against presbyters even when only one of them was deposed, especially if this deposition was not sanctioned by the rest of the presbyterate, for such deposition tackled the very essence of their common ministry.

Not insisting on the number of presbyters deposed, we proceed to the next question connected with this deposition. In the eyes of the church in Rome and of Clement, the deposition of presbyter or presbyters was so serious a matter that it was deemed necessary to intervene in this affair and even to dispatch some people to Corinth. We should naturally ask ourselves, why did this event become so significant? We cannot consider a deposition of one or another presbyter so exceptional an event in the church life of that time. Undoubtedly, occurrences of this kind did happen, just as they took place in previous epochs. For instance, from the letter of Polycarp we know of the deposition of the presbyter Valens (*Letter to Philippians* 11). Indeed, Clement insists that one should not remove from ministry the presbyters who are truly worthy of their calling, but this is not enough to explain the significance which Clement ascribed to this event. It is possible that in Clement's eyes it was not so much the fact itself as the reasons behind it that had a significance. But we do not know anything of these reasons. On the other hand, it is even less clear why the church of Corinth ascribed such a significance to the deposition of a presbyter that news concerning it had reached the church of Rome. The number of presbyters was not strictly limited, as was the number of deacons in the West. The number of presbyters could have been enlarged without difficulty. If some group within the church of Corinth, led by one or two individuals, had decided to sponsor their own people for the presbyterate it could have been done without deposing the old ones. Lobbying of such a sort would have certainly contradicted the basic principles of ecclesial life of that time, but the affair would still have stayed within the borders of the church in Corinth. Thus we are inclined to admit that the senior or the chief presbyters had been among the deposed. They could not ordain another one alongside him, for the chief presbyter was always one in every local church. If a group of individuals in the church of Corinth desired to ordain their leader as the chief presbyter, the one who previously held the office inevitably must have been deposed. Given this assumption, the deposition of the senior presbyter must have resonated differently than the deposition of one or another of the regular presbyters, however unjust it might have been in itself. We find some indirect indication to the fact in the letter itself. Having mentioned that the apostles appointed the first-fruits of the faithful as bishops and deacons, Clement adds that they had passed a rule that after their death others would undertake their ministry instead of those whom the apostles appointed. For this reason he considers it unacceptable to remove from the ministry those who offered the gifts (*prosenegkontas ta dôra*) without reproach. This term, "one who offered the gifts," identical with the term "one who offers thanksgiving," clearly indicates whom Clement had in mind. Moreover it is noteworthy that Clement distinguishes those who "offer the gifts" from other presbyters. With respect to the latter, he says that it is unjust to remove those who were ordained for their ministry with a good will of the whole church, while with respect to the former, he points out that it is not a small sin when we eject out of "episcopacy" those who piously and without reproach were offering the gifts. In the first instance, he says *ou dikaiôs*, while in another, *hamartia gar ou mikra*.[54] This distinction which Clement draws between presbyters confirms that the senior or the chief presbyter was among the deposed from the ministry or that he was the only one who was deposed. Then we will understand better why the "revolt" took such forms and reached the church of Rome. Indeed, it is no small sin to remove from ministry the senior presbyter who fulfills his ministry without reproach, for he presides at eucharistic assembly and offers gifts to God. But this, in turn, means that the church of Corinth did have its senior presbyter who occupied a central place in its assembly. Do we have to doubt that the same kind of senior presbyter was at this time in the church of Rome? If it was not, Clement would hardly have written his letter. The church tradition does not only confirm that the church of Rome had such a figure, but moreover, it has preserved his name: it was Clement himself.

4. The letters of Ignatius of Antioch lead us beyond the boundaries of the apostolic age. For this reason, we will not deal with them now, except for merely indicating that for Ignatius, the bishop is the unique and permanent presider of the eucharistic assembly. Clement and Ignatius are separated by a small interval of time. How could what is customarily called the monarchical episcopate have appeared in the local churches if no roots of it existed in the apostolic age? As we shall see later, the theory that accounts for existence of a permanent senior presbyter is the only one that can give adequate explanation to this mysterious fact.

However thoroughly we would scrutinize the letter of Clement in order to find a figure of the bishop as it appears in Ignatius's letters, we will not find such a figure. On the other hand, in Clement's letter, we have some indications of the manner in which the transition of the name "bishop" to the figure of the senior presbyter occurred. For Clement, as we have seen, it is unjust to oust from ministry the presbyters who blamelessly served to the flock of Christ (*ou dikaiôs nomizomen apoballesthai tês leitourgias*). *Leitourgia* is a common ministry of all presbyters as well as of all the members of the church. The senior presbyter among them, occupying a central place at the eucharistic assembly and "liturgizing" with other presbyters, fulfills a special function. He offers the gifts to God. This special function of the presbyterial ministry, one that pertains to him alone, is designated by Clement as episcopacy (*episkopê*). This usage of this term by Clement is hardly accidental. Rather, it is more likely that for him the episcopacy of the senior presbyter is not identical with the *leitourgia* of all the presbyters. We are ready to go even further in this direction. When in chapter 42 Clement said that the apostles were ordaining the first-fruits of the faithful to be bishops and deacons, his use of the term "bishops" included, as we saw, all the presbyters. But it was primarily the senior presbyters whom he meant here. This follows from the close connection in which he held bishops and deacons. We know that in Ignatius deacons are presented as the "fellow ministers" of the bishop rather than of the presbyters. Undoubtedly this was the situation in the apostolic age. Pointing out in chapter 44 that there will be a strife for the "episcopacy," Clement could be thinking of no one but the senior presbyters. This is indicated by the very term *episkopê*, which a little later he directly connects with the gift offering that belonged to the senior presbyter. Besides, the strife could have only taken place because of the dignity of the senior presbyter, rather than of the presbyters in general. Therefore, it is entirely possible for Clement to apply the term *episkopos* to the senior presbyter. However, as we indicated earlier, this cannot be a basis for conclusion that the term "bishop" was applied to the presbyters in the church of Rome. There is no ground for such a conclusion. Apparently, the terms used in the Roman church were *hêgoumenos, proêgoumenos,* and "presbyters," but perhaps Clement knew that in other churches, and maybe in the church of Antioch, the senior presbyter largely was styled as "bishop."[55]

5. When we approach the question of chief or senior presbyter in the apostolic age we cannot overlook the witness of 1 Peter. We must be cautioned, though, because this testimony is of a very special kind, and points at the senior presbyter only indirectly.[56]

> So I exhort the presbyters among you (*presbyterous en hymin*), as a fellow presbyter (*sympresbyteros*) and a witness (*kai martys*) of the sufferings of Christ as well as a partaker in the glory that is to be revealed. Tend the flock of God that is your charge, not by constraint but willingly (*prothymôs*), not for shameful gain but eagerly, not as domineering over those in your charge but being examples to the flock. And when the chief Shepherd is manifested you will obtain the unfading crown of glory. (5.1–4)

This is one of the most important passages in the New Testament, cited a number of times already. It allows us to define the ministry of presbyters. The apostle Peter both joins himself with and distinguishes himself from the presbyters. He exercised the ministry of the apostolate, which presbyters do not possess. The essence of his ministry is that he is "a witness (*martys*) of the sufferings of Christ as well as a partaker in the glory that is to be revealed."[57] Being an apostle he fulfills the ministry of presbyters, hence being a "fellow presbyter" to his addressees. If he would simply use the term "presbyter" in application to himself, he would have wholly identified himself with the presbyters. But St. Peter could not think of such identification, for to identify himself in this way would have meant for him to renounce his apostleship. We have to take the term "fellow presbyter" in its literal meaning rather than considering it purely a figure of speech.[58] The presbyterial ministry as it emerges in the verses cited above is a pastoral service/pastorship. Presbyters shepherd the flock of God which is with them (*to en hymin*) under the guidance of the Chief Shepherd. Pastoral service is a leadership in the local church which includes presiding at the eucharistic assembly. In what sense did St. Peter share the pastoral service with presbyters whom he was addressing? He could have meant the initial stage of the life of the Church when the first eucharistic assembly had been actualized through him and for some time after that he stood at the head of the church in Jerusalem. The Church had been actualized through Peter so that in the Church he was the pastor of Christ's sheep ("feed my sheep") in a very special sense, since the church of Jerusalem was the only local church at the time. It is quite doubtful that Peter would have this period in mind, for in his letter he spoke of the present, not of the past. Exactly at the moment of writing his letter he was fulfilling the pastoral ministry and therefore he was a "fellow presbyter" to other presbyters who, like him, were fulfilling the pastoral ministry. Where exactly, i.e., in which local church, he was fulfilling this ministry is a question directly relating to the interpretation of the letter itself. In any case, one should not proceed from the *a priori* assumption that Peter was not at the head of any church in the period of his life after Jerusalem, and put under doubt the actual pastoral ministry of Peter at the time when this letter was written. If we acknowledge the authorship of Peter, we must acknowledge that he stood at the head of a local church.[59] As a presbyter of this church he could only have been a chief or a senior presbyter, i.e., he occupied a central place in its eucharistic assembly and was the one who "offered thanksgiving." This church was *syneklektê* ("also chosen") in relation to the churches which St. Peter was addressing. When he associated himself with the presbyters of these churches, he first of all associated himself with their chief or senior presbyters. Perhaps the thought of St. Peter was focused upon the eucharistic assembly which proclaims Christ's passion and anticipates the "partaking in Christ's glory."[60] The fact of St. Peter being a "fellow presbyter" testifies that other local churches also had senior or chief presbyters.

This is exactly how the term "fellow presbyter" was perceived by the ecclesial consciousness of the first two or three centuries. The senior or chief presbyter began to apply the name "fellow presbyter" to himself. This designation suited him well, for it associated him with other presbyters but at the same time indicated his special position in the local church. Thus this term becomes almost if not completely a technical expression. We find evidence pointing to this in the work of an anonymous anti-Montanist writer: "The presbyters in the place, our fellow presbyter Zoticus of Otrous also being present, requested us to leave a record of what had been said against the opposers of the truth . . ."[61] This passage is especially important since it employs both terms "presbyter" and "fellow presbyter" at the same time. Only Zoticus, who is the bishop, is a "fellow presbyter" to the anti-Montanist writer, unlike all other presbyters. We do not know whether the expression "fellow presbyter" was used in the apostolic age in relation to the senior presbyter, but there is no serious objection against allowing this possibility. If in the third century this expression is applied to bishops, this speaks of its vitality, because the bishop of the third century only distantly corresponded to either the senior presbyter of the apostolic age or to Ignatius's bishop. Thus we find the expression "fellow presbyter" in the writings of Dionysius of Alexandria: "To our beloved brothers and fellow presbyters Dionysius and Philemon . . ."[62] Cyprian employs the expression "fellow presbyter" with two meanings. On the one hand he continues to apply it to the bishops alongside the expression *coepiscopus* ("fellow bishop"),[63] but on the other hand he applies it to the presbyters who comprise the bishop's presbyterium.[64] In the fourth and fifth centuries the expression "fellow presbyter" becomes virtually unnecessary. It is still used by force of habit to designate the priestly ministry of bishops and presbyters just as the expression *syndiakonos* is used to designate the same ministry of bishops and deacons.[65] The word usage of the fourth and fifth centuries cannot serve for us as valid testimony to the way in which the expression "fellow presbyter" was used in the first and second centuries.

V. The Ministry of the Senior Presbyter

The chief or senior presbyter of the early church did not differ in his ministry from other presbyters, just as they did not differ among themselves. He was a presider, just as they were. He was a pastor, just as they were. Compared to other presbyters he did not have any special ministry, since the early church did not have any ministry of administration other than that which all the presbyters fulfilled together. He was a presbyter, just as others were presbyters, or he was a bishop, just as others were bishops. But since he was the first among them he *de facto* manifested their entire ministry while the other presbyters already in the apostolic age formed a kind of council around him. When Ignatius designated the presbyterium as *synedrion* he was not introducing innovations into church life. From the very beginning in the church of Jerusalem, while the forms of church life which were then in use resembled the forms of life common for Judaism, there was no place for either conscious or unconscious imitation. This form grew out of the first eucharistic assembly where the Twelve, appointed by Christ, assumed the seats of the presiders.

The senior presbyter at the eucharistic assembly became the one who "offers thanksgiving," for this was the role of St. Peter at the first assembly of the church in Jerusalem. As a presbyter he took a place among the *prôtokathedritai*, but as the first or the senior one among them he took a central place in their midst, central to the whole eucharistic assembly. The "offering of thanks" was a manifestation of the priestly ministry which belonged not to the presbyters alone and consequently not to the senior one among them, but to all the people whom God has gathered in the body of Christ, as in the temple. Jewish meals had a religious character, but they were not precisely the sacred rites which were associated exclusively with the temple. The Eucharist, instituted by Christ, became a "spiritual offering" in a "spiritual temple." In this spiritual house, the priesthood is not a prerogative of one family, as in the Old Testament, but belongs to all people, for every one of the people is ordained into the office to be the priest of God. As priests, the entire people worships God but this priestly worship is made real through one person, for only one person can "offer thanksgiving" and this person is the one who occupies a central place at the eucharistic assembly. In the temple of the Old Testament all priests, including the high priest, actively offered their priestly worship even though they constituted only a portion of the people. In the "spiritual temple" it is one person who actively offers a priestly worship, even though all the people constitute the royal priesthood, because the "spiritual offering," celebrated by the people, requires it.

Assuming the central place, the senior presbyter "offered thanksgiving," manifesting the priestly ministry of the whole of God's people. He would not be able to offer thanksgiving if the priesthood did not belong to all the people, for, compared to the people's priesthood, he did not have any special priesthood himself. He was a priest just as all were priests in the "spiritual house." But it is only because all were priests that he, assuming the central place in the assembly, was offering thanksgiving. For this reason the ministry of priestly worship fulfilled by the chief presbyter was a function of the place that he occupied at the eucharistic assembly. As senior among the presbyters he occupied the central place, and since he occupied this place he celebrated the sacred rites.

Not being different from other presbyters in the ministry of administration, he did not differ from the people in the ministry of priesthood, just as the presbyters did not differ from the people. He had the charism of administration which the people did not have. But the charism of priesthood belonged to him by virtue of his being a member of God's people together with its other members. He actively offered the priestly worship due to his charism of presiding, rather than due to his charism of priesthood. Since the first eucharistic assembly where St. Peter was the one who "offered thanksgiving," there is an immutable rule that was established in the life of the Church, namely that it is the senior presider who actively offers the priestly worship together with the people.

The sacred rites of the Church were not exhausted by the "offering of thanks." The Eucharist encompassed all the sacred rites celebrated by the Church, for it was the central focus of all ecclesial life. Everything grew out of the Eucharist and everything was directed towards it. Apart from the "offering of thanks," the apostolic church celebrated the sacrament of reception into the Church, which included the ordination of laics, ordination to the special ministries of the prophets, teachers, presbyters-bishops, and deacons. Presiding over the eucharistic assembly, the senior presbyter presided over all sacred rites as well and, by virtue of his presiding, he actively offered a priestly worship. The senior presbyter never acted alone but always and everywhere together with the people and the presbyters. He was the "mouth of the Church" and the Church cannot be without the people just as the people cannot exist without those who preside over it, especially without a senior person among those.

VI. The Ordination of the Senior Presbyter

1. In the New Testament, the fact that bishops-presbyters were ordained appears indisputable. "When they had appointed presbyters for them in every church (*cheirotonêsantes de autois kat' ekklêsian presbyterous*), with prayer and fasting they (i.e., Barnabas and Paul) committed them to the Lord in whom they believed" (Acts 14.23). The question which must be raised in connection with this text concerns the manner in which the presbyters were ordained. Were they ordained by the apostles themselves or did the apostles ordain those who were elected by local churches? But we have no need to raise another question in connection with this one—was the primitive ecclesial organization aristocratic or democratic? At best this latter question is a misunderstanding. The church administration was neither aristocratic nor democratic, for it is not the will of man in whatever form but the will of God through the revelation of the Spirit that is active in the Church. If Barnabas and Paul were ordaining presbyters for the churches they founded they were not ordaining those whom they considered to be personally adept for this ministry, but those whom God had pre-ordained for this ministry.[66] Elsewhere in Acts the presbyters ordained by Paul are referred to as ordained by God: "Take heed to yourselves and to all the flock, in which the Holy Spirit has made you bishops (*en hôi hymas to Pneuma to Hagion etheto episkopous*), to care for the church of the Lord and God which he obtained with his own blood" (20.28). The ordination of the presbyter-bishops is accomplished by the Spirit according to the will of God.

With respect to the question of whether the local church participated in the ordination of presbyters, we have to seek the answer not in the texts cited above but in chapter 6 of Acts, in the narrative about the ordination of the "seven." When the apostles deemed it necessary to commend the "service of the tables" to the "seven," they did not ordain them on their own, but summoned "the body of the disciples" who they suggested should elect from their midst seven men "of good repute, full of the Spirit and of wisdom" (6.2–3). Possibly this was the course of action Paul and Barnabas undertook in the churches they founded, but this does not rule out the possibility of Paul's independent action if local circumstances prompted him to do so. Even if he acted in this way, which is less likely, one should not regard this as an expression of his authoritarian mood.[67] One has to give attention to the fact that the author of Acts situates the ordination of presbyters during the missionary journey of Paul and Barnabas, but on their way back. Consequently the local churches must have already existed for some time, during which the number of the faithful must have increased. Luke's remark concerning the presbyteries' ordinations must be placed in relation to Paul's commission to Titus: "This is why I left you in Crete, that you might amend what was defective (*hina ta leiponta epidiorthôsê*), and appoint presbyters in every town as I directed you" (1:5). The ordination of presbyters by Paul and Barnabas, too, was an amendment or completion of what was unfinished, i.e., what had been done at their first visit.

What then had been done at their first visit during their missionary journey? Can we make a conclusion from Luke's report that the churches founded by the apostles did not yet have any presbyters? If this were so, we would have to conclude that the preaching of Paul and Barnabas resulted in nothing but the emergence of a few believers. We cannot outrightly reject this suggestion, but neither can we accept it, for it stands in nearly open contradiction to the goals of Paul's missionary activity. He did not have in mind to convert a few people to Christianity, but rather to "build up" the churches. A church could not exist without the eucharistic assembly and the assembly could not exist without the person presiding over it. In this respect there is no disagreement between Luke's and Paul's understanding of the "building up" of the churches. Luke points out that Paul and Barnabas ordained presbyters for the local churches (*kat'ekklêsian*). We have reason to treat Luke's terminology with caution, but this does not mean that we must always doubt it, even if no indisputable evidence supports our suspicions. On their way back Paul and Barnabas completed what they did not finish at their first visit. Local churches had already existed when Paul and Barnabas ordained presbyters for them; therefore, they already had a eucharistic assembly and its presider. Put differently, Paul and Barnabas at their first visit ordained the senior presbyters in those churches. This suggestion fully corresponds to the report of Clement of Rome concerning the apostolic activity. He says that the apostles, preaching the gospel throughout cities and lands, were ordaining the first-fruits of the believers to be bishops and deacons "*tôn mellontôn pisteuein*," i.e., for the future believers.[68] We have indicated above that Clement here did not have in mind presbyters in general but the senior ones among them. Whatever had been the number of those who had come to the faith, if they had a presbyter then they constituted a church, not a group of disunited believers. "Always everyone and always together for the same thing (*epi to auto*) the Lord added day by day those who were being saved" (Acts 2.47). Thus it was not only in the first period of the church in Jerusalem but thus it was in every church founded by the apostles. In order that the Lord might add those who were being saved to the church, it was necessary that this church would have this *epi to auto*. The senior presbyter was not only a presider of those for whom he presided at the eucharistic assembly, but also of those who in the future will believe in Christ and will become members *epi to auto*.

2. If the presbyters were indeed ordained, there is no doubt that the first one among them was ordained as well. Did there exist any distinction between the ordination of the senior presbyter and of the rest of the presbyters? If we speak of the time which Luke describes in Acts 14, there can be no hesitation in answering this question. He was ordained in the same manner as other presbyters were ordained by the apostles. At the time when he was ordained, he was the only presbyter, hence he immediately occupied a central place at the eucharistic assembly. When other presbyters were ordained thereafter he *eo ipso* became the senior one among them and continued to occupy the central place at the eucharistic assembly. This still does not resolve the question concerning the ordination of the senior presbyter in the churches which already had presbyters. We cannot bypass this question, for it is a cardinal one. The way we solve it determines how we solve the problem of the episcopal ministry that was soon to emerge.

First of all, we have to reject the thought that anyone who felt himself to have greatest respect among the presbyters of the local church could on his own initiative occupy the central place at the eucharistic assembly. Actions based purely on one's own initiative were unknown in the early church. No one could ordain himself for a ministry in the Church, even a prophet or a teacher. If a presbyter could of his own will occupy the central place at the eucharistic assembly, this would signify the absence of structure and order in the early church. Besides, it would have certainly caused competition and rivalry between presbyters. We do not have evidence indicating that this was happening in the apostolic times. This lack of evidence of competition among presbyters is clearly suggestive, given what we know about the rivalry surrounding the appointment to the episcopal sees, in spite of the fact that this appointment was not executed on a random basis. The process of appointing a person for the central place at the eucharistic assembly was one of the most important aspects in the life of the local church, for the whole liturgical life rested upon it. Therefore this appointment had to have characteristics of an ecclesial act, i.e., charismatic nature, for everything which is done in the Church comes back to God as to the source of the gifts of grace in the Church. It was the one destined by God for this service who was called to occupy the central place at the eucharistic assembly.

3. Arguing that the senior presbyter was indeed ordained, we have not yet resolved the question of the manner in which he was ordained. Only modern theology can eliminate this latter question because for this theology the ritual of ordination totally exhausts the meaning of the sacrament. Hence it claims that the sacrament of ordination exists only if its ritual exists. If there is no ritual we are unable to speak of the sacrament of ordination, according to modern theology. Proceeding from the concept of the ordination sacrament which includes not one but three charismatic aspects, we have to ask whether the ordination of a senior presbyter involved all these three charismatic aspects, i.e., whether it involved the election, the ritual act, and the testimony of the people.

If presbyters were elected by the local church, there is no doubt that the senior presbyter was elected by the same local church as well. The local church designated him out of the group of presbyters because the senior presbyter was not elected for a special ministry but rather for a special place among the presbyters. It is possible that in this designation the presbyters had a decisive role because it was they who put forward from their midst a person who enjoyed the foremost authority. This election was subject to reception by the local church, which witnessed to the fact that the election made by the presbyters or the people accords with the will of God. Did this witnessing directly follow the election or was there a sacramental ritual performed over the elected person? On the basis of Luke's testimony (Acts 14.23) we know that presbyterial ordination involved the laying on of hands with prayer, the same attested by Acts 6.6: "These (i.e., the "seven") they set before the apostles, and they prayed and laid their hands upon them" (*kai proseuxamenoi epethêkan autois tas cheiras*).[69] All presbyters, from whose midst the senior presbyter was put forward, were ordained with prayer. The ministry of presiding for which the presbyters were ordained was one and was not sub-divided into ranks; therefore the ordination with prayer could not have been re-peated over a senior presbyter. If it were repeated it would mean that the senior presbyter was being ordained for a special ministry of priesthood. However, we know that such special priestly ministry did not exist in the early church. They could not have been asking for special charismatic gifts, for after his ordination he remained a presbyter. No additional charismatic gifts could have been asked for him since by his ministry the senior presbyter in no way differed from other presbyters.

Using the terminology of a later period, we could define the ordination of the senior presbyter through the term *probolê*. This term is used in canon 2 of the council of Chalcedon. It would be wrong to understand *probolê* as referring to someone's appointment for a position. *Probolê* is not some juridical act coming from a lower ecclesial authority but rather it is an ecclesial act in accordance with which some person is "promoted" for a certain position or for a place which en-tails certain acts or activity. According to the canon of Chalcedon, noted above, a presbyter or a deacon could have been promoted or put forward to be an *ekdikos* or an *oikonomos*. This meant that one of the presbyters or deacons could have been appointed to such a position or such a place among other presbyters or dea-cons, which entailed a certain kind of activity in the church. This does not involve a change in his ministry and hence was not accompanied by a petition for special gifts. This was a change of place, but it was not an official appointment; rather, it was an ecclesial act. We find this kind of promotion in the work of Hippolytus of Rome, but of course he does not use the term *probolê*. In the *Apostolic Tradition* we find rites of episcopal, presbyterial, and diaconal ordination. All these rites con-tain a laying on of hands accompanied by a prayer asking for sending down of the charismatic gifts. Apart from these, the *Apostolic Tradition* contains the "ordina-tion" of reader and subdeacon. Neither of these ordinations—of a reader and a subdeacon—includes the laying on of hands (*cheirothesia*) and prayers. The rite of ordaining the reader states that the bishop ordains him through handing to him a book,[70] while the ordination of subdeacon is performed through proclaim-ing his name.[71] In addition to this, both rites specifically indicate that the hands are not laid upon these persons. Modern scholastic theology observes the differ-ence between the clergy and church servers in that the former, in the sacrament of their ordination, receive special gifts of the Spirit, whereas the latter are merely appointed by church authorities through a blessing, without administering the charismatic gifts. Hence one ministry is recognized as possessing the grace, while the other does not. The Church in the third century did not know of ministries without grace. The ministry of a reader or a subdeacon was charismatic and it could not have been any other. Every ecclesial act takes place in the Church and, as everything in the Church, can occur only by the will of God. If a subdeacon, to use the terminology of Hippolytus of Rome, was "proclaimed" in the ecclesial assembly, this should be understood in the sense that one of the faithful was "promoted" for a special place that entailed an activity which other faithful did not have. For Hippolytus's time this meant that the ministry of subdeacon was based on the ministry of priesthood which all the faithful possessed. The distinction between a faithful who was "proclaimed" to be a subdeacon and the rest of the faithful was that a subdeacon had been put in a special position in the midst of the faithful. This promotion was done according to the will of God attested to by the church. This was a charismatic ministry, because all the faithful possessed a charismatic ministry of priesthood and, therefore, this was an ordination, even though a different one from the ordination of bishops, presbyters, and deacons.

In a similar manner a senior presbyter was "promoted" to a special place in the midst of the presbyters. Just as a presbyter or a deacon who, in accordance with canon 2 of Chalcedon, was promoted to be an *oikonomos* or an *ekdikos,* nevertheless remained presbyters and deacons, or just as one of the faithful who, in accordance with *Apostolic Tradition* was promoted to be a reader or a subdeacon, still remained one of the faithful and did not receive any degree of priesthood, thus also a senior presbyter, promoted for a central place at the eucharistic assembly, still remained a presbyter just as he was before, no different from all other presbyters.

The election of a senior presbyter, whatever form it took, was directly followed by the testimony of the people. This testimony was expressed in their assent for this person to occupy a central place at the eucharistic assembly in order to offer thanksgiving.

Thus the ordination of a senior presbyter comprised two aspects pertaining to the sacrament of ordination: the election and the testimony. The absence of the laying on of hands did not make ordination defective or incomplete for, as we already know,[72] the most essential and absolutely indispensable aspect of ordination was the witness of the Church that the ordination was done in accordance with the will of God.

VII. The Deposition of the Senior Presbyter and His Replacement

1. The fact that the senior presbyter was ordained bears the implication that his place at the eucharistic assembly was permanent rather than changing from one assembly to another. A person ordained through the witness of the Church could not have been deposed from his position without any special reasons. He occupied this place permanently, because the ministry of presbyter bishops was a permanent one in the local church where they have been ordained for their ministry. Certainly deviations from this order did happen, as the letter of Clement of Rome shows us. But this was far from being normative for ecclesial life and the mind of the Church could not give consent to these deviations because they went against the propriety and order. Propriety in ecclestical life, deriving from the Church's very nature, was guarded by the ministry of administration. Therefore it could not have been anarchical: "One today is a bishop, another tomorrow; today a deacon, tomorrow a reader; today a presbyter, tomorrow a layman."[73] If such conditions existed this ministry would not only cease to fulfill its purpose. It would cease to be the ministry of administration altogether. It must have been clearly defined rather than blurred if it would refer to an uncertain number of people. The presbyter-bishops were specific individuals ordained for their ministry in accordance with God's calling through communication of charismatic gifts. For this reason it was out of the question that the one who yesterday was a presbyter would be a laic today while a laic would become a presbyter. The ordination would lose all its purpose and would become excessive if the ordained people would alternate from one assembly to another. Those whom Christ called to be apostles, except for one who had fallen away from his ministry, remained apostles till the end of their lives.

> While I was with them, I kept (*etêroun*) them in your name, which you have given me; I have guarded them (*ephylaxa*), and none of them is lost but the son of perdition, that the scripture might be fulfilled. (Jn 17.12)

Christ preserved those whom he had called and he still preserves those whom God has called in Christ's body for the ministry of the Church. The seats of those who presided in the eucharistic assembly were permanent and so also were the individuals who occupied them permanent rather than alternating between assemblies. When the ecclesial assembly in fulfillment of the will of God ordained presbyters for the ministry of presiding, it could not replace them on the basis of their individual whims or desires. God, who had called these individuals to this ministry, kept them through the gifts of the Spirit in the fulfillment of this ministry, with the exception of those who had fallen away from it.

> For our sin is not small, if we eject from the episcopate those who have blamelessly and holily offered its sacrifices. Blessed are those presbyters who finished

their course before now . . . for they have now no fear that any shall move them from the place (*topou*) appointed to them.[74]

This is the sacred charter of any ecclesial ministry and particularly of the ministry of senior presbyters. As presiders they offer gifts to God. God is faithful to himself, and therefore to depose these from the places they occupy means to oppose the will of God which has called them to these places.

If we consider Clement's letter as one of the first instances of collision between law and grace, this collision must not be understood in the way suggested by Rudolph Sohm.[75] His fundamental mistake was to assert that Clement was founding the church discipline upon law and hence that it was he who put the first stone into the edifice of "Catholicism" in the history of the church. The deposition of presbyters or of the senior presbyter, as described in Clement's letter, could have happened only if the ecclesial assembly assumed its right to appoint those whom it pleased for the presbyterial ministry. Both ordination and deposition from the ministry in the Church occurs in accordance with the will of God. It requires a revelation of God's will, attested by the whole church. It was not Clement who was innovating, being the first, according to Sohm, to introduce the concept of divine law; rather, it was the assembly of the church in Corinth which was bringing ecclesiastical law into life. If the deposition happened in accordance with the will of God, the church of Corinth must have submitted to it and likewise the church of Rome, following the Corinthians. Clement could not have spoken of a "revolt" taking place in the church of Corinth, because the fulfillment of God's will cannot be regarded by anyone as a revolt. In this case, Clement himself would be violating the order that God had established in the Church. In fact, the deposition occurred against the will of God and for this reason the church of Rome could not accept it. It could not accept the deposition of the persons whom God did not deprive of the gifts of the Spirit.

In Clement's time the fulfilling of presbyterial ministry did not rest upon the divine law but rather upon the charism granted in return for the prayer of the Church. Presbyters occupy their places until God, who gave the gift of the Spirit, takes this gift back. These considerations are Clement's main argument against deposing the presbyters in the church of Corinth. The presbyters and the senior presbyter among them were ordained by apostles or other glorious men with the good will of the whole church and thus it is not a small sin to deprive of episcopacy a person who was blamelessly offering the gifts. "For we see that in spite of their good service you have removed some from the ministry which they fulfilled blamelessly."[76] If God, who called people to ministry, preserves those whom he called, this is the will of God rather than law, either divine, natural, or historical. This is the kingdom of grace. This is the Church of the Spirit manifest in the granting of grace and the keeping of those upon whom the grace was bestowed. It is human will which, in the name of the law, rebels against this state of things. This will wishes to establish itself in the Church and finally succeeds in doing so.

If Clement's letter effected the emergence of the doctrine of divine law, i.e., the emergence, to use Sohm's terminology, of "catholicism" in the church, it was not Clement's fault. He is still far from the statement which Hippolytus of Rome attributed to Pope Callistus, that a bishop should not be deposed even if he commits a mortal sin. Clement does not oppose the act of deposition *per se* but rather the fact that this deposition contradicts the will of God. The Roman church refused to receive the deposition of presbyter or presbyters since it could not witness in the Spirit that this deposition was in accordance with the will of God. Reception was not the expression of law but was founded upon the Spirit. The way the church of Rome reacted to the actions of the church of Corinth had a charismatic rather than a juridical nature. Later in history the right to depose presbyters and bishops was established. This precisely was a *right* which naturally was not attributed to the assembly of a local church but to a higher ecclesiastical authority. The manner of deposition based on law brought to life the right for appeal to the councils because in the realm of law there was no place for ecclesiastical reception. Clement's bishop-presbyters did not represent the religion of power and authority to the detriment of the religion of the Spirit.[77] They were charismatics and therefore as charismatics they could not have been deposed from their appointed places merely by the will of the ecclesial assembly.

The place which was reserved for the senior presbyter at the eucharistic assembly was unique. It was the same place which was reserved for Christ at the Last Supper and it was the same place where St. Peter sat when he celebrated the first Eucharist. At the eucharistic assembly this place could have been reserved only for the person called by God, who having called this person preserved him until the end of his days if he blamelessly and piously fulfilled his ministry. To depose him from this place was "not a small sin," but a sin against the Spirit.

2. The senior presbyter was the person who occupied the unique central place at the eucharistic assembly. Apart from him no other person "offered thanksgiving" in the local church. If another senior presbyter should stand next to the first one and offer thanksgiving, like the first one, the former would cease to be the chief presbyter. He was always at the head of the eucharistic assembly in the local church and being at the head of it he always offered thanksgiving.

In connection to this we have to clarify who could replace the senior presbyter at the eucharistic assembly if that became necessary. No question exists that one presbyter can replace another, because all of them had one and the same ministry. However, this is unquestionable only with respect to the pastoral ministry. The priestly ministry belonged to all the people, not to the presbyters alone. On this basis, could the senior presbyter entrust the offering of "thanksgiving" to any member of the church, who, like himself, had a charism of priesthood? Ignatius of Antioch points out that the Eucharist is valid when it is performed by the bishop or by the person whom the bishop allows to perform it (*ekeinê bebaia eucharistia hêgeisthô, hê hypo episkopon ousa ê hô an autos epistrepsê*).[78] If we take these words out of context we have the impression that according to Ignatius any member of the church could celebrate the Eucharist with the permission of the bishop. Was that indeed what Ignatius meant? It is hardly likely. Ignatius's statement that only *that* Eucharist is "valid" which is celebrated with the bishop's permission is preceded by the exhortation to follow the bishop and presbyterium which represents the college of the apostles and to revere deacons as the command of God. Hence Ignatius had no need to specify to whom exactly a bishop could entrust the celebration of the Eucharist. Nevertheless, we are left with some uncertainty. Was it a presbyter *or* a deacon or a presbyter *and* a deacon whom Ignatius considered a legitimate person whom the bishop could allow to celebrate the Eucharist? When the sacred liturgy was celebrated, according to Ignatius, the deacons, being the bishop's assistants in liturgical area, stood in the closest proximity to him. In several passages of his letters Ignatius calls deacons his concelebrants.[79] Due to this reason, he could have considered a deacon to be that person whom the bishop usually entrusted with substituting for himself at the eucharistic assembly. However he hardly could have dismissed presbyters completely from celebrating the Eucharist since their seats were closest to the bishop's at the eucharistic assembly.

If this theory is accurate, we find ourselves in the realm of concepts completely unfamiliar to the apostolic age. This is hardly surprising, because for Ignatius, as we shall see below, the high priestly status of a bishop did not derive from his function of presiding; rather, conversely, his function of presiding derived from his high priestly status. The senior presbyter was the one who "offered thanksgiving" due to his charism of presiding rather than due to the charism of some special priesthood. The apostle Peter was the first "offerer of thanksgiving" at the first eucharistic assembly. He remained one while he, with the rest of the apostles, stood at the head of the Jerusalem church. It is hard to imagine that the apostle Peter could in reality preside at each eucharistic assembly in the course of all this time. In his absence he was replaced by one of the apostles, for all of them at that time were fulfilling the ministry of presiding in the church of Jerusalem and all of them occupied front seats at the eucharistic assembly. After his departure from Jerusalem St. Peter was replaced in his role as the one who "offers thanksgiving" by a senior presbyter and other apostles—by the presbyters. Thus only a presbyter could replace a senior presbyter at the eucharistic assembly because he and the senior presbyter had one and the same ministry of presiding. The senior presbyter could not entrust the celebration of the Eucharist to any of the other members of the church for no one except for the presbyters had the ministry of presiding. The priestly charism itself was insufficient to offer thanksgiving and no special priestly charism existed in the early church. Substituting for the senior presbyter, another presbyter took his place at the eucharistic assembly and hence also offered thanksgiving. Such substitution could happen only in exceptional circumstances, when the senior presbyter could not physically stand at the head of the eucharistic assembly.

If none but the one who had the charism of presiding could substitute for the senior presbyter, this already solves the question of whether any people with special ministries could also substitute for him. The apostles must be separated from this group. Their status was exceptional, unique, and incomparable to anybody else's. Their places at the eucharistic assembly were filled by presbyters and for this reason whenever they participated in the eucharistic assembly they could preside over it at the invitation of the senior presbyter. The prophets, teachers, and evangelists did not fulfill the ministry of presiding either in their own or in any other church. For this reason they could not utter thanksgiving and the senior presbyter could not entrust them with doing it. We risk making this statement despite an extremely widespread opinion that it was precisely the prophet who, when present in the local church, would "offer thanksgiving." With the exception of Acts 13.2, this opinion is based entirely on the testimony of the *Didache*, which ascribes to the prophet a high priestly ministry. This testimony cannot be taken into account, for it is stands unparalleled in the Christian literature. We will not return to what we had already said concerning this text, except for emphasizing once again that the *Didache* reflected special tendencies of special circles in one way or another alien to the "Great Church." Besides, the attempt of the *Didache* to transpose the high priestly ministry onto a prophet was not historically successful. With respect to the evidence of Acts 13.2 ("While they were worshiping the Lord and fasting . . .") we can draw but one conclusion, namely, that the prophets and teachers indicated in 13.1 were the presiders of the church in Antioch and that Barnabas, mentioned first in their list, was possibly the one who "offered thanksgiving."[80] In other words, they were presbyters of the church in Antioch and Barnabas was the senior one among them. They headed the church of Antioch as presbyters, not as prophets and teachers. When the prophet happened to be in a local church he could be invited to "offer thanksgiving" only if he were the one who "offers thanksgiving" in his own church. We have already stated that in the apostolic church to join several ministries was a more or less common phenomenon, but we are dealing here with the joining of ministries, not with their mixing together. If a prophet as a prophet began to offer thanksgiving he would take upon himself a ministry for which God did not call him.

"And lo, a throne stood in heaven, with one seated on the throne. Round the throne were twenty-four thrones, and seated on the thrones were twenty-four elders ..." (Rev 4.2–4). At the eucharistic assembly the thrones of the elders were reserved for presbyters, whereas the throne of the "One Seated" was reserved for the senior or chief presbyter. God, who ordained him for his place at the eucharistic assembly, was keeping him in this ministry. But he in his turn from the height of his position was overseeing and keeping (*etêrei*), so that "fierce wolves not sparing the flock" would not steal the sheep of the flock where he and other presbyters were ordained by God to be shepherds.

Chapter 7

The Bishop

I. The Bishop as a Successor to the Senior Presbyter

1. *Nihil innovetur nisi quod traditum est.*[1] This saying of Pope Stephen contains the basic rule of church life. Nothing new should be introduced; everything should rest on the tradition of the church. If in the beginning of the second century in the letters of Ignatius we find bishops in the local churches, they could not have appeared there all of a sudden. Even less could they be a concoction of Ignatius himself. The ecclesial mind would not have accepted what did not exist previously. The figure of the bishop from Ignatius's letters was preceded by the figure of a senior or chief presbyter of the apostolic age. The senior presbyter *de facto* already possessed all the characteristics of the bishop in Ignatius's letters. He presided at the head of the local church and at the eucharistic assembly. Nevertheless, the bishop of Ignatius's letters is not wholly identical with the senior presbyter. Unlike the bishop-presbyters of the New Testament, the bishops we know from Ignatius's letters did not exist in apostolic times. Among these figures was the one who "offered thanksgiving," the senior among them. The bishop of Ignatius's letters stands apart from presbyters even though a connection between them had not yet been entirely lost. But the bishop-presbyters are no more; rather, there is a bishop and presbyters.

The starting point of the transformation of the senior presbyter into a bishop was found in the place that the senior presbyter occupied at the eucharistic assembly. Occupying the central place, he was the one who "offered thanksgiving." For this reason he became a chief or a senior priest in the midst of the priestly people of God. This did not constitute a special ministry with respect to the priesthood of all the people, but was rather a manifestation of this ministry. The senior presbyter became a bishop when his senior or first position among the nation of priests turned into a special high priestly or hierarchical ministry. This means that the episcopal ministry emerged from the priestly ministry of the people. This ministry was transposed to a person who, always occupying the first place among the presiders of the church and always performing the "offering of thanks," was *de facto* already a senior priest, though not yet endowed with a special ministry. If the central place at the eucharistic assembly had not been occupied by the same person but by different persons each time, this transformation of the "offering of thanks" into a special ministry would not have been possible. Thus, the episcopal ministry is founded upon the eucharistic assembly where from the very beginning the central place was always reserved for one and the same person. The connection of the bishop's ministry with the ministry of the senior presbyter was then preserved. One stood in the place of another without any break of succession between them.

Having emerged from the priesthood of the people the high priesthood of the bishop did not overshadow the former. Initially the genetic link between them persisted. The high priesthood of the bishop continued to remain within the range of the people's priesthood rather than outside of or above it. The bishop was the high priest of a priestly people, for all the members of the church, including presbyters, were priests. The ministry of priesthood remained the same. However, there appeared in it a higher degree of priesthood which, combined with presiding, became a special ministry.

The next stage in the development of the original ministry of senior presbyter was the priestly ministry of presbyters which became a second degree of priesthood. The presbyters acquired the status of a second degree of priesthood not only with respect to the bishop but also with respect to the priestly people. As deacons acquired a status of priestly ministry, the third degree of priesthood emerged. Seen in this context the priesthood of bishops, presbyters, and deacons can be regarded as a special priesthood if we understand it not as some heterogeneous priesthood, but as higher degrees of the one priesthood of the people. The segregation of higher degrees of priesthood from the common ministry of the people occurred under the influence of the doctrine of consecration. The latter led to the obscuring in the ecclesial mind of the people's priestly ministry which had already begun to weaken with the formation of higher degrees of priesthood. Scholastic theology brought to the extreme the movement that sought to segregate higher degrees of priesthood on the basis of consecration. Regarding those who bear higher degrees of priesthood as consecrated over against all other church members who do not receive consecration, this doctrine came into conflict with the Church's tradition. Scholastic theology presents basic principles of Church organization in such a manner that they cannot be substantiated by the Church's tradition or justified by historical facts. In so doing it does not ground these principles in the mind of the Church but undermines their status.

The concept of consecration, as we have seen, is not part of the doctrine of the Church but the result of theological speculation. To this day the Church in its liturgical life continues to confess the one priesthood that belongs to all the people of God, the higher degree of which is the special priesthood shared by the members of Church hierarchy.

2. The episcopal ministry grew out of the place that the senior presbyter occupied at the eucharistic assembly. This should not surprise us, for the ministries were formed in such a way throughout Church history. To draw upon historical analogies can actually be dangerous; nevertheless, one may use them with a certain caution. The position of the senior presbyter among other presbyters to some extent resembles the position of a metropolitan, the bishop of the major city of a province, among other bishops. When metropolitan districts began to take shape, the metropolitan differed from other bishops of his province in nothing except the place that he occupied among them, mainly at provincial councils. He was a bishop like all other bishops and his ministry was entirely identical to the ministry of any urban bishop. Gradually he began to rise among the other bishops not only in the honor deriving from the place he occupied, but also in his ministry. He secured for himself the episcopal ordinations within the borders of a province; however, this prerogative continued to belong to all the bishops and thus it was not particular to him. Thus the right of the metropolitan to celebrate episcopal ordinations was not reserved to him as his special function, one that belonged to a metropolitan only, so the place he occupied did not evolve into a special ministry distinct from the ministry of other urban bishops. The metropolitan's authority was superior to that of ordinary bishops. He even possessed some authority over those bishops, but essentially the metropolitan's ministry still remained a regular episcopal ministry.

The same situation applied also to the patriarchs. They managed to gain a greater influence over a greater number of bishops, as well as greater power over them, but they still continued to be bishops just like the rest. However, the more elevated the position they occupied became, the more this tended to turn the position into a special ministry. We discover such an attempt in Byzantium. The bishop of Constantinople, having become an imperial patriarch, *de facto* became the highest ranking bishop in the East. The teaching on the *kêdemonia pantôn* of the patriarch of Constantinople sought to vindicate theologically the *de facto* position that he had. According to this teaching he was the successor of an apostle (without specifying which one) to whom alone was entrusted the care of the entire universal church. For reasons of administrative convenience the patriarch transferred a portion of his authority to the metropolitans who acted as his representatives and governed parts of the universal Church in his name.[2] The patriarch became the father of all including the bishops, all of the members of the Church coming to be viewed as his children. The teaching about the *kêdemonia pantôn* appeared rather late, in the twilight of Byzantine history, and did not much influence its course. But had it developed, the ministry of an imperial patriarch would have turned into a special ministry. It is interesting to note that the teaching on the *kêdemonia pantôn* spread to the church of Moscow where first the metropolitan and then the patriarch of Russia began to put it into practice. It became unacceptable for the bishops to address the patriarch as brother—for he is not a brother to the bishops but rather their common father. The ministry of the patriarch came to be distinguished from the ministry of other bishops in his particular vestments, different from those of other bishops and metropolitans. This is also confirmed by the instances of special installation services for the bishops who were elected patriarchs. It is rather naïve to regard a special rite of patriarchal ordination as an expression of Russian theological illiteracy. Undoubtedly this service grew out of the idea of special patriarchal ministry distinct from the ministry of other bishops. The patriarch sought to gain for himself the position of a super-bishop or of a bishops' bishop. In Russia, just as in Byzantium, this attempt was unsuccessful, for historical circumstances did not support it.

These analogies can illustrate somewhat the process by which the position occupied by a particular person, under particular circumstances, can effect the formation of a special ministry. We have indicated above that the place that the senior presbyter occupied at the eucharistic assembly turned into a special ministry. Occupying this place from the very beginning, he was the only one who "made thanksgiving," as well as the celebrant of all the liturgical acts. The seniority of priesthood, connected with this status, was transformed into a special ministry, while he himself became a high priest or a hierarch.

II. The High Priestly Ministry of the Bishop

1. We do not know precisely when and where the high priestly ministry was finally appropriated to the figure of senior presbyter, and I doubt that we will ever know. Phenomena of this kind do not happen at once but gradually imprint themselves in the mind and, as it usually happens, not in one place but in several places at the same time. History is very stingy, leaving us with very few documents. In some cases this makes the task of a historian a lot easier but in others much more difficult. On the basis of the documents at our disposal, we are merely able to point to when the teaching about the high priestly status of a bishop was expressed for the first time. Hence our answer to a certain degree still remains speculative.

The question of why and how it happened is surrounded with even greater difficulty. Life is always unexpectedly complicated and when we subject it to scrutiny we always adjust it to fit a certain model. In real life there is not one but a whole complex of causes at work and we are unaware of most of these. In a way that is totally natural to us we tend to simplify the processes, focusing our attention on one cause alone which may not be the cardinal one. Historical perspective becomes especially distorted if we seek the cause in a wrong place. Putting the processes in the Church under our scrutiny we first of all have to seek the causes within the life of the Church itself rather than outside. We consider it necessary to reiterate that the Church has in its possession such creative power that it is able to create, out of itself, whatever is needed. This does not mean that we can disregard all exterior factors, but we must in all circumstances preserve a proper perspective.

2. The priesthood of the people was the foundation of ecclesial life in early Christianity. We have seen that the episcopal ministry grew out of this priesthood. The bishop became a high priest with respect to the priestly people. If this aspect contained an innovation, the idea of high priesthood itself was in no way unusual for the mind of the Church.

For the Jewish mind the priesthood was bound up with the temple, and without the temple it could not exist. If there is a priesthood there is also a temple and, conversely, if there is a temple there must also be a priesthood. In turn, the priesthood could not have been conceived without a high priest. If there are priests there must also be a high priest and conversely. For the mind of the early church the priesthood of the people stemmed from the priesthood of Christ. As living stones of the spiritual temple, Christians share in the high priesthood of Christ through his body, which is their temple. "For he who sanctifies and those who are sanctified have all one origin" (*hagiazôn kai hagiazomenoi ex henos pantes*) (Heb 2.11).[3] The high priesthood and priesthood both have one origin or, more precisely, they both constitute one reality.

The doctrine of the high priesthood of Christ is found in the New Testament. It is most eloquently expressed in the Johannine literature and in the letter to the

222 of the Holy Spirit

Hebrews.[4] The latter text directly calls Christ a high priest. "Therefore, holy brethren, who share in a heavenly call, consider Jesus, the apostle and high priest (*Apostolon kai Archierea*) of our confession" (Heb 3.1, cf. 10.20 et al.). We have to note once again[5] that the author of Hebrews does not construe Christ's high priesthood after the image of Aaron but after the order of Melchisedek, the king and priest of the Most High God (7.1–3). The Old Testament temple is replaced by the "spiritual house," the bloody sacrifices by the spiritual ones, the Aaronic priesthood by the ministry of the King of righteousness and High Priest, and the Levitic priesthood by the priesthood of the laics, all the people. In Paul's letters we do not find the idea of high priesthood explicitly but, as we noted above, he does not have a teaching on priesthood either, even though it underlies his entire teaching concerning ministries.[6] The question of whether Paul did or did not know the teaching on the high priesthood of Christ can be answered in different ways. More important, however, is that neither Paul nor the author of Hebrews gives any indication that the ministry of high priesthood may be entrusted to any persons who have special ministries in the Church. Does this mean that Christ's ministry of high priesthood rules out any possibility of other people fulfilling this ministry? This question is even more legitimate, given that Christ's ministry as Shepherd not only excludes but directly presupposes the ministry of pastors without which no local church can exist. The question of the special ministry of high priesthood is merely another form of the question of why St. Paul does not mention priesthood in his lists of ministries. The priesthood belongs to the Church as a whole. Being a common ministry of the entire people of God, it is headed by Christ. "He is the head of the body, the Church" (Col 1.18). A special ministry of high priesthood cannot be isolated from the priestly ministry of God's people because the priestly ministry itself is not a special ministry. If Christ's own ministry was construed in the pattern of Aaron's ministry, then priestly ministry would be a special ministry in the Church. It would not rule out a high priestly ministry within the sphere of a special priestly ministry. The teaching of the author of Hebrews concerning *ephapax*—"once and for all"—excludes the multiplicity of the high priestly ministry in the Church. For the ecclesial mind of the apostolic age there could not be any other ministry of high priesthood apart from the ministry of Christ. The fullness of the Church is revealed in the eucharistic assembly of every local church and the entire Church worships through the high priesthood of Christ.

The pastoral ministry found itself in a completely different position. In real life the unity and completeness of the "Church of God in Christ" is manifest through the multiplicity of local churches. Each local church must have the pastoral ministry, for without it the multiplicity of these churches could not exist. Without presiders there is no eucharistic assembly and consequently no local church, either. The ministry of presiding comes to be a special ministry, for only some of the members—not the entire people of God—are called to it. Having in common Christ as Chief Shepherd, the presiders act as pastors in the local church under the leadership of Christ.

3. The teaching concerning the high priesthood of the bishop was unknown to Clement of Rome, though his ideas were already approaching this teaching under the influence of the sacred establishment of the Old Testament. Yet, he completely shared the perspective of Hebrews, considering Christ as the unique high priest: *Iêsoun Christon, ton archierea tôn prosphorôn hêmôn.*[7] "Christ is the high priest of our offerings." A bishop, for Clement, is the celebrant of the Eucharist not due to his status as a high priest but rather to his status as a presider of his church, this demonstrated by the terms *episkopos* and *presbyteros.* Efforts to show that Clement applied the term "high priest" to a bishop will not be successful. The Old Testament sacred establishment was present in Clement's spiritual vision, but he hesitated to transpose it to the Church. He used it merely in order to prove that the churches, as in the Old Testament, must maintain the order and structure established by God himself. "For to the high priest his proper ministrations were allotted, and on the Levites their proper services have been imposed."[8] If one would relate these words to the church organization in the New Testament it would be historically inaccurate. In the time of Clement a special priesthood of presbyters did not exist and therefore he could not have likened them to the Old Testament priests. Even less could he liken the bishop to an Old Testament high priest, for to him a bishop was no different from a presbyter.

If we would date the composition of Clement's letters to 95–96 AD, as is the custom, then within ten to fifteen years thereafter we find a senior presbyter who becomes a bishop with the concept of the high priestly ministry underlying it. The letters of Ignatius of Antioch bear witness to this. Indeed, Ignatius did not yet apply the term "high priest" to the bishop.[9] But the absence of a term cannot prove beyond any doubt that the ministry which this term designated did not exist. Usually the term merely crystallizes what had already existed in real life. Such crystallization, in turn, gives to this phenomenon a precision and clarity which it did not have before the term appeared. Despite the absence of a term, the high priestly ministry of the senior presbyter features in Ignatius's letter with the utmost clarity.

In Ignatius's letters the term "bishop" lacks all the vagueness that it had before and is applied only to the head of a local church. The senior presbyter does not disappear in the midst of presbyters, as we still see in the letters of Clement, but is presented in Ignatius's work separately from the presbyters. The senior presbyter, having been detached from the midst of the presbyters, becomes a bishop because this detachment, as we saw, could only happen on the basis of his primacy or seniority among the priestly people. But the primacy of priesthood as a special ministry cannot be anything but the high priesthood. The bishop of Ignatius's letters does not represent a new figure having a completely new ministry. He is the senior presbyter of the apostolic age, one of whose functions became a separate ministry. That is why Ignatius's definition of the episcopal ministry has two aspects. On the one hand, the senior presbyter already had all the functions which Ignatius assigns to the bishop, but on the other hand, he also did not yet personally possess all of these functions.

> The Spirit was preaching and saying this: "Do nothing without the bishop."[10] Let no one do any of the things pertaining to the church without the bishop. Let that be considered a valid Eucharist, which is celebrated by the bishop, or by one whom he appoints. Wherever the bishop appears let the people be present; just as wherever Jesus Christ is, there is catholic church. It is not lawful either to baptize or to hold an agape meal without the bishop . . .[11]

> Be careful therefore to have one Eucharist. For there is one flesh of our Lord Jesus Christ, and one cup for union with his blood, one altar, as there is one bishop with the presbytery and the deacons, my fellow servants . . .[12]

Just as well, nothing could take place in the church without a senior presbyter: neither reception into the Church, nor the *agape* meal, nor the eucharistic assembly which from the very beginning was one in every church. But this is not the language of the apostolic age. It is not even the language of Clement's letter. This is the first and the most striking manifesto of the bishop's high priestly status. According to Ignatius, everything that constitutes the prerogatives of episcopal ministry pertains to the bishop's priestly ministry, shared by no one else. The New Testament is completely silent concerning the senior presbyter since his ministry was, on the one hand, a function of the presider's ministry, and on the other, a function of the common priestly ministry of the people of God. The senior presbyter did not personally possess any of these functions, for he did not have a special ministry distinct from the presbyterate. Ignatius of Antioch could not be silent concerning the bishop, as he understood him, for in his case, this ministry belonged to the bishop personally. It ceased to be a function of the ministry of presbyters and of the people.

In Ignatius, the old order became new, for this old order received a new and different clarification. It stands out particularly in the passages of his letters where he refers to the ministry of a bishop and to his status and role in the life of the local church. "He who honors the bishop has been honored by God; he who does anything without the knowledge of the bishop is serving the devil."[13] The author of interpolations into Ignatius's letters renders this idea differently: "Honor God as the source and the Lord of all, and the bishop, as a high priest who bears the image of God." He is absolutely correct, for it was the doctrine of the bishop's high priestly ministry which was at the base of Ignatius's reflections. "Be zealous to do all things in harmony with God, with the bishop presiding in the place of God (*eis topon Theou*) . . ."[14] "For Jesus Christ, our inseparable life, is the will of the Father (*tou patros hê gnômê*), just as the bishops, who have been appointed throughout the world, are in the will of Jesus Christ (*en Iêsou Christou gnômê eisin*)."[15] Christ is the *gnômê*, the will of the Father, and the bishops are within the *gnômê* of Christ. "Therefore it is clear that we must regard the bishop as the Lord himself."[16] "But . . . [the presbyters yield] not to him [the bishop], but to the Father of Jesus Christ, to the bishop of all."[17] "See that you all follow the bishop as Jesus Christ follows the Father . . ."[18] Neither St. Paul nor the author of Hebrews nor St. John could have written this, even though for them all the senior presbyter was indeed the center of a local church—not due to his own ministry but because he occupied the central place at the eucharistic assembly. His place came to be a special ministry and the person who occupied it came to possess a different status in the church.

4. From Ignatius's letters the episcopal ministry stands out quite clearly and distinctly. However, this does not solve the question of how much his letters are reflective of the actual state of the matter. Do they reveal the actual status of the bishop in Ignatius's time or do they reflect some of Ignatius's personal views that he sought to implement? If we respond affirmatively to the first question another would ensue, i.e., whether the process whereby the senior presbyter became a bishop was in its initial or in its final stage.

To regard Ignatius's letters as a vision or as a literary incarnation of an ideal hovering in his mind does not resolve the problem of his letters, but instead puts it aside. The letters of Ignatius are so vivid and the connection to the reality of church life is so evident in them that one has to lose all sense of history to detach these letters from real life. On the other hand, these letters are starkly polemical. If in the life of the church of his time everything was firm and stable, would there be a need for constant return to the same theme, as Ignatius did? If we leave aside the letter to the Romans, his basic theme concerns the bishop and everything that relates to his ministry and his status in the local church. These letters are a constant and persistent appeal of a great Christian figure who before his death wished to set a firm grounding for his life's work so that it would not disappear with him. His writing does not possess the epic tranquility of Clement of Rome, who does not even express distress concerning the "uproar" in the church of Corinth. Due to these characteristics of Ignatius's letters it is difficult for us to determine what the actual situation was not only in the churches that he addressed but also even in the church of Antioch itself.

Ignatius understood himself as a bearer of a special ministry that set him apart from the rest of the presbyters. Perhaps it would be true to say that he brought his ideas concerning the episcopal ministry to life due to his unprecedented authority in Antioch and beyond its confines. In the letter to the Ephesians he stated that bishops exist in all local churches: *hoi episkopoi, hoi kata ta perata horisthentes,*[19] i.e., the bishops in his sense of this term, rather than the bishops-presbyters of the New Testament. At the same time, Polycarp, whom Ignatius calls bishop in his letters to the church of Smyrna and to Polycarp himself, does not apply this title to himself. The same Polycarp is completely silent in his own letter concerning the bishop of the church in Philippi.[20] Even more striking is that in his letter to the Romans Ignatius is completely silent concerning the Roman bishop. May we infer from this that other individuals whom Ignatius termed bishops did not apply this title to themselves and may we thereby admit that Ignatius's words concerning the bishops existing throughout the Roman Empire amount to an overstatement, consciously or unconsciously made? Such a conclusion would be an overstatement as well. Ignatius could not have demanded from the churches to which he wrote a special deference toward an individual whom he himself called bishop if there were no basis for such attitude in the very life of these churches. In his letters Ignatius could develop an ideology of the episcopal ministry, but he could not make up the ministry itself. If Ignatius did not know the exact situation in all of the churches, he could at least be aware of the situation in the churches which he addressed. If he called Polycarp a bishop this could tell us that the status of Polycarp, as a senior presbyter, in the church of Smyrna, did in fact approximate the position of Ignatius himself in the church of Antioch. Polycarp, as well as the senior presbyters of other churches whom Ignatius addressed, may have not yet been applying the term "bishop" to himself. But from his point of view, Ignatius could well have considered them bishops.[21]

Just as the lack of the term "high priest" in Ignatius's writings does not indicate the absence of the high priestly ministry, so also the absence of the term "bishop" cannot be regarded as a proof that the ministry designated by that term did not exist. Polycarp may not yet have understood himself as a bishop, for in the initial period there was in fact no distinction between the offices of a bishop and of a senior presbyter. The distinction lay in the ideology of episcopal ministry, even if this ideology was not altogether foreign but existed in the *de facto* position of the senior presbyter. Hence the letters of Ignatius could have given an impetus for the appropriation of such ideology by the churches which Ignatius was addressing. Every senior presbyter could have understood himself as a bishop, i.e., have begun to view his primacy among the priestly people of God as a special high priestly ministry. The appropriation of the high priestly ministry by senior presbyters could not have happened in all the churches at once, and whenever it occurred in a given church it might not necessarily have gone together with accepting the title "bishop." As the writings of Irenaeus of Lyons show, even at the end of the second century the bishop was still called presbyter, even though at that time a bishop's ministry was clearly distinguished from the presbyterial office. The traditional use of the term continued to be implemented, even though this use did not reflect the actual situation.

All these considerations lead us to conclude that Ignatius's letters reflect a starting point or at least a first stage of the process by which the senior presbyter was transformed into the bishop. Whether Ignatius himself was the first senior presbyter who became a bishop we do not know, but this is precisely what the course of history made him to be. His life, work, and especially his death were among the major factors that ensured the success of this transformation. His writings made it possible for the idea of the bishop's high priestly ministry to be articulated. But the end result of this process depended on the position of the Roman church. Had the church of Rome not accepted the episcopacy as a special ministry, it would have remained a local movement rather than a matter of catholic or universal significance. Ignatius understood the importance of the Roman church, which he himself characterized as presiding in love in the multiplicity of local churches.[22] Perhaps this explains his silence concerning the bishop of Rome in his letter to the Roman church. We certainly cannot comprehend this matter fully, but we cannot bypass it either. Of what significance would it be if bishops existed throughout the Roman world while there was no bishop in Rome? It is of course possible to speculate that Ignatius did not know the name of the senior presbyter in the church of Rome, but this is most unlikely. Besides, this theory does not explain anything, because he could have mentioned the bishop without indicating his name.

For Ignatius the bishop did exist in the church of Rome and it was the senior presbyter who was the bishop; but the church itself did not consider him as such. Ignatius did not take the risk of imposing his ideas on the most authoritative church of his time. Perhaps he considered doing this in person rather than through a letter. What he managed to accomplish in this respect we simply do not know.

5. Rome lingered and hesitated due to its conservative stance, even though she perhaps sympathized with the novel ideas coming to her. We know that Clement of Rome was not aware of a special high priestly ministry of the senior presbyter. According to the witness of Justin Martyr, it was unknown to the Roman church even in his time. Describing the eucharistic assembly in his *Apology*, Justin used the term *proestôs* to designate a bishop, or more precisely, a senior presbyter,[23] whereas for the purpose of advocating Christianity before the Roman public opinion the title *archiereus* would be more suitable in view of the charge of atheism leveled against Christians; for Justin, like Clement the senior presbyter, celebrated the Eucharist not as a high priest of the church but as its presider. Following Clement, Justin considered Christ as the only high priest: "God has shown that His everlasting Priest, called also by the Holy Spirit Lord, would be Priest of those in uncircumcision."[24] But both of them had a subtle premonition of the concept about the high priestly status of the senior presbyter, which did not derive from theological presuppositions, but rather from his factual position in the church. Justin's "presider" (*proestôs*) is clearly endowed with the functions that approximate him to the bishop that we see in the Ignatius's letters.

Hermas, who was writing his *Shepherd* in Rome at approximately the same time, did not utter a single word with respect to this high priestly ministry. It is quite remarkable that he did not use the expressions "bishops and presbyters" but rather, "bishops and deacons" or "the presbyter and deacons."[25] For him, just as for Clement, the terms "bishop" and "presbyter" were synonymous. If we read in his text: "You shall therefore write two little books and send one to Clement and one to Grapte. Clement then shall send it to the cities abroad, for that is his duty . . ."[26]—then the most that we can infer from these words is that Clement was·the senior presbyter. In his letter to Pope Victor concerning the Paschal controversy, Irenaeus of Lyons relates that Polycarp of Smyrna and Pope Anicetas could not come to an agreement with respect to the celebration of Easter,

> [f]or neither could Anicetus persuade Polycarp not to observe what he had always observed with John the disciple of our Lord, and the other apostles with whom he had associated; neither could Polycarp persuade Anicetus to observe it

as he said that he ought to follow the customs of the presbyters that had preceded him.[27]

Polycarp did not apply the title of bishop to himself, but at least as it follows from Irenaeus's letter, Anicetus too is still a senior presbyter. Ignatius of Antioch could have rightfully called both of them bishops in his understanding of the term since both acted in a way in which the bishop of Ignatius's letters had to act. "But though matters were thus, they communed together, and Anicetus conceded (the celebration of) the Eucharist in the church to Polycarp, manifestly as a mark of respect . . ."[28] But both for Polycarp and, perhaps, for Anicetus, Christ was the only existing high priest:

> Therefore I praise you for everything; I bless you, I glorify you, through the eternal high priest, Jesus Christ, your beloved Son, through whom, with him, in the Holy Spirit, glory to you, now and for the ages to come, Amen.[29]

The *Second Letter of Clement*—the date and geographical origin of which is still subject to doubt, but which most likely comes from Rome in the second half of the second century—speaks exclusively about presbyters, without mentioning the bishops.

However, Rome could not have stayed indifferent for very long to the doctrine that it continued to receive with a growing persistence from all ends of the Christian world. The East was becoming quite comfortable with the title "bishop," applying it to only one person who stands at the head of the local church. Polycrates wrote to Pope Victor:

> For in Asia also great lights have fallen asleep which shall rise again on the day of the Lord's coming . . . among these are Philip, one of the twelve apostles . . . and, moreover, John, who was both a witness and a teacher, who reclined upon the bosom of the Lord, and, being a priest, wore the sacerdotal breastplate . . . and Polycarp in Smyrna, who was a bishop and martyr; and Thraseas, bishop and martyr from Eumenia, who fell asleep in Smyrna. Why need I mention the bishop and martyr Sagaris who fell asleep in Laodicea, or Melito, the Eunuch . . . Seven of my relatives were bishops; and I am the eighth. I could mention the bishops who were present, whom I summoned at your desire . . . [30]

In the East, the process by which a senior presbyter changed into a bishop was in its final stage. Not only did all the churches have bishops, but retrospectively, all senior presbyters were considered bishops as well. The developing doctrine of the apostolic succession begins to include the succession of the bishops' high priestly status, which in turn finalizes the acceptance of the apostolic succession doctrine. Through the apostles the high priesthood of Christ passes onto the bishops. This is what Hegesippus relates: "James, the brother of the Lord succeeded to the government of the Church in conjunction with the apostles . . . He alone was permitted to enter into the holy place; for he wore not woolen but linen garments."[31] We are not concerned about the historical validity of this witness. Whatever it may be, it attests to the idea apparent from then onward in the ecclesial mind that the apostles had a high priestly ministry. Apart from the Palestinian tradition represented by Hegesippus, we have a tradition coming from Asia Minor that naturally ascribed the high priestly status to the apostle John. This indication we find in the letter of Polycrates, cited above: "John, who was both a witness and a teacher, who reclined upon the bosom of the Lord, and, being a priest, wore the sacerdotal breastplate."[32] Without a doubt, Polycrates wanted to point out that John was a high priest. Later, this tradition concerning the high priesthood of James and John received a wide popularity. It is attested by Epiphanius,[33] Jerome,[34] and a number of other ecclesiastical writers of much later period. Certainly, the Church consciousness could not be satisfied with attributing high priesthood to James and John only—this status must naturally have come to include all the apostles. The *Doctrina Addai* mentions that on the day of his ascension, the Lord "raised his hands, put them on the heads of his eleven disciples and entrusted to them the gift of priesthood."[35] The Savior himself institutes the high priesthood.

The Roman church perhaps showed indifference both to the high priesthood of James, the brother of the Lord, which it learned from Hegesippus himself, and to the high priesthood of John, mentioned in the writings of Polycarp. The Roman church's characteristic realism hindered its acceptance of the high priesthood of the apostles as a continuation of the high priesthood of the Old Testament. Besides, the high priesthood of James and John had very little relevance for this church. The Roman church seemed to be awaiting the moment when the concept of high priesthood would be associated with the apostles and, in particular, with the apostle Peter, as a consequence of the idea of apostolic succession. While theological thought lingered and vacillated, life could not wait, and went on to evolve within the general tendency of the church development that was persistently requiring the transformation of a senior presbyter into a bishop. Probably, the senior presbyter in Rome *de facto* became the bishop earlier than in other churches. The process was advanced by the sense of discipline that became so vividly expressed in the letter of Clement of Rome. The significance of senior presbyter was growing both within and outside of the church of Rome. The succession of its senior presbyters had great significance. Apparently Hegesippus first put the list of succession for the church of Rome together.[36]

We can say only with approximation at what point the process whereby the senior presbyter became a bishop ended. Most likely it happened at the time of Pope Victor. He was indeed a bishop, rather than a senior presbyter of the Roman church. At the same time, Irenaeus writes in his letter to Victor:

> Among these were the presbyters before Soter, who presided over the church which you now rule. We mean Anicetus, Pius, Hyginus, Telesphorus and Xystus. They neither observed it themselves, nor did they permit those after them to do so. And yet though not observing it, they were nonetheless at peace with those who came to them from the parishes in which it was observed; although this observance was more opposed to those who did not observe it.[37]

Since we do not have the beginning of Irenaeus's letter with the address, we cannot be certain that Irenaeus applied the term "presbyter" to Pope Victor, as well, but neither can we assert that he used the term "bishop." We already know that, driven by a tradition, Irenaeus continued to designate those who really were bishops with the term "presbyter." In his letter to Victor he perhaps had special reasons for designating Victor with this term. Being in disagreement with Victor's stand towards the churches of Asia Minor in the question of Paschal celebration he might have been emphasizing not only that the attitude of the presbyters who preceded Victor in leading the church of Rome was different but also that their churchly status compared to Victor's was different. No matter how Irenaeus actually addressed Victor, he was in his eyes without doubt a "bishop instituted by the apostles" (*ab apostolis institutus episcopus*).[38] This was also Victor's understanding concerning his position. We may compare his stand in relation to Polycarp with the position of Clement of Rome toward the church of Corinth. Victor acts in his own name, as a head of the Roman church, whereas Clement acts in the name of the church itself, identifying himself with its presbyters. We will not err terribly if we suppose that it was exactly in his time or immediately following his rule that the Roman church adopted a special ordination rite for the bishop preserved for us by Hippolytus of Rome. "Grant that your servant, whom you have chosen for episcopacy, should shepherd your flock and should serve you as high priest without blame, serving by night and day . . ."[39] The senior presbyter of Rome became a bishop on the basis of the high priestly ministry. We shall not forget that, according to the *Liber pontificalis*, Victor was of African provenance and that the church of Carthage in Tertullian's time or maybe even earlier did know the terms *sacerdos* and *episcopus*. Rome had ended the transition from senior presbyter to bishop not only for Victor himself but had finalized this process for other churches as well. If after Victor some places continued to apply the term "presbyter" to bishops, it was already an anachronism.

6. The fundamental factor which caused the transition from senior presbyter to bishop was high priesthood as a special ministry. Having acknowledged this, we still lack an explanation of how and why the high priestly ministry emerged in the local churches. More exactly, the question should be put in the following way: How did it happen that the high priestly ministry of Christ became associated with the senior presbyter? We saw that for the understanding of the early church the high priesthood of Christ ruled out any special ministry of high priesthood in the Church. We have to admit openly that the question concerning the emergence of this special ministry is one of the most difficult.

Early Christian consciousness was in a way challenged by the idea of high priesthood. This challenge proceeded from the surrounding pagan world. Out of all the pagan cults, it was the cult of the emperors that most expressly illustrated this idea. Given an instinctive Christian aversion to everything that was pagan, even unconsciously, the imperial cult exercised the least influence on Christian thinking. It might well have had the reverse effect, slowing down the development of Christian teaching of high priesthood. To some extent this effect of the imperial cult is exemplified in the letters of Ignatius. We have pointed out that these letters do not contain the term "high priest," while the ministry of a bishop derives from the high priestly ministry. Without doubt Ignatius was wary of this term as being close to the imperial cult, and he chose instead to employ the usual term "bishop." This term reflected another major role of episcopal ministry, that is, the guarding of the right doctrine and the struggle against heresies.

To an even greater extent, the idea of high priesthood came to the Church from Judaism. Given the esteem the Old Testament writings enjoyed, the concept of high priesthood as laid out in the Old Testament must have had some attractive force. Without doubt this idea was highly influential, but its influence was stronger on the second stage of the emergence of high priesthood in the Church than on the initial one. We saw that Clement of Rome did not go further than drawing some analogies between the sacral organization of the Old Testament and the ecclesial organization of the New Testament. Justin Martyr, as his Dialogue with Trypho the Jew demonstrates, was quite familiar with the Old Testament, but even he did not cross the borderline between Old and New Testaments. For this reason it would be incorrect to seek the origin of the Christian high priest-hood only in the Old Testament. Even if we accept this explanation, the question remains: how did the idea of the Old Testament high priesthood penetrate Christian consciousness?

In its initial shape, the idea of high priesthood had no connection with the high priesthood of the Old Testament. This shape is reflected in the letters of Ignatius. In his teaching on the Church he wholeheartedly followed the apostle Paul. In every local church the eucharistic assembly manifests the fullness of the Church of God, itself being the "icon" of the Last Supper. The place of Christ at the Last Supper is taken, after the example of St. Peter, by the one who is seated in the center of the eucharistic assembly. For this reason the bishop, for Ignatius, is the image of the invisible Bishop, Christ. Ignatius found at hand the concept of the high priestly ministry of Christ and merely by way of "topological" comparison transposed it to the figure of senior presbyter. Ignatius expressed this in his famous formula, "Wherever the bishop is present let the community be present, just as wherever Jesus Christ is, there is the catholic Church."[40] The fullness in the unity of the Church is wherever Christ is, but Christ is present in the completeness of his body in the eucharistic assembly. Therefore the Church catholic is wherever the bishop is present, because without him, the eucharistic assembly, at which he takes Christ's place at the Last Supper, is impossible. Through his high priestly ministry Christ acquired for himself a royal priestly people, and the bishop, en-throned at the place of Christ, perpetuates this ministry, "gather[ing] together the number of those that shall be saved, and . . . offer[ing] to you the gifts of your holy Church."[41] From the topological perspective, the priestly ministry of senior presbyter becomes a special ministry of high priesthood.[42] Two degrees of priestly ministry, extant in the Church from the apostolic times—where the first degree is the ministry of Christ as a High Priest, and the second is the priestly ministry of all the people—transformed into the two degrees of ecclesiastical hierarchy, where the first degree was assigned to the bishop, as the image (typos) of Christ at the eucharistic assembly, and the second to all the people.

Ignatius's topological doctrine concerning the high priesthood of the bishop did not emerge merely out of his theological speculations. Rather, it mainly responded to the pressing need of contemporary church life. At first glance we might be perplexed by Ignatius's constant and persistent exhortation to be subject to the bishop and to keep full unity with him. The bishop of Ignatius's letters is the senior presbyter whose primacy in the area of worship became a special ministry. He inherited from his predecessor all that he had. Can we infer from this that neither submission nor unity with presiders or a presider existed in churches prior to Ignatius, and that it emerges precisely in connection with the episcopal ministry in Ignatius's time? "Unity of the Spirit in the bond of peace" is the Pauline idea: the unity of all in the Church and, of course, the unity with the presiders. The Third Letter of John bears witness to the fact that submission to the presiders was a reality of church life. The authority of a presider was so strong that it could challenge even the authority of the "elder" John himself. The "commotion" in the church of Corinth caused by the "uproar" of some people against the presbyters was an unusual event. The First Letter of Peter was meant to warn the presbyters against abusing their power, exhorting them not to be domineering over those in their charge but to be examples to the flock. The pastoral letters do not for a moment doubt the authority of bishop-presbyters. A bishop manages the church as the head of the family. The Church is the household of God (1 Tim 3.15), while the bishop is God's steward (Titus 1.7). For the ancient mind, the power of the *paterfamilias* was so indisputable that its existence did not need any justification.

Therefore Ignatius's appeal for complete submission to the bishop leads one to think that the church life of his time featured a process that threatened the unity of the church members with their bishop. Even though this process was a novel or relatively novel element in church life, it had no direct connection with the emerging episcopal ministry. It would have happened also with senior presbyters in charge, even though in this case it would have had a different direction. Ignatius fought this innovation, seeking to bring ecclesial life back to its pristine norm. We do not know whether this process took place in all the churches but we can be quite sure about Antioch and the churches to whom Ignatius wrote. Alongside the one eucharistic assembly which was the practice from the beginning, private assemblies appeared that brought together some but not all members of the church. One of the reasons for this novel phenomenon was that some members of the local churches, under the influence of Jewish practice, desired to celebrate the Eucharist on the Sabbath rather than on the "first day after the Sabbath," the day of the Lord. "If then they who walked in ancient customs (*hoi en palaiois pragmasin*) came to a new hope, no longer observing the Sabbath, but the Lord's day . . ."[43] They probably organized a eucharistic assembly under the presiding of one of the presbyters who shared their outlook. Was that the reason for Ignatius's words: "Let that be considered a valid Eucharist which is celebrated by the bishop, or by one whom he appoints"?[44] Apart from those people, the Docetists also organized separate assemblies: "They abstain from Eucharist and prayer, because they do not confess that the Eucharist is the flesh of our Savior Jesus

Christ . . ."[45] Ignatius recommends shunning the Docetists: "It is right to refrain from such men and not even to speak about them in private or in public . . ."[46] The celebration of the Eucharist by a small group of Christians breaches the unity of the local church since the members of it share one body and one cup of the Lord.

> It is right then, that we should be really Christians, and not merely have the name; even as there are some who recognize the bishop in their words, but disregard him in all their actions. Such seem to me not to act in good faith, since they do not hold valid meetings according to the commandment.[47]

The tendency to establish separate eucharistic assemblies becomes stronger as the local churches grow in numbers. The establishment of such separate assemblies was dictated by purely practical reasons, which is why this tendency was much more difficult to counter. If much later the ecclesiastical authorities gave way before the necessity to have separate eucharistic assemblies, Ignatius, by virtue of his eucharistic ecclesiology, did not wish and could not accept this. Despite all the tendency to the formation of separate eucharistic assemblies, he asserted its unity because within the limits of the polis there must be one altar and one bishop, for there is one Lord and one faith. It is not hard to see that the basic argument of Ignatius against the plurality of eucharistic assemblies amounted to the teaching on the high priestly ministry of the bishop. There can be only one high priest for all the Christians dwelling in one place, hence there can be only one altar and one assembly. The idea of the senior presbyter as a presider of a local church was insufficient ground for keeping one eucharistic assembly within the limits of one city. The senior presbyter would preside over those gathered for the Eucharist. The limits of the church were defined through the limits of the eucharistic assembly. If these limits went over the borders [of the assembly], Christians could form a new eucharistic assembly, i.e., a new local church, without transgressing the commandment of love and unity. This new eucharistic assembly would have a new senior presbyter. It must be noted that the concept of the high priesthood of a bishop did not overcome the tendency to form separate assemblies within the borders of the city, but it established the bishop as a high priest above all these assemblies. These were the consequences of Ignatius's thought which he himself could not anticipate. He was protecting the ancient principle of one single eucharistic assembly. For his time the topological concept of high priesthood indeed ruled out the possibility to have separate eucharistic assemblies.

Very soon the concept that the bishop is a high priest departed from Ignatius's theological presuppositions. In practical church life these proved insufficient when additional liturgical centers began to emerge within the limits of the city church. The ecclesial mind sought other clearer and firmer foundations that would correspond more closely to the reality of life. Naturally it turned to the sacral organization of the Old Testament. It was impossible to adopt the high priesthood of the Old Testament mechanically. Ecclesial organization did not match the sacral organization of the Old Testament. Local churches remained independent and self-sufficient and no bishop could claim the status enjoyed by the high priest in Judaism. The attempts to establish continuity between the Old Testament high priesthood and the apostolate of which we are aware could not have resonated well in the ecclesial milieu, especially in Rome. Such attempts would presuppose the concept of the universal church of which in the second century we still get but a glimpse. It is possible that the idea of the universal church was first accepted by Montanism. The term "high priest" first appears in *Didache*, where it is not applied to the bishop but to the prophet. Montanism could have given an impetus toward more distinct formulation of the bishop's high priestly ministry. What the church's thinking adopted from the Jewish sacral organization was just the idea of special high priesthood as a divinely established order. High priestly ministry began to be regarded as a special ministry which is traced back to Christ through the apostles. The concept of the bishop as a high priest thus interacts with the concept of succession and continuity (*diadochê*). As a result of this interaction the idea of high priesthood with which Christ endowed the apostles finally takes root. From the apostles this priesthood is said to pass on to the bishops, by way of apostolic succession. This was the new shape of the concept of Christian high priesthood, in contrast to the topological view of Ignatius. This latter, like Ignatius's eucharistic ecclesiology, did not survive through history. The doctrine of the Church becomes detached from the Eucharist, which is why the concept of the bishop's high priesthood completely departs from its eucharistic foundations. No longer does the high priestly ministry depend upon the Eucharist. Nevertheless, the content of the doctrine remains unchanged until it loses its connection with the priesthood of all the people of God. It was regarded as a special ministry within the priesthood of the people. Scholastic theology placed it outside of the people of God, for it construed the entire ministry of priesthood by the model given in the Old Testament, where it belongs only to specially ordained individuals. As a result of this, the people of God became deprived of the priestly ministry to which every member of the Church is ordained in the sacrament of his reception into the Church.

III. Changes in Church Life Caused by the Transition from Senior Presbyter to Bishop

1. The process of transition from senior presbyter to bishop happened surreptitiously, so that the mind of the church might not have noticed the change. No breach in the church life occurred. The old order changed into the new, still remaining preserved in this new order. Therefore no crisis, let alone a revolution, took place in the life of the church. Despite being one of the most substantial processes in church life, this change caused much less upheaval than other, less substantial processes of lesser consequences. At the time when episcopal ministry was instituted, the life of the church remained the same as it had been before. The high priestly ministry developed on the basis of the place occupied by the senior presbyter, and this place remained the same. Just as before, the bishop was seated in the central place in the eucharistic assembly, while the presbyters remained in their own places. The order at the eucharistic assembly remained exactly as it had been earlier. Just as earlier, the senior presbyter or bishop celebrated together with all the people and the people did not lose anything of its ministry. The understanding of the royal and priestly status of the members of God's people begins to be weakened not with the appearance of the bishop's high priestly ministry but with the emergence of the concept of the priesthood of presbyters. While the bishop remains the singular high priest, the priesthood of the people retains its significance and all its power. The people cannot celebrate [the Eucharist] without the bishop, but neither can the bishop act as the "mouth of the church" without the people. The high priesthood of the bishop actually safeguarded the priesthood of the people, while the priesthood of the people in fact created the high priesthood of the bishop.

2. Initially the appearance of the high priestly ministry of the senior presbyter, who thereby became a bishop, did not effect any noticeable changes in church life. Nevertheless it was the beginning of a profound reformation of dogmatic thinking that finally affected the entire life of the church. Indeed, early Christianity bore within itself the potentiality for the appearance of episcopal ministry. Yet once it appeared, due to its inner logic, it determined the further shape of this ministry. Episcopal ministry became something which it had not ever been and which did not at all correspond to the character of the early church. Like the senior presbyter before, the bishop was still the presider in the eucharistic assembly. But it was exactly here that the first essential change was to take place. By virtue of his central place at the eucharistic assembly, the senior presbyter was becoming the first priest in the midst of the priestly people. This latter seniority of his was wholly conditioned by his seniority among other presiders. He was the senior priest because he was the senior presbyter. At the eucharistic assembly his priestly ministry, expressing the priestly ministry of the people, originated from his ministry as a presider. But when the bishop started to possess a special ministry of high priesthood established by Christ, the correlation between his ministry as a presider and his ministry as a priest was reversed. Now, at the eucharistic assembly only the person who had a charism of high priesthood could take the place of Christ at the Last Supper, the place taken by St. Peter in the church of Jerusalem. And so the bishop became the presider of the local church by virtue of his status as a high priest. Receiving the charism of high priesthood through a special rite of ordination, the bishop thus acquired the status of the presider in the church for which he was ordained a bishop.[48] This hardly noticeable shift in the dogmatic area had enormous consequences. The eucharistic assembly was the source and starting point for the ministry of the senior presbyter. *Epi to auto*—"always everyone and always together for the same thing"—as the manifestation of the Church created the senior presbyter, but having created him, it could not exist without him. A bishop as a high priest is ordained in the Church, but he is not created through *epi to auto*, that is, through the people of God "always everyone and always together." *Epi to auto* becomes dependent on the bishop. It can exist without him, if the presider is a person delegated by the bishop. Already Ignatius espoused the thought that Eucharist is valid when it is celebrated by the person assigned by the bishop, but Ignatius still had one single eucharistic assembly in mind. A bishop can assign the celebration of the Eucharist to whomever he wishes, and still retain the high priestly status. By virtue of this fact, several eucharistic assemblies can emerge within the borders of one local church but its unity will not be broken, for the bishop remains the one single high priest at all the assemblies. The presiders at additional eucharistic assemblies would be the bishop's delegates. The bishop remains a part of the central eucharistic assembly where he presides in person, but at the same time he is situated above the additional assemblies where the presbyters at his commission celebrate the Eucharist. The boundaries of a local church are extended and defined through the boundaries of the power of the bishop as a high priest. The episcopal principle of unity of the local church replaces the eucharistic one.

With the appearance of the high priestly ministry, the position of presbyters became the most vulnerable. The changes in this area were revealed quickly even though they did not immediately follow the emergence of episcopal ministry. Retaining their places at the eucharistic assembly, they still were the *prôtokathedritai*—

that is to say that to all appearances they retained their ministry of presiding and all that pertained to it. Here is precisely the nerve center of the whole process that followed. Paradoxical as it is, the entire weight of the problem of the ecclesial hierarchy does not rest on the bishop but rather on the presbyter. The bishop inherited all functions of the senior presbyter, whereas the presbyterial ministry, as it is gradually established beginning from the third century, did not have any direct points of connection with the previous era. The priestly ministry of presbyters did not directly derive from the eucharistic assembly despite being connected with it. Therefore, it was much more novel than the primitive episcopal ministry.

The early history of the development of the episcopal ministry is primarily the history of presbyters' loss of their ministry in favor of the bishop, indeed a temporary one, since comparatively soon they reacquire the priestly ministry, receiving it from the hands of bishop. Seated in the center of the eucharistic assembly the senior presbyter expressed or made incarnate the entire ministry of presbyters, but the presbyters still retained their ministry of presiding, for only under this condition could the senior presbyter be seated at his place. Meanwhile the bishop, now bearing a special ministry of high priesthood, no longer needed the presidency of presbyters since his own presidency no longer derived from their ministry. Having ceased to be presiders, presbyters kept their places at the eucharistic assembly at the two sides of the bishop, the only high priest and presider of a local church. These closest and most honorable seats that the presbyters continued to occupy could only belong to the bishop's associates, who formed the presbyterium. When Ignatius of Antioch calls the presbyterium or college of presbyters a *synedrion* this does not signify exactly the same thing as what the presbyterium has become at the end of the second or in the beginning of the third century. "Be zealous therefore to have one Eucharist . . . as there is one bishop with the presbytery . . ." (*hama tô presbyteriô*).[49] Ignatius still sees the bishop as organically connected with the presbyterium. This formula strikes us as almost similar with the formula of Polycarp: *Polykarpos kai hoi syn autô presbyteroi*. "Polycarp and the presbyters with him . . ."[50] Polycarp totally identifies himself with the presbyterium while Ignatius distinguishes himself from it without yet totally separating himself from the presbyters. "Also be subject to the presbytery, as to the apostles . . ." (*hôs tois apostolois*).[51] "Be zealous to do all things in harmony with God, with the bishop presiding in the place of God and the presbyters in the place of the council of the apostles . . ." (*eis topon synedriou tôn apostolôn*).[52] According to Ignatius, presbyters constitute the apostolic *synedrion* which includes the bishop, who occupies a special place in it. He cannot be excluded, because no ecclesial *synedrion* can exist without a bishop. They are his associates in the area of administration but not concelebrants in the area of liturgical worship. More precisely, they are his concelebrants in this area as far as every member of the Church is a priest to God and Father.[53] "God and Father of our Lord Jesus Christ, look upon this your servant and impart the Spirit of grace and counsel of presbyterate so that he might assist and guide your people with a pure heart . . ."[54] This prayer for presbyterial ordination found in Hippolytus of Rome asks for the "Spirit of grace and counsel" for the presbyters so that they might guide the people. The "Spirit of counsel" becomes the charism of presbyters because as the senior presbyter became the bishop, the entire presbyterial ministry consisted of being assistants and advisors to the bishop, together with whom they governed the church. Nevertheless, during the entire pre-Nicene period the presbyterium remained the council of the local church, not the bishop's council.

When the external circumstances of ecclesial life dictated the necessity of splintering the single eucharistic assembly of the local church into many, the church's thinking handled this problem with ease. Ignatius of Antioch affirmed the unity of the altar and the episcopacy in every local church, but in the course of the development of his teaching concerning the bishop's high priesthood, the Church's thinking retained the unity of the episcopacy but abandoned the unity of the altar. The bishop as the one high priest in his church became the principle of unity in the local church.[55] When a concept is appropriated only partially this not only deforms the concept but also often produces its exact opposite. This is precisely what happened historically with Ignatius's idea of a single eucharistic assembly. In a local church there must be one bishop but there can be, if necessary, several eucharistic assemblies. Just as in the area of pastoral work the bishop can have assistants, so he could have such in liturgical worship. Quite naturally presbyters became just such assistants. This once again revealed historically the ancient role of presbyters as ecclesial presiders. If there were some hesitations in this issue they were local and provisional. The bishop remained the eucharistic celebrant for the main assembly while sending presbyters to the additional liturgical centers. They became the ones who "offered thanksgiving," not on their own authority but dependent upon their bishop. The eucharistic celebration was the primary content of the bishop's special ministry of priesthood and thus it naturally had to be expanded to the presbyters when they began to preside at the additional eucharistic assemblies. When the notion of priesthood began to be applied to presbyters, they could get only a second degree of it since the high priesthood is by its nature united in every church. In connection to this I would wish once again to make note of the position of the Roman church. We know that for a while it hesitated in ascribing the high priesthood to the bishop. Due to this conservatism this church strove for a long time to avoid the multiplicity of eucharistic assemblies in one single church. Given the numbers of its members it was a more difficult task for Rome than for any other church. On the level of theological speculation, it regarded the additional centers as the spatial expansion of one single eucharistic assembly, and therefore the bishop remained the eucharistic celebrant within the limits of the city church. Here I have in mind the teaching and practice of the Roman church concerning the *fermentum*. We do not have evidence that other churches knew this concept, although we have some grounds to suppose so. As such this concept is most significant theologically, but practically it surely could not overcome the multiplicity of eucharistic assemblies.[56]

IV. Apostolic Succession

1. The doctrine of apostolic succession is a subject deserving a special study. I consider it only for the sake of defining its connection with the doctrine of the high priesthood of the bishop. Concerning the linkage between these doctrines, one must not represent it in terms of a cause-and-effect relationship. As I have noted already, it is more proper to speak of the interaction of these doctrines. The doctrine of apostolic succession gave the final touch to the doctrine of the high priesthood of bishops, but, in turn, the doctrine of high priesthood confirmed the doctrine of apostolic succession.

Remaining faithful to the point which I expounded before, I do not consider it possible for me to accept a view, quite widespread at the present time, that the doctrine of apostolic succession arose at some historical moment under the influence of a number of reasons mostly originating from outside of the church. At best, it was Gnosticism that could have given impetus to the formulation of this doctrine. The nucleus of this doctrine was located in the Church from the very beginning, while the shape of this doctrine naturally changed throughout the history of its development.

2. The idea of succession in relation to ministries and the figures fulfilling those was quite widespread in both pagan and Jewish antiquity.[57] We have no grounds to think that it was not present in the Church from the very beginning. Tradition was the foundation of the life of the early church. "For I received from the Lord what I also delivered to you . . ." (1 Cor 11.23). "For I delivered to you as of first importance what I also received . . ." (1 Cor 15.3). The succession of tradition was not a foreign idea to Paul, who himself, before his conversion, was raised at the feet of Gamaliel (Acts 22.3). The idea of succession of tradition implies the idea of succession among the individuals who keep the tradition. Even this idea was not foreign to Paul from his childhood, for it was in the tradition that he was raised by Gamaliel. For Paul the Twelve kept the primordial tradition, especially Peter. Trusting that the coming of Christ would happen in his lifetime, Paul at first could not be especially concerned about securing the succession of what he committed to the churches. This fact does not in any way undermine the existence of succession in Paul's lifetime: from the Twelve to Paul and from Paul to the churches he founded. When the peril of death threatened him, the succession of tradition became the source of an even greater anxiety. "Therefore, be alert, remembering that for three years I did not cease night or day to admonish every one with tears" (Acts 20.31). The idea of succession among the individuals who keep the tradition becomes most manifestly expressed in the Pastoral letters: "And what you have heard from me before many witnesses entrust to faithful men (*pistois anthrôpois*) who will be able to teach others also" (2 Tim 2.2). The apostle hands down the doctrine of faith to the churches where it must be kept unharmed through the succession and continuance (*diadochê*) of individuals entrusted with the guarding of the doctrine. This, at least, is the sense of this difficult verse from 2 Timothy.

3. The idea of *diadochê* was not merely present in the Church, but it was present in several forms in which the keeping of tradition was ascribed to different individuals. For Clement of Alexandria the *didaskalos* was such individual. In *Hypotyposes*, he says that

> [t]he Lord after his resurrection imparted knowledge (*gnosis*) to James the Just and to John and Peter, and they imparted it to the rest of the apostles, and the rest of the apostles to the seventy, of whom Barnabas was one.[58]

The true *gnosis* [*Editor's note:* knowledge] originating with Christ himself is handed down through apostles from one generation of *didaskaloi* to another, while in some part this *gnosis* remains secret and is handed down secretly.[59] We cannot allow ourselves to think that Clement was the only author within the "Great Church" who espoused the doctrine of the succession among the *didaskaloi*. The Letter of Barnabas cited by Clement contains the same teaching. However, this doctrine concerning the *didaskaloi* as guardians of apostolic tradition was not sustained by the Church, not only due to its suspicious affinity with the teaching of Gnostic sects but also because there was no firm ground for it in the early church. In Origen's writings this teaching appears less distinctly, and in general it is much more toned down there in view of safeguarding it from false *gnosis*. Nevertheless, even in Origen we find the concept of spiritual hierarchy, the hierarchy of the Word, represented by a *didaskalos*, which Origen contrasted with the church hierarchy. For him the true bishop is the one who has *gnosis*, not the one who has a front seat at the ecclesial assembly.[60]

Apparently among the Montanists there was a doctrine of succession with regard to the prophetic ministry.[61] This is abundantly clear from one text from the Oxyrhynchus Papyri.[62] It is curious to note that some orthodox opponents of Montanism did not deny the concept of prophetic succession. Rather, they doubted that Montanist prophets could prove that their line of succession was unbroken. Thus according to Eusebius, Miltiades wrote: "For if after Quadratus and Ammia in Philadelphia, as they assert, the women with Montanus received the prophetic gift, let them show who among them received it from Montanus and the women."[63] This remark is most curious since it shows the significance of *diadochê* in the eyes of the orthodox, but it could have such significance only if this idea was present in the Church itself. On the other hand, Miltiades' words do not prove that the Church embraced the doctrine of prophetic succession. We have no indication of this fact. Even Irenaeus of Lyons, who, as we know, did not take an extreme stand toward Montanism, does not mention it.

The Church could not accept the doctrine about the *diadochê* of either the *didaskaloi* or the prophets since it already had the doctrine about the *diadochê* of the presbyters-bishops contained in the very doctrine concerning the Church. The former doctrines were derivative from the doctrine of the *diadochê* of the presbyter-bishops and doubtlessly are of later origin. They presuppose the concept of the universal church which the understanding of the early church did not contain. It was impossible to assert the doctrine about the succession of *didaskaloi* or prophets in the limits of a local church, for not all local churches always had one or the other. In this situation not only could the breach in succession of *didaskaloi* or prophets happen, it in fact did happen when one *didaskalos* did not follow immediately after another, just as one prophet did not follow another. The local church could not always safeguard their succession because it was not responsible for caring about these ministries. If, due to the death or departure of a prophet or teacher, prophetic or teaching ministry ceased, the church could not ordain other people in their places so that new individuals could receive the ministry of the old. Even within the limits of the Church catholic one could have only a slight chance of establishing the succession of these persons, let alone establishing it in local churches. This was the view of Miltiades, cited above. Clement of Alexandria proceeded from the notion of a "spiritual church" when he argued for the succession of *didaskaloi*. As a result of the doctrine of the universal church, the "treasury of faith" was not entrusted to the Church, but rather to particular individuals, which in turn favored the rise of secret *gnosis*. For allegedly the universal church does not have its empirical manifestation and thus cannot be the guardian of tradition. In fact it was the Church catholic, fully manifested in every local church, to which the "treasury of faith" was entrusted.

4. Before we proceed to examine the doctrine of succession of presbyter-bishops we should note that this doctrine was expressed by means of two paradigms. According to the first, the substance of the doctrine concerning succession is that the ministry of presbyter-bishops, ordained by apostles or other persons who had necessary authority for this, does not cease in a local church but continues without interruption. One generation of presbyter-bishops succeeds another, forming an unbroken chain of persons exercising one and the same ministry. The second paradigm is distinct from the first in arguing that apostles not only ordained first bishops but also commended to them their own ministry, preserved in the Church through the unbroken chain of bishops. In this paradigm, the episcopal *diadochê* has a merely instrumental role since by means of it the apostolic ministry is preserved. These two paradigms are not mutually exclusive, because the idea of transmission of ministry is not completely alien to the first paradigm. Rather the difference lies not in this idea but in the understanding of what exactly was handed down from the apostles.

We find the first unambiguous indication to the episcopal *diadochê* in the letter of Clement of Rome. But this was merely an indication rather than a full exposition of the doctrine concerning succession of bishop-presbyters. Clement never occupied himself with such task. The concept of the *diadochê* was, for Clement, one of the arguments in support of his point that one must not remove presbyter-bishops who fulfill their ministry without reproach. If Clement used the *diadochê* as an argument, this means that it was present in the church's understanding rather than being just his personal opinion.

Let us try to define the substance of Clement's theory. It consists of three main theses. The first thesis: Christ is sent from God (*Iêsous Christos apo tou Theou*).[64] The second: Christ is from God and the apostles are from Christ—both one and the other in an orderly manner derive from God's will (*Ho Christos oun apo tou Theou kai hoi apostoloi apo tou Christou; egenonto oun amphotera eutaktôs ek thelêmatos Theou*).[65] There exists some parallel between these two theses, but what is its exact nature? Clement could hardly consider the ministries of Christ and of the apostles as parallel. Christ gave the apostles their ministry; that is, the source of their ministry is in Christ, just as the ministry of Christ rests in God. But both one and the other proceed from God, for everything derives from his will. Here is where the parallel ends. Clement's third thesis is as follows: the apostles, being instructed by Christ after his resurrection, being faithful to God's word, and being given the power of the Spirit for their ministry, went out to preach the gospel of the kingdom of God. Preaching throughout lands and cities, they ordained the first-fruits of the faithful, after testing them by the Spirit, to be bishops and deacons of the future believers.[66] The apostolic ministry was to build up local churches rather than to convert specific individuals to Christianity. The latter task was entrusted to the churches they founded. In the course of building up the churches, the apostles ordained the first-fruits of the faithful to be bishops, for without the episcopal ministry, local churches cannot exist. It is not hard to see some hiatus between the first and the second theses on the one hand, and the third, on the other. It would not have existed, if Clement's third thesis was: the bishops come from the apostles. But precisely this could not be. The apostles could not give a ministry to the bishops in the same way as they themselves were given a ministry by Christ. However elevated the apostles' position in the Church would be and however exceptional their ministry, the source of the bishops' ministry does not lie in them, but rather—just like the general source of all ministries—in God through the Spirit.[67] That is why the third thesis contains the thought that not only apostles but also bishops are from Christ and, through Christ, from God. Therefore, despite the hiatus, all three theses are strongly connected with each other.

Having certified the initial chain of the *diadochê*, Clement comes to his second fundamental statement:

> Our apostles also knew through our Lord Jesus Christ that there would be strife for the title of bishop. For this cause, therefore, since they received perfect foreknowledge, they appointed those who have been already mentioned, and afterwards added a law that if they should fall asleep, other approved men should succeed to their ministry. We consider therefore that it is not just to remove from their ministry those who were appointed by them, or later on by other eminent men, with the consent of the whole church, and have ministered to the flock of Christ without blame, humbly, peacefully and worthily, and for many years have received a universally favorable testimony.[68]

Even though this passage from Clement's letter is extremely difficult to interpret, its general sense is sufficiently clear.

The line of the *diadochê* must not be broken in the Church. After the falling asleep of those bishops ordained by the apostles, other individuals should assume their ministry. This is an unquestionable law of ecclesial life which derives from the very nature of the Church. No local church can exist without the eucharistic assembly and no assembly can exist without a senior presbyter. Any interruption in their ministry would signify interruption in the existence of the local church. The *diadochê* not only preserves the succession of episcopal ministry—it also safeguards its charismatic nature. First presiders were tested by the Spirit (*dokimasantes tô pneumati*). Their successors should likewise be tested (*dedokimasmenoi*) and ordained with the assent of the whole church. In and through the Spirit the apostles were ordained for their ministry, in and through the Spirit the apostles ordained the first bishops, and in and through the Spirit, with the assent of the whole church, must their successors be ordained. Clement of Rome clearly emphasizes the charismatic nature of not only the apostolic ministry but of the episcopal ministry as well. For this reason, it is quite risky to speak, as it is custom, of the institutional nature of the apostolic and episcopal ministry in Clement. The contrasting of institutional and charismatic types of ministries in the early church proceeds from a misunderstanding of the nature of ministry. Apostles were appointed by Christ, but they became apostles on the day of Pentecost, as Clement himself says (*meta plêrophorias pneumatos*). Bishops were ordained by apostles, but the goal of this ordination was so that the gifts of the Spirit would be sent down upon those who were already chosen by God.

This is a general sense of the cited passage from Clement's letter. In commenting on this passage we must not forget that Clement's goal was far from convincing the church of Corinth to accept the doctrine concerning the *diadochê*. This concept was beyond dispute for both the Roman and Corinthian churches. The individuals who caused the "uproar" in the church of Corinth certainly were not aware that they were transgressing the letter of the law concerning the *diadochê* of presbyters-bishops. They did not intend to replace forever or for a time the presbyterial ministry with another one, e.g., the prophetic ministry, as we see in the *Didache*. They wanted to replace one group of presbyters with another, without thus interrupting the succession of their ministry. Hence, Clement had no need to justify the doctrine concerning the *diadochê*. If this is so, what did he seek to prove? From the context of chapter 42 of his letter, it is clear that his emphasis is not so much on the concept of the *diadochê* as on the claim that one group of presbyters should come in the place of another. The commandment or an order which the apostles had given did not mean to establish the *diadochê* among the bishops, but to ensure their orderly succession. Since the apostles through Jesus

Christ knew of the future strife for the position of episcopacy, i.e., they knew that the order of succession would be upset, they prescribed that new bishops should come into the places of the old ones only following the death of the latter. Therefore, to remove the bishops who fulfill their ministry without reproach is to transgress the commandment of the apostles. The Corinthians' fault was not that they rejected the *diadochê* but that they had upset the order within the *diadochê* itself.[69]

The concept of the *diadochê* among the bishops implies the succession of their ministry. By means of ordination one bishop receives his ministry from another. Can we state on this basis that bishops, being ordained by apostles, received their ministry? The apostolate, as we pointed out above, was an exceptional phenomenon, and as such could not be succeeded to at all. Hence the bishops cannot be regarded as the apostles' successors in the same sense as one bishop is a successor of another. We do not find this idea in Clement. For Clement, the ministry of bishops-presbyters and the ministry of apostles were special ministries. To confuse these ministries would be to transgress the will of God, which is not the confusion of ministries but their diversity. The succession can only occur among homogeneous, not heterogeneous, ministries. The concept of heterogeneous ministries itself refutes the idea of succession. If the ministry of apostles could be succeeded, apostles, not bishops, would succeed it. In the understanding of the Church, the senior presbyters began to be regarded legitimately as bishops since they indeed had accepted their ministry. But never were the bishops regarded as apostles. Nevertheless, this answer does not exhaust the whole question, only a part of it. Before we proceed to examine the issue further we should give a résumé of what we find on the issue of the *diadochê* in Clement. The beginning of episcopal ministry was the apostles' ordaining the first bishops whose ministry was to be exercised continuously in the local churches. A proper order should be preserved in the Church, the order that proceeds from the will of God, and this must be observed through the *diadochê* of the bishops. It is expressed through the due succession in which new bishops come into the place of the deceased ones.

5. The apostles ordained the first-fruits of the faithful to be bishops and deacons. The church's thinking assigned great significance to this fact since it established a link between the ministry of bishop-presbyters and the ministry of apostles. Luke specifically mentions the ordination of presbyters by Paul and Barnabas: "And when they (i.e. Barnabas and Paul) had appointed elders for them in every church, with prayer and fasting they committed them to the Lord in whom they believed" (Acts 14.23). It does not matter whether Clement of Rome depended on

Luke as a source or not, for the appointment of the first-fruits of the faithful to be bishops was a living tradition of the Church which was at the foundation of all its ecclesial structure. Given the significance of this fact we have to be precise about its proper meaning. We have to reject firmly the notion that the ordination of the first-fruits of the faithful to be bishops was an individual act on the part of the apostles that derived from their power. This is how scholastic doctrine sees it being influenced by individualism that has penetrated Church life. On the basis of a random comment of Jerome,[70] it regards the right to ordain as an exclusive pre-rogative of episcopal ministry. Our modern individualism was unknown to the life of the early church. Ordination was an ecclesial rather than an individual act of the one in charge. We must not imagine that the apostles, preaching the gospel throughout lands and cities, were ordaining the first among the faithful to be bishops and deacons, afterwards forming a local church. Ordination cannot be done outside of the church because ordination is an ecclesial act that postulates the church's existence. If ordination does take place, this means there is a local church, but if there is no local church, there is no ordination. Apostles were or-daining the first-fruits of the faithful within the local churches rather than apart from them. But how were these churches formed? Just as the Church of God was actualized in the figure of Peter at the first eucharistic assembly so also were the local churches actualized in the figures of the apostles. The actualization of the local church was an actualization in it of the ministry of presiding. The local church was formed when an apostle, together with the first-fruits of the faithful celebrated in it the first Eucharist. Episcopal ordination was performed in the eucharistic as-sembly of a local church. At this assembly the newly ordained bishops took the seats that the apostles had at the first eucharistic assemblies of the Jerusalem church. In particular the senior presbyter took the place that before him was occu-pied by an apostle who celebrated the first Eucharist in this church. Celebrating the first Eucharist, an apostle was the first presider of this local church. Topologi-cally the ministry of presbyters and of the senior presbyter in particular continued the ministry of the apostles. Presbyters ordained by the apostles received from them the ministry of presidency. It was one of the functions of the apostolate, but it was not their special ministry. It becomes a special ministry for the bishops ordained by the apostles. Therefore, receiving from the apostles their ministry of presidency, bishops were not the successors of their apostolic ministry but rather merely of their place in the eucharistic assembly.

The connection between the apostolate and episcopate is not only that the apostles ordained the first bishops but also that the latter received their ministry of presidency from the apostles. Thus the episcopal *diadochê* equals an unbroken chain of episcopal ministries beginning from the first bishop ordained by the apostles, from whom he received his ministry of presidency. In this sense the apostles are a part of the chain of the *diadochê* of bishops.[71]

6. It has been an accepted point of view that we do not find any indications of episcopal succession in the letters of Ignatius. Moreover, the letters of Ignatius are used to prove that our first ideologue of episcopal ministry had no knowledge of such a concept.[72] Such an opinion seems suspicious to us. Indeed, how could the Roman church appeal to the doctrine concerning the *diadochê* if it had not been already widely accepted? But is it certain that Ignatius knew nothing of the concept of succession? He did not speak about it directly since it was irrelevant to the goals he was pursuing. He sought to establish in the church's understanding the singularity of the senior presbyter who had become a bishop on the basis of his ministry as a high priest. The concept of the *diadochê*, the way it was presented in his time, did not provide him with a decisive proof in order to ground the notion of the senior presbyter becoming a bishop in the church's thinking. Nevertheless, the letters of Ignatius allow us to argue for his knowledge of this concept. The topological concept of bishop-presbyters taking their succession from the apostles must have been close to Ignatius's understanding. He himself construed his theory of the bishop's high priesthood on the basis of topology. We find indications in support of this view in his letters. We have shown above[73] how we should read the statement of Ignatius that the presbytery takes the place of the council of the apostles. Probably he was thinking at the same time of the first eucharistic assemblies of the church in Jerusalem where apostles, in a certain sense, stood as the council around St. Peter, and of the Last Supper of Christ, where all the apostles were a council around Christ. But he unwittingly gave preference to the image of the Last Supper in connection with his doctrine of episcopacy. In the same Jerusalem church the presbyters, appointed by the apostles, took their places at its eucharistic assembly. It would be incorrect to conclude from this that Ignatius argued only for the topologic aspect of apostolic succession of the presbyters. We should not forget that Ignatius lived in the age of transition. The senior presbyter, having become a bishop, was a figure distinct from presbyters, but not yet separated from the presbytery. He occupied a special place within the presbytery just as he occupied a special place at the eucharistic assembly. Affirming the topological succession of presbyters Ignatius confirmed to an even greater extent the apostolic succession of the senior presbyter who became a bishop.[74] The topological high priesthood of a bishop does not in any sense contradict this understanding. As proof we can cite the fact that thereafter the high priesthood became connected with the concept of apostolic succession.

7. In the understanding of Clement of Rome the *diadochê* applies to all bishop-presbyters including even the deacons, but *de facto* it applies, most of all, to the senior among them because in and through him the *diadochê* is manifested. If our conjecture is correct then, as we have already seen, the whole letter of Clement was provoked by the fact that the senior presbyter was among the deposed. When the ecclesial consciousness tried to express in concrete terms the commonly held teaching on the succession of presbyter-bishops by citing the consecutive list of names, it naturally focused only on the names of senior presbyters. The memory of the Church could not retain the names of all presbyters. Moreover, it was impossible to determine the proper order of succession for some presbyters because one could not tell which presbyter assumed the place of which in the presbytery. Senior presbyters were in a different position. Their identity was always specified and they always followed in succession one after another. The succession of the senior presbyter secured the succession of everybody else. Sooner or later the need must have been felt for creating the lists of succession. Naturally only senior presbyters were included in these lists. One can hardly suppose that Hegesippus was the first who began to compile such lists but apparently he was the first to make such a list for the church of Rome.[75]

> And when I had come to Rome I made a list of succession until Anicetus, whose deacon was Eleutherios. And Anicetus was succeeded by Soter, and he by Eleutherios. In every succession, and in every city (*en hekastê de diadochê kai en hekastêi polei*) that is held which is preached by the law and the prophets and the Lord.[76]

It is impossible to get an impression of the view on the *diadochê* that Hegesippus held on the basis of this brief reference by Eusebius. Without constructing a larger theory we will limit ourselves just to the content of this quote. Hegesippus indicates in precise terms that he compiled the list of succession for the church of Rome. With respect to other churches the assertion of Hegesippus that every church has this kind of succession is merely his own conclusion. This conclusion is quite legitimate because the doctrine of succession itself was contained in the church tradition, but we can hardly expect it to find expression in every church. The list for the church of Rome which Hegesippus composed ends with Eleutherios. Should we then think that St. Peter was at the head of the list? It is doubtful because the *diadochê* for Hegesippus meant only the continuation of the ministry of senior presbyters or bishops, without any indication that this succession somehow preserves the apostolic ministry.[77] Given the stage the *diadochê* doctrine was at in the time of Hegesippus, especially in the Roman church, it could not have included apostles, because apostles were never regarded as senior presbyters. If in fact Hegesippus did compile the succession lists for other churches, aside from the Roman one, he was by far not always able to put the name of some apostle in the beginning of the list.

The second half of the second century was a turning point for the doctrine of episcopal succession. The "hiatus" which we have found in Clement of Rome with his concept of the *diadochê* was gradually compensated for by the idea of the high priestly ministry of the bishop. When the Church's thinking accepted the idea that Christ bestowed this ministry upon the apostles, it found a concrete link between the high priestly ministry of Christ and the one of the bishops. Christ entrusted the high priesthood to the apostles who ordained bishops, handing this ministry down to them. Meanwhile, a missing link was found in the doctrine of the *diadochê* connecting apostles and bishops. The doctrine of the succession of bishops evolves into the doctrine of apostolic succession. The task had become so much easier, given that from the very beginning an existing connection was recognized between the apostolate and the episcopal ministry. Topological succession of bishops evolved into the direct apostolic succession. The apostles, laying the foundations for the churches, were their first high priests and therefore they qualified to be put at the head of the lists of episcopal succession. Every bishop in his local church becomes a direct successor of the apostles.[78]

Irenaeus stands on the border between the topological and direct doctrines of apostolic succession, but he leans toward the second. According to Irenaeus the bishops are "instituted by the apostles" (*ab apostolis instituti*),[79] and "have the succession from the apostles" (*successionem habent ab apostolis*).[80] How did Irenaeus understand the *successio ab apostolis*? We have no ground to think that Irenaeus was not aware of the doctrine concerning the high priestly ministry of bishops. However, he brings to the foreground not their status as high priests but rather as teachers. This was dictated by the goals of his struggle against the heresies. The "treasury of faith" is entrusted to churches but is guarded by bishops, for at their ordination they receive the "reliable charism of truth" (*charisma veritatis certum*).[81] They are witnesses and guardians of tradition coming from the apostles, for each bishop in succession through the apostles receives the charism of fidelity to the apostolic tradition. This charism exactly comprised the essence of episcopal succession from the apostles. If we view Irenaeus's concept of succession exclusively from this perspective, his concept finds affinity with the concept of the *diadochê* of *didaskaloi* as expounded by Clement of Alexandria and Origen. One essential difference is that in Irenaeus it was not the *didaskaloi* who were the keepers of the tradition, but rather the presbyters who were ordained by the apostles and to whom the apostles entrusted the churches.[82] Therefore the succession of bishops from the apostles secures the authentic character of faith held by the churches which are governed by the bishops,[83] for in these churches the *charisma veritatis* never runs out. For this reason, for Irenaeus, the succession lists become extremely significant. Irenaeus claimed that he could have compiled a similar list for every local church but that there is no need to do that.[84] It sufficed to give the list of bishops for one church—the Roman church, "the very great, the very ancient, and universally known Church founded and organized at Rome by the two most glorious apostles, Peter and Paul" (*maximae, et antiquissimae, et omnibus cognitae, a gloriosissimis duobus apostolis Petro et Paulo fundatae et constitutae ecclesiae*).[85] Due to this special status of the Roman church every other church should conform its teaching with Rome: "It is a matter of necessity that every church should agree with this church" (*necesse est ad hanc ecclesiam convenire omnem ecclesiam*).[86] However, it seems that Irenaeus does not yet seem to think that Peter and Paul, who founded the church of Rome, were also its bishops.[87] Nevertheless, he clearly expresses the idea of succession from apostles. Through the ordination of the first bishop or bishops, the apostles handed over to them the *charisma veritatis*. The bishops are the apostles' successors as teachers and guardians of the ecclesial tradition, but the function of teaching can hardly be isolated from high priesthood.[88] Irenaeus must have regarded the teaching as a function of presidency with which high priesthood was firmly connected. Topological succession here is clearly evolving toward the direct succession.

The church of Rome accepted Irenaeus's concept of succession because it was possible that this teaching was already extant there. The Roman church gave the final formulaic shape to this teaching, drawing from the idea of high priesthood of bishops that includes teaching and guarding of faith. This is the shape in which we encounter the doctrine of succession in Hippolytus of Rome. The apostles were the first to receive the gifts of the Holy Spirit which the bishops now possess, being their successors who received from them the high priesthood and the function of teaching.[89] It is hardly possible to consider this teaching belonging to Hippolytus's personal theology. More likely Hippolytus only formulated what he already found in Rome and what Pope Victor and Hippolytus's later rival, Pope Callistus, actually practiced. Possibly another rival of Callistus, Tertullian, also assisted in the final formulation of the doctrine of apostolic succession.[90] Perhaps it is not a coincidence that Tertullian called Callistus by the name *pontifex maximus*, but it is a difficult challenge to rely on Tertullian due to his passionate nature and the extremely polemical character of his writings. If we leave Tertullian aside, Hippolytus would be the most faithful witness to the fact that the doctrine of apostolic succession had been formed on the basis of the doctrine of high priestly ministry. Since this time, on the level of dogmatic teaching, the high priesthood of the bishop includes his apostolic succession and the latter presupposes the former. This is very much in agreement with the historical development of the doctrine concerning the bishop's apostolic succession and his high priestly ministry.

8. With this we conclude our study of the transformation of the senior presbyter into a bishop. Thereafter all understanding of what episcopal ministry contains develops on the basis of the concept of apostolic succession that includes high priesthood and teaching. We needed to turn to the first pages in the history of this process in support for our description of the original organization of the Church. We did not seek its origin outside of the Church but within the Church, assuming that in the Church nothing can come out of nothing because everything it contains has its roots in the Church's past, even if this past had been swept aside by what came to replace it. We deliberately avoided discussing how the empirical factors influenced this process since their influence at this time was negligible. Just as a force [in physics] has to have a certain point of application in order to be able to function, so the empirical factors have to have their own point of application in the Church in order to influence ecclesial life. This point of application for the empirical factor was found in what the Church contained in itself and was developing from within. Our task was to show that the starting point for the development of episcopal ministry was to be found in the Church itself. It did not emerge at a certain historic moment as something new, something never before found in the Church. The early church possessed in potential the foundations of this ministry even though it did not have the ministry itself. Instead it knew one single ministry of bishop-presbyters, the first of whom presided over the others at the eucharistic assembly.

Chapter 8

The Power of Love

---

1. The Church's thousand-year history since its first millennium has significantly modified its life, creating forms radically different from those of the primitive era, establishing ecclesial ideas which no longer contain its ancient teaching. In reality it is now quite difficult for us to understand the first pages of the history of the church. It is a struggle for us to abstract these forms from those to which we have been accustomed, so much so that other structures than those we know now seem almost impossible. All of the modifications which have occurred in the life of the Church and which still are taking place are the consequences of its historical existence. From the beginning, the Church found itself surrounded in the common course of human existence. It lives in history; that is, history is where it realizes its mission. It is impossible to exclude the Church from history, for it itself has a historical dimension. One also cannot separate history from the Church, for it is in the Church that history finds its meaning and fulfillment.

There were only concrete churches in early Christianity, located in a specific places. There was no distinction between an abstract idea and a concrete view of the Church, for the Church resided, lived, and was revealed in all the fullness of its unity and in all the unity of its fullness in each local church. The historical aspect of the Church has to do neither with its essence nor its nature, but with all its manifestations in empirical life. The external forms of the Church's life, which proceed from its nature, are influenced by empirical factors. This influence is completely legitimate and natural with respect to the external, but it is unjustifiable and inappropriate when empirical factors burst into the Church and affect its internal life, leading the very essence of the Church into the historical process. Empirical principles replace the ecclesiological ones and most certainly provoke distortions that are more or less profound. The Church's history has known just such distortions. Most often they were corrected, but not all of them and not all the time. During nearly two thousand years of history, under the influence of empirical factors that have penetrated the Church, a "sediment" has formed, one which has concealed the true life of the Church almost entirely. Most of the time we slide across the surface of this outer covering without attempting to penetrate to the authentic essence of the Church. Finally we see the Church as it appears on this surface and we take this external manifestation for the actual essence of the Church.

External, empirical factors are thus "ecclesialized" and the empirical principles that are their foundation come to play the role of ecclesiological principles. Thus they lose all contact with the empirical reality which was their source. But even then, when they no longer are relevant in empirical life, they continue to shape the life of the Church. This creates a rupture between the empirical stratum of the Church's life, which corresponds to a given historical moment, and the general history of humanity. Thus we can see why it is that the life of Byzantium, with all its particularities long since having disappeared from the stage of history, has been preserved, immutable and unchangeable, in our ecclesial life. Byzantium survives in the Church. The shadow of the Byzantine emperor remains present during certain liturgical actions when we reconstitute the ceremonial of the Byzantine court. Meanwhile, the true spiritual heritage of Byzantium is hardly known to us. We are not always able to distinguish the action of authentic ecclesial sources from those of empirical factors assimilated by the Church over a long period of time. And what is more, in constituting a kind of historical moment fossilized in ecclesial life, these empirical factors progressively distance the Church from the progress of history, preventing the legitimate effects of new factors due to the mutations of history. The true nature of the Church is no longer able to be manifest in the actual historical conditions and this prevents the Church from fulfilling its mission in the historical life of humanity. Our era demands that in our ecclesial life dead empirical factors be distinguished from the truly ecclesial ones so that the life of the Church may be opened to the impact of the new and the historical aspect of the Church's existence be brought back to life. This is the only condition under which a true renaissance of the Church's life would be possible.

As with all of history, that of the Church is irreversible. We cannot return to the time of early Christianity, not only because of radically changed historical conditions but also because the experience of the Holy Spirit's guidance of the church, accumulated through the passage of time, cannot be laid aside. Nevertheless, the time of early Christianity remains an ideal for us, according to which we must check our ecclesial life. It was the time when the nature of the Church shone clearly through the fabric of history. Examining this first era should assist us in eliminating the superficial deposit formed by historical events and show us more clearly the path to follow.

2. The Church was actualized on the day of Pentecost by the Spirit and in the Spirit.[1] The Church is the place where the Spirit acts and the Spirit is the principle of its life and activity. The Church lives and acts by the Spirit, with the assistance of the charismatic gifts which God distributes in it, as he wills. Grace is the "only thing that moves" everything within the Church. The tradition of the Church has its origin in the Spirit, not in any human actions. On the first day of Pentecost, the Church appeared already with the fundamental principles of its organization, founded upon the same Spirit who created it. Consequently, the organizing principle in the Church is the Spirit and this excludes every other principle, since every other principle would be external to the Church.

In the course of history, law penetrated ecclesial life and gradually became its organizing principle. External factors belonging to the "former age" found their way into the Church, which was the beginning of the "last days." Law belongs to the "former age" and is alien to the Church. The nature of law is not transformed in the Church, for if it were so changed, law would not be law. Once established in the Church ecclesiastical law was created, based upon Roman law. The ecclesial consciousness approximated the ecclesiastical canon (*kanôn*) to civil law (*nomos*). In both, the Church recognized realities of the same order. From an empirical perspective, for such is the verdict of history, law helped to consolidate ecclesiastical organization and government, making for a number of modifications in them. At least such seems evident to church historians. Concerning the consolidation of ecclesial life, our judgment is unilateral at best, for we really do not know what this life would have been like had it not been penetrated by law. On the one hand, this opinion seems to manifest a skepticism about the action of charismatic principles and a conviction, avowed or not, that only law is able to be the organizing principle of life, the Spirit being able only to create anarchy. Such an approach would have been impossible among the first leaders of the Church because they knew that the power of God is accomplished through weakness (2 Cor 12:9). On the other hand, does this point of view not see law as absent in the early church, the only principle of its life and its organization being grace?[2]

Do not be mismated with unbelievers. For what partnership have righteousness and iniquity? Or what fellowship has light with darkness? What accord has Christ with Belial? Or what has a believer in common with an unbeliever? (2 Cor. 6.14–15)

Under Constantine the Great, the Church received the peace which it had hoped for and which it needed, but it was constrained to be harnessed to an alien yoke, that of Caesar and Roman law. Thus appeared what St. Paul had feared, the mixture of light and darkness, and the believers sharing with non-believers. While the great miracle of history was that the emperor became Christian, the Christians would forget the problem bearing on them: would Caesar be able to become a Christian and remain Caesar? The conversion of the emperor had obscured Christian consciousness. Enchanted by this conversion, Christianity could not see that the Roman empire did not change, but remained the same except for the persecutions, and that spiritually and morally Constantine's empire was inferior to those of Trajan or Marcus Aurelius. No change, no *metanoia* took place which could make the empire Christian. Caesar could not see any usefulness in repentance for the state, certainly nothing useful in rejecting the very principles upon which the empire was itself built. Even if the empire had wanted to, it would not have been able to change without destroying the *pax Romana*, the unique principle of which remained law. Thus in becoming Christian Constantine did not cease to be Caesar and brought pagan imperial consciousness into the Church. He set about ruling the Church just as he had ruled the state, all the more since the lines dividing the Church and state were blurred. Did not one of the emperors say that the fundamental principles of church life and their laws rested in him, the emperor, and thus the Roman state became the church under the rule of a Caesar? Despite all of this, or perhaps all the more because of this and for the same reason, the new and shining horizons which opened before the Church led one to believe that the kingdom of Caesar had now become *civitas christianorum*, the city, the kingdom of the Christians. Several Christian authors would continue to reject the kingdom of Caesar. St. Augustine contrasted Christ to Caesar, noting that the Jews and following them others, had preferred Caesar to Christ—*non habemus regem solum Caesarem*—"we have no king but Caesar." However, he believed that a joining of the two was possible; two cities could become one, if *rex terrenus sub rege caelesti, rex caelestis super omnia*: "the earthly king is subject to the king of heaven who reigned over all things."[3] St. Augustine was a rare exception. It is significant that the fall of Rome inspired in him hardly a word of regret while for St. Jerome the same seemed to mark the very end of the world. And even St. Augustine saw Rome as *mater nostra in hac nati sumus*—"our mother in whom we are born and have life."[4] The majority of other writers would believe the possibility of the city of God being realized in the Roman empire. They welcomed Caesar as the king of the city of God on earth, forgetting that Christians have no permanent city but seek for the one that is to come (Heb 13.14). Or better yet, had they not come to believe that the city to come was the kingdom of Caesar? In the second century, the ardent expectation of the coming of Christ in glory had diminished somewhat. By the fourth century Christians seemed no longer to think of it, for the anointed one of God ruled on the earth. The protests of Christians against a total submission to the alien yoke did not produce much in the way of tangible results, because it was not the emperor who was seen as problematic, only the abuse of imperial power. We do not know what was the reaction of the twelfth-century church to the solemn declaration of the emperor which said:

> Everything is permitted to the emperors, because there is on earth no difference between divine and imperial power. All is allowed the emperors and they can use the name of God together with their own, because they have received the imperial dignity of God and there is no distance between God and themselves.[5]

But we do know that in twelfth-century Byzantium they believed firmly that the anointing of the emperor washed away all his sin.[6] One could ask if the imperial cult had disappeared in the Christian empire or if it continued even to the very fall of Byzantium. The Christian Caesar remained an *Augustus*. Everything that had any relationship to the person of the emperor became by this very fact sacred.

The kingdom of Caesar could not exist without law and the church of the state had recognized this. The church did more. It itself took law as the foundation of its organization and administration, modeling its life upon that of the Christian city. This was easily done, since law had already begun to penetrate the life of the church from the time of Cyprian of Carthage. In accepting the law, had not the church renounced grace? "I do not nullify the grace of God; for if justification were through the law, then Christ died to no purpose" (Gal 2.21). The historical church could not consider rejecting grace, for in so doing it would be rejecting its very self. Also important here would be the modifications brought about by law, which had not distorted its essence but had succeeded only in creating around it an empirical dimension, the visible church. In pursuing this direction ecclesial thinking attempted a synthesis of grace and law. Was it successful? It does not seem so, for such an approach would always limit grace rather than the law. Such a synthesis is in fact impossible, for there is nothing common to grace and law, which are realities of two completely different orders.

The doctrine of the visible and the invisible churches which appeared after the formation of this empirical dimension, which in turn brought in its own principles and rules, became a fatal temptation for theological consideration. This doctrine of the visible and invisible churches, which stemmed from an empirical event, confirmed the legitimacy of the existence of law in the life of the Church. The visible church is the church on earth. The invisible church is the church triumphant in heaven. The two churches were not completely identical and their identity was further weakened by the affirmation that the church on earth is directed by the vicars of Christ. The heavenly church is that of the saints. The church on earth has to do with sinful human beings and is directed with account taken of the corrupted nature of its members. Consequently, it becomes normal that the same laws that rule the empirical life would also rule in the earthly church. Law exists in this church because of the corrupt nature of mankind manifest in empirical human life and manifest also in the life of the church. The church on earth and the Christian state are of the same character. At their foundation is the same corrupt and non-transfigured human nature, that of humanity living life on earth.[7] This is why the Byzantine situation could not distinguish whether the church was in the state or the state was in the earthly church. Grace was sufficient for the heavenly church just as the earthly church needed law.

The so-called synthesis of grace and law which claimed to realize the doctrine of the visible and invisible churches then was made at the cost of the integral body of Christ. Could one admit the division of this body? To divide the body of the Church is to divide Christ himself. "Is Christ divided? Was Paul crucified for you? Or were you baptized in the name of Paul?" (1 Cor 1.13). According to the doctrine of the catholicity of the Church, the unity of the Church is absolute. There are not two churches, the invisible and the visible, the heavenly and the earthly. There is only one Church of God in Christ which dwells in all the fullness of its unity in each local church with its eucharistic assembly. In using the terms cited above, we could say that the invisible church manifests itself fully in the visible church and that the latter manifests itself in the invisible church. This is made real in every Eucharist and we attest to it in confessing the true body and blood of Christ. The local church lives in empirical reality but this does not exhaust this reality, for it is not of this world. If the Church were to be defined completely by empirical reality, that is, the reality of this world, it would be a mixture of the old and the new ages, and this would mean that the Church remains always in the old age. Scholastic theology approximates this position. Now, in being in the Church we are in the Spirit, for the Church is the Church of the Holy Spirit. The Church, which is manifest in a visible manner in all its fullness in the course of the eucharistic assembly of the local church, cannot live according to disparate principles which contradict each other. The synthesis of grace and the law would not be possible except if law, as grace, had been made part of the very essence of the Church. If law cannot exist in the "invisible church," then it cannot exist in the one which is "visible." Reciprocally, if the existence of law is justified in the "visible" church, it ought also to be the same in the church which is "invisible."

The primitive Church did not recognize law. This was not because its organization was merely in a primitive or embryonic stage. Neither was it because this organization was badly determined or unstable to the point of approaching anarchy. It had no need of law because it existed out of that which was its nature, not from that which was alien to its being.

3. Law remains the foundation of empirical social life.[8] It may be said to be humanity's supreme achievement in the course of history. Law governs relationships among people, establishing above all what its subject ought not to do.[9] The negative character of law is by no means a fault, but something good. Because of it, law protects the individual from all sorts of aggression, not only on the part of other persons but also on the part of society and the state. Every modification or violation of the nature of the law leads to oppression of the human being. Some would actually want to attribute a positive character to law. Temptations to modify law's nature put into question its very existence. If such a law were to exist, it would not be able to accomplish its function of protecting the individual in his or her life in society. It would bestow enormous power upon the collective dimension of society, its institutions, by placing them above the human person, in effect making the individual dependent upon the collectivity.

To change the negative character of law into a positive one is a breakdown of value in social life. It makes the state greater, more significant than the individual. The problem of the relationship between the state and the individual cannot be completely resolved. Can one find an equilibrium between the individual and the state which at once respects the inviolability of the individual and allows the state to accomplish its purposes? If these were limited to protecting the person in social and public life and protecting this social life, then the problem would be easily resolved. But this would be on the condition that the state may be in the second position with respect to the individual and be in the service of the individual, not the individual in the service of the state. The empirical individual tends in his own social relationships to be dependent on the existence of others and even on that of the state. In order to protect other individuals and itself, the state must limit or control the individual in his tendencies. But by its nature the state would not recognize limits to its own expansiveness either externally or internally and would not fear absorbing the personality of its members. By nature, every state is "ecumenical" because its identity contains that of a worldwide state; internally, it is "global" in that it absorbs all that it contains. Law limits every individual, thus serving the interests of the state. But law also limits the state in any aggression against the individual. The threshold of this limitation ought to be the individual, for in legally limiting the latter the state ought not to destroy the individual, even if its own interests and those of other individuals might demand this. The law indicates both to the individual and to the state that which it ought not to do, meaning to protect the one from the other.

But if one recognizes the primacy of the state over the individual, all the efforts of the state would be in its own defense against the individual and not in protection of the individual. In taking itself to be the superior value and sometimes even the ultimate value, the state comes to consider the individual as a means and not as an end. The individual used by the state as a means to attain its own purposes then ceases to be an individual. The individual having primary value over the state recognizes the latter, insofar as the state having the superior value, alienates or negates the individual. "Human rights" would be inviolable if the state recognized the primacy of the individual and because of this submitted itself to a superior value that is not empirical, but abstract. When the "human rights" are determined and provided only by the state they are clearly relative. The state can annul them temporarily or definitively if its own interests demand this. As regards supreme value, the state tends toward the domination of the individual, attempting to submit the individual to its own interests. The limitation of this domination is not to be found in the individual but in the state. The state's norms become positive, for it shows less interest in hindering its members from hurting other individuals (and, consequently, the state itself) than in their accomplishing its own demands. At the same time, the state does not always take account of the interests of individuals. The law then indicates not only what one ought not to do, but also that which one must do, again concerning those who are members of the state. Positive norms are not limited to saying what one ought to do. By their very natures they tend to monopolize the conscience of individuals. And the state is forced to create among its members a sensibility which is adequate to guarantee positive norms. Meanwhile, even if the étatist ideology prevails, the state remains legitimate as long as it does not attempt to dominate the consciousness of its members. From the moment the first step in this direction is taken, an alarm is sounded and the state built upon law becomes transformed into a totalitarian state.

In such a state, there are no longer any limits on its domination of the individual. In principle, it is no longer believed that the law can limit the state in favor of the individual. The state now demands the entire person, seeking to dominate his inner world, as well. Law becomes almost completely positive; it ceases to protect the individual from the state. The totalitarian state has no need of individuals. To it they are essentially a problem, since the features which comprise an individual are incompatible with the idea of a totalitarian state. Whether the state admits that the individual has a meaning in himself is secondary here. In either case this kind of state tends to dominate all its members. It protects their interests only insofar as these correspond to those of the state, for it is not the individual as such that the state protects but the collectivity. A totalitarian state is also able to sacrifice totally the interests of its members for its own purposes.

The great difference between a legitimate state and a totalitarian one has to do with law and the role that it plays in the state's life. The transformation of a legitimate state into a totalitarian one is not so difficult as one would like to believe, for the nature of the state is essentially the same in either case. In a totalitarian state the nature of this reality is denuded, while in a legitimate one it is veiled by the law. To the extent that the action of law is weakened and its character changed, the legitimate state then tends to become a totalitarian one.

4. The Church recognizes the place of the law in empirical social life. It considers the law as the most important factor in the public life in which it itself participates. The Church cannot be disinterested in public life because it is the life in which its members exist and are active and because its own empirical life intimately depends upon the basic principles structuring the social and public life which is governed by the law. In protecting the individual, the law guarantees in a certain measure the life and activity of the members of the Church both within and outside the state, that is to say, the free and independent existence of the Church within the confines of the state. The situation of the Church within a legitimate state or a state which, in attacking the private life of its members, is tending toward totalitarianism, can actually be more difficult than existing within a state that is totalitarian. Nevertheless, whatever its perversions, the legitimate state cannot refuse the Church a possibility of free existence, for such a state, if it remains faithful to itself, cannot refuse religious freedom to its members. This is why the Church recognizes law in empirical existence and strives without wanting to direct them to maintain the structures of public and social life within the limits of authentic law, that which has as its mission to protect the individual.

The totalitarian state is able to recognize the Church and allow it a certain freedom of action within limits which it determines. But it is also able to deny the Church's existence and limit its activity to such a point that practically speaking, its existence becomes nearly or even completely illegal. The protection accorded to the Church by the totalitarian state almost always demands sacrifices of the Church, for the totalitarian state never sacrifices anything to its members or to the organizations within its confines. Under certain conditions, a balance between the Church and the totalitarian state can be attained, but it always remains precarious because the Church can never recognize the totalitarian state, just as the state can never really recognize the Church. Conflict between them is inevitable even if this can be postponed for a shorter or longer period of time. The totalitarian state rejects the Church because it cannot allow the existence of an autonomous spiritual domain. The Church cannot recognize the totalitarian state because it demands a certain renunciation of itself or, in any case, the renunciation of its mission in the world. Independently of the ideology which it professes, the Church cannot recognize the totalitarian state, for it cannot give its approval to the enslavement of the individual even to the most sublime purposes. History has not known of an ideological state that did not seek to dominate the individual. Consequently if one proposes to the Church to choose between a "lay" or secular state that is legitimate and a "Christian" one which is totalitarian the Church clearly ought to prefer the former.

5. The Church which defends the law existing beyond its own sphere and which even has need of such law, nevertheless rejects this kind of law within its own life.[10] Whatever the importance of law in empirical life, it is this life which the law expresses, with all its imperfections. Law makes its appearance when reciprocal love among people has been weakened. Law protects the individual who does not need such protection if relationships among people are governed by love. Being imperfect, empirical life has no love and the individual is imperfect because of his non-regenerated nature. Thus there is the need for protection, not only in relationship to other individuals but also with respect to the state and society. The imperfection of empirical human life is transcended in the Church by renaissance, a rebirth. Life which is lived under the law becomes charismatic. In the charismatic order of things, there is no place for the law since the individual has no need of being protected. By its very nature grace excludes the law just as grace eliminates the law of the Old Testament by fulfilling it. One of the great contributions of St. Paul is his having posed to Christian consciousness the problem of law and grace.

For I through the law died to the law, that I might live to God. I have been crucified with Christ; it is no longer I who live, but Christ who lives in me; and the life
I now live in the flesh I live by faith in the Son of God, who loved me and gave
himself for me. I do not nullify the grace of God; for if justification were through
the law, then Christ died to no purpose. (Gal. 2.19–21)

The death to the law of the Old Testament is simultaneously the death to law in
general. In the Church we are born to new life so that we can "live for God." The
foundation of this new life is love because "God is love" (1 John 4.8). According to
Ignatius of Antioch the Church itself is love (*agapê*). The Church is love because it
has been created by the love of Christ who loved us and gave his life for us. "By
this we know love, that he laid down his life for us; and we ought to lay down our
lives for the brethren" (1 John 3.16). Being in God, Christians are in love, a love
which has as its model the love of God who has sent his Son into the world. "So
we know and believe the love God has for us. God is love, and he who abides in
love abides in God, and God abides in him" (1 John 4.16). Life in the Church is life
in Christ and it is the life of Christ which is anyone who lives in the Church. "It is
no longer I who live, but Christ who lives in me" (*zô de ouketi egô, zê de en emoi
Christos*). By his life in Christ a man becomes a person in the Church. The absolute
person is God, for only he possesses the fullness of life, and man becomes a person by the adoption which is given in the Church through the Spirit as interme-
diary. "See what love the Father has given us, that we should be called children of
God; and so we are. The reason why the world does not know us is that it did not
know him" (1 John 3.1). The one who lives in love should not want to live at the
expense of others, for in each of them it is Christ who lives. On the contrary,
such a one is ready to renounce himself for the others, even to giving his life for his
brothers. We also ought to give our life for our brothers, for "he who finds his life
will lose it, and he who loses his life for my sake will find it" (Matt 10.39). The sacrifice of oneself for the sake of Christ means the renunciation of individual rights
which are essential to empirical life: the protection of physical existence is in effect
the principal mission of the law which, in practice, it is not capable of realizing.

To give up the law is to transcend it. One transcends an imperfect reality in
order to seek perfection. The primitive Church professed this renunciation of the
law in relationships with others. "You have heard . . . but I say to you . . ." That
which was given to the ancients was the perfect law, not only for that time, but
perfect law as such. No matter its perfection, this law has been surpassed by that
love which is the free manifestation of the love of the children of God, free in the
Spirit and by the Spirit. Love in the New Testament writings is always connected to

the Spirit. It is the supreme gift of the Spirit who "remains," even though "prophecies will pass away; tongues will cease; knowledge will pass away" (1 Cor 13.8). This is not a new law based upon juridical principles. It is purely and simply the annulment of law, for what Christ said in the Sermon on the Mount does not enter the category of law. The descent of the Spirit on the day of Pentecost signifies the end of the Law. The new Sinai was not the Sinai of the Law but that of the Spirit, which entails love. The one was replaced by the other at the moment when the Church came into being.

The Sermon on the Mount was the announcement of love, which had no need of the law because it had transcended it. No longer is there any place for law in human relationships for those who, having become children of God by adoption in the Church, can say with St. Paul, "It is no longer I who live, but Christ who lives in me." Christ lives in each of us, for all are his body. He lives in the Church. Can the law govern the life of Christ? This apparently blasphemous question is posed by us each time we admit law into the life of the Church, but we do not realize this. "The Lord is the Spirit" (2 Cor 3.17). To accept the law is to refuse the gifts of the Spirit, it is to return to the law that Christ "nailed to the cross, having disarmed the principalities and powers and made a public example of them, triumphing over them in him" (Col 2.14–15). It is the return to the domination of these powers and the refusal to recognize the death of Christ, "for if justification were through the law, then Christ died to no purpose."

If the Church has no need of law to protect an individual with respect to others, it has even less need of it to protect an individual from itself. This cannot even be an issue in the Church. Since the Church has given birth to the individual as a person it would never want to put such a one into subjection. The Christian lives as a person in the Church, entering and remaining as such. The Church speaks to the unique and irreplaceable human person, not to the masses or the mob. In the Church one person is not set in opposition to another or to the Church because one is shoulder to shoulder with other members of the Church without whom one would not be able to exist. The individual "I" or "me" is always surrounded in the Church by the "we," the "us" without whom one could not be. However, the "we" is not merely a conglomerate of separate, individual "I's," but the Church itself as the one body of Christ. On the one hand, there is the human person aspiring to the union of his whole life with the others "in Christ Jesus." On the other hand, there is the individual-as-robot. Such is the extreme antithesis of the Church with the totalitarian state. Both do away with the law, but the Church does this uniquely for and in itself without affecting empirical, social life.

"A former commandment is set aside because of its weakness and useless-
ness, for the law made nothing perfect" (Heb 7.18–19). Law is abolished in the
Church because it is powerless and of no use. The Church insofar as it is love is
uniquely able to create relationships in love which exclude the law. The eruption
of law into the Church is the restoration of the "earlier commandment," the penetration of non-charismatic powers into charismatic life, the mixing up of light and
darkness.

6. The problem of law in the Church essentially concerns the ecclesiastical hierarchy and their relationships with the members of the Church. Here we find the
point of law's insertion back into the Church, the occasion which allows it to penetrate and remain there.

The hierarchical ministry is the principal ministry of the Church. It is also
as ancient as the Church's history. From the moment of their appearance the local
churches had the ministry of the presider. The apostles were the first presiders,
then there were the bishop-presbyters appointed by the apostles. The local
churches actively shared in the institution of these ministries, for it was done during the eucharistic assembly. These ministries became an assurance of continuity
from the moment they were instituted by the apostles. We know that the local
churches chose their own presiders. This election was the recognition of the will
of God. The local church would elect for the ministry those who were predestined
to it by God.[11] They are pastors because God has predestined and established
them by the sending of charismatic gifts and not because they had been chosen
by the people for their service. They served the Church because they had a particular charism for their ministry and vice versa. Neither the beginning nor the ter-
mination of their ministry was determined by law, for the grace necessary to their
ministry had its source not in the law, but in God, who gives charismatic gifts "to
each in particular, as he wishes."

To base the ministry of the presider on legal power would be an historical
temptation resulting from the penetration of law into the Church. From the Constantinian era, the power of bishops was based on law and, as a result, all of the organization and administration of the churches as well, for the bishop is the supreme
bearer of the ministry of administration in the church. In the ancient Church the
authority of the bishop came from the eucharistic assembly. The one who presides over the people of God, united with them in the eucharistic assembly—the
senior presbyter—manifested the authority of the ecclesial assembly, that is to
say, the authority of the Church. The authority the senior presbyter represented
from apostolic times was always within the church and not external to it. He was

the pastor of his church because like all the other members he belonged to the flock of Christ. If he was found to be outside the flock he would cease to belong to it and would not be able to be its pastor or shepherd. Here is why there is no other authority above the local church, certainly not that of another local church and its presiders. The Church is the place where the Spirit acts. The Church of God in Christ manifests itself in all its fullness in every local church. Consequently there is no action of the Spirit outside the local churches. If such is the case then there cannot exist a ministry which is superior to the local churches, and authority, in the Church, is a ministry.

While the eucharistic assembly remained one under the presidency of the bishop, his authority did not overstep these limits. Ignatius of Antioch urged the churches to follow their bishops but did not demand them to obey him, insofar as he was the bishop of all of Syria, in the same way as the churches obeyed their own bishops. The bishop was the one and only high priest of one eucharistic assembly, but his high priesthood *per se* implied the possibility of extending his authority beyond the limits of the eucharistic assembly. The breaking of the link between the bishop and the eucharistic assembly did not occur in the pre-Nicene period, for the authority of the bishop, despite all the modifications which happened to his ministry in the course of the third century remained always founded upon the eucharistic assembly. The imperial church rejected this source by affirming that to preside over the church of a small town or little village would lessen the dignity of the bishop.[12] Having rejected the eucharistic foundation of episcopal authority, the consciousness of the church needed to borrow a juridical principle from empirical social life, since nothing else in the Church could justify this authority. This was the most important mutation which occurred in the life of the Church and it happened at a moment in which one began to determine the limits of the local church by those of episcopal power, based on law. The idea of legal power introduced the institution of juridical relationships between the bishop and the members of his church and also the institution of a legal power above the bishops, the heads of local churches. The legal power of the bishop would necessarily lead to a legal limitation of this power, which, as we have seen, occurred at the Council of Moscow of 1917–18. Following a long historical process, the hierarchical ministry, whose existence stemmed from the very essence of the Church, received a foundation external to the Church.

7. Law generally manifests itself in the Church as divine law. This is why it is so difficult to determine where the authority founded upon law ends and that founded upon divine principle begins. The idea of theocracy is as ancient as the state itself,

perhaps even more ancient. It is one of the most grandiose dreams of humanity, an illusion very difficult to conquer, for it weaves together "both night and day, both light and darkness."[13] It is a mixture of the present and the future, or better, an anticipation of the future in the present. The kingdom of God is replaced by that of Caesar, the heavenly Jerusalem by an earthly one. It is an alteration of the Lord's prayer, "may your kingdom come," words by which Christians welcomed their Lord at the eucharistic assembly while awaiting his glorious coming when "God will be all in all" (1 Cor 15.28). In the theocratic order, it is in the course of the ancient era, the former times, that the kingdom of God arrives.

By nature every state tends toward theocracy under this or that form, openly or in a more hidden fashion, for it cannot find any sufficient legitimation in empirical reality on which to base itself. It was not just the madness of madmen on the throne which led Rome to divinize its emperors. The beginning of this cult dates to the time of Augustus, one of the wisest Roman emperors, whom the Christians particularly respected. This cult was the culmination of a natural development of an idea of power which sought to found itself upon itself. Divine authority demanded neither justifications nor foundations, while the authority of one man above another man is always suspect. Augustine understood this perfectly when he affirmed that man was able to dominate only the animals but not other human beings.[14] The cult of the emperors was rather easily accepted since it responded to a kind of inner human need of that time. No one in the ancient world opposed it except the Christians, for whom human wisdom was foolishness before God. With the skepticism proper to the Roman mind the divinized emperors knew perfectly well that they were far from being gods and would say bitterly and mockingly of themselves that only in death would they become immortal gods. Nevertheless, they also perceived in this cult the foundation of the Roman empire and, both wise men and madmen, they persecuted the Church cruelly because it opposed the Lord Jesus to the Lord Caesar. Even a power which had rejected its religious foundations preserves a mystical character, however perverted. Totalitarian states have their own atheistic mystique where the supreme representative of power is seen or considered, if not a god, then at least a "super-human."

8. The consciousness of the Church has often encountered theocracy as an idea not only outside the Church, when the kingdom of Caesar was considered as the realization of the kingdom of God, but also within the Church itself. In taking this path, in seeking a visible incarnation of divine power, ecclesial thinking overlooked the power of Christ in the Church. Pastors are chosen and ordained by God. Does this mean that the source of their power resides in God, who transmits to them his power, just as in the theocratic state God transmits his power to his anointed one? Did this not mean that the pastors then led the flock of Christ in his name, that they are his vicars in the Church? In the East, the charismatic act of episcopal ordination in the Church never included anointing. In the celebration of this sacrament there was prayer for the charismatic gifts for pastors in their ministry in the Church. However, one did not ask for the translation into the Church of divine power. If the Church's pastors possessed such a power then they would not be themselves part of the flock of God but would be above it. The ecclesiastical hierarchy cannot in actual existence replace the one and only Shepherd, for no one can replace Christ. They are not his vicars in the Church, for Christ is the only Anointed One.

By nature, power as such is not service to others. The one who has power rather is the one who is served. The idea of power as *diakonia*, that is ministry or service, was first formulated by St. Paul, who based it upon Christ's own teaching. Paul's famous words addressed to Rome state that "those who have authority (*hoi archontes*) are ministers of God (*leitourgoi Theou*)" (Rom 13.6).[15] This approach was alien to the Roman mentality. In republican Rome power was honor and in imperial Rome the power was divinity. These words of St. Paul were not heard at that time since Roman power did not wish to consider itself as a ministry. Only such an understanding of power, though, would be acceptable to Christian consciousness. The power, as divinity, was the "infernal beast."[16] Nearly two centuries later, Origen again used this Pauline approach to the subject of power with respect to the presiders of the churches.

> I think he ought to be called "guide" (*hêgoumenos*), the one we call "bishop" in the Church. He ought to be the servant of all in his ministry, in order to be of use to all in the work of salvation.[17]

The power of pastors considered to be vicars of Christ destroys the very doctrine of ministry in the church. This concept, though, has been able to appear in the Church's thinking following upon the understanding that the one Church of God must be divided into the heavenly church and the church on earth. The head of the heavenly church is Christ and on earth his vicars reign. The earthly vicariate represented by the pastors weakens the pastorate of Christ (the question of the degree of this weakening is irrelevant). The pastorate of Christ is limited to the invisible domain of the invisible church. The visible portion on earth belongs to his vicars. The ecclesiastical doctrine has been able to conquer such perversions as the idea expressed in the *Apostolic Constitutions* that "the bishop is, after God, god upon the earth."[18] Nevertheless, the Church did not transcend the very notion of a vicariate which is still contained in dogmatic theology.

9. The relationships betweens pastors and the faithful are not to be based on the authority given to the first, the apostles, because in the Church there are neither those who dominate nor those who are dominated.

> You know that the rulers of the Gentiles lord it over them, and their great men exercise authority over them. It shall not be so among you; but whoever would be great among you must be your servant, and whoever would be first among you must be your slave. (Matt 20.25–27)

The Pauline doctrine of ministries is based upon these words of Christ. The pastors serve the flock of Christ as presiders before God without dominating them. Guides and leaders, they lead the flock of God, but not on their own authority as representatives of power. They lead the flock through the gifts of the Spirit which remain in the Church and by which the Church exists. Within the people of God who constitute the Church, each one of the faithful, and not just the pastors, is established priest and king by his God. In destroying the doctrine of the "work of ministry" of the Church, the religious authority of the pastors destroyed at the same time the teaching about the royal dignity of the members of the people of God. Christ "has made us kings and priests to God and his Father" (Rev 1.6); all of us, and not just some. For if the kingdom belongs only to one group, then the rest are deprived of it. The Church, however, does not anoint pastors at their ordination; it anoints every one who enters it. The religious authority belongs to empirical existence, to social life where only a power of divine origin is able to be independent and absolute. There is no place for such a power in the Church, for it is "the beginning of the last days," the beginning of the new age (*aeon*). All are given charismatic gifts insofar as all are priests and kings.

10. Can it then be said that there is no power in the Church? The absence of all power would mean the absence of any structure and order. We have rejected the idea that in the course of the apostolic era, when the church, according to general consensus, did not have law, the Church was in a state of anarchy.[19] We have seen that order was there from the beginning. This order (*taxis*) was not artificial or alien to the Church but derived from its very nature. Structure and order presupposed the existence of a hierarchical principle protecting them and which involved all the members of the Church. Since every person is in the Church, each member together with all the others has Christ as head. "He has put all things under his feet and has made him the head over all things, of the church ..." (Eph 1.22). Submission to Christ, beneath whose feet God has placed all things, this is also reciprocal submission of all the members of the Church to each other, for one submits himself to Christ in the Church, which is his body. Submission to Christ and to one another is also expressed by service to God and to all.

> [He], though he was in the form of God, did not count equality with God a thing to be grasped, but emptied himself, taking the form of a servant, being born in the likeness of men. And being found in human form he humbled himself and became obedient unto death, even death on a cross. Therefore God has highly exalted him and bestowed on him the name which is above every name, that at the name of Jesus every knee should bow, in heaven and on earth and under the earth ... (Phil 2.6–10)[20]

This self-emptying (*kenosis*) proceeded from the very nature of God who is love, and the ministry of Christ was an expression of kenotic love. This love is at the foundation of all the ministries of the Church, for it can have no other foundation than that given by God. The ministry of Christ is a model for all other ministries.

> In this the love of God was made manifest among us, that God sent his only Son into the world, so that we might live through him ... Since God has loved us so much, we too should love one another ... (1 John 4.9, 11)[21]

Submission to Christ and our mutual submission to one another is the love of Christ and reciprocal love. It is the same as the love shown by Christ in his ministry. "For the Son of Man himself did not come to be served but to serve, and to give his life as a ransom for many" (Mark 10.45). The same love is expressed in the service of one another, because all of this occurs in the Church for which Christ has given his life. In the Church there is no love without ministry and there is no ministry without love. Love surrounds all the members of the Church and thus ministry belongs to them all. Every ministry is charismatic, for grace is one. Consequently all ministries are like in nature but different according to their charismatic gifts. The differences in the gifts create the differences among the ministries, the importance of which is their function in the life of the Church. The hierarchical principle manifests itself in the Church in the hierarchy of ministries, which is also that of love. The hierarchy of ministries culminates in that of the bishops, which is the most important in the Church. As the highest hierarchical ministry, it is the highest model of love and the most complete imitation of Christ's self-sacrificing love. This is culmination point of all ministries, their beginning and end being in love. Among the differing gifts from which stem the differences among ministries, the greatest is the charism of love and this charism belongs to all.

> But earnestly desire the higher gifts. And I will show you a still more excellent way. . . . If I have prophetic powers, and understand all mysteries and all knowledge, and if I have all faith, so as to remove mountains, but have not love, I am nothing. (1 Cor 12.31, 13.2)

Without love every ministry is nothing and is outside of the Church, for the Church is love. "And this commandment we have from him, that he who loves God should love his brother also." (1 John 4.21) The ministry of administration, of direction both external and internal, would cease to be without love, for without love there is no charism, no gift. Insofar as it is the chief ministry of the Church, the pastoral office is by nature the chief expression of love.

Those who bear the ministry of administration, the pastors, are also representatives of authority without which the ministry would be impossible. Authority is part of the life of the Church, which has this ministry of administration. But the ecclesial authority ought to conform to the nature of the Church and not be in conflict with it. If such authority claims to be superior to the Church then it must also be superior to Christ. This is why neither the Church nor its authority can ever be founded upon a juridical principle, for the law is external to love. Such authority cannot belong to the vicars of Christ on earth, since God has not delegated his power to anyone but has put all people in submission to Christ, "put all things under his feet." In the Church, which is love, there is only the power of love. God gives the pastors not the charism of power but that of love and, through it, the power of love. The bishops who exercise the ministry of administration are the bearers of the power of love. The submission of all to the bishop takes place in love and it is by love that the bishop submits to the faithful. All submission of one to another is realized through the mediation of the love we have for Christ. The submission of all to the bishop is actualized by the love he has for all and by the reciprocal love of the faithful for him. There can be no other foundation of power in the Church, for Christ is the only foundation of power in it. The pastors are able to have only that which Christ gives to the Church. Law as a foundation of authority in the Church is not sent down as a charismatic gift, for Christ does not possess any law. "Take my yoke upon you, and learn from me; for I am gentle and lowly in heart, and you will find rest for your souls" (Matt 11.29). The power of Christ in the Church is the power of love, acquired by the love which he has for it.[22]

11. If the power founded upon love is insufficient in actual life, which has lost the principle of love, it is on the contrary completely sufficient in the Church, where love is the first and the last principle. Juridical power is a substitute for love in actual social life, a substitute as perfect as possible in a very imperfect life. In the Church, where perfect love dwells, there is no need for such a substitute.

> So I exhort the elders among you, as a fellow elder and a witness of the sufferings of Christ as well as a partaker in the glory that is to be revealed. Tend the flock of God that is your charge, not by constraint but willingly, not for shameful gain but eagerly, not as dominating over those in your charge but being examples to the flock. (1 Peter 5.1–3)

To dominate or command (*katakyrieuô*) the flock of God means to use a power not based upon love. The Letter of Peter demands of the bishops who are fellow pastors that they govern by being examples to the flock (*typoi ginomenoi tou poimniou*). They must be a model or image for the flock, a model or image of love by means of which they govern the flock of God. The power of love with which the shepherds or pastors are clothed is the sacrificial offering of oneself for the others and a self-sacrificing ministry, of which St. Paul gives an example.

> As servants of God we commend ourselves in every way: through great endurance, in afflictions, hardships, calamities, beatings, imprisonments, tumults, labors, watching, hunger; by purity, knowledge, forbearance, kindness, the Holy Spirit, genuine love, truthful speech, and the power of God; with the weapons of righteousness for the right hand and for the left . . . Who is weak, and I am not weak? Who is made to fall, and I am not indignant? . . . For though I am free from all men, I have made myself a slave to all (*emauton edoulôsa*), that I might win the more . . . I have become all things to all men, that I might by all means save some. (2 Cor 6.4–7, 11.29, 1 Cor 9.19, 22)

It is only in the love of Christ and in him that the charism of Love is acquired, the gift which permits one to give oneself to others so that at least some may be saved. To win all not for oneself but for Christ is the content of the power of love in the Church. The opposition of *katakyrieuô* to *douloumai*, of domination to servitude is the opposition of the power not based upon love to the power of love. The first demands that one be served, the second serves the others. The first dominates, the second makes oneself the servant of all.[23] I repeat here nearly word for word the saying of Origen: "Let the rulers of nations exercise lordship over them, but let the rulers of the Church be to it as servants."[24] Such a power does not create superiors and inferiors, masters and slaves. It does not provoke division in the Church, but by it all are reunited in love. It does not dominate by fear or force, but "takes the form of a servant," for the fear has no love. "There is no fear in love, but perfect love casts out fear. For fear has to do with punishment, and he who fears is not perfected in love" (1 John 4.18).

In recognizing in the Church the existence of a power other than that of love, one diminishes or even denies grace, for this would be to diminish or deny the common charism of love without which there could be no ministry. The power of vicars of God as divine power has no need of the gifts of the Spirit. It is this power which gives all ministries, and all is accomplished in the name and authority of this power. Juridical power no longer has any need of grace. The existence of such a power in the Church would signify that the life of the church is directed according to the norms of law. These would then have imposed limits upon the Spirit who blows in the Church when and where he wishes. The norm of law would prefer that the Spirit blow there, where law itself is respected. Even if these norms of law were of divine origin they would constitute a kind of sealed treasure, formed at the moment of the birth of law from which the Church would then draw, not by grace but by law. Only love, as the common content of the ministries of the Church, as well as the power based on love and flowing from love, cannot banish the grace from the life of the Church.

> I do not nullify the grace of God; for if justification were through the law, then Christ died to no purpose. (Gal 2.21)

Notes

Author's Foreword

1. Dionysius the Areopagite, *Ecclesiastical Hierarchy*, 2.2.7.
2. P. Batiffol, *L'Eglise naissante et le catholicisme* (Paris, 1922), x.

Chapter 1. The Royal Priesthood

1. The Russian translation views *oikodomeisthe* as an imperative, but it seems more correct to view it as an indicative: "you are built into a spiritual house, where you are a holy priesthood."

2. The critical text: *basileian hiereis.*

3. The critical text: "has made them a kingdom and priests, and they shall reign on earth." Concerning the second part of the phrase, it would be more proper to take into account one more variant, *basileuousin:* "and they reign on earth." Cf. E. G. Selwyn, *The First Epistle of Peter* (London, 1949), 159.

4. G. Dix, "The Ministry in the Early Church," in *The Apostolic Ministry,* ed. K. E. Kirk (London, 1946), 285. [Translator's note: Throughout this work I have consistently used two different English words to translate two different terms in the original. I have used "laic" to translate Fr. Afanasiev's *laik* in Russian—in Greek, *laikos*—and I have used "lay person/people" to translate his Russian *mir'anin*, Gr. *biotikos.* It would become confusing if only "lay person" were used to translate both terms, since their connotations are very different. It seems that in the author's text they are actually opposed to each other. As I understand Fr. Afanasiev's terminology, he uses *mir'anin* in the ordinary sense of a "non-cleric," as it is widely used in practice today. That is not the case with *laik.* Strictly speaking, there is no such word in Russian, at least there was not until Afanasiev. It seems that he coined the word on the basis of the Greek to create an analogy to the term "cleric." He uses this term so as to connote the "sacred rank" which "laic" is—the "laic" is not a non-cleric in a modern sense of "lay person," i.e., one not initiated into a sacred order. The very next chapter speaks about the setting apart of the laics. The secular connotations of the adjective "lay"

as "non-expert," "not initiated" into some area of knowledge, a "non-specialist," are especially misleading here. Precisely, the laic is an initiated person. Through baptism he or she is initiated into a sacred clerical order, the royal priesthood of God in Christ. When speaking about laics, Fr. Afanasiev deliberately makes it sound as if he is speaking about a clerical rank, an ecclesiastical office. I think that by deliberately introducing a term *laik* he intended to "fence off," terminologically, a common connotation of the word *mir'anin*, that is, "lay person."

5. The translation of *basileion hierateuma* offers certain difficulties. See on that subject E. G. Selwyn, *First Epistle of Peters'* 165 ff. The difficulty concerns only the term *basileion*, but not the term *hierateuma*. (See G. Kittel, *Theologischens Woerterbuch zum N. T.*, 3:249–251, the article by G. Schunk.) Whether we translate the expression *basileion hierateuma* as "a kingdom of priests" or as "royal priesthood" or, finally, as "a priesthood proper to a king," the meaning of the expression does not change: the kingship and the priesthood belong "in Christ" to the Church and through the Church—to each of her members. This is particularly clear if we compare this expression in the Epistle of Peter with the corresponding expressions in the book of Revelation. If we assume that the Seer of Mysteries [St. John the Theologian] was developing the ideas of the First Epistle of Peter, then for him the *basileion hierateuma* of Peter meant that "kingship and priesthood" which belong to the Church and are realized at the eucharistic assembly. See Bishop Cassian (Bezobrazov), *Christ and the First Generation of Christians* [in Russian] (Paris, 1950), 295.

6. See W. D. Davies, *Paul and Rabbinic Judaism* (London, 1948), 177 ff.

7. The teaching concerning the Messiah from the tribe of Levi was known in ecclesiastical circles. Hippolytus of Rome accepted it (see L. Maries, "Le Messie issu de Levi chez Hippolyte de Rome," *Religieuses Sciences Revue* 39 (1951): 381–396), as well as Ambrose of Milan, Hilary of Poitiers, et al. It was known to the contemporary of Hippolytus, Julius Africanus, who, while himself not accepting it, viewed it as an attempt at harmonization of genealogies in Matthew and Luke. Cf. A. J. B. Higgins, "Priest and Messiah," *Vetus Testamentum*, 3 (1953): 321–357.

8. Cf. Heb 3.6. See Michel, "*oikos*" in *TWNT*, 5:129–130.

9. See J. Behm, "*thusia*" in *TWNT*, 3:181 sq.

10. See E. G. Selwyn, *First Epistle of Peter*, 161 ff.

11. According to verse 9, Christians have to declare the wonderful deeds of him "who called them out of darkness into his marvelous light." This ministry is not a function of their royal priesthood, but their mission as a nation of God among other nations. In the Old Testament, Israel had to declare God's praise (Isa 43.21), but in the New Testament this mission has gone over to the Church.

12. The plural of *kleroi* does not disrupt the unity of God's *kleros*, just as the plural of *ekklesiai* does not disrupt the unity of the Church. The plural of the term *kleros* corresponds to the empirical plurality of the churches, each of which manifests all the fullness of God's Church in Christ. God's *kleros*, over which the presbyters preside at the eucharistic assembly, is the God's *kleros* in all its fullness, but not merely a part of it.

13. See A. Lebedev, "*Kleros*" in *Encyclopaedia of Theology* [in Russian] (St. Petersburg, 1910), 11:242.

14. I am citing this text from the Russian translation, the accuracy of which is not significant for me here.

15. Tertullian, *On Exhortation to Chastity,* 7; cited after *The Ante-Nicene Fathers,* volume 3.

16. Ibid.

17. Justin Martyr, *First Apology,* 67; cited after *The Ante-Nicene Fathers,* volume 1. See A.-M. Roguet, *Amen, acclamation du peuple sacerdotal* (Paris, 1947).

18. Dionysius the Areopagite, *Ecclesiastical Hierarchy* 2.2.4.

19. Ibid., 6.1.2.

20. Irenaeus, *Against the Heresies* 4.8.3. See Paul Dabin, *Le sacerdoce royal des fideles dans la tradition ancienne et moderne* (Brussels-Paris, 1950), where one finds gathered the Patristic testimonies on the question of royal priesthood.

Chapter 2. **The Ordination of Laics**

1. Hippolytus, *Apostolic Tradition* 19 [English translation is cited from Hippolytus, *On the Apostolic Tradition,* trans. A. Stewart-Sykes (Crestwood, NY: Saint Vladimir's Seminary Press, 2001)].

2. On the meaning of *latreuô* and *latreia* see the article by H. Strathmann in *TWNT,* 4:62 ff.

3. In the pre-Nicene period, baptism by water and the Spirit constituted a single event. The separation of this single sacrament into baptism and chrismation occurred in the Nicene era. See G. Dix, *The Theology of Confirmation in Relation to Baptism* (Westminster, 1946). It must be noted that even in the present time in the Orthodox Church the sacraments of baptism and chrismation liturgically constitute a single whole where it is difficult to determine when baptism ends and chrismation begins.

The question concerning confirmation is much more complicated for Roman Catholic than for Orthodox theology since in the Roman Catholic Church baptism and chrismation (confirmation) are two distinct sacraments not only dogmatically but also liturgically. See the excellent article by P. Th. Camelot, "Sur la theologie de la Confirmation" in *Revue des Sciences philosophiques et theologiques* 38 (1954): 637–657. Insisting on a primordial unity of baptism and chrismation, he considers that "the separation of the two sacraments was neither an accident nor a 'disintegration,' but should be seen in the light of the meaning proper to each sacrament." ("la separation des deux sacrements n'a pas ete un accident, ni une 'desintegration,' mais la mise en lumiere des valeurs propres de chacun") (657).

4. See S. Bulgakov, *The Orthodox Church* (Crestwood, NY: St. Vladimir's Seminary Press, 1966), 113. It is curious to note that in modern Roman Catholic literature we find attempts to present the sacrament of confirmation as a "sacrement de l'Action Catholique." L. Bouyer in his article "La signification de la Confirmation," *La vie spirituelle,* Supplement 29 (1954): 162–179, finds this idea "extravagante" (169).

5. Or in three aspects, if we count the preliminary anointing with the holy oil performed by the presbyter (see G. Dix, *Theology of Confirmation,* 12).

6. Hippolytus, *Apostolic Tradition*, 21. The French translation is by Dom B. Botte, *La tradition Apostolique*, Sources chrétiennes 11 (Paris, 1946), 52. In the Latin translation, apparently a more reliable witness of Hippolytus's text, this prayer reads as follows: "Lord God, you made them worthy to deserve the remission of sins through the laver of regeneration of the Holy Spirit: send your grace upon them that they may serve you in accordance with your will; for to you is glory, to the Father and the Son with the Holy Spirit in the holy Church both now and to the ages of ages. Amen."

7. See Paul Dabin, *Le sacerdoce royal des fidèles dans les livres saints* (Paris, 1941), 314–316.

8. The question of whether the sacrament of baptism or chrismation expressed the idea of the setting apart of the laics was not an issue for the ancient Church, since at that time baptism and chrismation constituted a single unit. When St. Jerome said that the baptism of laics is their priesthood (*Altercatio Luciferiani et orthodoxi*, c. 2), he certainly meant not only baptism, but chrismation as well; and when St. Augustine spoke of the anointing as the basic element of the setting apart, he had baptism in mind as well (St. Aug. *In ps.* 26). Among the modern scholars who studied this question, G. Dix considers confirmation a setting apart for the only existing order in the Church—that of laics (*The Shape of the Liturgy* [London, 1945], 23, 34–35).

9. We have some reason to believe that anointing was done already in the apostolic times. "It is God who establishes us with you in Christ, and has anointed us (*chrisas hèmas*); he has put his seal upon us and given us his Spirit in our hearts as a guarantee" (2 Cor 1.21–22). There is virtually no doubt that it is baptism that is meant here. (See E. B. Allo, *Saint Paul: Seconde épître aux Corinthiens* [Paris, 1937].) But this is not the only place among the writings of the New Testament which speaks of the anointing of the faithful (see 1 John 2.20, 27). The identical expression in both Paul and John permits us to think that we are dealing with an actual anointing. On the other hand, nowhere in Acts is the anointing mentioned in connection with baptism but in all instances the administration of the gifts of the Spirit is associated with the imposition of hands. That is why we cannot exclude a possibility that the anointing mentioned in the writings of the New Testament is only a metaphor taken from Isaiah 61.1. (See "Sur la theologie de la confirmation," P. Th. Camelot, 638.) However, we have to point out that this suggestion could be true only if we were to assert that *sphragis* was not done by anointing. (See E. Dinkler, "Jesu Wort vom Kreuztragen," *Neutestamentliche Studien für R. Bultmann* [Berlin, 1954], 110–129.) In Justin Martyr we learn that in his time the forehead of the newly baptized was anointed possibly in the form of the letter *tau* or *chi* to seal the baptism. (*Discourse with Tryphon the Jew* 113–114; see L. S. Thornton, *Confirmation: Its Place in the Baptismal Mystery* [Westminster, 1954], 33 ff.; P. Th. Camelot, "Sur la theologie de la confirmation," 638).

10. P. Th. Camelot ("Sur la theologie de la confirmation," 655) states that "confirmation is for the baptized the royal and priestly anointing which gives him his title and the right to participate actively in the priesthood and sacrifice of the Church." Unfortunately, this very important statement is still quite unclear because the author fails to say "explicitly" how laics participate in the priesthood.

11. [Translator's Note: The English translation of the Rite of Baptism is taken from the home page of the Monastery of St. Andrew (Manchester, England), http://www.anastasis

.org.uk/baptism.htm (last accessed November 30, 2006). Translation is made by Archimandrite Ephrem Lash.]

12. When compared with the rite described by Hippolytus of Rome, contemporary chrismation with holy oil corresponds more closely to the anointing done by the presbyter immediately after the baptism in water rather than to the pouring of the holy oil by the bishop and the imposition of his hands. From this it follows that the meaning of the sacrament of chrismation was ascribed to the first anointing. (See G. Dix, *Theology of Confirmation*, 12–13.)

13. In [the classic exposition of Orthodox dogmatics by] Metropolitan Makary, we read: "In baptism, a person is sacramentally born into a spiritual life; in chrismation, he receives grace that raises and strengthens him spiritually ..." *Orthodox Dogmatic Theology* [in Russian] (St Petersburg, 1895), 2:314. This definition of the essence of the sacrament of chrismation was without question influenced by the medieval Western teaching on confirmation (Cf. G. Dix, *Theology of Confirmation*, 21 ff.). It remains completely unclear what the words "the seal of the gift of the Holy Spirit" mean, given such a definition of the sacrament of chrismation. Interestingly, Metropolitan Makary himself cites excerpts from Tertullian and Cyprian asserting that through chrismation the newly baptized becomes "God's anointed." Thus, in Tertullian, we read: "After this, when we have issued from the font, we are thoroughly anointed with a blessed unction (*perungimur benedicta unctione*), [a practice derived] from the old discipline, wherein on entering the priesthood, *men* were wont to be anointed with oil from a horn ..." (*De Baptismo* 7; English translation: *Ante-Nicene Fathers*, vol. 3). And Cyprian wrote: "It is also necessary that he should be anointed who is baptized; so that, having received the chrism, that is, the anointing, he may be anointed of God (*unctus Dei*), and have in him the grace of Christ" (Epist. 70[69], 2; English translation: *Ante-Nicene Fathers*, vol. 2). We are reminded once again that only kings and priests were God's anointed ones in the Old Testament. A similar lack of clarity with respect to the character and nature of the sacrament of confirmation is also present in the Roman Catholic theology. Following debates in the Anglican Church, confirmation began to be a subject of discussion also in the Roman Catholic Church. P. Th. Camelot in "Sur la theologie de la confirmation" openly denounces the classic formula of Pseudo-Melchiades: *Augmentum gratiae—robur ad pugnam*, which has influenced Orthodox scholastic teaching on chrismation.

14. See W. L. Knox, *St. Paul and the Church of the Gentiles* (Cambridge, 1939), 138.

15. Ambrose of Milan, *De Mysteriis* 34. Tertullian's reference in *De Pudicitia* 9 to *vestis prior* has no real relation to the sacrament of baptism. Rather, it coincides with his interpretation of the parable on the prodigal son. There is no mention of clothing the newly baptized in Tertullian's *De Baptismo*, nor in Cyprian of Carthage. By itself, the lack of any reference in one or the other could not incontrovertibly imply that the Church of Carthage did not know this custom.

16. Cyril of Jerusalem, *Mystagogical Catechesis* 4.8.

17. Dionysius the Areopagite, *Ecclesiastical Hierarchy* 2.2.7.

18. A. Dmitrievskij, *Opisanije liturgicheskikh rukopisej*, vol. 2, *Euchologion* (Kiev, 1901), 202–209.

19. It is possible that the words of the apostle Paul themselves in Gal 3.27 were inspired by the Lord's parable on the called and the chosen. Cf. L. Boyer, "Le mystère pascal" *Lex orandi* (Paris) 4 (1945): 437.

20. In the late post-exilic period, the setting apart of an Old Testament high priest was done by his being clothed in a special garment. Of his two garments, the white linen garment had an especially sacral significance, for after being dressed in it he entered the holy of holies. The lesser priests had white garments as well. According to the Babylonian Talmud, Moses wore a white garment in the course of the seven days when the tabernacle was built. At the same time, the white garment also possesses an eschatological character. It is possible that this is precisely the character of the reference to the white garments in the book of Revelation which does not in the least undermine the association of white garments with baptism. (Cf. J. Bonsirven, *Le judaïsme palestinien au temps de Jésus Christ* [Paris, 1934], 1:65; W. Michaelis in *TWNT*, 4:248 ff.; H. Riesenfeld, *Jésus transfiguré* [Lund, 1947], 118 ff.). The clothing of the faithful to which the New Testament texts allude, particularly in Eph 6. 11–18, has a sacerdotal character. See Paul Dabin, *Le sacerdoce royale des fidèles*, 308.

21. In the *Apostolic Constitutions,* we read: "When this is done, let the deacons bring the gifts to the bishop at the altar; and let the presbyters stand on his right hand, and on his left, as disciples stand before their Master. But let two of the deacons, on each side of the altar, hold a fan, made up of thin membranes, or of the feathers of the peacock, or of fine cloth, and let them silently drive away the small animals that fly about, that they may not come near to the cups. Let the high priest, therefore, together with the priests, pray by himself; and let him put on his shining garment (*lampran estheta metendus*), and stand at the altar, and make the sign of the cross upon his forehead with his hand, and say . . ." (8.12.3–4). I would like to point out one detail in this excerpt which is generally important in many respects. The bishop, surrounded by the presbyters, stands before the altar. He alone is clothed in the "shining garment," for he alone celebrates the sacred service. This is not yet a special garment, but only a more solemn one. The term *lampra esthês* thus reminds us of the baptismal garments which were designated by the same term.

22. Rev 1.6.

23. J. Goar, *Euchologion* (Paris, 1647), 366; A. Dmitrievskij, *Opisanije liturgicheskikh rukopisej*, 2:79 and 94.

24. H. Denzinger, *Ritus Orientalium* (Wuerzburg, 1862), 287–288. Cf. the prayer from the Ethiopian ritual: *Domine Deus qui sanctis tuis coronas incorruptibiles proebuisti, tu qui proeparari has coronas benedic eis . . .* (idem, 209).

25. In all possibility, the custom of "crowning" the newly baptized emerged under the influence of the Old Testament. We know that the crown represented the royal authority of Israelite kings. It was assumed afterwards by the high priests as a part of their solemn garments. Additionally the crown undergoes democratization and serves as an expression of joy at the feasts, as, for example, at the Feast of Tabernacles and at the marriage ceremonies. Finally, this idea receives an escatological significance: the righteous will receive a crown in the age to come. See J. Bonsirven, *Le judaïsme palestinien* 1:521; H. Riesenfeld, *Jésus transfiguré* 50 sq.

26. Symeon of Thessalonica, *On the Sacraments* 68.

27. Hippolytus, *Apostolic Tradition* 21.

28. Ibid., 4.

29. Dionysius the Areopagite, *Ecclesiastical Hierarchy* 2.2.7.

30. [Translator's Note: In Russian, the word for "lay person, layman"—*mirianin*—derives from the word *mir*, i.e.,"world."]

31. Hippolytus, *Apostolic Tradition* 23. See E. Dinkler, *Jesu worte vom Kreuztragen*, 124.

Chapter 3. The Ministry of Laics

1. Justin Martyr, *First Apology* 1.65.

2. Hippolytus, *Apostolic Tradition* 21 [Stewart-Sykes, 112].

3. In the Septuagint, the terms *leitourgeô* and *leitourgia* normally designate the offering of sacrifices by priests, as opposed to *latreia*, which designates in general any cultic service. In the writings of Paul, with the exception of one passage where the word *leitourgos* refers to the ministry of civil servants (Rom 13.6), *leitourgia* bears an expressly religious connotation, which has connections, in one way or another, with the eucharistic assembly. As early as J. B. Lightfoot it was noted that *leitourgia* in Phil 2.17 relates to 1 Peter 2.5 and signifies the royal priesthood (*Saint Paul's Epistle to the Philippians*, 119). Using *leitourgeô* and *leitourgia* to designate collections for the Jerusalem church (Rom 15.27 and 2 Cor 9.12), the apostle Paul saw the collections as an expression of one of the kinds of priestly ministry of the faithful connected with the eucharistic assembly. There is no doubt that collections took place at the eucharistic assembly (1 Cor 16.1–2). Therefore they constituted a part of the common *leitourgia* of the faithful. The collections were manifestations of love as foundational for the entire life of the Church (1 Cor 13). Cf. E. Schweitzer, *Das Leben des Herrn in der Gemeinde und ihren Diensten* (Zuerich, 1946). On the meaning of *leitourgeô* and *leitourgia* see H. Strathmann in *TWNT*, 4:225–229, 232–236.

4. See Hippolytus, *Apostolic Tradition* 4.

5. Ignatius, *Letter to the Smyrnaeans* 8.2: "Wherever the bishop appears let the congregation be present; just as wherever Jesus Christ is, there is the catholic Church." [English translation: *The Apostolic Fathers*, trans. K. Lake, vol. 1, Loeb Classical Library 24 (Cambridge, MA: Harvard University Press, 1977)].

6. Origen, *In Leviticum homilia* 9.1 ["Therefore, you have a priesthood because you are 'a priestly nation' and for this reason 'you ought to offer an offering of praise to God." In Origen, *Homilies on Leviticus 1–16*, trans. G. W. Barkley, Fathers of the Church 83 (Washington, DC: Catholic University of America Press, 1990), 177].

7. Canon 4 of the Council at Gangra. The idea that the worthiness of the sacramental act depends on the personal worthiness of the bishop who celebrates it apparently was for the first time proposed by Origen. "But when those who maintain the function of the episcopate make use of this word as Peter, and, having received the keys of the kingdom of heaven from the Saviour, teach that things bound by them, that is to say, condemned, are also bound in heaven, and that those which have obtained remission by them are also loosed in heaven, we must say that they speak wholesomely if they have the way of life on

account of which it was said to that Peter, 'Thou art Peter'; and if they are such that upon them the church is built by Christ, and to them with good reason this could be referred; and the gates of Hades ought not to prevail against him when he wishes to bind and loose. But if he is tightly bound with the cords of his sins, to no purpose does he bind and loose" (*In Matth.* 12.14). See J. Danielou, *Origène* (Paris, 1948), 83.

8. On the time of the emergence of the iconostasis, see the article by K. Holl, "Die Entstehung der Bilderwand in der griechischen Kirche" in *Gesammelte Aufsätze zur Kirchengeschichte II: Der Osten* (Tübingen, 1927).

9. Canon 69 of the council in Trullo [English translation for the canons of the council in Trullo: G. Nedungatt and M. Featherstone, eds., *The Council in Trullo Revisited*, Kanonika 6 (Roma: PIO, 1995)].

10. Balsamon, *Commentary on Canon 69 in Trullo.*

11. Canon 13 of Laodicea.

12. Zonaras, *Commentary on Canon 69 in Trullo.*

13. Ibid.

14. Balsamon, *Commentary on Canon 69 in Trullo.*

15. N. Milaš, *Canons of the Orthodox Church with Commentaries* [in Russian] (St. Petersburg, 1911), 558. Balsamon was already aware of a different canon of the Western Church: "I know concerning Latins that not only lay men, but women as well come into the holy altar and sit even when the celebrants celebrate the sacred mystery stand" (Balsamon, *Commentary on Canon 69 in Trullo*).

16. Justin Martyr, *First Apology* 1.65.

17. See Archimandrite Cyprien Kern, *Evkharistiia* [The Eucharist] (Paris, 1947), 166.

18. Funk, *Doctrina duodecim apostolorum* (Tübingen, 1887).

19. Canon 101 of the Council in Trullo.

20. The distinction in the way the laics receive the holy mysteries in the Orthodox and Roman Catholic Churches is not a qualitative, but a quantitative, one. It is not this distinction that is important, but rather the distinction in the way of receiving communion between clerics and laics, equally present in both the Roman Catholic and Orthodox Churches.

21. Balsamon, *Commentary on Canon 101 of the Council in Trullo.*

22. "No one amongst the laity shall give himself the divine Mysteries if there is a bishop or presbyter or deacon present. Anyone who dares to do this, acting contrary to what has been ordained, shall be excommunicated for one week, that he might learn not to presume more than he ought" (Canon 58 of the Council in Trullo).

23. Balsamon, *Commentary on Canon 58 in Trullo.*

24. Concerning those orders, see Archimandrite Cyprien Kern, *Evkharistiia*, 42–134.

25. The falling to the ground represents an individual prayer of every member of the Church, whereas the standing upright at the time of prayer expresses his priestly ministry in the Church. "Every priest stands daily at his service . . ." (Heb 10.11).

26. The emphasis is mine.

27. John Chrysostom, *Commentary on the Second Corinthians* 18.3 [English translation is from *Nicene and Post-Nicene Fathers*, First Series, vol. 12 (slightly adapted).]

28. Justin Martyr, *First Apology* 1.65. [Editor's note: In the celebration of the liturgy in many Orthodox churches today, the threefold "amen" at the calling down of the Spirit on the gifts (*epiklesis*) is once more said aloud by the whole congregation.]

29. Eusebius of Caesarea, *Church History* 7.9.2–4 [English translation is from *Nicene and Post-Nicene Fathers*, Second Series, vol. 1 (slightly adapted).]

30. Theodoret of Cyrus, *Commentary on the Second Corinthians*, 1.20. See B. Sove, "Evkharistiia v drevnei Cerkvi i sovremennaia praktika" [The Eucharist in the Ancient Church and Modern Practice] in *Zhivoe predanie* [Living Tradition] (Paris, 1937), 171. [Editor's note: See English text at: http://www.holy-trinity.org. Last accessed November 30, 2006.]

31. "... *laon periousion, basileion hierateuma, ethnos hagion* ..."

32. Liturgy of St. Basil.

33. Concerning this, see my study *The Lord's Supper* (Paris, 1952). [Editor's note: This study is forthcoming in English translation by Alvian Smirensky.]

34. See the corresponding prayer in the liturgy of the *Apostolic Constitutions*. It is offered by the bishop himself who celebrates the Eucharist: "We further pray to Thee for me, who am nothing, who offer to Thee, for the whole presbytery, for the deacons and all the clergy, that Thou wilt make them wise, and replenish them with the Holy Spirit ... We further offer to Thee for this people, that Thou wilt render them, to the praise of Thy Christ, 'a royal priesthood and an holy nation' ..." (8.12; English translation is from *The Ante-Nicene Fathers*, vol. 7). What we have here is the ecclesial prayer uttered by the bishop in the name of all the people who take part in the Eucharist.

35. Cyril of Jerusalem, *Mystagogical Catecheses* 5.6–8 [English translation is cited from E. Yarnold, *The Awe-Inspiring Rites of Initiation* (Collegeville, MN: Liturgical Press, 1994), 92–93].

36. *Apostolic Constitutions* 8.15.

37. Canon 2 of the Council in Antioch. Even if this canon had in mind the Docetists, its general sense still remains the same.

38. Apostolic canon 9 (cf. Ap. canon 10). Both canons—second of the Council in Antioch and Apostolic canon 9—coincide in their basis, but differ in details. Thus, Apostolic canon 9 mentions those who depart after the scriptural readings, i.e., prior to the common prayer of the faithful, and thus do not stay until the end of the eucharistic assembly and do not receive communion. In turn, the second canon of Antioch encompasses not only these people but also those who remain at the eucharistic assembly but refrain from participation in communion. Consequently the latter canon indicates a second phase in the changing ecclesiastical practices: in the first stage the people who for one reason or another wished to refrain from communion left the assembly before the common prayers with the faithful, but all who stayed participated in communion. The indication of Nicodemus Milaš (*Canons with commentaries*, 1:68) that the catechumens took part in some of the prayers with the faithful is incorrect and does not reflect the data contained in *Apostolic Constitutions* (book 8) to which Milaš himself refers. The catechumens left the assembly after the homily and before the common prayers. This order is clearly indicated in the canons cited above.

39. Apostolic canon 8.

40. Zonaras, *Commentary on Canon 2 of the Council in Antioch*.

41. Aristenus, *Commentary on Canon 2 of the Council in Antioch.*

42. Zonaras, *Commentary on Apostolic Canon 9.*

43. Balsamon, *Commentary on Apostolic Canon 9.*

44. Balsamon, *Commentary on Canon 2 of the Council in Antioch.*

45. Balsamon, *Commentary on Apostolic Canon 8.*

46. Balsamon, *Commentary on Canon 2 of the Council in Antioch.* Here I leave aside the question of the authenticity of Balsamon's note on the origin of the antidoron, as being the purely liturgical problem.

47. Ibid.

48. Basil the Great, *Letter* 93 [English translation: St. Basil, *Letters, Volume 1 (1–185),* trans. A. C. Way, Fathers of the Church 13 (New York: Fathers of the Church, 1951)].

49. Milaš, *Canons of the Orthodox Church,* 69. [Editor's note: At the time Afanasiev was completing *The Church of the Holy Spirit,* i.e., from 1947 into the early 1950s—it was defended for the doctorate July 2, 1950, and parts were published in Russian in *La pensée orthodoxe* in 1948, 1949, 1954, and *The Lord's Supper* was published in 1952—his observation in the following sentence of the text above was accurate, namely, that even the once a year requirement for reception of communion was not always observed.]

50. Justin Martyr, *First Apology* 1.67.

51. Ibid.

52. *Apostolic Constitutions* 8.33.

53. Origen complained at the faithful who avoid attending ecclesial assemblies regularly: "Does it not cause her [the Church] sadness and sorrow when you do not gather to hear the Word of God? And scarcely on feast days do you proceed to the Church, and you do this not so much from a desire for the word, as from a fondness for the festival and to obtain, in a certain manner, common relaxation. What then shall I do, to whom the dispensation of the Word is commited? . . . Where or when shall I find your due season? You spend most of the time, no rather almost all of it in mundane occupations; you pass some of it in the marketplace, some in business . . . No one or very few have time to hear the Word of God." (*In Gen.* 10 [English translation: Origen, *Homilies on Genesis and Exodus,* trans. R. E. Heine, Fathers of the Church 71 (Washington, DC: Catholic University of America Press, 1982)]; cf. J. Danielou, *Origène,* 54). Which gatherings are spoken of in Origen, is not clear. Most probably, these are *synaxeis* rather than eucharistic gatherings, since it is unlikely that in his time the latter took place on the days other than feast days. If this is so, was Origen correct in reproaching the faithful that they never or rarely attend his sermons? Was he correct in his reproach that the faithful more eagerly gather to the church festivals, rather than at the hearing of him interpreting the Word of God? In his spiritualistic view the interpretation of the Word prevailed over the eucharistic assembly, but were the people wrong indeed in preferring the eucharistic gathering to the *synaxis* where Origen preached his homilies?

54. Jerome, *Apology Against Jovinian* 2.29; St. Ambrose, *De sacramentis* 4.6; St. John Chrysostom, *In Eph.* 3.

55. *Apostolic Constitutions* 8. 2.

56. Encyclical *Mediator Dei* (1947).

57. The idea of spiritual communion probably originates with Origen. As Jean Daniélou himself establishes in his book *Origène*, 74 ff., despite his own attempts to present Origen's teaching on Eucharist as an orthodox one, Origen discerns between two kinds of communion: actual—the communion of Christ's body and blood at the eucharistic assembly, and spiritual—the communion of God the Word through his word. "But we are told that we drink the blood of Christ not only by the sacramental ritual, but also when we receive his words" (*In Num.* 16.9). On the basis of this, Origen asserted that "Neither by not eating, I mean by the very fact that we do not eat of the bread which has been sanctified by the word of God and prayer, are we deprived of any good thing, nor by eating are we the better (*perisseuomen*) by any good thing; for the cause of our lacking is wickedness and sins, and the cause of our abounding is righteousness and right actions; so that such is the meaning of what is said by Paul: 'For neither is eat are we the better, or if we eat not are we the worse'" (*In Matt.* 11.14). Apart from its general meaning, this text is extremely interesting in applying the words of the apostle Paul concerning food in general to the eucharistic sacrifice. In any case, for Origen, spiritual communion—the communion of God's Word—does not count any lower than an actual communion of the eucharistic gifts.

58. Hippolytus of Rome, *Apostolic Tradition* 8.2.

59. Apostolic canon 39.

60. Cyprian, *Epist.* 14.4.

61. Hippolytus of Rome, *Apostolic Tradition* 2.

62. Ibid., 3.4.

63. Cyprian, *Epist.* 38.1.

64. Cyprian, *Epist.* 29.1. Cf. *Epist.* 39.1.

65. Eusebius, *Ecclesiastical History* 6.43.17.

66. Ignatius, *Ephesians* 4.2.

67. *Didache* 13.4.

68. Cf. F. E. Vokes, *The Riddle of the Didache* (London, 1938).

69. Canon 64 of the council in Trullo.

70. Canon 64 of the council in Trullo. The quote from Gregory the Theologian is taken from his Homily 32.11, 13, 21.

71. On this subject, see below, p. 129 ff.

72. Justin Martyr, *First Apology* 67.

73. Eusebius, *Ecclesiastical History* 6.19.17–18.

74. Cf. H. v. Campenhausen, *Kirchliches Amt und geistliche Vollmacht in den ersten drei Jahrhunderten* (Tübingen, 1953), 275.

75. As we know, the sermons by Augustine, still a presbyter at that time, caused a great consternation in Hippo, even though he spoke in church upon the request of his bishop. On the other hand, according to the witness of *Peregrinatio Aetheriae*, in Jerusalem in the end of the fourth century all presbyters took turns in preaching during the liturgy, the bishop speaking after all of them. Even before he occupied the see of Constantinople, John Chrysostom was already known as an outstanding preacher, thus it is beyond doubt

that he preached while a presbyter at Antioch. These facts, as well as others, point out that beginning with the fourth century different churches held different practices with respect to allowing the presbyters to preach in churches.

76. Balsamon, *Commentary on Canon 19 of the Council in Trullo.*

77. Balsamon, *Commentary on Canon 64 of the Council in Trullo.*

78. Ibid.

79. Balsamon, *Commentary on Canon 19 of the Council in Trullo.*

80. On the consensus of the believers in the matters of faith, one can read in P. Dabin's *Le Sacerdoce Royal des Fideles dans la tradition ancienne et moderne,* 21: "The consensus of the faithful in the matters of faith, also called the *catholic sense,* is a definite criterion of divine tradition, if one presents it as something definite, clear and unanimous. The scriptural texts usually cited in favor of this consensus are John 17.20–21; Romans 1.5, 1 Cor 3.22, Eph 4.16, 1 John 2.20, 21, 27. The unity in true faith is one of the essential characteristics of the Church. The Church will be weakened if it will not encounter anything except the concept of the teaching Church. Most illustrious fathers and theologians ascribed dogmatic importance to the consensus of the faithful. St. Hilary rendered homage to the soundness of their catholic sense. When certain bishops favored Arianism, but the people remained firm in the Nicene faith, he wrote: 'The ears of the faithful are holier than the heart of the bishops.'" Dabin, however, immediately minimizes his statement, saying: "The object of the consensus of the faithful does not extend to most subtle of the truths: as Melchior Cano (16th century Roman Catholic author) justly said, to ask of the common people their opinion is to interrogate the blind on the subject of colour."

81. Cf. Matt 23.8.

82. Balsamon, *Commentary on Canon 64 in Trullo.*

83. Zonaras, on the same canon.

Chapter 4. The Work of Ministry

1. Cf. the dictum of the Sophists: "How can a man be happy if he is a slave to anybody at all?" (Plato, *Gorgias* 491c). [English translation: Plato, *Lysis, Symposium, Gorgias,* trans. W.R.M. Lamb, Loeb Classical Library 166 (Cambridge, MA: Harvard University Press, 1925).] I cite this dictum from the article by W. Beyer, "*Diakoneô*" in *TWNT,* 2:81.

2. *Contra* R. N. Flew, *Jesus and His Church* (London, 1943), 183, who argues that all the gifts are given to the Church as a whole. Cf. also E. Schweitzer, *Das Leben des Herrn.*

3. [Translator's note: The author cites the excerpt from Romans 12.6–9 from the Russian Synodal translation which gives "the superior" for the translation of *ho proistamenos* in 12.8.]

4. C. Spicq, *Les épîtres pastorales* (Paris, 1947), xliv.

5. In the list of the gifts of the Spirit (1 Cor 12.8–10), there is no indication at "helpers and administrators" (*antilêmpsis* and *kybernêsis*) that are mentioned in the list of individuals having particular ministries (v. 28). On this subject see below, chapter 5, II, 3.

6. See M. Goguel, *L'Eglise primitive* (Paris, 1947), 124.

7. On this subject, see below, chapter 4, II, pp. 106 ff.

8. This opinion, predominant until this day, has slowly begun to change. The thesis, which is becoming more and more popular now, argues that all ministries in the apostolic times were regarded as charismatic. E.g., this is the opinion of E. Schweitzer. Curiously enough, G. Dix in his article "The Ministry in the Early Church" in K. E. Kirk, *The Apostolic Ministry*, 232 ff., again, in some way, brings back the old view of Harnack.

9. On this subject, see O. Linton, *Das Problem der Urkirche in der neueren Forschung* (Uppsala, 1932).

10. See my article "Two Concepts of the Universal Church," *Put'* (Paris) 45 (1934): 16–29.

11. Even if in the Jerusalem Church some regarded the local churches as her spatial extension, this view was not predominant, not even in the Jerusalem church itself. See W. G. Kümmel, *Kirchenbegriff und Geschichtsbewusstsein in der Urgemeinde und bei Jesus* (Uppsala, 1943), 16–19.

12. According to the *Didache*, a prophet could only stay in the local church indefinitely if he chose this church as his permanent residence.

13. Clement of Alexandria, *Stromateis* 6.5.

14. H. Greeven, "Propheten, Lehrer, Vorsteher bei Paulus" in *Zeitschrift für die neutestamentliche Wissenschaft* 53 (1932): 1–2, p. 9.

15. See below, chapter 6, IV, p. 191 ff.

16. I Clement 63.3.

17. F.X. Funk, *Doctrina duodecim apostolorum* (Tübingen, 1887).

18. Hippolytus, *Apostolic Tradition* 2.

19. By this statement I do not mean to offer an immediate solution to the question concerning the relation between Acts 15 and Gal 2.1–5. On the state of this question, see J. Dupont, *Les problèmes du livre des Actes d'après les travaux récents* (Louvain, 1950), 51 ff.

20. Cf. Dionysius the Areopagite, *Ecclesiastical Hierarchy* 5.3.5: "The sacred announcement by the hierarch concerning the rites of consecration and those being consecrated denotes the mystery that the performer of consecration in his love of God is the exponent of the choice of the divinity, that it is not by virtue of any personal worth that he summons those about to be consecrated but rather that it is God himself who inspires him in every hierarchic sanctification." [English translation: Pseudo-Dionysius, *The Complete Works*, trans. C. Luibheid and P. Rorem, Classics of Western Spirituality (New York: Paulist Press, 1987), 241.]

21. Hippolytus, *Apostolic Tradition* 3.

22. [Translator's note: The author here means the *Epitome of the Apostolic Constitutions*, book 8, preserving the Greek version of Hippolytus's *Apostolic Tradition* 3.]

23. Hippolytus, *Apostolic Tradition* 2.

24. "To the nearest kin, the inheritance is given of the fields and land; but the leadership of the people is given to the one whom God has chosen . . ." Origen, *In Num.* 22.4.

25. Origen, *In Matth.* 24.

26. Hippolytus, *Apostolic Tradition* 3.

27. Hippolytus, *Apostolic Tradition* 4.

28. Cyprian, *Epist.* 55.8.1.

29. Clement of Rome, *Epistle to the Corinthians* 44.1–4.

30. Ibid., 42.4.

31. Ibid., 44.3.

32. Hippolytus, *Apostolic Tradition* 2.

33. Ibid., 15.1.

34. Cyprian, *Epist.* 55.8.

35. Ibid., 67.5.

36. The apostles, especially the Twelve, must be singled out as a separate group due to exceptional character of their ministry. They were not elected by the local church, for they were selected and ordained by Christ himself.

37. Here I do not intend to give an exhaustive exposition of the apostolic ministry, as well as of other ministries of the primitive church. For the most part, I concentrate on the aspects of these ministries which directly relate to my primary goal. On the history of the question concerning ministries, see Linton, *Das Problem der Urkirche*.

38. Cf. *Epistle of Barnabas* 5.9.

39. St. Paul expresses the same idea in 1 Cor 3.10–11: "According to the grace of God given to me, like a skilled master builder (*architektôn*) I laid a foundation, and another man is building (*epoikodomei*) upon it. Let each man take care how he builds upon it. For no other foundation can any one lay than that which is laid, which is Jesus Christ."

40. See below, chapter 4, I, 3, p. 86.

41. Cf A. V. Gorsky, *The History in the Gospels and the History of the Apostolic Church* [in Russian], 2nd ed. (Moscow 1902), 420: "This ministry could not have been handed on, and the apostles as such did not and could not have successors." See also M. Fiveisky, *Spiritual Gifts in the Primitive Christian Church* [in Russian] (Moscow, 1907), who develops the same idea.

42. See G. Kittel's article "*Eschatos*" in *TWNT,* 2:694 and the article by Schneider, "*Ektrôma*" in *TWNT,* 2:463.

43. See L. Cerfaux, *Le Christ dans la Théologie de S. Paul* (Paris, 1951), 51.

44. What is even less probable is J. Munck's supposition, namely, that Paul changed the meaning of the term "*apostolos*," which prior to him was used to denote the messenger of a Christian community or a travelling missionary sent by Christ. For Paul, as J. Munck speculates, to be an apostle meant to be called for a special and exceptional ministry. Paul is an "apostle to the Gentiles" and only he is "the apostle"; therefore, the "apostleship" signified a highest degree of authority. After Paul, this understanding of apostleship was applied to the "Twelve." Therefore, the collegium of the "Twelve" does not have a new apostle added to it, but rather the "Twelve" were endowed with the same authority that Paul possessed as an "apostle to the Gentiles." See J. Munck, "Paul, the Apostles and the Twelve," *Studia Theologica* 3 (1949): 96–110.

45. Luke's comment that Matthias "was enrolled with the eleven apostles" (Acts 1.26) cannot support the statement that the Twelve were already apostles at this time. Luke employed the term which was in common use in his time. Besides, Luke could not say that Matthias was enrolled with the Twelve, since in fact he was enrolled with the eleven disciples. Cf. J. Wagenmann, *Die Stellung des Apostels Paulus neben den Zwölf in den ersten zwei Jahrhunderten* (Giessen, 1926), 66–67.

46. O. Cullmann, *Königherrschaft Christi und Kirche im Neuen Testament* (Zürich, 1950), 21.

47. Irenaeus, *Against Heresies* 3.1.1: " For, after our Lord rose from the dead, they were invested with power from on high when the Holy Spirit came down, were filled with everything, and had 'perfect knowledge': they departed to the ends of the earth . . ." [English translation: *Ante-Nicene Fathers*, vol. 1].

48. Cf. J. L. Leuba, *L'institution et l'événement* (Paris-Neuchâtel, 1950).

49. See M. Goguel, *L'Eglise primitive*, 98–99; G. Sass, *Apostelamt und Kirche* (Munich, 1939), 38, 105.

50. W. G. Kümmel, *Kirchenbegriff*, 7, 11; E. Percy, *Die Probleme der Kolosser und Epheserbriefe* (Lund, 1946), 340; Campenhausen, *Kirchliches Amt*, 24. Cf. also K. Holl, "Der Kirchenbegriff des Paulus in seinem Verhältnis zu dem der Urgemeinde," *Gesammelte Aufsätze zur Kirchengeschichte II: Der Osten*, 46 ff.; E. Schweitzer, *Das Leben des Herrn*, 72.

51. I leave aside the theory of "schaliach" that seems to me improbable. Quite recently, this theory was proposed by G. Dix in "The Ministry in the Early Church" in K. E. Kirk, *The Apostolic Ministry*. This theory aimed not so much at clarifying the notion of apostleship, as at solving the question of the origin of episcopate. On this theory see also K. H. Rengsdorf, "*Apostolos*" in *TWNT*, 1:424 ff.

52. This statement made by Paul does not in any way diminish the ecclesiological nature of his apostleship. Paul himself asserted that "God has appointed in the church first apostles . . ." The indication that Paul's apostleship was not from men refers not to his ordination, but to his election. We saw above that Paul's apostolic activity began with the participation of the church of Antioch.

53. See E. Hoskyns and F. N. Davey, *L'enigme du Nouveau Testament* (Neuchâtel, 1949), 125 ff.

54. Contrary to E. Schweitzer, *Das Leben des Herrn*, 72. See on this subject L. Cervaux, *Le Christ dans la théologie de saint Paul*, 135 ff.

55. It appears to me that O. Cullmann in his book *Sainte Pierre* (Paris-Neuchâtel, 1952) greatly overestimates the significance of this agreement, considering it as effective for the whole apostolic period. However, he himself acknowledges that there were no churches that were comprised of Jews or Gentiles exclusively. Due to this fact, he is ready to admit that one and the same church could have depended both on St. Paul, heading the mission to the Gentiles, and on St. Peter, the leader of the mission to the Jews. This supposition can hardly be justified with the evidence we possess.

56. Irenaeus, *Against Heresies* 3.1.

57. Contrary to W. G. Kümmel, *Kirchenbegriff*, 6.

58. I leave aside all the difficulties of text, structure, and meaning for the cited excerpt from Corinthians. Here I would like to note that I deem it unlikely that in the excerpt concerning the appearances of Christ, cited above, there are two separate parts, structured symmetrically: in the first part (v. 3–5), Paul renders the original tradition, which he himself supplements in the second part (v. 6–11). (See W. G. Kümmel, *Kirchenbegriff*, 5). I find K. Holl's hypothesis more plausible ("Der Kirchenbegriff des Paulus," 46–47), which states that verse 5 speaks about Christ's appearances in Galilee, but the rest of the passage about

his appearances in Jerusalem. See also A. M. Farrer, "The Ministry in the New Testament," in K. E. Kirk, *The Apostolic Ministry,* 129.

59. Thus, e.g., J. Hering, *La première épitre de St. Paul aux Corinthiens* (Neuchâtel-Paris, 1949), 136; H. Lietzmann, *An die Korinthier I–II* (Tübingen, 1949), 77–78.

60. Cf. A. Harnack, "Die Verklärungsgeschichte Jesu, der Bericht des Paulus und die beiden Christusvisionen des Petrus," in *Sitzungsberichte der Berliner Akademie,* Phil.-hist. Klasse, 1922, 65ff.

61. The Twelve were included among "all the apostles" at any rate. The reason behind the distinction between the terms "the Twelve" and "the apostles" is that only verse 7 has a direct relation to the establishment of the apostolate. Paul was handing over to the Corinthians the tradition which he himself received concerning the death of Christ "for our sins," his burial, and resurrection. Then he lists the individuals to whom Christ has appeared and who were the witnesses of his resurrection. These were the people to whom the Corinthians could turn, if they wished. Clear witness to this is Paul's own indication that among the five hundred brethren to whom appeared the risen Christ "most . . . are still alive." All individuals indicated in vv. 5–7 were not yet apostles when Christ appeared to them. Therefore, these verses do not give any indication whom Paul did consider to be apostles. Speaking of Christ appearing to "all the apostles," Paul hands over the tradition concerning the establishment of the apostolate. He emends this tradition in v. 8 where he speaks of his own apostleship. Cf. L. Cerfaux, "Pour l'histoire du titre *Apostolos* dans le Nouveau Testament," *Revue des Sciences Religieuses* 48, nos. 1–2 (1960): 79.

62. See K. H. Rengsdorf, *TWNT,* 1:432; W. G. Kümmel, *Kirchenbegriff* 45.

63. With respect to Acts 4.36, it indeed could be used as an argument in favor of Barnabas's apostleship, if it is translated as follows: "Joseph who was surnamed Barnabas, who was among the apostles . . ." (Foakes Jackson and K. Lake, *The Beginnings of Christianity,* 4:49). But this translation has no support in the Greek text.

64. M. J. Lagrange, *Epître aux Romains* (Paris, 1922), 366.

65. There is no need to introduce an additional hypothesis, as does K. L. Schmidt (*Die Kirche des Urchristentums: Festgabe für A. Deissmann* [Tübingen, 1927], 290ff.), that originally only the Twelve and Paul were counted as apostles, but later the notion of apostleship became widened, only to get narrowed once again due to the abuse of the apostolic title.

I leave aside the question concerning the "apostles of the churches" (*apostoloi ekklêsiôn*) to whom Paul is referring in 2 Cor 8.23 and Phil 2.25. Both these passages deal with a mission which was temporarily entrusted to certain people. In this sense, the Greek term "*apostolos*" corresponds with the Hebrew term *shaliach.* See G. Sass, *Apostelamt und Kirche,* 17 ff.; E. Mollard, "Le développement de l'idée de succession Apostolique" in *Revue d'Histoire et de Philosophie Religieuses* 34, no. 1 (1954): 1–29: "*Hoi apostoloi* and *hoi dôdeka* are synonyms. This is the terminology found in the synoptic Gospels, in the Acts, with Paul (at least, it seems to me, in 1 Cor 15 and Gal 1) and in the book of Revelation" (9).

66. See the article by G. Friedrich, "*Euaggelistês*" in *TWNT* 2:734–735. The absence of the term "evangelist" in 1 Cor 12.28 cannot serve as a proof that in the time when this epistle was written, those who were called "evangelists" in Eph 4.11 did not exist. Apparently, St. Paul did not have need to designate specifically those who were preaching the gospel at

the time when 1 Cor was composed. Mostly, they did not act on their own, but in close contact with St. Paul, as his co-workers and assistants. He customarily referred to them as his brethren. Thus, Paul applied the name "*adelphos*" to Timothy (2 Cor 1.1; Col 1.1; Philem 1) who in 2 Tim 4.5 is designated as an "evangelist." Paul called as "brothers in Christ" those people who "*ton Christon kêryssousin*" (Phil 1.15), "*ton Christon kataggelousin*" (v. 17) and, although he knew that some of them do it from "envy and rivalry" (v. 15), he still was regarding them as his co-workers. At the time when the Epistle to the Ephesians was written, those who were "*ton Christon kataggelousin*" acted independently of St. Paul or any other apostles. Their preaching of Christ's gospel became a special ministry that had to be designated by a special term. It is quite possible to admit that, as E. Percy supposed (*Die Probleme der Kolosser,* 342), it was they who founded the church or the churches to which the Epistle to the Ephesians was addressed.

67. Eusebius, *Ecclesiastical History* 3.37.1: "*tên prôtên taxin tês tôn apostolôn epechontes diadochês.*"

68. Ibid., 3.37.2–4.

69. Ibid., 5.10.2–3.

70. See O. Linton, "Das Problem des Urkirche"; also E. Fascher, *Prophêtês* (Giessen, 1927).

71. Until this day, the question remains unsolved, whether Eph 2.20 refers to the Old Testament or the New Testament prophet. The majority of scholars (e.g. L. Cerfaux, *La theologie de l'Eglise selon saint Paul* [Paris, 1948], 106; M. Goguel, *L'Eglise primitive,* 104; E. Percy, *Die Probleme der Kolosser,* 329) are inclined to the latter opinion. This view seems to me to be accurate, especially if Eph 3.5 is taken into consideration.

72. See M. J. Lagrange, *Epître aux Romains,* 298; H. v. Campenhausen, *Kirchliches Amt,* 66; H. Greeven, "Propheten, Lehrer," 5.

73. Eusebius, *Ecclesiastical History* 5. 17.4.

74. See C. Spicq, *Les épîtres pastorales,* 48.

75. E. Percy, *Die Probleme der Kolosser,* 379.

76. Chapter 7. *Didache* 11.1. [English translation: *The Apostolic Fathers,* trans. K. Lake, vol. 1, Loeb Classical Library 24 (Cambridge, MA: Harvard University Press, 1977).]

77. Eusebius, *Ecclesiastical History* 5.16.7.

78. Ibid., 5.17.1.

79. Ibid., 5.17.3.

80. "And the spirits of prophets are subject to prophets" (1 Cor 14.32). See E. Fascher, *Prophêtês,* 185.

81. See P. de Labriolle, *La crise montaniste* (Paris, 1913); but this does not exclude the possibility of Johannine circles strongly influencing Montanism. Cf. W. Schepelern, *Der Montanismus und die phrygischen Kulte* (Tübingen, 1929), 159.

82. See above, chapter 3, IV, 2, pp. 59–65. My view is contrary to the opinion of H. Greeven, "Propheten, Lehrer," 11–12, who thinks that the charism of testing pertained to the prophets themselves. H. v. Campenhausen holds to the same opinion (*Kirchliches Amt,* 67), however conceding that the charism of testing may be granted to other people. Nevertheless, he considers that: "Die Verantwortung für das, was geschieht, wird der Gemeinde darum nicht abgenommen."

83. Eusebius, *Ecclesiastical History* 5.16.8.

84. Commandment 11. Cf. Irenaeus, *Against the Heresies* 3.24.1: "'For in the Church,' it is said, 'God hath set apostles, prophets, teachers,' and all the other means through which the Spirit works; of which all those are not partakers who do not join themselves to the Church, but defraud themselves of life through their perverse opinions and infamous behavior."

85. *Didache* 11.1.

86. See J. P. Audet, "Affinités littéraires et doctrinales du *Manuel de Discipline*" in *Revue Biblique* 59, no. 2 (1952): 219–238.

87. *Didache* 11.10.

88. Ibid., 11.8.

89. Ibid., 11.7.

90. Ibid., 13.3.

91. Ibid., 10.7.

92. Cf. G. Dix, *The Shape of the Liturgy*, chapter "The Lord's Supper, or Agape," 82 ff.

93. *Didache* 15.1.

94. Commandment 11.12.

95. Vision 3.1.

96. Lucian tells about Peregrinus that he was "a prophet and a thiasarch and a head of the congregation and he alone was all this ... They chose him as their presider" (*De morte Peregrini*, p. 11). Even here the prophetic ministry coexists with other ministries, rather than incorporates them in itself.

97. *Didache* 9.4.

98. Ibid., 10.5.

99. See K. H. Rengsdorf, "*Didaskalos*" in *TWNT*, 2:150 ff.; H. Greeven, "Propheten, Lehrer."

100. *Stromateis* 7.16 (English translation: *Ante-Nicene Fathers*, vol. 2, p. 554, the translation altered to correspond to N. Afanasiev's text).

101. Origen, *In Rom.* 9.2.

102. See H. v. Campenhausen, *Kirchliches Amt*, 66. H. Greeven, "Propheten, Lehrer," 24: "Es ist kaum zu viel gesagt, wenn man feststellt, dass ohne die *didaskaloi* der christlichen Gemeinden die Entstehung einer Überlieferung und letzlich des Kanons nicht zu denken ist."

103. See G. Bardy, "L'Eglise et l'enseignement pendant les trois premiers siècles," *Revue des Sciences Religieuses* 22 (1932): 1–28.

104. See the commentary of H. I. Marrou, *A Diognète*, Sources chrétiennes 33 (Paris, 1951), 266.

105. *Epistle to Diognetus* 11.

106. Similitude 8.6.

107. Irenaeus, *Against the Heresies* 2.28.3.

108. Ibid., 28.6.

109. Ibid., 27.1.

110. Tertullian, *De Praescriptione* 7.

111. Clement of Alexandria, *Stromateis* 1.9 (English translation: *Ante-Nicene Fathers*, vol. 2, 309).

112. Origen, *Contra Celsum* 6.40.

113. There exists no basis whatsoever for wholly identifying pastors and teachers. If in Eph 4.11 *poimenes* and *didaskaloi* are joined together under the same definite article, this does not indicate that their ministries are identical. Teaching was part of the ministry of pastors, as it follows from the requirement set in 1 Tim 3.2 that the bishop must be "an apt teacher—*didaktikos*." Alongside the episcopal ministry, there might have existed a separate ministry of teacher. There is even less ground for the view that teaching is an isolation of one function of apostleship into an independent ministry. (Cf. K. H. Rengsdorf, "*Didaskalos*," 161.)

Chapter 5. **"Those Who Preside in the Lord"**

1. We find classic expositions of this view in J. Réville, *Les origines de l'épiscopat* (Paris, 1894); A. Sabatier, *Les religions d'authorité et la religion de l'Esprit* (Paris, 1903). In the meantime, the argument concerning charismatic anarchy was significantly weakened, but did not altogether disappear. M. Goguel, *L'Eglise primitive*, 160, writes: "The apostle Paul was not content to found the churches, he also organized them." However, it still remains unclear what was the principle of church organization. See also K. Holl, "Der Kirchenbegriff des Paulus" in *Gesammelte Aufsätze zur Kirchengeschichte II*, 44–67; H. v. Campenhausen, *Kirchliches Amt*, 62.

2. Cf. M. Goguel, *Introduction au Nouveau Testament*, vol. 4 (Paris, 1926).

3. Hippolytus of Rome, *Commentary on Daniel* 3.8.

4. Tertullian, *De fuga* 12.

5. Tertullian, *De ieiunio* 13.

6. Origen, *Commentary on Matthew*, 16.8 [Translator's note: English translation is mine.]

7. The term *hoi hagioi* in the writings of St. Paul still remains a subject of debate (see O. Procksch, the article "*Hagios*" in *TWNT*, 1:107ff.). If we admit that Paul applied this term to Jewish Christians, then the expression *en pasais tais ekklêsiais tôn hagiôn* would signify the Palestinian churches. The ecclesiastical structure of the Palestinian churches must have been the model for the life of the Hellenistic churches. Thus, Paul accepted the principle of order and structure from the ecclesial tradition, and for this reason could not go against this principle for the sake of charismatic anarchy that allegedly predominated the churches he founded. See also E. B. Allo, *Première épître aux Corinthiens* (Paris, 1935), 371 ff.; W. G. Kümmel, "Kirchenbegriff," 16).

8. See O. Linton, *Das Problem der Urkirche*; F. M. Braun, *Aspects nouveaux du problème de l'Eglise* (Fribourg, 1942; German translation, *Neues Licht auf die Kirche*, 1946). Also see the article by K. L. Schmidt, "*Ekklêsia*" in *TWNT*, 3:502–539.

9. See R. Grosche, "Das allgemeine Priestertum" in the collection of essays, *Pilgernde Kirche* (Freiburg im Bresgau, 1938).

10. See above, p. 87 ff.

11. See P. Bonnard, *Jésus-Christ édifiant son Eglise* (Neuchâtel-Paris, 1947).

12. These are not different people that are spoken about here, but the same individuals possessing different functions of the ministry that they fulfill. This is indicated by the article *tous* which unites all three participles. See W. Neil, *The Letter of Paul to the Thessalonians* (London, 1950), 121.

13. On the meaning of *kopiaô*, see F. Hauck, *TWNT,* 3:827 ff. In the New Testament writings, *kopian* and its derivatives mean "die christliche Arbeit an der Gemeinde und für die Gemeinde." See also A. Harnack, "*kopos (kopian, hoi kopiôntes*) im frühchristlichen Sprachgebrauch" in *Zeitschrift für Neuen Testament* 26 (1928): 1–10.

14. See E. Schweitzer, *Gemeinde nach dem Neuen Testament* (Zürich, 1949), 5.

15. See H. Lietzmann, *An die Korinther I–II* (Tübingen, 1949), 63–64. H. Lietzmann considered the bearers of such charismata as *antilêmpsis* and *kybernêsis* as not belonging to the charismatics in an exact sense of the word. See also the note by W. G. Kümmel, *Kirchenbegriff,* 188.

16. See above, p. 86.

17. See H. Greeven, "Propheten, Lehrer," 33. In his opinion, *spoudê* has nearly a technical sense, signifying "die eifrige Tätigkeit für die Gemeinde."

18. See F. Buchsel, "*Hêgeomai*" in *TWNT,* 2:909–911.

19. See Bishop Cassien (Besobrasoff), *Christ and the First Generation of Christians* (in Russian; Paris, 1950), 260. Cf. C. Spicq, "L'origine johannique de la conception du Christ-prêtre dans l'Epître aux Hébreux" in *Aux sources de la tradition chrétienne: Mélanges offerts à M. Goguel* (Neuchâtel-Paris, 1950), 265–266. It is entirely possible to admit that the author of the letter lived for a long time in Asia Minor, but he could hardly borrow this term from there, for we have no evidence that this term was ever in use in the churches of Asia Minor. If, however, as H. Strathmann supposes ("Der Brief an die Hebräer," *Das Neue Testament Deutsch* [Göttingen, 1949], 65), the Hebrews was addressed to Rome, the compiler of the letter apparently reckoned with the terms that were current in the church of Rome.

20. Clement, *Letter* 1.3, 21.6; Hermas, *Shepherd,* Vision 2.2, 3.9.

21. In Acts, the term "hegoumen" is one of the archaic terms. If we are to allow for the existence of "Proto-Lk" (see H. Sahlin, *Der Messias und das Gottesvolk* [Uppsala, 1945]), this term undoubtedly existed in the Aramaic original. Luke preserved this term in connection to Judas and Silas alongside the term "presbyter." The term *hêgoumenos* is also found in the Gospel of Luke 22.26.

22. I leave open the question concerning the authorship of Hebrews. On this, see Bishop Cassien, *Christ and the First Generation,* 260.

23. Clement, *Letter* 5.7, 9.4, 37.2, 3, 55.1. Cf. Acts 14.12.

24. Sirach 33.19: *hêgoumenoi ekklêsias.* On the meaning of *hêgoumenos,* see C. Spicq, "Alexandrinismes dans l'Epitre aux Hébreux," *Revue Biblique* 58 (1951): 496–497.

25. I am inclined to stay with what follows from the text itself, namely that the expression *tous de poimenas kai didaskalous* designates two categories of individuals rather than one. (See L. Marchal, "Origine divine des éveques" in *Supplément au Dictionnaire de la*

Bible, 2:1324; P. Battifol, *Etudes d'histoire et de théologie positive*, série II [Paris, 1926], 233). The absence of the article before *didaskalous* cannot be a decisive argument in favor of the second opinion. The absence of the article is most likely explained by the fact that teaching was one among the functions of the pastors. If we assume that the terms "pastors" and "teachers" are completely identical, we will be facing an insoluble problem: how, then, did the ministry of the *didaskaloi* originate, who had no connection at all with the ministry of the presiders? Besides, given this assumption, we will be facing another question: why in 1 Cor 12.28 did St. Paul mention the ministry of administration alongside with the teachers? In this instance, just as in many others, we are faced with the unstable terminology of New Testament writings, partly caused by the unstable character of the ministries. The same person could have possessed different charismata, only one of which was a principal one, which defined his ministry.

26. There is no basis for differentiating *hêgoumenoi* of Heb 13.7 from *hêgoumenoi* of Heb 13.17, understanding the first as evangelists or apostles who first preached the Word of God to the faithful. If it were the evangelists who were spoken about here, they could not have been an example to imitate for all the members of the church, for some part of these members might as well not have known them. However, it is entirely possible to admit that the expression "*hoitines elalêsan hymin ton logon tou Theou*" has a wider meaning, denoting, generally, everybody having a special ministry in the Church. In the *Didache*, we find the same expression "*lalountes ton logon tou Theou*" (4.1) encompassing apostles, prophets, and teachers, i.e., denoting a category of people who exercised a ministry in the Church on the basis of special gifts of the Spirit. If, as it is entirely probable, the compiler of the *Didache* took this expression from the letter to the Hebrews, even in this letter, it has to indicate that *hegoumenoi* belong to the same group as do prophets and teachers.

27. Cf. 1 Tim 5.17; Titus 1.9.

28. See above, p. 131.

29. Cf. Tertullian, *De praescr. haer.* 21.4: "quod ecclesiae ab apostolis, apostoli a Christo, Christus a Deo accepit"; Irenaeus of Lyons, *Against Heresies* 3, preface.

30. This interpretation is substantiated by the *Ecclesiastical Canons of the Apostles*: "For there are twenty-four presbyters, twelve on the right and twelve on the left. For those on the right side, taking the vessels from the archangels, bring them to the Master, while those on the left face the multitude of angels." (Chapter 18.1–2; Funk, *Doctrina duodecim apostolorum*, 62). The ecclesial assembly is designated as the choir of angels. Cf. E. B. Allo, *S. Jean. L' Apocalypse* (Paris, 1921), 18–19. Angels of the churches in the book of Revelation undoubtedly correspond to the angels of the nations in Judaism. See O. Cullmann, *Christ et le Temps* (Paris-Neuchâtel, 1947), 138. I do not intend to solve here the difficult question concerning the angels of the Revelation. A widely spread opinion states that they are personifications of the bishops. In Russian theological literature, this opinion was shared by such an authoritative figure as Metropolitan Philaret of Moscow. (See *Collected Correspondence of Metropolitan Philaret* [in Russian], 4:394). As it is clear from my own text, I do not totally adhere to this point of view, the simple reason being that at the time when the book of Revelation was written, the bishops did not yet exist. See also the article by G. Kittel,

"*Aggelos*" in *TWNT,* 1:85 ff. It is hardly possible to regard these angels as celestial beings. With this supposition, the words of reproach and reprimand which the Seer of mysteries addresses to the angels, sound very strange indeed.

31. Shown by O. Cullmann, the term *kôluein* has liturgical connotation. (See *Le baptême des enfants* [Paris-Neuchâtel, 1948], appendix, 62 ff.). Therefore, 1 Cor 14.33 deals with liturgical assemblies. Based on this, we can also reason that the term *aphienai* has liturgical connotation too.

32. Irenaeus of Lyons, *Against Heresies* 3.14.2.

33. Until the present time there exist the proponents of a theory that the singular of *episkopos* here indicates a person distinguished from presbyter. See the article by A. M. Farrer, "The Ministry in the New Testament" in K. E. Kirk, *The Apostolic Ministry.* His constructions appear to me as little convincing. The hypothesis which appears as even less convincing to me, states that the singular of *episkopos* in the Pastoral letters is used for designating a group of people (see E. Schweitzer, *Gemeinde nach dem N. Testament* 109). H. W. Beyer's suggestion, which appears to me as more probable, argues that "the term bishop is meant as a model / type and says nothing about the number of bishops at one place" (*TWNT,* 2:614). C. Spicq seems to adhere to a middle position: "While the terms 'presbyter' and 'bishop' are more or less synonymous and could have been applied indiscriminately to the same person, it nevertheless seems that the functions exercised by them were not always identical . . . One is thus entitled to think that at the time of the Pastoral epistles, a bishop was a presbyter possessing, here and there, a higher authority or better, a ministry more particularly defined, an 'episkope.'" (Spicq, *Les épîtres pastorales* [Paris, 1947], xlvi–xlvii). H. v. Campenhausen (*Kirchliches Amt,* 117) contends that in the Pastoral letters we are dealing with the monarchical episcopate. However, he situates the composition of the letters in the second half of the second century.

34. Verse 5.17 of the same letter speaks about "the presbyters who rule well" (*kalôs proestôtes presbyteroi*). The pending conclusion is that "*proestôtes presbyteroi*" are the same as the bishops in the third chapter of the same letter. If we insist that the bishop and presiding presbyter are different figures, Paul's authorship has to be sacrificed. Even given these conditions, many things remain unclear. Why did the author of the letter fail to mention the requirements set for the presbyters if they are different from bishops? The only suggestion one could make is as follows: at the time when 1 Timothy was written, the ministry of bishops and deacons—at least of the former—had emerged quite recently, while presiding presbyters already existed for a long time. That is why the author of the letter did not have to refer specifically to the requirement set for the presbyters. We will observe later that a separate episcopal ministry emerges by the time of Ignatius of Antioch. It is highly improbable to affix the composition of 1 Timothy to this period. J. Jeremias in "Die Briefe an Timotheus und Titus" (*Das Neue Testament Deutsch* [Göttingen, 1949], 32–33) argues that the term "presbyters" in the Pastoral letters denotes the elders, i.e., the eldest members of a local church, who did not have any specific ministry. Jeremias suggests that this archaic usage of the term "presbyter" offers a proof in favor of the letter's authenticity. Concerning the "*proestôtes presbyteroi*," he argues that this term designates the elders entrusted with certain official duties. The relation of these "ruling presbyters" to bishops and deacons still

remains unclear. To some extent, J. Jeremias's opinion returns to A. Harnack's theory concerning the "charism of eldership" and can hardly be agreed with. Besides, he offers no decisive proof in favor of his view.

35. Cf. H. W. Beyer, "*Episkopê*" in *TWNT,* 2:602–604.

36. F. Prat, *La théologie de S. Paul* (Paris, 1949), 1:369.

37. I firmly refuse to associate myself with the view that Luke's use of the term "presbyter" is a transposition from the ecclesial organization of his time. On this subject, see below.

38. Jerome, *Commentary on Titus* 1.5.

39. Cf. L. Marchal, "Origine divine des eveques," 1306.

40. F. Prat, *Théologie de Saint Paul,* 2:365; A. Michiels, *L'origine de l'Episcopat* (Louvain, 1900), 218–230.

41. The complexity of the issue concerning the transition from apostolate to episcopate, and the issue caused by the hypothesis about apostles-bishops, is shown in the recent work by G. Dix, "The Ministry in the Early Church" in K. E. Kirk, *The Apostolic Ministry* (London, 1946) 185 ff. However cunning his constructions are, they are far from being convincing. L. Marchal, who supports this hypothesis (the article "Evêques" in *Dictionnaire de la Bible,* Suppl. vol. 2, pp. 1297–1333), was pressed to acknowledge the following: "What concerns the manner in which the transition from the apostolate to episcopacy took place, we here are left with conjectures only" (1327).

42. It should be noted that a "rod" in 1 Cor 4.21 (*hê rhabdos*) does not necessarily signify the symbol of authority. According to Philo (*De Poster. Caini* 97), <*rhabdos*> designates a symbol of rearing of a child, the uninitiated one, whereas the expression "*en agapê, pneumati te prautêtos*" is applied to the initiated. (See Goro Mayeda, *Le langage et l'Evangile* [Genève, 1948], 137). In 1 Cor 3.1, Paul indicated to the Corinthians that he could not "address" them "as spiritual men (*pneumatikois*), but as men of the flesh, as babes in Christ." St. Paul could have had a fear that he would again find Corinthians as "babes in Christ," not as spiritual adults.

43. R. Knopf, *Das nachapostolische Zeitalter* (Tübingen, 1905), 194 ff; Michiels, *L'origine de l'Episcopat,* 210 ff.

44. Cf. J. Réville, *Les origines de l'épiscopat,* 148 ff.

45. Paul's silence about the term "presbyter" cannot serve as proof to the absence of presbyters in the churches that St. Paul had founded. We cannot reject the evidence of the Pastoral letters, despite the controversy surrounding Paul's authorship. We will attempt to demonstrate below that presbyters existed in Pauline churches from the very beginning. Paul had all the reasons to avoid using the word "presbyter" since it did not have fully terminological significance and could have led to misunderstandings.

46. J. Réville, *Les origines de l'épiscopat,* 108; Weizsäcker, *Das apostolische Zeitalter der christlichen Kirche* (Tübingen, 1902), 604 ff.

47. Cf. A. Harnack, *Die Quellen der sogenannten Apostolischen Kirchenordnung, Texte und Untersuchungen,* vol. 2 (1886) Heft 5.

48. Hermas, *Shepherd,* Vision 3, 9.7.

49. 1 Clement 42.4.

50. Ibid. 54.2. Cf. 1 Tim 5.17: *"proestôtes presbyteroi."*

51. E. Hutch, *The Organization of the Early Christian Churches* (Oxford, 1880).

52. *"ton Poimena kai Episkopon tôn psychôn hymôn."* To whom exactly the title "Shepherd and Guardian" refers in the cited text from the letter of Peter, still remains to some extent an open question. It would be most natural to see Christ as "Shepherd and Guardian," to which conclusion we are entitled by the context of verses 21–25 in the second chapter of the letter. In verse 21 it says that "Christ also suffered for you, leaving you an example, that you should follow in his steps." Those who follow in the steps of Christ, follow him as their Shepherd. The verses that follow are taken almost word for word from Isaiah 53 and describe the redeeming act [*podvig*] of Christ. Besides, the image of Christ as Shepherd is grounded in the very words of Christ—John 10.11. Nevertheless, one cannot exclude the possibility of seeing God the Father as this Shepherd and Guardian. Through Christ's redeeming act, the straying sheep have returned to God. We find the image of God as Shepherd in Ezekiel: "I myself will be the shepherd of my sheep, and I will make them lie down, says the Lord God" (34.15). Even if we consider that the apostle Peter in verse 25 speaks of God the Father, that does not at all change our conclusions in the text above. See H. W. Beyer, *"Episkopos"* in *TWNT,* 2:611; C. Spicq (*Les épîtres pastorales,* xlvi and 86) applies the title "Shepherd and Guardian" to Christ.

53. See pp. 139–140.

54. Eusebius, *Ecclesiastical History* 3.23 [English translation: *Nicene and Post-Nicene Fathers,* Series II, vol. 1].

55. Origen, *Homily on Joshua* 7.6 [English translation: B. J. Bruce, ed. C. White. Fathers of the Church 105 (Washington, DC: Catholic University of America Press, 2002)].

56. Cf. Hermas, *Shepherd:* "If he find some of [the sheep] fallen away, it will be woe to the shepherds. But if the shepherds themselves be found fallen away, what shall they answer to the Master of the flock? That they have fallen away because of the sheep? They will not be believed, for it is incredible that a shepherd should be harmed by the sheep, and they will rather be punished for their lie. And I am the shepherd, and am very exceedingly bound to give account for you" (Sim. 9.31).

57. See pp. 145–146.

58. See the article by G. Delling, *"Antilêmpsis"* in *TWNT,* 1:576.

59. One has to note that the gift of assistance is not present among the gifts listed in 1 Cor 12.8–10.

60. On this subject, see below, p. 182.

61. See B. Reicke, *Diakonie, Festfreude und Zelos* (Uppsala, 1951), 21 ff.

62. Ignatius, Trallians 2.3, 3.1; Magnesians 6.1. On this subject, see below.

63. Hermas, *Shepherd,* Sim. 9.26.

64. Hippolytus, *Apostolic Tradition* 9.

65. *Didache* 15.1.

66. *Apostolic Constitutions* 2.44; 3.15, 19.

67. Hippolytus, *Apostolic Tradition* 30.

68. A. Harnack, *Quellen der sogen. Apostol. Kirchenordnung,* 11.

Chapter 6. "The One Who Offers Thanksgiving"

1. This is indicated by the words which connect the letters to the seven churches and the vision: "After this I looked, and lo, in heaven an open door . . . at once I was in the Spirit" (vv. 1–2). The door leading to heaven was the door to the eucharistic assembly. "At once I was in the Spirit . . ." This vision, like the vision described in the first chapter, took place at the eucharistic assembly: "I was in the Spirit on the Lord's day (*en têi kyriakêi hêmerai*) and I heard behind me a loud voice . . ." (1.10). When the doctrine concerning the heavenly church comes into existence, the signs of which are already found in the book of Revelation, the earthly church is regarded as the icon of the heavenly one (Clement of Alexandria, *Stromateis* 4.8).

2. We have at our disposal an official stenographic report of the confiscation of church possessions from the church in Cirta (modern Constantine in Algeria) during Diocletian's persecution. By its tragic force, the dry stenographic record made by a Roman official obliged to be present at the confiscation of possessions and books surpasses all pietistic novels. The church was situated in a private home, remodeled for the purpose of Christian gatherings. Notified in advance about the forthcoming search, the bishop gathered with his clerics in the church premises. When the seizing of church property began, all the clergy assumed their customary places: the bishop at his throne, the presbyters at their seats on both sides of him, and next to the bishop, on either side, the deacons stood. The date of the record is 19 May 303, but we are fully entitled to think that this order in which the bishop, presbyters, and deacons arranged themselves existed from the very beginning, for it had its origin in the eucharistic assembly itself, as we shall see below (cf. G. Dix, *The Shape of the Liturgy,* 24).

3. Cf. H. Lietzmann, *Histoire de l'Eglise ancienne: Les commencements* (Paris, 1950), 153–154.

4. See A. Loisy, *L'Evangile et l'Eglise* (Paris, 1902), 111: "Jesus announced the Kingdom of God, and it was the Church that had come."

5. Cf. F. Kattenbuch, *Der Quellort der Kirchenidee: Festgabe für A. Harnack* (1921).

6. I leave open the question whether the Last Supper was a paschal evening meal, as it follows from Luke's testimony. However important this question and its solution may be, it does not really matter for my study. There is currently no consensus on this question in the modern theological scholarship. See Bishop Cassien, *Christ and the First Generation;* J. Jeremias, *Golgotha* (Leipzig, 1926); M. Goguel, *L'Eglise primitive.*

7. I consider the existence of the Twelve a historical fact and therefore refuse to discuss the question of whether the concept of the Twelve was a concoction of the early church. See F. M. Braun, *Aspects nouveaux du problème de l'Eglise,* 68–73; Rengsdorf, "*Dôdeka*" in *TWNT,* 2:325 ff.

8. See the article by G. Kittel, "*Akoloutheô*" in *TWNT,* 1:210 ff.

9. In relation to *chabûrah,* I mainly rely on the study of G. Dix, *The Shape of the Liturgy,* 50 ff., which cites a bibliography on the issue. To the studies indicated there, I have to add R. Otto, *Reichgottes und Menschensohn* (Munich, 1934).

10. On the time of the descent of the Spirit on the day of Pentecost, see Bishop Cassien, *Christ and the First Generation*, 130–131.

11. If Theophilus, to whom Luke addresses his Acts, was a pagan, it is quite possible that Luke's silence on the procedure of the eucharistic celebration is clear by itself. See J. Jeremias, *Die Abendmahlsworte* (Göttingen, 1949), 65.

12. On the chronology of Acts, see the article by E. Jacquier in his *Les actes des apôtres* (Paris, 1926) and a number of points by H. Sahlin in *Der Messias und das Gottesvolk*.

13. Contrary to E. Jacquier, *Les actes des apôtres*, 187. If the apostles themselves exercised the service of the tables, it follows that in the church of Jerusalem, until the institution of the "seven," there were no other people who fulfilled the same ministry. For this reason, we can rule out the possibility of there being a special ministry of deacons from the Jews.

14. I utterly refuse to accept the theory that the "*hellênistai*" of Acts 6 were Gentile Christians. With this presupposition, "*hebraioi*" would be merely Jews, rather than the Aramaic-speaking Jews. (See H. J. Cadbury, "The Hellenist" in *The Beginnings of Christianity* [London, 1933], 5:59–74; H. Windisch, "*Hellên*" in *TWNT*, 2:508–509). This theory has no solid ground. Undoubtedly, it grew out of the intention to show that Paul was not the first missionary to the Gentiles and that the Hellenistic religious outlook influenced Christianity at its starting point. In particular, this theory tries to show that the term *sôtêr* which Peter employs (Acts 5.31) originated with the Greeks. (See W. G. Kümmel, *Kirchenbegriff*, 12).

15. I find unlikely the suggestion made on the basis of Matt 15.27, that the "service of the tables" was the distribution of monetary aid to the needy members of the church. Cf. E. Jacquier, *Les actes des apôtres*, 187.

16. See P. Gaechter, "Die Sieben (Apg. 6.1–6)," *Zeitschrift für Katholische Theologie* 74 (1952): 134. Gaechter thinks that "daily distribution" does not signify the distribution of aid at daily meals. On the basis of Lk 13.3, he supposes that "*kathêmerinê*" means the distribution "for the purpose of every day," rather than "every day."

17. Cf. M. Goguel, *La naissance du christianisme* (Paris, 1946), 192.

18. See E. Jacquier, *Les actes des apôtres*, 186.

19. It is usually assumed that the conflict between Hellenists and Jews happened within the church itself. In the main body of the text, I stay with this usual understanding, but, in a footnote, I would like to voice an alternative theory. Luke is quite certain in pointing out that the matter was about the support to the widows, without mentioning the support to other needy members of the church. Meanwhile, in the near future, if not at that very time, there were many needy people among the members of the Jerusalem church. Why does Luke fail to mention them? The second comment that needs to be made concerns the very fact of supporting the widows. If this support caused conflict to ensue, one could naturally be led to think that the number of widows was a significant one. Whence could they originate in such numbers at that time in the church of Jerusalem? Were they indeed the widows of Christians, that is, having converted to Christianity before the death of their husbands? This is very unlikely, since we know that as there were either no or extremely few occasions of death among the first Christians (see Ph. M. Menoud, "La mort d'Ananias et de Saphira" in *Mélanges offerts à M. Goguel* [Paris, 1950], 146). Or did they convert to Christianity by themselves? This is also highly improbable. Finally, the third com-

ment concerns the terms "*hellênistês*" and "*hebraios*" which Luke does not usually apply to the members of the church (see H. Windisch, "*Hellên*" in *TWNT,* 2:508). If we stay with the assumption that this conflict erupted among the members of the church in Jerusalem, these questions remain unanswered. But if we suppose that the conflict between Hellenists and Jews erupted outside of the church, it eliminates all these questions. The ministry of support in the church of Jerusalem did not amount to helping its own members only, but rather meant helping the needy in general and, first of all, the widows, which was the sacred duty of Old Testament Jews. It is very obvious that the number of needy widows in Jerusalem was significant, which necessitated the "daily distribution." The administrative division of Jerusalem into seven districts could have given the idea of appointing seven men so that each of them would have a certain part of Jerusalem under his supervision. The help provided for the Jerusalem widows had its origin in the eucharistic assembly, and for this reason the institution of the "seven" could not fail to influence the structure of the church in Jerusalem. On the other hand, the conflict that had erupted among the inhabitants of Jerusalem in connection with the help to the widows, shows that the state of the Jerusalem church found resonance in the general Judaic milieu, whose attitude toward the church itself experienced changes depending on the currents that at the moments were prevailing in this milieu.

20. P. Gaechter, "Die Sieben," 148 thinks that the appointment of the "seven" took place at the assembly of Hellenists, rather than of the whole church. This assertion of his has no basis in Luke's narrative, but derives, rather, from his assumption that the apostles, having ordained "seven," whose names Luke reports, for the Hellenists, ordained another "seven" for the Jews. This, in P. Gaechter's opinion, resulted in the split of the Jerusalem church in two sections, each of which had its own assembly and its own network of assisting the poor.

21. See E. Jacquier, *Les actes des apôtres,* 185–186; P. Gaechter, "Die Sieben," 147.

22. E. Jacquier, *Les actes des apôtres,* 190.

23. It is not necessary to stress in a special way the connection of different currents within the Jerusalem church with the two groups of which it consisted: "Hellenists" and "Jews." Hellenists were far from always being a liberal faction in Judaism. In some instances, they were even more rigorist than Palestinian Jews. See W. D. Davies, *Paul and Rabbinic Judaism.*

24. Irenaeus of Lyons already regarded the "seven" as deacons (*Against Heresies* 1.26.3; 3.12.10).

25. Canon 18 of Trullo.

26. John Chrysostom, *Commentary on Acts* 14.

27. Ignatius, *Smyrneans* 8.1. Cf. the interpolated text: ". . . And reverence the deacons as ministering according to the command of God."

28. Ignatius, *Magnesians* 6.1.

29. Ignatius, *Trallians* 3.1.

30. Ignatius, *Smyrneans* 8.1.

31. It has no significance for me whether Paul's name was present in the source document used or, rather, translated by Luke (see H. Sahlin, *Der Messias und das Gottevolk,*

359–360). Rather, for me it is important that the relief that was gathered was laid at the feet of presbyters, not at the feet of the apostles.

32. On this subject, see a short but good summary in P. Bonnard, *L'épître de saint Paul aux Galates* (Paris-Neuchâtel, 1953), 47. See also W. L. Knox, *The Acts of the Apostles* (Cambridge, 1948), 40 ff.; H. Sahlin, *Der Messias* 361–362.

33. This connection was already noted by K. Holl in "Der Kirchenbegriff des Paulus" in *Gesammelte Aufsätze zur Kirchengeschichte II: Der Osten,* but he did not draw from it all possible conclusions.

34. As an example, I can cite a suggestion that chapter 15 of Acts is not in its right place. Its proper place is before chapter 12. Even with this suggestion, a lot of chronology still remains unclear: the Apostolic council could have taken place in 43, or at the latest, in 44 AD (the year when Agrippas I died), or else in some interval prior to 50 AD (the beginning of the reign of Agrippas II). Then, the death of St. James falls not in the reign of Agrippas I, but in the reign of Agrippas II (see H. Sahlin, *Der Messias,* 359; see also E. Jacquier, *Les actes des apôtres,* cclxxxvii, which features different datings of major events in the book of Acts suggested by various scholars). Even more radical remodeling of the Acts material was made by J. Knox, *Chapters in a Life of Paul* (New York, 1950). In his opinion, the Jerusalem council took place after Paul's second missionary journey and at the time of his second visit to Jerusalem, which falls, according to J. Knox, in the years 50–51 AD (Acts 18.22).

35. The suggestion that the "seven" were both future presbyters and future deacons, was made by F. X. Funk, *Lehrbuch der Kirchengeschichte,* 1:83–84.

36. P. Gaechter, "Die Sieben," 153 ff., considers the Seven to be presbyters who, in his opinion, were assistants to the apostles. The latter, together with the presbyters, formed the "council" of the Jerusalem church, which joined together its two separate factions, made of Jews and Hellenists.

37. We do not know of either an Aramaic or a Hebrew equivalent for the term *hê-goumenoi,* just as we do not know the similar equivalent of the term *presbyteroi.* It is possible that *hêgoumenoi* is a translation of the term *parnasim* (from *parnes,* meaning *pascere, nurtire, gubernare*). Every independent community in Palestine had at its head a college of seven members, or *parnasim* (Strack-Billerbeck, *Kommentar zum Neuen Testament aus Talmud und Midrasch,* 4/1:145; cf. P. Gaechter, "Die Sieben," 149–150).

38. In the opinion of P. Gaechter, it was the apostle Peter who appointed James. Cf. W. L. Knox, *St. Paul and the Church of Jerusalem,* 169.

39. See E. Jacquier, *Les actes des apôtres,* 368; P. Gaechter, "Die Sieben," 157.

40. Cf. Clement of Rome, *1 Corinthians* 5.7; 37.2, 3; 51.5; 55.1; 60.4, where the term *hegoumenos* signifies a person holding a secular office.

41. This is the method used by O. Cullman in his study *Le baptême des enfants et la doctrine biblique du baptême* (Paris-Neuchâtel, 1948) in the issue of infant baptism. He writes: "But it is not from the point of view of scriptural attestation that the question of infant baptism should be posed. If we keep in mind our sources, the answer to this question cannot be found anywhere else than in the general New Testament *doctrine* on this subject" (22).

42. The hypothesis of the rivalry between the *desposynoi* and the apostles does not have serious backing. At any rate, the claim made in support of this theory that Matthew 16.18 emerged at Antioch as the apology of Peter against James (F. J. Foakes Jackson and K. Lake, *The Beginnings of Christianity,* Part I, Vol. 1, 330) is no longer acceptable, since it is without doubt that the saying of Christ, "You are Peter," could emerge only in Palestine, and more precisely in Jerusalem (cf. J. Jeremias, *Golgotha,* 68 ff.).

43. Concerning James the Lord's brother, Hegesippus reports that the former succeeded to the government of the church in Jerusalem in conjunction with the apostles (Eusebius, *Ecclesiastical History* 2.23.4). However, Clement of Alexandria already reports that "Peter and James and John after the ascension of our Saviour, as if also preferred by our Lord (to other disciples), strove not after honor, but chose James the Just bishop of Jerusalem" (Eusebius, *Ecclesiastical History* 2.1.3). On the basis of this evidence, Eusebius considered James to be the bishop of Jerusalem (Ibid., 2.23). Epiphanius (*Against Heresies* 78.7) and John Chrysostom (*Comm. on the Letter to the Corinthians,* Homily 33.4) ascribed the installation of James as the bishop of Jerusalem to the Lord himself.

44. Cf. R. Knopf, *Das nachapostolische Zeitalter,* 206; cf. F. M. Braun, *Jean le Théologien et son Evangile dans l'Eglise Ancienne* (Paris, 1959), 60.

45. See M. Goguel, *L'Eglise primitive* (Paris, 1947), 136–137, and also H. Chirat, *L'assemblée chrétienne à l'âge apostolique,* Lex Orandi 10 (Paris, 1949), 60.

46. Contrary to E. Schweitzer, *Das Leben des Herrn,* 92 and W. Bauer, *Rechtgläubigkeit und Ketzerei* (Tübingen, 1934), 97.

47. Irenaeus, *Against Heresies* 1.9.2.

48. This fact was noted by M. Goguel, *L'Eglise primitive,* 138.

49. See 1.3; 3.3; 21.6. Contrary to the opinion of R. Knopf, *Das apostolische Zeitalter,* 163; Weizsäcker, *Das apostolische Zeitalter der katholischen Kirche* (Tübingen, 1902), 615. The term *hegoumenos* is also employed in a double meaning: it designates both those who have an ecclesial and secular ministry (5.7; 37.2, 3; 51.5; 60.4). In the instances when Clement wants to specify that he is referring to the presbyters of the church, he employs the following expression: *"presbyteroi kathestamenoi"* (54.2).

50. Clement of Rome, *1 Corinthians* 42.4.

51. Ibid., 44.5.

52. If we accept this theory, the term "presbyters" in 21.6 designates the presbyters of the church, rather than senior members of the church.

53. 47.6.

54. 44.3–4.

55. I regard as unlikely the suggestion of M. Goguel that the term "bishop" was used in Rome, while the term "presbyter" was used in Corinth. However, M. Goguel himself puts this suggestion in a conditional form (*L'Eglise primitive,* 141).

56. I cite the witness of 1 Peter after the letter of Clement, due to the special character of the former, and not because I consider that it was composed later than Clement's letter. I leave aside the Pastoral letters which, in my point of view, do not give indications concerning the chief presbyter. However, C. Spicq supposes that in the epoch when the Pastoral

letters were written, among the presbyters there was a *presbyteros kat' exochên* (*Epîtres pastorales*, 94).

57. The witnessing of Christ's passion and his glory (*doxa*) implies the witnessing of Christ's resurrection, which is not mentioned *explicite*. This diversion from a usual formula encapsulating the apostolic witness found in the New Testament writings (cf. Acts 1.22; 2.32) appears somewhat strange. It cannot be explained by the fact that the sufferings are one of the main themes of the letter. Cf. E. Selwyn, *The First Letter of Peter*, 228.

58. There is no basis for diminishing the literal content for the word *sympresbyteros*, regarding it as an expression of St. Peter's humility or of his feelings of sympathy toward the presbyters. See E. Selwyn, *The First Letter of Peter*, 228. The New Testament writings do not allow for such an interpretation. Nowhere did the apostles identify themselves, for reasons of humility, with the persons who did not have their ministry. When we deal with the ministries for which God himself ordains, there is no place for "humility."

59. Bishop Cassien argues that 1 Peter was written in Rome (*Christ and the First Generation*, 292). By this he gives an answer to the question of which church Peter was heading. He could have had a temporary stay in the church of Rome, but then he could not have been a presbyter there; however, if he was a presbyter, he could have been nothing but a senior presbyter. 1 Peter, if it was written by Peter in Rome, is one of the arguments in favor of the theory that Peter stood at the head of the Roman church.

60. Cf.: "For as often as you eat this bread and drink the cup, you proclaim the Lord's death until he comes" (1 Cor 11.26).

61. Eusebius, *Ecclesiastical History* 5.16.5. To this testimony we must adduce another remark which we find in the letter of Polycarp: "*Polykarpos kai hoi syn autô presbyteroi.*" This is an almost exact rendering of the form "fellow presbyter" in Peter's letter.

62. Eusebius, *Ecclesiastical History* 7.5.6.

63. Cyprian, *Epist.* 44.1–2.

64. Cyprian, *Epist.* 41 and 45. We do not find the expression *compresbyter* in Tertullian.

65. See J. B. Lightfoot, *St. Paul's Letter to the Philippians* (London, 1890), 96, 230; H. Achelis, *Das Christentum in den ersten drei Jahrhunderten* (Leipzig, 1912), 2:16.

66. See above, chapter 4, I, 6.

67. See W. L. Knox, *St. Paul and the Church of Jerusalem* (Cambridge, 1925).

68. Clement of Rome, *1 Corinthians* 42.4.

69. If we assume that Acts was written at the end of the first century, there is still no basis for speculating that the evidence concerning the ordination of the Seven is a transposition of the church practice contemporary to Luke. The church practice may have preserved the order of the ordination of the first presbyters which at that time assumed the characteristics of being a tradition of the church.

70. Hippolytus, *Apostolic Tradition* 12.

71. Ibid., 14.

72. See above, chapter 4, I, 6.

73. Tertullian, *De praescreptione haereticorum* 41. See H. v. Campenhausen, *Kirchliches Amt*, 100: "The presumption that the spiritual leader and the teacher at the divine

service were originally freely interchanged, is an arbitrary hypothesis which, as we have seen, has in itself little probability within the scope of the Pauline churches."

74. Clement of Rome, *1 Corinthians* 44.4–5.

75. R. Sohm, *Kirchenrecht* (Munich and Leipzig, 1923), 157 ff.

76. Clement of Rome, *1 Corinthians* 44.6.

77. Cf. A. Sabatier, *La religion d'autorité et la religion de l'Esprit* (Paris, 1903).

78. Ignatius, *Smyrneans* 8.1.

79. Ignatius, *Philadelphians* 4; *Smyrneans* 12.2.

80. E. Jacquier, *Les actes des apôtres*, ccxiii and 379.

Chapter 7. **The Bishop**

1. Cyprian of Carthage, *Letters* 74.1.2.

2. P. Sokolov, *A Russian Hierarch From Byzantium* [in Russian] (Kiev, 1913), 167 ff.

3. See C. Spicq's translation "L'Epître aux Hébreux" in the series *La Sainte Bible* (Paris: Les Editions du Cerf, 1950), 40. See also the article by O. Procksch, "*Hagiazô*" in *TWNT*, 1:112–114.

4. C. Spicq, "L'origine johannique de la conception du Christ-prêtre dans l'Epître aux Hébreux" in *Aux sources de la tradition chrétienne* (Neuchâtel-Paris, 1950), 258 ff.; also H. Sahlin, *Zur Typologie des Johannesevangelium* (Uppsala, 1950).

5. See above p. 12.

6. It appears to be expressed *implicite* in many passages of his letters, in particular in Rom 3.25. For the interpretation of this verse, see W. D. Davies, *Paul and Rabbinic Judaism*, 232 ff.

7. Clement of Rome, *1 Corinthians* 36.1. Ignatius of Antioch apparently shared the same view, as one may draw from *Philadelphians* 9.1, if we agree that the term "high priest" refers to Christ, rather than to the high priest of the Old Testament: "The priests likewise are noble, but the High Priest who has been entrusted with the Holy of Holies is greater, and only to him have the secret things of God been entrusted. He is the door of the Father, through which enter Abraham and Isaac and Jacob and the prophets and the apostles and the Church."

8. Clement of Rome, *1 Corinthians* 40.5. The Greek text is as follows: *Tô gar archierei idiai leitourgiai dedomenai eisin, kai tois hiereusin idios ho topos prostetaktai, kai leuitais idiai diakoniai epikeintai: ho laikos anthrôpos tois laikois prostagmasin dedetai.*

9. I consider the term *ho archiereus* of *Philad.* 9.1 as most likely referring to Christ or to the Jewish high priest. See P. Th. Camelot, *Ignace d'Antioche: Lettres*, Sources chrétiennes 10 (Paris, 1951), 150.

10. Ignatius, *Philadelphians* 7.2.

11. Ignatius, *Smyrneans* 8.1–2.

12. Ignatius, *Philadelphians* 4.

13. Ignatius, *Smyrneans* 9.1.

14. Ignatius, *Magnesians* 6.1.

15. Ignatius, *Ephesians* 3.2.

16. Ibid., 6.1.

17. Ignatius, *Magnesians* 3.1.

18. Ignatius, *Smyrneans* 8.1.

19. Ignatius, *Ephesians* 3.2.

20. W. Bauer (*Rechtgläubigkeit*, 77) suggested that Polycarp avoided mentioning the bishop of Philippi, since the latter was a heretic, but this suggestion is not well founded.

21. In the letter of the church in Smyrna concerning the martyrdom of Polycarp (16.2), he is already called "the bishop of the catholic church of Smyrna" (*episkopos tês en Smyrnê katholikês ekklêsias*).

22. The inscription of his letter to Romans.

23. Justin Martyr, *First Apology* 1.65.3.

24. Justin Martyr, *Dialogue with Trypho* 33.2.

25. Hermas, *Shepherd*, Vision 2.4.2–3; 3.5.1; Similitude 9.27.2 et al.

26. Hermas, *Shepherd*, Vision 2.4.3.

27. Eusebius, *Ecclesiastical History* 5.24.

28. Ibid.

29. *Martyrdom of Polycarp* 14.3; Eusebius, *Ecclesiastical History* 4.15.35.

30. Eusebius, *Ecclesiastical History* 5.24.2–8.

31. Ibid., 2.23.4–6.

32. Ibid., 5.24.3.

33. Epiphanius, *Panarion* 29.4.

34. Jerome, *De viris illustus* 3.2.

35. F. Nau, *La didascalie des douze Apôtres* (Paris, 1902).

36. Eusebius, *Ecclesiastical History* 4.22.3. This is indicated by the word used by Hegesippus—*epoiêsamên*, 'I have made.'

37. Ibid., 5.24.14.

38. Irenaeus, *Against Heresies* 3.3.1.

39. Hippolytus, *Apostolic Tradition* 3.4. Cf. Nicolas Afanassieff, "Quelques réflexions sur les prières d'ordination de l'évêque et du presbytre dans la *Tradition Apostolique*," *Pensée Orthodoxe* 1/12, Paris, 1966.

40. Ignatius, *Smyrneans* 8.2: *hopou an phanê ho episkopos, hekei to plêthos estô, hôsper hopou an ê Christos Iêsous, ekei hê katholikê ekklêsia*.

41. *Apostolic Constitutions* 8.5.

42. The idea of topological high priesthood finds its most stark expression in the passages from Ignatius's letters where he uses the term *synedrion*, certainly if we presume that he employed it in its specific meaning deriving from Judaism, rather than in a usual sense of the Greek. The first alternative is most likely. Thus, in the letter to Philadelphians, he designates presbyteral college as "*synedrion tou episkopou*" (8.1). He employs the same term to designate the congregation of the apostles (*synedrion tôn apostolôn; Magn.* 6.1). By this he points out that at the eucharistic assembly, the presbyteral college occupies the place of the apostolic college, whereas in the letter to Philadelphians he refers to the apostles as

the presbyteral college of the church (*hôs presbyterion ekklêsias;* 5.1). The term *synedrion*, deriving from the designation of the *synedrion* of Jerusalem, implies the idea of a high priest. The topological role of presbyteral college, as *synedrion,* presupposes the topological high priestly role of a bishop.

43. Ignatius, *Magnesians* 9.1.

44. Ignatius, *Smyrneans* 8.1.

45. Ibid., 7.1.

46. Ibid., 7.2.

47. Ignatius, *Magnesians* 4.

48. This is shown with absolute clarity in the prayer for the ordination of a bishop which we find in the work of Hippolytus of Rome: "God and Father of our Lord Jesus Christ . . . grant that your servant, whom you have chosen for episcopacy, should shepherd your flock and should serve before you as high priest without blame, serving by night and day, ceaselessly propitiating your countenance and offering the gifts of your holy Church. And let him have the power of high priesthood, to forgive sins according to your command, to assign duties according to your command, to loose every tie according to the power which you gave to the apostles . . ." (*Apostolic Tradition* 3). All the liturgical functions enumerated above grow out of the spirit of high priesthood. The bishop is ordained as a high priest of his church and therefore, the bishop is a high priest, and, being a high priest, he is the presider of his church. The power to offer thanksgiving, to assign duties, to loose the ties and to forgive sins belongs to him personally as to a high priest. At the time of Hippolytus, the bishop could not use this power on his own. It was given to him in the Church, which is why he could use it only in the Church, when the whole people concelebrates him, as its presider.

49. Ignatius, *Philadelphians,* 4.

50. Ignatius, *Letter to Philippians.* See H. de Genouillac, *L'église chrétienne au temps de Saint Ignace d'Antioche* (Paris, 1907), 157: "Around the bishop, there was a small group of associates, who listened to his orders . . ." I consider this interpretation to be wrong, since it does not correspond to Polycarp's actual position in the Church.

51. Ignatius, *Trallians* 2.2.

52. Ignatius, *Magnesians* 6.1.

53. If our interpretation of the term *synedrion* in Ignatius's letters is correct, it bears witness to the fact that Ignatius was still far from the idea of the special priesthood of presbyters. (On the composition of the Jerusalem *synedrion,* see the excursus in E. Jacquier, *Les Actes des apôtres,* 772.) At the same time, this same term attests to the fact that Ignatius did not yet have a concept of a special priesthood or high priesthood of the apostles.

54. *Apostolic Tradition* 7.

55. See above, chapter 7, II, 6.

56. See F. Cabrol, "Fermentum et Sancta" in *Dictionnaire d'Archéologie Chrétienne et de Liturgie,* 5:1371–1374. [Ed. note: This is the fragment of the eucharistic bread from the principal celebration sent to the additional assemblies' celebrations, there to be added to the eucharistic cup as a sign of the unity of all eucharistic celebrations.]

57. See Elie Bikermann, "La chaîne de la tradition pharisienne" *Revue biblique* 59, no. 1 (1952): 44–45.

58. In Eusebius, *Ecclesiastical History* 2.1.4.

59. Clement of Alexandria, *Stromateis* 6.7. Cf. P. Th. Camelot, *Foi et Gnose: Introduction à l'étude de la connaissance mystique chez Clément d'Alexandrie* (Paris, 1945), 90 ff.

60. See J. Daniélou, *Origène*, 52 ff.

61. The idea of succession among the prophets was also known in Judaism. See E. Bikermann, "La chaîne de la tradition," 50–51.

62. "For the prophetic spirit is the corporate body of prophetic rank, which is the body of the flesh of Jesus Christ mixed with humanity through Mary" (Grenfell-Hunt, *Oxyrhynchus Papyri* [London, 1898]; cf. Pierre de Labriolle, *La crise montaniste* [Paris, 1913]).

63. Eusebius, *Ecclesiastical History* 5.17.4.

64. Clement of Rome, *1 Corinthians* 42.1.

65. Ibid., 42.2.

66. Ibid., 42.3–4. In these words of Clement we find the doctrine of apostleship almost fully expounded. We see here all the aspects we have noted above, which defined the apostolic ministry: the election of the Twelve during the earthly ministry of Christ, their instruction, the appearance to them of the Risen one and, finally, the descent of the Spirit upon them at the day of Pentecost.

67. Cf. G. Bardy, *La Théologie de l'Eglise de saint Clément de Rome à saint Irénée* (Paris, 1945), 44.

68. Clement of Rome, *1 Corinthians* 44. This passage is usually called upon by the proponents of the apostles-bishops theory. They interpret this passage in this way: having ordained the first-fruits of the faithful to be bishops and deacons, the apostles added a law that upon their deaths, other tested persons would accept their ministry upon themselves. For this reason, one must not remove from ministry those who were ordained by apostles or their successors. (Cf. A. Michiels, *L'origine de l'épiscopat*.) Quite recently, G. Dix came back to this interpretation ("The Ministry in the Early Church" in K. E. Kirk, *The Apostolic Ministry*, 253 ff.). Thus, Clement did not affirm the succession of ministry among bishops and presbyters and the order of their replacement, but the apostolic succession in the exact sense of the word. It seems that, according to Clement's own words, apostles provided a law so that their successors could ordain bishops and deacons. If we accept this interpretation, the question naturally arises, why did Clement write about this at all? What did the apostolic succession have to do with the case of the church in Corinth? The only answer to this confusion must be that Clement himself was as such a successor of the apostles (G. Dix, "Ministry in the Early Church," 265). Then the whole affair in Corinth comes to be seen in a new light. The "scandal" was not that the Corinthians removed the presbyters, but rather that they trespassed on Clement's rights, ordaining new presbyters without him. We have to reject this interpretation firmly, for it has no ground in the church tradition. Besides, the very text of Clement does not entitle us to such a reading. In his text, the term *leitourgia* does not designate the apostolic ministry, but the ministry of bishops-presbyters. Therefore, bishops, not apostles, are the subject of the expression "*ean koimêthôsin.*" There is no basis to think that "approved men" and "eminent men" were the apostles' successors. At any event, there is no doubt that "approved men" were bishops. Concerning "eminent men," these were either bishops or individuals who, together with the apostles, were founding

churches on their commission. Lastly, one more comment: one cannot be absolutely certain that "*metaxy*," which Clement uses twice in chapter 44, means "after." In the first instance, "*kai metaxy epinomên dedôkasin*" does not appear to mean that after ordaining the first-fruits of the faithful, apostles made the law of apostolic succession. This is a logical nonsense.

69. Clement of Rome, *1 Corinthians* 44.2.

70. Jerome, *Epist*. 146.1.

71. Cf. E. Caspar, *Geschichte des Papsttums* (Tübingen, 1930), 1:10 ff.

72. Cf. H. Lietzmann, *Histoire de l'Eglise ancienne* (Paris, 1937), 2:57.

73. See above, chapter 7, II, 6, note 42.

74. In his letters to the Romans and to the Trallians, Ignatius contrasts his own person with the apostles, but this juxtaposition has more a literary than an actual nature. Most of all, I have in mind here a famous passage from the first letter I have mentioned: "I do not order you as did Peter and Paul; they were apostles, I am a convict; they were free, I am even until now a slave" (4.3). It does not matter for me whether Ignatius tied the names of Peter and Paul with Rome, or with Antioch. When he wrote those lines, he most probably had both in mind. What is important for me is this: it is as if Ignatius wants to indicate that he, being a convict, cannot yet speak with the same authority as the apostles did. Behind this literary juxtaposition, we can discern the idea concerning succession from the apostles. Moreover, we find the same thought—in the same form—in the letter to the Trallians. (I give it here in the translation by P. Th. Camelot, *Ignace d'Antioche: Lettres*, 115:) "Je n'aurais pas la pensée, étant un condamné, de vous donner des ordres comme un apôtre." (3.3) ["I did not have the thought then, being one condemned, to give orders as an apostle."] Here, Ignatius's thought is perhaps expressed even more clearly: he would be able to give instructions with the authority of an apostle, but he does not wish to do this, being convict. In any event, Ignatius's understanding contained the perception of his ministry, as a bishop of Antioch, as having succeeded from the apostles, of course in a topologic sense.

75. See M. Goguel, *Les premiers temps de l'Eglise* (Paris-Neuchâtel, 1944), 212; H. v. Campenhausen, *Kirchliches Amt*, 181.

76. Eusebius, *Ecclesiastical History* 4.22.3.

77. See Einar Molland, "Le développment de l'idée de succession apostolique," *Revue d'Histoire et Philosophie Religieuses* 34, no. 1 (1954): 19–20.

78. Topologic succession could not evolve into a concrete apostolic succession on the basis of the ministry of administration, which the apostles handed down to presbyters they ordained. This transmission was closely linked with the presidency at the eucharistic assembly. Meanwhile, by the middle of the third century at the latest, we find several eucharistic assemblies within the limits of a local church, one of them presided over by a bishop, and the rest by presbyters.

79. Irenaeus, *Against Heresies* 3.3.1.

80. Ibid., 4.26.2.

81. Ibid. On the meaning of the expression *charisma veritatis certum*, see D. Van den Eynde, *Les normes de l'enseignement chrétien aux trois premiers siècles* (Paris, 1933), 186 ff.

82. Irenaeus, *Against Heresies* 3.4.1.

83. As E. Lanne accurately points out in his article "Le ministère apostolique dans Saint Irénée," *Irénikon* 25 (1952): 130, for Irenaeus, "it is the churches which have the apostolic succession, and in the thought of St. Irenaeus, the bishops—successors of the apostles, possess it in that they direct the Church."

84. Irenaeus, *Against Heresies* 3.3.1.

85. Ibid., 3.3.2.

86. Ibid.

87. E. Caspar, *Die älteste römische Bischofsliste* (Berlin, 1926), 426–472; H. v. Campenhausen, *Kirliches Amt*, 184. Even Eusebius does not begin the list of bishops of Rome with the apostles. See *Ecclesiastical History* 3.2, 4.1.

88. For Judaism, high priesthood encompassed the idea of succession. See Josephus Flavius, *Jewish Antiquities* 13.3.4, par. 78; E. Bikermann, "La chaîne de la tradition," 54.

89. Hippolytus, *Philosoph.* 1.1. The full text of the passage: "These things no one else refuted, but the Holy Spirit which is handed down in the Church. Having attained this Spirit first, the apostles shared it with those who believed rightly—of these we [are] successors, attaining the same grace, sharing in the high priesthood and teaching, being reckoned as the guardians of the church . . ."

90. E. Caspar, *Geschichte des Papsttum*, 1:26–27.

Chapter 8. The Power of Love

1. See above, chapter 6, II.

2. The efforts to find the theological foundations of law were unsuccessful so far. All these efforts seem to be limited to the Old Testament, that is to say, to the "former age." The Old Testament foundation of law, supposing that it existed then as we know it now, cannot assure the existence of the same in the New Testament. See J. Ellul, *Le fondement théologique du Droit* (Paris-Neuchâtel, 1946).

3. Augustine in Ps. 55.2.

4. Augustine in Ps. 26; En. 2.18.

5. See A. Lebedev, *Historical Essays on the Eastern Byzantine Church* [in Russian] (Moscow, 1902) 106 and following.

6. "In applying this canon (canon 12 of the Council of Ancyra) the most holy patriarch, lord Polyeuctes, had banished from the precincts of the most holy and great church of God the emperor, lord John Tzimiskes insofar as he was the murderer of emperor and lord Nicephoras Phocas, but afterwards he received him. For it was said in accordance with the holy synod of the council which had convened then and as the acts of the council preserved in the archives of the *chartophylax* indicated, that as the anointing at holy baptism removes all previous sins, whatever they may be, even so the anointing at the imperial coronation had removed the sin of the murder which Tzimiskes previously perpetrated" (Balsamon, *Commentary on Canon 12 of the Council of Ancyra*).

7. See J. Bonsirven, *Théologie du Nouveau Testament* (Paris, 1951), 91: "The Church would then be the social and earthly realization, of the Kingdom of God, imperfect in that

it included both good and evil, an incomplete realization equally in that it did embrace the righteous ones who did not belong to the body of Christ except in their own hearts . . ."

8. I leave aside here the problems of the origin of law and its content, for these would require separate examination. As for the question of knowing if the object of law is the individual or society (see P. Roubier, *Théorie générale du Droit* [Paris, 1946]) it seems to me that the question is poorly posed. The subject of the law is an individual person, not in and of itself, but taken in its relations with other individuals. This is why, when one law protects the individual, it protects society, and conversely, when it protects society, it protects the individual—certainly, if a given society recognizes the value of the individual.

9. In governing human relationships, law defends order in society. Saying this does not at all prejudice the problem of interdependence of law and order.

10. The existence of law in the Church is denied both from juridical and theological perspectives. For me this is of no importance here. Naturally, the absence of legal norms in the Church does not signify the absence of rules of life. The question then does not concern the existence of some norms in the Church, but their nature.

11. See above, chapter 6, III, 3.

12. Canon 6 of the Council of Sardis. See my article, "A Failed Ecclesiastical Diocese" [in Russian], *Pensée orthodoxe* 9 (1953): 7–30.

13. [Translator's note: This is an allusion to the quote from Mikhail Lermontov's poem *The Demon*, strophe 16. The original has *ni noch', ni den', ni mrak, ni svet!*]

14. Augustine, *De Civitate Dei* 19.15.

15. In the history of Christian thought one often hears these Pauline words cited to justify that which Paul would never have wished to justify. The Barthian school considers these words of Paul as a justification of the state (even though this has no need of being justified) and of the power of the sword, including capital punishment. See, e.g., F. J. Leenhardt, *Le chrétien doit-il servir l'Etat? Essai sur la théologie politique du Nouveau Testament* (Geneva, 1939).

16. See Bishop Cassian, *The Kingdom of Caesar Judged by the New Testament* [in Russian] (Paris, 1949).

17. Origen, *Commentary on the Gospel according to Matthew* 16.8.

18. *Apostolic Constitutions* 2.26.

19. See above, chapter 5, I, 1.

20. Concerning this hymn, see L. Cerfaux, *Le Christ dans la théologie de Saint Paul*, 283 ff. and his bibliography.

21. See Eph 5.25–27.

22. If the supposition of M. E. Boismard, "Dans le sein du Père (Jn 1.18)," *Revue biblique* 59, no. 1 (1952): 34, is correct, and the idea of *charis* is based upon the *hesed* of the Old Testament, which is "practically identical to love," then it would be necessary to translate John 1.14 in the following way: "The Word became flesh and he dwelt among us, full of love and truthfulness." In this case John 1.14 would confirm what has been written here in our text.

23. See Phil 2.7.

24. Origen, *Commentary on the Gospel according to Matt.* 16.8.

Index

Michael Plekon is professor of sociology at
Baruch College-CUNY and a priest of the Orthodox
Church in America. He is the author of *Living Icons:
People of Faith in the Eastern Church*
(University of Notre Dame Press, 2002).

Vitaly Permiakov received his M.Div. from St. Vladimir's
Orthodox Theological Seminary and is a Ph.D. student
in theology at the University of Notre Dame.